LEAN COST MANAGEMENT

Accounting For Lean
By Establishing Flow

James R. Huntzinger

Copyright © 2007 James Huntzinger

ISBN-13: 978-1-932159-51-6

Printed and bound in the U.S.A. Printed on acid-free paper
10 9 8 7 6 5 4 3 2 1

Library of Congress Cataloging-in-Publication Data
Huntzinger, James, 1964-
  Lean cost management : accounting for lean by establishing flow / by James Huntzinger.
  p. cm.
  Includes bibliographical references and index.
  ISBN-13: 978-1-932159-51-6 (hardcover : alk. paper)
  1. Manufacturing industries—Accounting. 2. Cost accounting. I. Title.
  HF5686.M3H86 2006
  657′.867042—dc22

2006034323

Phone: (954) 727-9333
Fax: (561) 892-0700
Web: www.jrosspub.com

This book is dedicated to Garek and Quinnie, my angels in the flesh.

CONTENTS

FOREWORD: THE MEANS
ARE THE ENDS IN THE MAKING

H. Thomas Johnson

For a long time this book will be the definitive work on lean accounting for both edu-
cators and manufacturing practitioners. It is comprehensive, informative, judicious,
well-organized, and well-written. Jim Huntzinger surveys and assesses virtually
everything ever written about the role of accounting in a lean manufacturing setting.
His coverage of published sources is exhaustive. Moreover, his personal experience
working in one of Toyota's premier suppliers, Aisin Seiki, gives him unique insight
and skill for interpreting these sources.

A notable feature of Huntzinger's work is the attention he pays to the historical
context for lean manufacturing and lean accounting. His thorough coverage of historical records from the 1880s through the 1950s sheds new light on American precur-
sors to lean accounting and lean manufacturing. Especially revealing in this regard are
his story about the evolution of a flow manufacturing process at Henry Ford's pre-
World War I Highland Park facility in Detroit and his in-depth discussion of
Alexander Hamilton Church's prescient prewar ideas for managing costs in a manufacturing environment. Equally revealing is his account of the U.S. government's
manufacturing acceleration program during World War II known as Training Within
Industry (TWI). It seems that very little written today about lean manufacturing or
lean accounting was not visible in those early examples from Highland Park, A.H.
Church, or TWI. However, today's writings on lean focus on present-day examples
from Toyota, not on those earlier American examples that, until Huntzinger's book,
were largely buried in the past.

Huntzinger's analysis raises an intriguing question. How much did Toyota learn
from those early American examples? Certainly some members of the Toyota executive team visited Ford's River Rouge facility, perhaps as early as the 1930s. But that
plant, as we now know, did not embody one-order-at-a-time flow processes as thoroughly as did the older Highland Park plant, and even less so after World War II, when
Toyota people again visited the Rouge. However, Toyota people before World War II
translated and studied Henry Ford's writings from the 1920s, especially his book
Today and Tomorrow, which described practices in the original Highland Park plant.
More to the point, perhaps, Toyota was introduced to the TWI program when the U.S.

government brought it to Japan in the late 1940s to help Japanese industry recover from its wartime devastation. Huntzinger shows a direct connection between certain TWI practices from 1944 and similar practices found many years later in Toyota plants.

The next obvious question, of course, is why Toyota later enjoyed such stunning success by apparently following these early American practices, while American manufacturers seemed oblivious to their significance or even their existence. A possible answer is that Toyota's modern operations may reflect its own unique thinking and history more than its copying of American practices that seemed to pass under the radar of American companies. This is the conclusion that today seems to me most probable. My suggestion is that Toyota's thinking could have brought the company to the point it is at today even if Ford had never built and shown the world his early flow lines at Highland Park, or even his later semi-flow lines at River Rouge. Moreover, the thinking present in Toyota's modern operating system may not have been present in Ford's early operations any more than it was in American manufacturing operations generally. In other words, the presence of flow in Toyota's operations today may reflect entirely different thinking than was present in either Ford's early flow operations nearly a century ago or TWI sixty years ago.

The thinking I refer to concerns how one views the relationship between ends (or results) and means (or causes). I show in several writings that Toyota's system reflects the view that means and ends are related holistically, as one observes in all natural living systems. A living system is what scientists call a complex system at the edge of equilibrium that is highly sensitive to initial conditions and responds non-linearly to multiple feedback loops that help maintain the system's unique identity. The complex living system is a community of infinitely interdependent parts, each of which embodies a pattern (or spirit) that is common to the whole. That pattern connecting the system's parts is "the means that is the making" of the system's emergent features and outcomes (or ends).

In contrast to living systems thinking is the view that means and ends are related mechanistically, as in a machine. A mechanistic system is simply a collection of inert independent parts, connected only by external force or instruction. The mechanical system's outcomes are a linear and additive sum of the magnitudes of all the parts. The parts, and not patterns connecting them, are the ends in the making. In other words, in a mechanistic system the ends are merely and simply the sum of the parts.

For over a century Americans have viewed any business organization as a mechanical system in which outcomes are the sum of its parts. To produce a change in outcomes (or results) one needs only to make an appropriate change in the magnitude of the parts—the means. I contend that this was as true of Henry Ford's thinking at Highland Park as it was of all other American business thinking then and after. In that view, if the desired outcome of a manufacturing operation is lowest possible cost per unit, then the means to lowest cost is to produce the most output of each part in the least time. The whole, the unit cost of each final product, is the sum of the unit cost to produce each component part. Where only one variety of a product is produced, as was the case in Henry Ford's operation that produced black Model-T's in Highland Park and for a while at the Rouge, one can maximize output and minimize unit cost by running all lines in a continuous flow as fast as possible. Ford did just that with fabulous financial results in the first fifteen years or so of his company's history.

However, flow seems to have lessened in Ford's operations in the later 1920s and the 1930s as the company produced components and vehicles in increasing varieties. By the late 1940s, after Henry's death, flow was all but gone except in final vehicle assembly. So, I would conclude that the flow observed in Ford's pre-1920s Highland Park plant was more an accident of history than evidence of the same thinking we observe some forty years later in modern Toyota plants, where *both* continuous flow *and* product variety went hand in hand in component making as well as final vehicle assembly.

For Toyota, the means and the ends always focused on human considerations. The end is a satisfied customer served by the creative talents of satisfied workers and suppliers. The "means" that are those "ends in the making" are an operating system in which each person, employee, or supplier views themself as simultaneously an upstream supplier to a downstream customer and a downstream customer to an upstream supplier. Everyone performs activity that they design to meet the needs of an identifiable, immediate customer. Everyone knows in this context what are normal expectations, and they know to stop and take corrective action the minute they spot an abnormal outcome. The "ends in the making" produced by these "means" are ultimately a safe environment that consistently turns out the highest quality and lowest cost vehicles while generating the highest profits in the industry year after year.

Flow is a central feature of Toyota's operating system, but perhaps more important is the spirit embodied in and connecting each part of the system. That embodied spirit, resembling the pattern of connections one observes in a living system, was not really present in the flow lines present at Ford's Highland Park or Rouge plants. Ford's system, despite its flow features, did not focus on human considerations. He clearly saw the means to be a collection of independent parts that he manipulated mechanically to achieve his financial ends. Thus, from his dealers Ford demanded cash on delivery, forcing them to borrow from local bankers while he bragged about Ford Motor Company never borrowing money. He forced his suppliers to bid against each other and then he purchased from the lowest bidder. And Henry Ford was as responsible as anyone for the adversarial, sometimes violent, nature of labor-management relations in American industry after the 1920s. His famous "five-dollar-a-day" wage policy notwithstanding, he treated workers with disdain, ultimately hiring a small army of armed guards to deal with labor unrest at the Rouge plant in the 1930s. For these reasons, and more, the fact that his operations exhibited continuous flow, at least in his company's first fifteen years or so, hardly suggests that Ford offers an early foreshadowing of what would appear many years later at Toyota. His early Highland Park plant shows an intriguing exception to American manufacturing practice in the 20th century, but on closer inspection it does not reflect different thinking than what prevailed at almost all American companies.

Turning to his discussion of lean accounting, one of the main points Huntzinger makes is that flow processes, especially when reflected in product-specific cellular layouts, enable better product costing by providing an easy way to trace all costs to specific products, leaving almost none to allocate as indirect costs. In other words, almost all costs in a lean flow system become direct costs, virtually eliminating the category known as overhead. However, this does not reflect the approach to managing operations costs that one observes at Toyota. There one sees attention to the process or system, what I call the "means," in the belief that if one gets the means right, then satisfactory results will follow. Tracing costs to products is not germane to managing operations costs at Toyota. The accounting system tracks financial results, but only to know and report costs, not to manage them. Managing costs is done by managing the operations system, what I refer to as "managing the means," or MBM. As I have said here and elsewhere, Toyota acts as if "the means are the ends in the making." Had that thinking been present at Ford in the early years, I don't think flow would have died out when increasing product variety made flow more difficult to achieve. I think flow might have continued to flourish at Ford, and Ford's thinking might have spread to other American companies that would have done likewise. But that never happened.

What I say here about lean accounting and about flow at Highland Park is not meant to detract from the great value of this important book. This is a landmark study that should be required reading for anyone seriously attempting to understand lean accounting and lean manufacturing.

PREFACE

The Introduction provides a brief overview of what will be discussed in this book. It also indicates the three factors that are necessary for developing and implementing a lean cost-management system. The final message is focused on how thinking, or a change in thinking, is the key to accomplishing changes in the business enterprise to support lean accounting. This is accomplished by revisiting the past to bring past thoughts toward the future of business.

Chapter 1 explains the failure of current or traditional accounting practices and why accounting must reflect the operation and not vice versa. This notion has slowly taken shape in recent years but has not moved most firms away from traditional methods. The chapter also explains why traditional accounting practices fail to provide the manufacturing enterprise with needed or usable information.

Chapter 2 uncovers the roots of accounting and its development during the Industrial Revolution. The use and development of accounting methods during the period provide answers to how businesses today should view and use cost-managerial accounting to support business enterprise. It also discusses the main failure, overhead, of traditional systems and just why they cannot provide the informational support that is needed.

A real example, from my own experience, shows the failure of traditional cost-managerial accounting methods, particularly standard costing techniques. The traditional method's failure to provide accurate information is coupled with timeliness and motivational pressure toward poor or even wrong business and operational decisions.

Chapter 2 continues with a brief overview of how cost-managerial accounting has become an offshoot of financial accounting and how the two have completely different purposes. This situation leads into the difference between a business viewing its function through a flow mindset instead of an economies-of-scale mindset. There is also detailed discussion on just how the two views manifest into completely different thinking about how to operate the business: *flow* versus *economies of scale*.

Chapter 3 provides a brief example of a company, Toyota, that operates under flow thinking and the level of success that it has been able to achieve and maintain for a sustained period of time.

Chapter 4 compares and contrasts the difference between traditional thinking and lean thinking; traditional thinking manifests in management by results and lean thinking manifests in management by means (MBM). Explanations and examples of each type of thinking are given. The MBM approach is discussed as the much superior philosophy, and its successful execution is described.

Chapter 5 ties together with Chapters 3 and 4 by providing a background on the philosophies and methods of Alexander Hamilton Church. Church, one of the innovative figures in the accounting arena during the Industrial Revolution, developed principles that apply MBM philosophy to cost accounting and are applicable to today's lean enterprise. These principles connect ideas developed during the early twentieth century to concepts espoused by the lean enterprise today. A deeper understanding of these principles is provided by the transformation into a lean enterprise, with the results of enterprise excellence, as reported in Chapter 4, becoming a possible reality.

Chapter 6 begins to build the previous chapters' techniques, principles, philosophies, and thinking into a physical system. It discusses the characteristics that should be obtained and achieved by transforming the business system into a lean enterprise system. Cost information and its development change dramatically by value stream (defined as the activities required to design, order, and manufacture a product or information, taking it from raw material to the customer) development and move most incidences of cost into alignment with a product's value stream, thus simplifying the entire system.

Chapter 7 discusses the issue of excess capacity. Although only briefly discussed, excess capacity is an important factor because of its role in overhead costing and its contribution to inaccurate costing by traditional methods.

Chapter 8 continues the discussion started in Chapter 7, the physical implementation of lean manufacturing into the business enterprise. More details of the attributes of the lean enterprise are discussed. Critical items such as flow, pull, and takt time are used to develop standard operations, which play the key role in achieving the performance level and function of the lean enterprise. Without this level of execution, the cost-management system proposed in this book is difficult or impossible to achieve.

Chapter 9 discusses the basic measurements to maintain the high and constantly improving performance of the lean enterprise. The Five S's receive extra discussion because firms frequently improperly handle their application.

Chapter 10 dives into specific detail about the concept of right designing, after Chapters 6, 7, and 9 discuss the building of the lean enterprise as a system and introduce right-designing principles, techniques, and philosophies that must be understood and applied to all aspects of the system. Equipment, value streams (cells or a collection of cells), support functions, and resources must all be right designed to achieve a functional lean system. This chapter explains how and why to apply the concept of right designing.

Chapter 11 ties the physical implementation of and transformation to a lean enterprise (discussed in Chapters 6, 7, 9, 10, and 11) to the cost-management system (discussed in Chapters 2, 3, and 5). The physical implementation of lean provides the changes and environment necessary to apply the cost-management system. Without the transformation, the lean cost-management system would not be possible.

Chapter 12 gives a detailed discussion on teamwork and how it applies to the lean enterprise. Although this chapter may seem out of context with this book, it is critical to developing the functioning lean system. It is integral to connecting parts of the physical systems with each other at both the micro (single cell or value stream) and macro (focus factory or multiple cells of a product's value stream) levels. Unfortunately, most firms completely misunderstand and typically misapply the function and use of teamwork. It must be understood and applied properly to ensure a successful transformation to a lean enterprise.

Chapter 13 gives an overview of the three fundamental feedback loops that will cause the system to evolve. As with any discussion of lean manufacturing, continuous improvement is an integral part of the system. However, detailed discussion of continuous improvement is not given in Chapter 13 because it is thoroughly discussed in a wide variety of books, articles, and training presentations. This chapter reviews the main source for developing and implementing improvement ideas back into the system.

Chapter 14 discusses the impact lean has on informational and physical transactions within the business enterprise. Since much of this book focuses on systems and the thinking needed for understanding and developing a different type of system—a lean one—a view from a theoretical business position is discussed. The chapter provides a perspective of what is accomplished from an overall business model level. As Chapter 14 reveals, the lean transformation drastically eliminates or simplifies transactions at all levels. The result of the transactional reduction is an exceptionally effective business enterprise, which Chapter 4 reveals is true about Toyota. With lean management, a firm becomes more effective operationally, financially, developmentally, and in terms of customer satisfaction.

Chapter 15 ties a theoretical view to a practical view of the multidimensional gear train. The lean enterprise functions more like a gear train than it does a linked chain, which is a commonly used analogy because of the multifaceted aspects of a manufacturing company, which link and mesh at multiple rates and dimensions, not just linearly, as with a chain. The flows and connections of Dr. Steven Spear's Five Rules-in-Use and Dr. H. Thomas Johnson's view of a business as a living entity (with both individual functions and interdependent functions) provide views of a "well-oiled" synchronous gear train that meshes independent gears into a functioning system, which transfers movement throughout. Ronald Coase's transactional theory provides a simplified version (or simplified product design) of Dr. Spear's and Dr. Johnson's theories through the analogy of a gear train.

Chapter 15 also discusses how the view of the lean system as a gear train with every function, cell, and value stream linked promotes the simplified transactional movement of products and information. The view of each element stepping through the system effortlessly and automatically simplifies gathering and tracking cost information.

Chapter 16 provides an overview of activity-based costing (ABC). ABC is often mistaken for lean's solution to accounting practices. This chapter explains why ABC is not the best solution and elaborates on some of its failings.

xx Lean Cost Management

Chapter 17 discusses the application of Church's production factors method to a model factory operating as a lean enterprise. The chapter provides a practical account of costing methods discussed in previous chapters. It is meant to offer an understanding of how costing can be applied in the lean environment using the principles, philosophies, and methods discussed in this book. It is Church's method applicable to today's world.

Chapter 18 reviews a summary of the main points, ideas, and thoughts presented in this book and ties them to the change in critical thinking that must take place for successfully understanding and transforming any business enterprise into a lean enterprise. This must take place in order to achieve a lean cost-management system.

Chapter 19 discusses the "how to" of changing from a traditional way of operating the organization to a lean cost-management operation. This is presented not as a step-by-step procedure but as a discussion of the application of a series of lessons learned: practices that can be followed in order to leverage, or learn and understand, the thinking and methods that create a lean enterprise. Every company and situation is unique. No two kinds of implementation will be the same, but by adhering to common lessons and leveraging these lessons, successful change can be achieved. These lessons also invoke the common principles or means that need to be applied to achieve a higher level of learning and accomplishment.

Chapter 20 provides a conclusion to the points established in Chapter 1. As put forth in Chapter 18, thinking must precede action and action must happen to enable better thinking.

ACKNOWLEDGMENTS

I would like to extend great appreciation to Bob Pomeroy and Dan Glusick. Bob and Dan have been cohorts throughout the development of my understanding of lean and the Toyota Production System (TPS) during the last fifteen-plus years. The hours upon hours of thought, discussion, and implementation with these two individuals have been the most enlightening and enjoyable during my own lean journey. They understand the vision that is needed not only to implement lean but also to move it beyond its present state. My knowledge is every bit their knowledge as it has been jointly developed with them.

I wish to thank Jeff Futrell for helping me in the development of the *production factors spreadsheet*. Jeff is the original architect of the production factors spreadsheet (except for Church). He accomplished the original design, not by any intrinsic desire to implement lean but because he was trying to support what the manufacturing engineers were doing—the physical implementation of lean. He developed the production factors spreadsheet for the right reasons. Jeff is an accountant and also a genuinely nice and gracious person. I could not have re-created the spreadsheet and fully developed my thought process without his guidance and support.

I would like to thank Scott Larson, also an accountant, for his friendship and support and for indulging an engineer's ramblings and rants about subjects that are not in the engineer's repertoire. His insight from an accountant's perspective has been most helpful in understanding the connections between the two worlds of accounting and manufacturing. Scott also has the uncanny willingness and desire to "hang out with a bunch of engineers."

I would like to thank Dr. Jeffrey Liker, Dr. Robert "Doc" Hall, Dr. James Womack, Dr. H. Thomas Johnson, and Dr. Richard Vangermeersch for their kind and gracious help and work and for sharing their knowledge, ideas, and thoughts with me. The stories and insights which they have shared have been a wealth of knowledge that contributed to my own thought processes and ideas. Without the work and thinking of these five gentlemen, my own ideas could not have developed to their current level and definitely could not have evolved so rapidly.

I would like to thank Dr. Jeff Liker and Dann Engels for allowing me the opportunity to expand my lean horizons in areas I would have never been able to discover on my own. The information, experience, and knowledge I have gained have developed my thinking process about lean dramatically.

I would like to thank Gary Shimek and Anne Mosgaller of the Milwaukee School of Engineering's Walter Schroeder Library. Throughout my thesis project,

Anne diligently and promptly supplied me with articles, theses, and books that without her I would never have found or would have spent a huge amount of time searching for instead of focusing on writing and research. I greatly appreciate her professionalism and support as they contributed to making the research an enjoyable process.

Gary gave me substantial support in proofreading, helping me correct the technical format, and advising me on aspects that I did not have the skill to write myself. Receiving the professional help, skill, and insight from him was also a much-appreciated contribution.

I would also like to thank my thesis advisor, Joe Papp, who gave me valuable guidance and support during the thesis process. Joe also has a shared passion and interest in "all things lean," which has made the process much more insightful and enjoyable. We also have been able to share ideas about lean and industry beyond my specific thesis topic, which has been an extra and pleasurable feature of his support.

And finally I would like to thank Drew Gierman, the editor of this book. He gave me tremendous guidance over an extended period of time while I worked to modify my writing from a thesis to a book format. Because this is my first venture in writing a book it has taken much patience and guidance from Drew, and I greatly appreciated his help and support in the effort.

ABOUT THE AUTHOR

 **Jim Huntzinger** has over eighteen years of experience developing lean enterprises through system design and the development, implementation, and guidance of organizations both strategically and tactically through the transformation process. He began his career as a manufacturing engineer with Aisin Seiki (a Toyota Group company and manufacturer of automotive components) when it transplanted to North America to support Toyota. He spent eight years at Briggs & Stratton (a manufacturer of small engines) in a range of engineering and management positions, evolving lean and implementing it into its manufacturing operations and business practices. Huntzinger also spent over nine years as a manufacturing consultant helping businesses ranging from huge global corporations to small privately held companies to implement lean tools and strategies for the entire business enterprise. He has broad experience in lean implementation within machining assembly and fabrication for a wide range of companies and products.

Huntzinger is the founder and president of the Lean Accounting Summit. This event and the group of "thought leaders" associated with it are collectively working to develop, educate, and research accounting's role in the lean enterprise and business. He is also the cofounder of the TWI Summit, which is an event to contribute to the redeployment of the Training Within Industry (TWI) program throughout the United States and to the understanding of TWI's connection to the lean enterprise.

Huntzinger has also researched at length the evolution of manufacturing in the United States with an emphasis on lean's influence and development. He has researched and worked to redeploy TWI and uncovered its tie with the Toyota Way. He is also developing the history of Ford's Highland Park plant and its direct tie to Toyota's business model and methods of operation.

Huntzinger graduated from Purdue University with a B.S. in Mechanical Engineering Technology and received an M.S. in Engineering Management from the Milwaukee School of Engineering.

Web
Added
Value™

Free value-added materials available from
the Download Resource Center at www.jrosspub.com

At J. Ross Publishing we are committed to providing today's professional with practical, hands-on tools that enhance the learning experience and give readers an opportunity to apply what they have learned. That is why we offer free ancillary materials available for download on this book and all participating Web Added Value™ publications. These online resources may include interactive versions of material that appears in the book or supplemental templates, worksheets, models, plans, case studies, proposals, spreadsheets and assessment tools, among other things. Whenever you see the WAV™ symbol in any of our publications it means bonus materials accompany the book and are available from the Web Added Value™ Download Resource Center at www.jrosspub.com.

Downloads for *Lean Cost Management: Accounting for Lean by Establishing Flow* include a lean accounting implementation case study and slide presentations covering right designing for effective cost management and lean cost-management accounting.

INTRODUCTION

Accounting practices are important to any manufacturing enterprise. Obtaining and developing useful accounting information is required for any manufacturer to disclose information for both internal and external purposes. This book is focused on accounting—specifically managerial-cost accounting—for internal purposes; the relationship between internal and external will be discussed throughout the book to enhance understanding of each particular context.

Current cost-managerial accounting practices are not optimal and are most often misleading. The key points presented in these chapters will reveal the following:

1. How current cost-managerial accounting practices fail
2. The original purpose of cost-managerial accounting practices in early industry
3. How cost-managerial accounting should not be about accounting per se but about designing, executing, and improving the business system
4. How becoming a lean enterprise is the foundation for achieving superior performance and cost-managerial accounting (referred to as cost management)
5. What three factors are key to developing a superior cost-management system

These five points will be supported by reviewing a combination of historical references, management philosophy, and enterprise design and tying these to the three elements that are the foundation for a lean cost-management system:

1. Moving all costs to be direct costs
2. Developing and implementing flow production
3. Utilizing desktop hardware and software

It will also be shown that transforming a firm into the position from which it can develop and use a superior cost-management system consists of complete changes both in thinking and also in physical operations. The changes in thinking and in physical methods jointly drive a firm to become a lean enterprise via the three elements described above, leading to the ability to establish an outstanding cost-management system.

Without the change in accounting information, manufacturing firms will be left behind as more progressive companies learn and apply these superior practices. Dynamic change has been a part of industry since its beginning, and successful companies are the ones that can continually learn and apply needed change.

ACCOUNTING: WHERE WE ARE AND WHERE WE MUST GO

How did the organization get to this point? Cyril Northcote Parkinson, in his famous 1957 commentary on organizational bureaucracy, *Parkinson's Law, And Other Studies in Administration*, describes the condition of senior management as "plodding and dull," while middle management is "active only in intrigue against each other," leaving the people at lower levels of any organization "frustrated or frivolous." Unfortunately, Parkinson's humorous observations hit firms too squarely on the mark and led to the conclusion that "little is being attempted. Nothing is being achieved. And in contemplating this sorry picture, we conclude that those in control have done their best, struggled against adversity, and have admitted defeat."[1] To counter the abysmal picture painted by Parkinson, according to *Japanese Management Accounting*, "*to keep up with the new state of today's manufacturing environment, traditional management accounting functions must change*" (emphasis added).[2]

What Monden and Sakurai are referring to, as the countermeasure to Parkinson, is lean accounting or what could also be referenced as lean cost management. To develop lean accounting a company must first develop lean as a manufacturing system or an enterprise-wide system. Because the real goal of cost and managerial accounting is to serve operations, manufacturing systems must be developed and implemented so that accounting systems can be created to give proper information to operations for making correct and timely decisions. Orest Fiume and Jean Cunningham, two prominent CFOs with extensive lean experience, emphasize this point: "What accounting should do is produce an unadulterated mirror of the business—an uncompromisable truth on which everyone can rely.... Only an informed team, after all, is truly capable of making intelligent decisions."[3] Unfortunately, most manufacturing systems are designed to serve accounting systems instead of vice versa. Robert Kaplan explains why:

The internal management accounting function has now become subservient to the external financial reporting function in U.S. firms. Recall that the cost accounting and management control practices that developed in U.S. corporations between 1850 and 1925 evolved from demands of senior executives to help them understand their internal operations, to make new product and investment decisions, and to motivate and evaluate the performance of their employees. Contemporary U.S. practice, in contrast, is characterized by the internal use of accounting conventions that have been developed and mandated by external reporting authorities.[4]

What manufacturing systems must develop are accounting systems to provide them with the needed information. Today, accounting systems grossly distort the information reflected back to management about operations. Dr. H. Thomas Johnson and Anders Bröms stress this point in their Shingo Prize–winning book, *Profit beyond Measure*: "Management accounting simply takes accounting revue, cost, and profitability information, which is appropriate for measuring the overall financial results of a business, and inappropriately attempts to trace it to the particular activities and products of the business that give rise to those results."[5] Therefore, much of this book is focused on the physical operation system that must be developed and implemented and will conclude with a discussion of the accounting systems (cost and managerial) that will be an appendage of that system and serve its needs. The final result of the accounting system will be a simple and straightforward servant system of the operating system. The operating system will be based on the Toyota Production System (TPS) and its focus on waste elimination through creating value-added (*muda* free) flow of products and information by greatly simplifying everything associated with the business enterprise. Fiume and Cunningham also support this approach: "We believe that the natural evolution of the lean movement is toward streamlining and simplicity, and that accounting systems can and should become simple and even elegant."[6]

Over the last several decades, there has been little development of methods in cost managerial accounting to directly support the physical implementation of a lean enterprise-wide system. A few companies—very few, in fact—with innovative financial leaders have developed some internal and improved procedures for their own operations. Very little of this methodology has trickled down to mainstream manufacturing. In the last couple of years, a few articles, books, and seminars have begun to shed some light on the accounting dilemma, but much work and development in the lean accounting arena needs to be done. Lean accounting is one of the most underdeveloped frontiers in the lean manufacturing world, and as Jerry Solomon, a veteran in the lean arena, states: "As companies continuously improve their operations and move toward the Lean enterprise, many are finding barriers and brick walls to their initiatives—disguised as Accounting Departments."[7]

One interesting book published in 2000 by Emanuel Schwarz[8] touches on some of the issues revealed in this book and supported by the work and research of accountants and accounting historians like Brian Maskell, Dr. H. Thomas Johnson, and Robert Kaplan. Schwarz's book is aptly titled *Internal Accounting*. Even though Schwarz focuses in his book on the chart of accounts—that is, credits and debits associated with the transactions in T-account[9] charts of assets, liabilities, and equity—he correctly reviews the misuse, misunderstanding, and nonfunctional reality of present and traditional accounting methods and procedures.

Schwarz works to remedy these issues and develops methods to do so. He also very poignantly explains the necessary separation of financial and managerial accounting, the mistakes created by not separating these procedures, and issues caused by commonly accepted methods and terms:

> As a consequence, all accounting literature stated: Cost accounting is to establish inventory values. This is incorrect. We should not mix External needs of inventory values with Internal needs of production cost values. Determination of production cost is the primary objective of Cost Accounting.[10]

Schwarz continues his explanation:

> An accurate Chart of Accounts should not have any account called "Work-in-Process." The reason is very basic: We should not name an account referring to its ending balance. The name of an account should tell us the basic purpose of the account. And the purpose of this account is not to establish the amount of the work-in-process at the moment of the closing of the month, but it is to inform management of the production cost of the period.[11]

Schwarz then explains the source of the underlying issue:

> Over the last 50 years our university professors have tried to include procedures exclusively related to Internal Accounting as a part of Financial Accounting. This development is absolutely not acceptable.... No more using ridiculous terminology as Overhead.... No more mixing Financial Accounting with Internal Accounting.... This new Internal Accounting System will give management information never before received.[12]

Schwarz's book is one of the few writings that provide detailed methods to follow to create an improved accounting system as opposed to what is taught throughout academia.

Emanuel Schwarz brings into play this book's first point about cost-managerial accounting: its failure to produce useful information to help operation managers make decisions. Monden[13] has researched and published works revealing a wide variety of accounting and cost management issues. He studied Toyota's methods in accounting and production systems for many years. In his work he discloses the second point that this book develops: the accounting system must be a subservient system to the production system. The development of cost management accounting is completely dependent on the development and implementation of a lean manufacturing system or physical operation system. Monden notes that "there is an increasing tendency to believe that applying accounting controls is impractical or even redundant. What is important, however, is to control the *physical elements of production* that can influence cost standards. Cost control in this sense implies *workplace reforms*. It is now believed that the JIT [just-in-time] production system is crucial to this type of workplace reform" (emphasis added).[14] In this statement, Monden emphasizes that financial information is not the important factor to managing cost, but instead it is the design and operation of the production system. This point will be discussed later in more detail.

Glenn Uminger[15] reviewed this same philosophy and structure at the University of Michigan's 2003 Lean Manufacturing Conference.[16] Mr. Uminger was the architect of the Toyota Georgetown, Kentucky, manufacturing facility's management accounting system. He also emphasized that the management accounting system's goal must be to make the needs of the operation rightsized and right fitting.[17] Uminger learned this because in order to understand his assignment of setting up the Georgetown, Kentucky, plant with its first management accounting system, Toyota sent him to their plants in Japan and in the United States for six months to "[learn] by doing—actually working in manufacturing." This vital experience working in the plants taught him "that he did not need to set up the same complex accounting system he had set up at a former company."[18] Again, the system must serve the customer:

> The [accounting] system [that Uminger created in his new position at Georgetown] was simpler because Uminger took the time to understand the manufacturing system, the *customer* for which he was a *supplier* of services. He needed to build an accounting system that supported the real needs of the actual manufacturing system that Toyota set up.[19]

OVERLY COMPLICATED SYSTEMS

Today's cost and managerial accounting systems have many problems, one of which is overcomplication. Accountants often have difficulty accurately explaining what and how the system is doing and tracking. As a practitioner I have experienced this situation firsthand many times. These accounting methods are so cumbersome and use such outdated information that in my own experience reviewing systems with accountants the phrase that inevitably arises is, "well it *could* give accurate information *if* people would or knew how to follow procedures and *if* the engineers would *update* the standards." Assuming a company "could," *if* people "would," and *if* engineers would "update" is a big assumption. And even then the information would only be usable and accurate if the system is designed to give useful and accurate information in the first place. This is not the case, as will be shown.

The company cannot, the people (operators) will not, and the engineers do not follow procedures and update standards, and the company basically has a system that is not maintained. The reason is simple. Traditional systems are just too complex and time consuming to be properly maintained. In addition, the company will not (nor should they) employ resources to handle the problems of gathering and updating the information system. As Maskell states:

> Rather than approaching a complex problem by devising a complex solution, it is better to simplify the problem so that the solution is clear to everyone involved.
>
> The traditional Western approach to the solution of management problems has been to create complex systems and mathematical solutions. This "operations research" approach to the solution of business problems has contributed to the development of highly sophisticated but poorly performing companies—reliant upon technicians and specialists—whose production personnel are alienated and unproductive.[20]

The solution is to "dump" the system and develop a new system. Or better yet, develop and implement a lean manufacturing system. Accounting falls into the same dilemma as material management systems, such as Material Requirements Planning (MRP) systems. Complicated information systems are developed and implemented to manage complicated operation systems. Accounting tries to manage a business by tracking a complicated system and MRP tries to manage an operation by tracking a complicated system. *Simplify it and it will not be needed*! One result of lean is simplified systems. In both situations, accounting information and scheduling information, lean simplifies the overall system and thus simplifies the information systems. Dr. Steven Spear,[21] in his doctoral dissertation, provides proof of how Toyota accomplishes simplification with their system. His Five Rules-in-Use are the underlying principles that guide the operation and development of TPS. Rule 3 states that each good, service, and piece of information must have a *simple*, prespecified, self-diagnostic flow-path over which it will travel as it takes form.[22] Throughout his dissertation he stresses that simplification is absolutely necessary in order to achieve many of the requirements of the system and other rules. The simple flow-path, as referred to by Dr. Spear, is the development and implementation of one-piece flow.[23] The concept of one-piece flow as a prerequisite for simplification and a lean accounting system will be explained in detail later. It is brought up here to illustrate the absolute need for the elimination of any complex system that is indicative of traditional accounting, material management, scheduling, and manufacturing systems.

The conclusion is to simplify everything so that anything complicated is no longer needed and can be "dumped," as was stated at the beginning of this section. Lean accomplishes this if it is properly understood and implemented. Simplification is an underlying principle of the tools used for operating a lean enterprise. As Dr. Spear presents in his dissertation, the tools are a manifestation of trying to achieve this simplification (and the other requirements of his Five Rules-in-Use), which in turn results in the lean accounting methodology that is presented in this thesis. Simplification results in simplification. Or simplification results in flow manufacturing (one-piece flow), which results in a simple and very reflective cost-managerial accounting system.

TOO LITTLE TOO LATE

Another common issue with traditional cost management accounting is that it supplies information too late to have a significant or direct impact on operations. Locating the source of operational issues is key to resolving them and instituting countermeasures[24] to insure that the same concern will not return. If feedback is delayed, the ability to pinpoint and correct problems is greatly compromised. Henry Gantt[25] stressed this point in the early part of the twentieth century:

> Manufacturers in general realize the vital importance of the cost of their product, yet but few of them have a cost system upon which they are willing to rely in all conditions.
>
> Many accountants are so long in getting their figures in shape that they are practically worthless for the purpose intended, the possibility of using them has passed.
>
> The man who knows what to do and how to do it shall gradually supplant the man who knows what was done and who did it.[26]

Henry Gantt delivered this statement during a presentation to the American Society of Mechanical Engineers in 1915. He had originally written it in 1897. The realization of cost management accounting's failure to give timely information is not new. The same point was continually stressed in most of the research on present-day accounting methods done for this book.

WHY A DIFFERENT ACCOUNTING PRACTICE IS NEEDED

As discussed, traditional accounting methods are not acceptable when developing and implementing a lean manufacturing enterprise. (In fact, they may be unacceptable for any manufacturing environment.) When a manufacturing company operates using lean principles, the entire landscape of the business enterprise changes. This leads to a needed change in the management accounting area as well. Lean manufacturing has completely different needs and methods, which must be addressed. In order to support lean concepts, accounting procedures must change. The information needs for the lean environment are completely different than for traditional manufacturing. In a lean operation, physical attributes become increasingly more important and the information supporting the operation becomes directly associated with its physical actions. What this means is that the information flow becomes intertwined with the physical flow of the product.[27] As will be shown later, the information system for cost accounting is a direct reflection of the physical attributes of the flow of products.

In traditional cost-managerial accounting systems, information is extracted from the operation, sent through a separate system, and calculated under parameters separate from the activities on the floor. In lean accounting, as will be shown, cost information is formed and calculated by a direct reflection of the physical flow of products within the value stream.[28] This is a result of the approach that Dr. Spear, in his previously mentioned dissertation, defines as simplification of flow-paths. Current accounting practices do not achieve this; they also do not reflect accuracy of product and operational costs, as will be shown. One question that needs to be answered is why traditional cost-managerial accounting methods fail to provide information and support that is needed, particularly for a lean manufacturing enterprise.

THE NEW SYSTEM MUST REFLECT PHYSICAL OPERATIONS

As provided by Dr. Spear in his dissertation, simplification is one key to TPS or the lean enterprise. What this means is that the information that supports the operation, is intertwined with the flow of products.[29] Lean implementation pushes the support information flows down on the product flow. This means that as product flows along its value stream path—the process known as the flow-path—the information flow moves "on" the product. For example, as a product moves along its value stream, standard operations dictate exactly what the next process will do. The part moving in one-piece flow indicates what will and must be accomplished at the next step along the value stream. This principle enforces information that reflects exactly what the part requires during the physical operation.

As Dr. Spear's third rule (as well as the others in the set of Five Rules) states, *pre-specified* activities take place. This principle translates to the idea that every activity along the value stream or flow-path is predetermined, meaning predesigned and pre-learned. From a higher-level view, the entire manufacturing operation is completely designed and trained for direct and specific activities to happen and occur in only one way. So if in the lean operation everything is predesigned or predetermined to function in a specific manner, then support functions, like the cost-accounting system, must reflect these activities to give accurate and useful information to support the operation. This point will be expounded upon through the rest of the book.

NOTES

1. Parkinson, *Parkinson's Law*, 78.
2. Monden and Michiharu, eds., *Japanese Management Accounting*, xiii.
3. Fiume and Cunningham, *Real Numbers*, viii.
4. Kaplan, "The Evolution of Management Accounting," 409.
5. Johnson and Bröms, *Profit beyond Measure*, 145.
6. Fiume and Cunningham, *Real Numbers*, 3.
7. Rubrich, "From the Publisher." Solomon implemented a direct cost system and teamed up with the operating folks to provide user-friendly reporting that facilitated the improvement process taking place on the production floor ("About the Author" in *Who's Counting?*, by Jerrold M. Solomon).
8. Dr. Emanuel F. Schwarz is a Professor Emeritus at San Francisco State University.

9. A T-account is a format in the shape of a "T" used in accounting that provides the same basic accounting figures as a formal ledger account and is commonly used as a teaching aid.

10. Schwarz, *Internal Accounting*, 20.

11. Ibid., 4.

12. Ibid., v.

13. Yasuhiro Monden is Professor of Managerial Accounting and Operations Management at the University of Tsukuba Institute of Socio-Economic Planning in Tsukuba-shi, Japan.

14. Monden and Sakurai, eds., *Japanese Management Accounting*, 37; Monden, *Cost Management in the New Manufacturing Age*, 68.

15. Glenn Uminger, although currently manager of production control for Toyota Motor Manufacturing in North America, has a background and education in accounting and was a key architect of Toyota's management accounting system in North America.

16. The conference was held in Ypsilanti, Michigan, on May 5–7, 2003, and was chaired by the Japan Technology Management Program at the University of Michigan, Ann Arbor, Michigan.

17. Uminger, "Lean."

18. Liker, *The Toyota Way*, 287.

19. Ibid.

20. Maskell, *Performance Measurement*, xvi.

21. Dr. Steven J. Spear is a visiting assistant professor at MIT and a senior fellow at the Institute for Healthcare Improvement, both in Cambridge, Massachusetts. He has been a faculty member in Harvard Medical School programs since 2000, and he was an assistant professor at Harvard Business School for six years. He has also won three Shingo Prizes.

22. Spear, "The Toyota Production System," 5.

23. Ibid., 74. Although specific pages are identified in notes 21 and 22, Spear reiterates these points continually throughout his dissertation, as they are important and fundamental to the conclusions of his research.

24. Within lean firms, problems are addressed with countermeasures instead of solutions. This is because a countermeasure suggests that improvements are ongoing and continually evolving while solutions suggest a permanent situation.

25. Henry L. Gantt was one of the more influential management thinkers of the early part of the twentieth century. His ideas and writings covered a wide variety of management issues and methods. He is most famous for the Gantt chart.

26. Gantt, "The Relation Between Production and Costs," 19.

27. Rother and Shook illustrate this point very well. See Rother and Shook, *Learning to See*.

28. A value stream is defined as the activities required to design, order, and manufacture a product or information, taking the product from raw material to the customer.

29. "Products and information" means both manufactured products and also information that uses other information as a support function. For example, the product development process is a value stream of information (whereas product manufacturing is a value stream of physical items), and other informational support, like cost tracking, is information that supports the main information flow of the product development procedure.

2

WHY TRADITIONAL ACCOUNTING METHODS FAIL

For the most part, traditional accounting methods have failed the test. Indeed, rather than being part of the cure to what ails American business, management accounting systems have been part of the disease.[1]

Traditional cost-managerial accounting methods seem to have been around forever and are well established as solid methods for operating. But with a closer look at their history one can learn how and why they fail for a lean enterprise as well as for traditional manufacturers.[2] Although much valuable research and writing exists on where and how traditional cost and managerial accounting came into being, few manufacturing people (at any level) are aware of why it was developed or who developed it. M. C. Wells of the University of Illinois divulges this history, noting that "members of the accounting profession could not claim to have made any substantial contributions to the theory or practice of cost accounting prior to 1914."[3] Dr. Wells explains further that "the concern for costs and cost records is particularly interesting because it arose some time before there was any general interest in those matters amongst accountants."[4]

THE ROOTS OF COST AND MANAGERIAL ACCOUNTING

In a 1993 article for the Engineering Society, Audrey Taylor discloses some interesting history about cost and managerial accounting:

> Most companies attached all costs to the product before 1889. By 1915, most companies only attached manufacturing costs to the product. Due to the lack of automated information systems, it was easier for accountants to apply overhead to all products using a single rate. Even though a single rate was used to attach overhead to products, the distortion which resulted was minor due to the relatively small portion of overhead in the cost of the finished product.[5]

Cost accounting's roots trace back to about the fourteenth century during the Medieval Era. It grew out of the commerce in Europe and the growth of industrial enterprises by a variety of partnerships and individuals involved in the manufacture and trade of goods like woolen products, silk cloth, books, and other common products.[6] Although some of the basics of cost accounting were developed and used starting around the fourteenth century, it was not until the Industrial Revolution that significant changes developed that would shape our industry even to the present.

The Industrial Revolution[7] began the consolidation of activities in the manufacture of products. Prior to the Industrial Revolution manufacturers were single-product and single-activity entities. The marketplace determined price or exchange rates and the manufacturers were tied to whatever the market presented. There was simply no need for calculating internal costs. An individual or company would, for example, weave cloth (single activity and product) and introduce it into the market. Even if an individual or company might include a second activity—for example, dying the cloth—the operation was so small that there was no need to develop any system for an internal cost structure. Just like very small businesses today, simple double-entry bookkeeping was all that was needed and often this was not even done by the manufacturer. According to Dr. H. Thomas Johnson, "Market prices supplied all the managerial information he needed: namely, prices for finished goods and prices for all the inputs going into his cost of production. Input prices encompassed purchase prices of raw materials, market piece-rates paid to artisans, and market prices paid for inputs other than raw materials and labor."[8]

If any information was tracked using the double-entry method, the company needed simply to know inputs (material and labor[9]) and outputs, those products sold to the market. Enterprises prior to the Industrial Revolution were simple and straightforward and required little or no formal information system. With the advent of the Industrial Revolution, businesses began to take on multiple activities, although early on they retained the single-product focus. As the manufacturing of metal products came into play, the multiple activity and multiple product enterprise came into being. This type of manufacturing enterprise would drastically change the needs of industry in the cost-accounting arena, as Dr. Johnson asserts:

> The vertically integrated industrial firm is quite unlike a mid-nineteenth century firm. The vertically integrated industrial combined into one centrally managed enterprise each specialized activity formerly carried out separately by independent firms. However, in order to control and coordinate these combined activities, the vertically integrated industrial firm had to develop new organizational methods (...the design of complex accounting systems).[10]

With manufacturers now becoming responsible for multiple products and processes, the market could not tell them what the costs of particular processes or component products were. The market could only let them know the cost of the final product delivered to the market.[11] The cost-accounting methods that existed at the time were in no way capable of supplying cost information for internal activities now becoming increasingly present inside single enterprises. Cost accounting was a product of the Industrial Revolution and was taking on new forms and covering new needs.[12] According to Dr. Johnson,

> the typical manufacturing firm operating before 1900 apparently expected its accounting system simply to provide information on short-run operations. Cost accounting records were the basic and most highly developed source of such information ... such firms used their relatively advanced cost systems almost exclusively to monitor material and labor costs at the factory level. This emphasis on shop and factory efficiency reflects, of course, the bias of such industrial engineers as Frederick W. Taylor, who designed many of the complex cost systems used by large manufacturing firms during the late nineteenth century.
>
> What is noteworthy in this necessarily brief description of accounting practices in typical manufacturing firms prior to 1900 is the fact that such firms evidently did not concentrate upon commercial efficiency and assessment of overall company performance.[13]

Engineers play the key role in developing accounting methods and practices.[14] The accounting methods used today were the result of innovative ideas that engineers such as Frederick Taylor, Alexander Hamilton Church, and many others devised during this critical period of change in the industrial landscape. As Dr. Johnson states above, these engineers had no interest in accounting. Their interest lay in measuring and managing internal activities that evolve by the growth of multiproduct and multiprocess firms. Dr. Johnson states that

> ironically, many of those authorities who wrote about product costing from 1885 to 1914 were not interested in accounting, but in estimating. They were writing as engineers interested in devising rational, uniform systems for pricing unique products in non-competitive markets. For this reason, they paid attention to the problems of how to allocate fixed costs to products in manufacturing enterprises. They had no fundamental interest in accounting *per se*.[15]

Dr. Wells adds that

> the engineers were not, in fact, concerned with accounts at all. Their references were all to "cost records." Those records were not necessarily double entry, or connected with the firm's general accounting system. They were seen, rather, as something designed and maintained by the engineer, for the engineer.... Failure to recognize the distinction between cost records and cost accounts may explain some of the confusion surrounding the origins of particular costing techniques.[16]

He further explains that "it seems likely that the highly complex systems of cost accounting being described by 1900 had their origins in simple daily diaries. We cannot conclude that they ... were originally devised as accounting systems at all."[17]

How engineers of this period developed cost-accounting methods will be further expanded upon later in this book, and Church's ideas are expounded into lean cost and managerial accounting.

RELEVANCE LOST: WHY COST ACCOUNTING FAILED INDUSTRY

Today's cost-managerial accounting has failed to fulfill it intentions. Its use has evolved from its original objectives to a purpose it was not intended for and utterly falls short to achieve. Dr. H. Thomas Johnson and Robert Kaplan's 1987 book, *Relevance Lost*, vividly illustrates this point, noting that "by 1925 virtually all management accounting practices used today had been developed."[18] Johnson and Kaplan explain how this happened:

> By the time these events [multiple processes and products] unfolded, the spirit and the knowledge of management accounting systems design, developed, and sustained throughout the hundred-year period from 1825 to 1925, had disappeared. Organizations become fixated on the cost systems and management reporting methods of the 1920s. When cost systems became automated on digital computers, starting in the mid-1960s, the system designers basically automated the manual systems they found in the factory. Left unquestioned was whether these systems were still sensible given the great expansion in information technology represented by electronic, digital computers and the already changed nature of the organization's operations.
>
> One might wonder why university researchers failed to note the growing obsolescence of organizations' management accounting systems and did not play a more active or more stimulative role to improve the art of management accounting systems design.[19] ... Sixty years of literature emerged advocating the separation of costs into fixed and variable components for making good product decisions and for controlling costs. This literature, very persuasive when illustrated in the simple one-product settings used by academic economists and accountants, never fully addressed the question of where fixed costs came from and how these costs needed to be covered by each of the products in the corporations' repertoire ... while actual organizations attempted to manage with antiquated systems in settings that had little relationship to the simplified model researchers assumed for analytic and teaching convenience.
>
> Ironically, as management accounting systems became less relevant to the organization's operations and strategy, many senior executives began to believe they could run their firms "by the numbers." Early twentieth-century organizations such as Du Pont, General Motors, and General Electric had been created by owners who understood the technology of their products and processes. In succeeding decades, however, chief executives

were selected whose entire career had been spent in staff functions such as accounting, finance, and legal. Lacking knowledge in their organizations' underlying technology, executives increasingly made decisions based upon their projected impact on short-term financial measures.[20]

As Dr. Johnson and Kaplan report and as this book will discuss in detail later, cost and management accounting methods developed in order to assist the decision-making process for single-process and product-focused organizations. With the evolution of multiproduct and multiprocess enterprises, the needs for internal measures to motivate and evaluate efficiency developed with no intention of measuring the profit of the overall business.[21] The innovation of the early engineers was completely directed at improving the effectiveness of the factory floor. As Johnson and Kaplan reveal, during the twentieth century accounting shifted from using the accounting information for the efficiencies of the factory floor, to using the information for overall financial results, back to the factory floor. The unfortunate result (the relevance lost) is that the factory floor systems are still in the form of the overall financial methods and thus incapable of supplying beneficial information for managing the shop floor.[22] Kaplan reports that

> contemporary researchers' knowledge of managers' behavior is based not on studying decisions and procedures of actual firms, but on the stylized models of managerial and firm behavior that have been articulated by economic theorists who, themselves, have limited first-hand knowledge of the behavior they have modeled. These models have not been developed for or tested on actual enterprises.[23]

THE EVIL OF OVERHEAD

Wells explains there is "clear evidence of the confusion which abounds in ... cost accounting systems. That confusion relates primarily to the allocation of overhead costs."[24] Bruce Baggaley of BMA Inc., a lean consulting firm, explains in further detail what Wells expresses:

> One assumption of standard costing is that all overheads need to be assigned to the product and that these overheads relate (in most cases) to the amount of labor required to make the product. This leads to the distortion of product costs. Some products appear to cost more than they really do and other products appear to cost less. These costs mislead people and cause them to make wrong decisions relating to pricing, profitability, make/buy, and so forth.[25]

The biggest culprit of today's cost-managerial accounting irrelevancy is the overhead methods of standard costing. Its fallacy has been well documented since Dr. Johnson and Kaplan's *Relevance Lost* in a number of books and articles. Unfortunately, little attention has arisen and little change has happened in manufacturing. The issue with overhead allocation is that it achieves exactly what used to exist over one hundred years ago but does not exist today in the vast majority of manufacturing enterprises—single process and product operations. Dr. Johnson and Kaplan reveal that "overhead costs were combined into large, frequently plant-wide, overhead pools. The large overhead pools were then allocated to cost centers in different ways. Some factories simply allocated all costs directly to cost centers based on estimated direct labor hours or dollars. Others were somewhat more scientific. For each overhead pool, they chose some measure for allocating the pool to individual cost centers."[26]

Dr. Johnson and Kaplan's explanation is typical for most operations using overhead allocations. The problem with such a method is that for its allocation directive it uses an item that is generally below 15 percent of product costs; typically, it is even in the 3 to 8 percent range. So why would an operation use this method? According to Dr. Johnson and Kaplan,

> Such a system is simple to install, simple to operate, and simple to understand. Only one account is needed to transfer the cost of a component or subassembly from one stage to the next, thereby saving storage and processing time (probably an important consideration when the system is operated manually). The system generates product costs that satisfy all external reporting constituencies—stockholders, tax authorities, regulators, and creditors. *That for managers it is at best useless, and more likely misleading, seems less important* [emphasis added].[27]

This quote describes the crux of the problem. As stated previously, traditional accounting procedures for cost and managerial means are actually a result of the needs for external or financial accounting systems, *not* for internal system needs. Brian Maskell makes the same point very explicitly in his 1996 book, *Making the Numbers Count*: "There is no value to integrating the management accounts and the financial accounts. Each is serving a different purpose and linking them is irrelevant and harmful."[28] "In addition," he adds, "overhead absorption variance is a measure so complex and intangible that very few people in the company really understand it—let alone see its relevance—so the people are being driven by something they don't understand to do things that harm the company and do not serve the customers."[29]

The reason behind the development of complexity from a system that was originally a simple system is that it is being forced into enterprises with very complex dynamics. This is due to the wide variety of processes and products or components that make up a single product or a small number of products. For example, the engine manufacturing that will be used for a model operation in this book will be focused on manufacturing a small single cylinder engine. In order to manufacture this engine, the operation must assemble the final product (the engine), assemble several subassemblies, fabricate a number of components for the assembly and subassemblies, and machine a wide variety of components (crankshafts, cam-gears, cylinders, pistons, and so on) in order to make the final product. Obviously, this type of operation leads to a complex system of a vast variety of products and processes even though the final product is just one engine model.

Maskell illustrates nicely the shortfalls of traditional management and cost accounting using overhead methods and boldly and delightfully presents a grand prize competition by challenging any reader to apply for the prize if they can provide a valid purpose for an overhead absorption variance report.[30] He confirms Dr. Johnson and Kaplan's points with clear poignancy. The very designers who developed the methods, the engineers of the industrial revolution, also recognized these points in the very early part of the twentieth century.

Eli Goldratt's famous 1984 manufacturing novel, *The Goal*, which is based on the Theory of Constraints, warns of the potential disaster associated with absorption costing of traditional cost-management accounting. One such view states: "Any system such as absorption costing that rewards managers for building inventory to manipulate profits can be far more dysfunctional than even the critics of the 1950s imagined."[31]

RELEVANCE REGAINED: REFLECT
THE NEEDS OF THE FACTORY FLOOR

Dr. Johnson and Kaplan also present the point illuminated in Chapter 1: cost systems must be a reflection of operations and servant systems to support operational needs. They affirm that "the cost control system should build on the production control system, likely already in existence. Cost control system designers will need to leave their offices and work closely at the production process to learn what information can be captured and reported back to production supervisors to enhance their process and cost control activities."[32] An important term used by Dr. Johnson and Kaplan here is *enhance*. It is important, as they point out, that system developments help to enhance shop-floor management rather than controlling the decision-making process on the factory floor. As will be discussed later in more detail, in a lean manufacturing environment proper support information, not controlling information, is key to implementing and sustaining proper flow. And as was shown, the loss of accounting's relevance was driven by accounting information inaccurately controlling actions in operations driven out of the purpose of external reporting. Control of the system becomes implicit within the system and not explicit from the external reporting system.

The development, implementation, and execution of the physical lean system will be discussed in detail in later sections of this book. It is important to understand how the cost system must support this effort, but that will not be possible until at least some of the physical implementation is underway. As explained above, this is because the lean cost system will reflect the physical operations. The very cost system proposed in this book is dependent on the successful transformation from batch manufacturing to flow manufacturing in operations. Mark DeLuzio, former Danaher Corporation accounting executive, discloses: "The thing about finance is you cannot lead it, you have to follow the changes in the company. You can't go make changes in your financial systems without the company making the changes first."[33]

THE TRUTH ABOUT GAAP

Many manufacturing executives and leaders[34] are reluctant to drop traditional cost and managerial accounting practices. The major reason is their lack of understanding of what is needed and what existing systems and methods are and are not capable of doing. The biggest factor in this misunderstanding is the constraint (or the misconception of constraint) of generally accepted accounting practices (GAAP). GAAP is a very important part of accounting and critical to maintaining basic standards to give people and institutions credible and valuable information for decision making in the market.[35] But the truth about cost-managerial accounting is that GAAP should have *nothing* to do with a firm's cost-managerial accounting system. Cost-managerial accounting is for internal decision making and GAAP covers external, or financial, accounting decision making and methods. Maskell states:

> The spurious argument given time and again by reluctant accountants is that they must adhere to general accepted accounting practice (GAAP). This *is* *true* of financial accounting because the government has a bad habit of putting financial accountants in jail if they violate accounting practices. But the internal control of an organization is entirely under the control of the company itself.... This means that the accounting systems must become the servants of production, marketing, and engineering—not the other way round.[36]

Maskell further explains that

> financial accounting is the task of preparing and presenting an accurate representation of the company's business to outsiders.... Cost and management accounting, on the other hand, is used internally to help the company's managers control and improve the business ... there is no legal requirement to perform these tasks in any particular way or to perform them at all.[37]

Maskell's point is reinforced by a book published by the Institute of Management Accountants research foundation, which is focused on accounting issues present in implementing lean manufacturing. GAAP is most concerned with consistent methodology and overall total inventory costs, not the accurate costs of individual product families. Again, GAAP is an appendage of financial or external accounting practices, not internal cost-management accounting methods, although unfortunately that is its use today. Dr. Dileep Dhavale[38] of Clark University's Graduate School of Management points out: "A financial accountant is interested in an estimate of costs of total ending inventory and goods sold. Whether or not cost estimates of hundreds of individual products are accurate is unimportant as long as the totals are accurate. Furthermore, these estimates, as far as generally accepted accounting practices (GAAP) are concerned, can be obtained by consistent application of any systematic and rational procedure."[39]

Orest Fiume[40] and Jean Cunningham[41] poignantly express the reality between lean management accounting and GAAP when they state, "Nothing in Lean Management Accounting violates GAAP."[42]

HOW COST-MANAGERIAL ACCOUNTING FAILS THOSE IT SHOULD SERVE

Dr. Johnson states: "The fundamental reason for the lost relevance of modern management accounting is the belief that businesses can both plan and control their affairs with accounting information that is compiled for financial reporting purposes."[43]

Maybe the worst dilemma of accounting is that it fails the very people it was developed for and meant to serve: the operations folks. It is widely recognized that manufacturing managers and supervisors who sit in on monthly meetings get berated by management for not making the numbers because of variance problems, underabsorb, and so on. Most of these managers and supervisors do not have a clue of what exactly to do in regard to these missed numbers that they get lambasted about each

OVERHEAD, AN OLD-TIME SOCIALISTIC POLICY: *INDUSTRIAL SOCIALISM*

So • cial • ism (sō'shə-lĭz'əm)

n. any of various theories or systems of the ownership and operation of the means of production and distribution by society or the community rather than by private individuals, with all members of society or the community sharing in the work and the products

Source: Webster's New World Dictionary

Socialism tries to divide assets evenly for the entire population. It promotes that we all have equal input or generation of goods and therefore we all should have an even distribution of the goods. The thought is nice in theory but it is very far from the truth. There is not an equal input or generation of goods. The same analogy applies to overhead when used in accounting. The use of overhead indicates that operations have costs generated equally by everyone or by every process; therefore, we must distribute its expense equally to every department or product. The analogy can also apply to the practice of companies doing such a poor job tracking costs and those who generate or use them that it is only *fair* to equally charge all departments for it. Such an example is an inadequate response to this situation although it is a widely accepted practice. The real solution is to create a better and simpler tracking system. If you apply lean principles, you do just that.

Lean principles demand that companies align their operations around products and not processes, or the value stream. In doing this it becomes much simpler to focus all assets, resources, and utilities (for example, electricity) against a particular product. Doing this helps create what companies are interested in knowing: a product's cost. (See Chapter 10 on right designing and rightsizing equipment and processes where it reviews the financial reasons to right design and rightsize.)

month. I have, on many occasions, witnessed these types of meetings and felt a deep sympathy for the managers and supervisors as they scramble to explain and make sense of these monthly accusations. Most are very knowledgeable and capable manufacturing people, but they cannot relate to what countermeasures are needed to specifically address the variance reports that are blamed on them. Three primary failures result from this shameful situation.

The First Failure: No Help for Those in Need

The first failure is that management accounting reports are of *little help to operating managers* as they attempt to reduce costs and improve productivity.[44] The reports are not timely and do not give any indication of what type of actions to take. They are generally focused on direct labor utilization in a context unrelated to customer requirements. These operational inputs often represent only a small percentage (generally 4 to 12 percent) of the cost of the product(s) being manufactured. This charge frequently sends managers off in the wrong direction, pursuing actions that can be very detrimental to customer requirements.

Most factory managers and companies are always pursuing cost reduction projects. This approach is *wrong* when cost reduction is not focused on improvements in the value stream or the implementation of flow. Unfortunately, cost reduction typically is pursued to satisfy a flawed accounting system that may be grossly unrelated to long term success or profitability. As will be discussed in more detail later, the goal should not be cost reduction or cost reduction activities in and of themselves. Instead, companies should be developing flow manufacturing and teaching, directing and adjusting resources to accomplish this goal. This is the world of the lean enterprise.

The Second Failure: No Accuracy Here

Management accounting reports *do not give accurate information* on product costs. Simply by the nature of the method explained previously, the allocation through absorption methods and procedures used today were developed for single processes and products, not for multiple processes and products, which are typical of most of today's manufacturers. (Also see the insert on page 19 explaining the socialistic nature of overhead allocation.) Today, costs are distributed to products by simplistic and arbitrary measures, usually direct labor that does not properly represent the resources consumed by each product as it is being produced. The unfortunate result is that major operational decisions are made using the incorrectly derived cost information.[45]

The Story of the Crankshaft Machining Dilemma

A number of years ago, I experienced difficulty developing information to show the cost savings of implementing machining cells. The product was a crankshaft with an annual volume of approximately one million. There were about forty variations of the crankshaft, and traditional standard costing was used to track the cost of machining

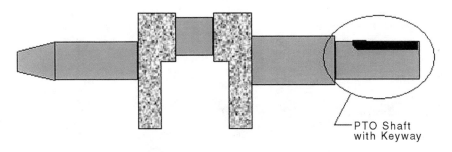

PTO Shaft
with Keyway

Figure 2.1 The "high runner" straight-keyed or straight PTO crankshaft

the product. Using the standard costing and data collection system that was used throughout the company, I compared the highest volume variation, which was approximately 67 percent of the annual volume, to one of the lowest volume variations, which was under 3 percent of the annual volume.

The "high runner" was a straight power take-off (PTO) shaft with a keyway, simple and straightforward to manufacture. It was typical to most of the crankshafts for this model, which usually varied only in diameter and length of the PTO shaft and size and length of the keyway (see Figure 2.1).

The "low runner" had a completely unique PTO shaft. It had an extra diameter and a pinion gear, which required the extra operations of turning the second diameter, the groove, and the pinion diameter; hardening the pinion diameter; and shaping the gear teeth for the pinion gear (see Figure 2.2).

The standard costing system showed the pinion crankshaft (with its extra operations) to be less costly to manufacture than the straight-keyed crankshaft. This obviously erroneous information about costs was very disturbing since the company used this information for a wide variety of business decisions—including the monthly

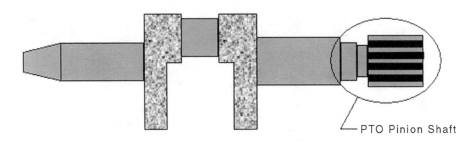

PTO Pinion Shaft

Figure 2.2 The "low runner" pinion gear PTO crankshaft

berating sessions the factory managers and supervisors had to go through because of incorrect information.[46]

The incorrect information about costs provided by the standard costing system in this example vividly illustrates the failure of traditional standard costing systems to provide relevant information for business decisions or operation decisions.

The Third Failure: Driving the Wrong Direction

The third failure of management accounting reports is *the questionable actions it drives factory managers to make* during their daily, weekly, and monthly decision-making processes. Such reports compel managers and supervisors to focus on the short-term cycle of the profit-and-loss statement rather than on long-range sustainable profitability. Most manufacturing people have heard of the hockey-stick effect in which production activities in the last week of the month increase substantially in order to "make the numbers." This situation causes extreme stress on a monthly basis for everyone involved with the operation—operators, managers, inventory, and machines—and frequently detracts from overall profitability. Dr. Johnson opines in his *Relevance Regained* that department supervisors will, without regard to customer demand, keep their people busy and machines running needlessly in order to reduce their standard cost variances. This action leads to an increase in product lead times, inventory of in-process and finished products and quality issues because by "using such targets and variances" it "encourage[s] high utilization of worker and machine time." He writes: "With so flawed a system, people sometimes put in hours creating defects, just so the department can report enough direct labor hours to be classified as 'efficient.'"[47]

This short-term mentality also propels a cut in short-term spending on direct improvement activities in order to "make the numbers." The financial accounting system treats many cash outlays as expenses of the period in which they are made even though these outlays will benefit future periods.[48] This will have a negative impact on training, improvement activities, preventative maintenance, and employee morale.

Ohno Recognizes Accounting's Failure

Taiichi Ohno (see Figure 2.3),[49] the renowned creator of the Toyota Production System (TPS), stresses caution when accounting practices are used. He writes: "When we want to evaluate something, we usually end up doing some kind of cost accounting. There is nothing wrong with cost accounting, but it sometimes leads top executives to faulty judgments."[50]

Ohno's statement may be a bit milder than his actual opinion. He is known to have credited Toyota executives for keeping the accountants out of his way while he worked on the shop floor to develop the techniques, methods, and principles that have become TPS.[51] John Shook[52] reports that Ohno's "battles with the chief accountant were legendary."[53] Ohno gratefully credits Eiji Toyoda for encouraging him to go on and for trusting his efforts.[54] In *Workplace Management*, Ohno references the illusions of arithmetic cost calculations forced by "number-pushers,"[55]

Figure 2.3   Taiichi Ohno
Source: Courtesy of Toyota Motor Corporation, Toyota City, Japan.

obviously not an endearing comment by Ohno. Ohno continues to express his displeasure of accounting methods in a later chapter of *Workplace Management*:

> This is nonsense—a particularly flagrant example of what happens when you go along with conventional bookkeepers' wisdom.
>
> The fact remains, however, that many people simply go by the numbers and fail to understand clearly whether costs are high or low....
>
> What happens is that from an accounting point of view costs will rise and fall. When they do, I hear everyone complain that the situation is intolerable, yet they continue to come up with silly reasons to explain why they can't rationalize operations in indirectly related departments. This way of thinking about things is widespread, but in my opinion, it's a big mistake to be deceived into thinking costs have really dropped.[56]

Ohno clearly maintained his focus on developing a better system and executing it properly. The same focus is key to the premise of this book: right designing a manufacturing system (and its support systems) and correctly executing its function.

Ohno also reveals the issue with the disconnection of departments and subsystems,[57] stating that "everyone has the impression that accounting is responsible for cost-cutting, but if you think about it, accounting is entirely incapable of reducing costs."[58]

Ohno also confirmed his opinions with Eli Goldratt a number of years later in a discussion they had. He writes: "When I met Dr. Ohno, the inventor of Kanban, the JIT system of Toyota, he told me that cost accounting was the one thing that he had to fight against all his life. 'It was not enough to chase out the cost accountants from the plants, the problem was to chase cost accounting from my people's minds.'"[59]

Ohno was not alone in his distaste for financial folks. Henry Ford, whose writings were intensely studied by Ohno, had an aversion to the financial community as well. Ford writes: "And that is the danger of having bankers in business. They think solely in terms of money. They think of a factory as making money, not goods. They watch the money, not the efficiency of production."[60]

Ohno was not alone in recognizing management accounting's failure. Peter Drucker also warned manufacturing management about the failure: "Peter Drucker, in a 1963 *Harvard Business Review* article, warned manufacturers that traditional cost accounting systems were preventing them from seeing the actual costs of their 'product clutter' strategy. He foresaw how traditional cost systems cause high-volume products to subsidize the manufacture of customized specialty products."[61]

WHY FINANCIAL ACCOUNTING BECAME
COST-MANAGERIAL ACCOUNTING[62]

How did cost-managerial accounting become financial accounting and in turn reappear as today's cost-managerial accounting? It happened as a result of the development of methods for inventory valuation. Dr. Johnson and Kaplan summarize the misguided loop of accounting methods, which was critical to the use of and way of thinking about accounting methods:

> Engineer-managers in metal-working firms between 1880 and 1910 had developed procedures for computing managerially relevant product costs. But those procedures disappeared from manufacturing accounting practice and writing after 1914. In their place appeared the costing procedures that twentieth-century accountants developed to value inventories for financial reports. While those procedures yield cost information that apparently aids financial reporting, the same information is generally misleading and irrelevant for strategic product decisions.[63]

Unfortunately, the process and methods for costing information used by the early engineer-managers, which was separate from accounting and used to help manage the manufacturing operation, has been forgotten or ignored and is completely unacceptable for a lean enterprise. Its use came about because of its ease of use and simplicity for auditors to develop inventory values. Again, these auditors borrowed the method from the engineers and had no intention of it being used for factory management purposes.[64] Dr. Johnson writes:

> The term management accounting appropriately describes the textbooks and courses that since 1960 have taught students how to adjust financial information for management decision-making. The subject is closer to accounting—the accumulation of financial information for public reporting—than it is to cost management. It bears little resemblance to pre-World War I cost management.[65]

Some of the innovators of accounting methods during the early part of the twentieth century also knew of such a problem. One of them, Church (whose ideas and methods will be reviewed in detail in later sections of this book), warns in his 1910 book of the misuse of deriving costing information and how it leads to misguided decisions.[66]

Dr. Johnson and Kaplan provide a final point about the misdirection and misguidedness of traditional cost-management accounting. Even though engineers developed industry's accounting methods during the period of 1885 through 1925, financial accountants of the World War I through World War II period never considered using the methods for operational control but *only* for developing information for external reporting.[67] The change occurred post-WWII.

FROM COST ACCOUNTING TO COST MANAGEMENT

According to Dr. Johnson:

> The purpose of cost accounting is to prepare information needed for financial reporting, and it has fulfilled that objective admirably. Cost accounting has failed managers because cost information compiled for financial reporting can rarely be used to manage costs, except under conditions that almost never exist in real manufacturing organizations. Manufacturing managers do not need better cost accounting; they need better information for cost management.[68]

As Dr. Johnson explains, many of the methods that have been discussed and developed over the last decade are very similar to the methods that manufacturing managers developed and advocated over ninety years ago, decades before cost accounting became the unfortunate source of information for today's cost management activities.[69] Dr. Johnson defines cost management:[70]

> Cost management uses cost information to evaluate how efficaciously a business consumes resources to create products or services that have value to customers. It is much older than cost accounting, having roots in the origins of managed enterprise—in the US, the first or second decade of the 19th century.[71]

Johnson differentiates further between the two:

> The difference between cost accounting and cost management information is based in how indirect costs are treated. Cost accounting treats indirect costs in the least costly manner possible—aggregating them in a few cost pools and usually attaching them to products with a single denominator. Cost management, on the other hand, requires that indirect costs be traced carefully to the consumption of specific resources that cause costs. Product cost accounting information, therefore, is not useful for product cost management if there is any diversity among products.[72]

With the proliferation of products and processes in industry between 1885 and 1925, companies needed information that would help manage internal processes and product lines and help them compare internal costs to the cost in the market. The engineers of the time worked to develop innovative methods to cover these needs. Their influence was significant and important because they were students of manufacturing technology and could directly relate to operational needs and methods, and they used their intimate knowledge to develop, build, and debate costing methods, unlike those who had no connection to or direct understanding of manufacturing who developed many models and theories, particularly the models of allocation, during the middle part of the twentieth century. Dr. Johnson concurs: "These practices were devised by engineers and industrialists, working in actual organizations, rather than by academic researchers."[73]

Johnson continues by explaining that

> managers needed information on how decisions about product mix could affect overall profits. To estimate the impact of individual products on a firm's overall profitability, engineer-managers in the late 19th-century metal-working firms sought to develop accurate product cost information.[74]

In conclusion, Johnson points out that "Until the early 1900s, manufacturers invariably developed cost information to facilitate management, not accounting."[75]

This same theme of helping management decisions instead of accounting processes will be the objective of the procedures and methods developed and discussed later in this book. The aim of accurate product costs is another central premise that will be discussed later, along with how this type of information should be used with other types of information to contribute to good decision making in the lean firm. It must be emphasized that the reason for the development of the cost-accounting method for inventory valuation at the turn of the century was for financial accounting purposes and was *never* intended for cost management purposes by those engineers that developed the method or by those auditors that used the method.

Dr. Robin Cooper[76] of Emory University's Goizueta Business School asserts:

> Cost accounting systems (as opposed to cost management systems) are the primary source of cost information. Cost accounting systems have different

objectives from cost management systems. Cost accounting systems support the financial accounting process by determining the costs of good sold and inventory values. These systems report distorted product costs and do not provide powerful mechanisms for cost management or control. In contrast, cost management systems are designed to help the firms manage costs. Their objectives include accurate product costs and the creation of pressures to reduce and control costs.[77]

The engineers that developed many of the costing procedures from 1885 through 1925 focused much effort on finding methods that would directly associate cost to products—not arbitrary allocation methods, but ways to assign the actual resources that each product consumed. They—in keeping with the engineer stereotype—wanted to get straight facts on exactly what each product would cost. Dr. Johnson believes that one reason this method eventually fell by the wayside is that it was too cumbersome to put into actual use. At that period in time, the costs exceeded the benefits.

Based on the failures that the misuse of cost-accounting has created and continues to generate in today's manufacturing industry, management accounting in the remainder of this book will be considered *dead*. Cost management is the philosophy and the methodology developed and discussed within these pages, although the term cost accounting may be used in reference to the issues it has created in the past. The cost-management philosophy is the only concept that can support the lean enterprise; cost accounting simply is not capable of fulfilling its operational needs. Dr. Cooper concurs:

> The power of these new systems rests on the principle that people cannot manage costs—they can only manage what causes costs. That is what cost management is about. Information for cost accounting has nothing to do with it.[78]

This viewpoint is held by all of the leading lean accounting thinkers today. Fiume and Cunningham conclude that "instead of cost accounting, the lean accountant's focus should be on cost management, which includes a different kind of cost accounting. We have learned that it is far less important to know the cost of making an individual product than it is to manage the costs of the business as a whole. In short, traditional cost accounting is narrow-minded."[79]

The failure of cost-accounting information to have the capability to manage operations was not an idea only realized in the latter half of the twentieth century. Frederick Taylor discusses the potential misuse of cost information in the last decade of the nineteenth century. He writes:

> There was a certain community of feeling, in those days, between the boys in the shop and the master, which I think passed away when machine-shop owners became corporations, when they were managed by a board of directors who never saw the workmen, who knew nothing of them, individually, and, as I fear, cared less.... The directors look only at the balance sheet.... If any way can be devised by which this can be remedied, it will be certainly an advantage to each.[80]

Taylor was not alone in this warning, as will be shown later. Church also stressed this point in the 1910s. Also, the concern was much of the driving force behind why Taylor, Church, and others worked to develop better management and cost-management methods.

FROM COST MANAGEMENT TO FLOW MANUFACTURING

Even with the methods developed from 1885 through 1925 to help manufacturers with cost management, the seemingly most effective method would eventually fall out of favor due to the difficult requirements to collect information and decipher it into product cost information. With manufacturing firms growing larger and having to manage more processes, products, and markets, the amount of information to track and gather became staggering. And with the increase of batch-style manufacturing[81] the amount of information only continued to grow.

With batch manufacturing becoming the predominant production system world-wide, the innovative cost-management ideas developed around 1900 appear to be nothing more than a blip on the industrial timeline. Two major reasons for the downfall of the direct costing method are the difficulty of gathering cost data due to the complexity of batch manufacturing and the lack of information systems with the capability to digest and present cost information. The unfortunate default has been the use of cost-accounting techniques of overhead, standard costs, and inventory valuation.

However, there is hope. The hope rests in developing a lean enterprise. Through such a development the first of the major issues preventing the use of direct product cost is eliminated. If a manufacturing company truly converts to lean, then it removes the batch-style manufacturing methods and inserts flow manufacturing. Flow manufacturing destroys the process-focused departments and in their place establishes product-focused value streams. Because of the very nature of product-value streams, a focus of resources to a specific product or product family is created.

If designed and implemented correctly, this change in physical manufacturing eliminates the complex and confusing network of product movement that is inherent to batch manufacturing. Not only does the lean value stream focus the product flow and resources required to manufacture it, it in turn eliminates the huge amount of information generated by the batch-manufacturing environment. Also, the much smaller amount of information generated by the value stream is directly focused on and around the product's value stream. This situation creates an ideal operation and supports the methods developed around 1900.

FLOW VERSUS ECONOMIES OF SCALE

Dr. Johnson and Bröms concluded that "thinking has led companies to optimize cost with 'economies of scale.' They run large-scale plants as fast and as full as possible, to achieve the highest possible throughput for the existing level of costs."[82]

Dr. Johnson and Bröms contrast Toyota by explaining how Toyota "views customers and workers as parts connected in a web of interrelationships." This approach allows Toyota to focus on everyone within the system and "produce to order" following a few basic principles and also frees them from not driving results "by manipulating external stimuli."[83]

In *Profit beyond Measure*, Dr. Johnson and Bröms explain how Ohno described TPS as a "limited production" system. Ohno's thinking was to avoid doing anything in excess of what it takes to produce what could be sold and no more.[84] The concept of right designing systems and machines will be further discussed in more detail in a later chapter. It is a very key concept to becoming a lean enterprise and to the success of developing a lean cost-management system.

The quote from *Profit beyond Measure* illustrates the contrast between traditional batch production and lean production. This is the very reason why James Womack and Daniel Jones named their 1996 book *Lean Thinking*. To truly implement lean into a manufacturing enterprise, a completely different thought process must be understood. The traditional viewpoint of manufacturing and economies of scale must be abandoned. This change in thinking has been extremely difficult to achieve and is most likely the reason why so few companies have successfully transitioned from traditional manufacturing to lean manufacturing. Mark DeLuzio,[85] in a 2001 interview with *Manufacturing News'* Richard McCormack, refers to "how you think" as a precursor to successful lean transformation.[86]

Another interesting point is that this different thinking originally was developed and implemented in the United States at the Ford Motor Company. Lean thinking was innovated at Henry Ford's Highland Park plant (see Figure 2.4). The Highland Park plant was the cradle of this thought process and achieved significant accomplishments in flow manufacturing.[87]

Figure 2.4 Highland Park in the fall, 1913
Source: Collection of the Henry Ford Museum, Benson Ford Research Center, Greenfield Village, Photo No. P.833.700.

Toyota executives, particularly Ohno and Eiji Toyoda, understood the methods Ford developed and implemented and brought them to Japan, applying them to their own operation and market situation. Toyota was able to raise the flow principles to a higher level after World War II and continues to evolve the system to the present.[88]

River Rouge, Toyota, and a Different Way of Thinking

The interesting aspects of Henry Ford's River Rouge plant were twofold. First, the business model applied at the River Rouge plant was a transition not only for the Ford Motor Company but also for industry in general. The River Rouge plant was a vast industrial machine, which Ford intentionally developed into a completely vertically integrated industrial complex. At the Rouge, the manufacturing flow of Highland Park was transformed into manufacturing of scale economies. The massive Rouge contained elements of both the flow and economies of scale philosophies.

The second aspect of the Rouge rode directly on top of the first. Members from Toyota visited the Rouge plant in 1950.[89] Inspired by the Toyota Motor Company's founder, Kiichiro Toyoda, the Toyota executives who visited the Rouge saw something much different than their counterparts from the Big Three automakers—Ford, General Motors, and Daimler-Chrysler—had seen.[90] What the Toyota folks saw was the ghost of Highland Park: *flow*. The flow principles onto which they latched were the very essence that made Highland Park and the Model T such a tremendous success for so many years. They were the principles of a system, which Kiichiro Toyoda had aspired to several years before. The Toyota members took what they saw and applied it vigorously to their young company.[91]

Executives for the Big Three viewed something entirely different at the Rouge. They saw economies of scale in action and took its principles and methods back to their own companies and applied it vigorously. This type of thinking become the predominant business mentality applied in industry worldwide, and it still prevails today. This industrial thinking and the issues it creates were discussed in the early sections of this book.

In *Profit beyond Measure*, Dr. Johnson and Bröms enumerate this story that was told in the book *The Reckoning*:

> Toasting Philip Caldwell, the head of Ford who in 1982 was visiting Japan, Eiji Toyoda, of the Toyota company, said, "There is no secret to how we learned to do what we do, Mr. Caldwell. We learned it at the Rouge."[92]

Johnson and Bröms further recall that

> it must have been obvious to Mr. Caldwell in 1982 that he and his colleagues at Ford, as well as his counterparts in the other Big Three companies, had definitely not viewed the operations at Henry Ford's Rouge River plant in the same way as had Toyota.[93]

Johnson and Bröms elaborate that

to understand the differences in how Toyota and the Big Three interpreted operations at the River Rouge plant is to understand the difference between Toyota's distinctive thinking and the thinking that has dominated management practice in most of the world's other businesses during the past five decades.[94]

As Dr. Johnson and Bröms illuminate, in this story it is crucial "how different *methods of thinking* affect long-term performance" and that "is the lesson to be learned."[95]

The lessons learned by the Toyota executives about the importance of flow manufacturing are often missed by executives in business today. The lesson of flow learned is a result of the Highland Park plant.[96] This vision viewed by Eiji Toyoda and Shoichi Saito at the Rouge plant features a foundation, principles, and methods built and implemented at the Highland Park plant. For without Highland Park, the Rouge would have never been possible.

This convergence of thinking illustrates the power of the thinking process in business. It has shaped industry worldwide for nearly a century and has only begun relenting in the last twenty years with the rise of Toyota and TPS. Thinking[97] of how business is operated shapes how business is managed and in turn how we design and use the systems for operating and managing, hence cost-management accounting versus cost management.[98]

Flow

Dr. Johnson and Bröms maintain that "when work links customer with customer in a balanced, continuous flow every step of the way, it satisfies every new customer demand with minimum resources. Toyota's 'produce to order' system, for example, balances resources at every stage to the amount needed to advance one customer's order."[99]

Flow is fundamental to lean manufacturing. Flow manufacturing is key to establishing the most effective principles and methods for a manufacturing enterprise. Flow ties an operation directly to the customer's needs and demands. Effective implementation of flow creates an enterprise, that utilizes the minimum amount of resources to satisfy the customer's requirements. Toyota has accomplished this and continues to refine it in the pursuit of perfection. Ford's Highland Park plant was the origin of these principles and methods. The engineers of Highland Park also relentlessly pursued principles of flow as Dr. Jeffrey Liker,[100] a professor of industrial and operations engineering and the director of the Japan Technology Management Program at the University of Michigan, explains: "A focus on 'flow' has continued to be a foundation for Toyota's success globally in the 21st century."[101]

Flow aligns everything to meet only what the customer requires. This pursuit is how TPS achieves the most cost effective manufacturing environment. Many of today's companies drive cost-reduction activities. Toyota does not. Cost reduction is the wrong approach. It promotes point improvements, sometimes referred to as cherry picking, and does not address the actual need, which is to establish flow. Truly lean companies work to develop and establish flow through creating value streams. Unless a company is ready and willing to do this, no number of cost-reduction programs will achieve the improvements and effectiveness of instituting flowing value streams. Dr. Johnson stresses this point:

> A more productive exercise would begin by recognizing that the fundamental problem is not "cost." Rather, the problem is a failure to organize work so that everything needed to satisfy customer expectations is part of one continuous, self-organizing stream of activity. To the extent that it is necessary to perform activity outside of that stream, more resources are consumed, and costs are greater than would be the case if all work were integrated in a continuous flow.[102]

Implementing flow is about developing one-piece flow throughout the value stream of product families. Almost every piece of literature on TPS or lean refers to the establishment of one-piece flow. One-piece flow is key to the pursuit of perfect flow. No one has achieved this goal, but a few relentlessly pursue it, such as Toyota and its group companies. It is the reason why Womack and Jones included "perfection" as the fifth and final principle in their book, *Lean Thinking*.[103] It provides a never-ending drive to eliminate waste from the system, or as Ohno explained, a vision to achieve "limited" production. If one were to view all of the principles and tools in TPS, they all can be viewed as simply a means to an end with flow (ideally one-piece flow) being the end. All of the techniques and tools are methods and functions to support flow (see Figure 2.5). Dr. Liker explains that "all the supporting tools of lean such as quick equipment changeovers, standardized work, pull systems, and error proofing, were all essential to creating flow."[104]

As discussed previously, lean thinking got its start at Ford's Highland Park plant and Toyota took these basic principles and applied them to their specific situation to develop what is known today as TPS. Figure 2.5 illustrates that all methods and tools are there to support flow. These techniques are "countermeasures" to either establish flow where it does not currently exist or resolve interruptions in flow. Toyota very well may have acquired their countermeasure mentality from Ford. Many of Toyota's early executives, such as Kiichiro Toyoda, Eiji Toyoda, and Taiichi Ohno, studied Ford's writings and work. Hartley Barclay, in his 1936 book, *Ford Production Methods*, squarely hits the attitude that is alive and well at Toyota and was learned from Henry Ford: "It is evident that Ford progresses by solving difficulties rather than by evading them."[105] This is the very day-to-day behavior and mentality that drives Toyota today.

Two authors, Dr. H. Thomas Johnson and Dr. Steven Spear,[106] have written about the principles and ideas essential to TPS, but a close examination of their brilliant and well-written work supports that what they suggest manifests itself as flow. Their writings illuminate what I call the Zen of TPS.

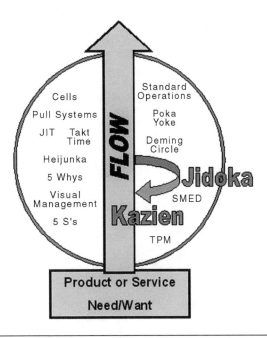

Figure 2.5 It's all about ... *flow!*

In a keynote address for the 1997 Lean Manufacturing Conference at the University of Kentucky, Mike Kitano, then president of Toyota Motor Manufacturing North America, disclosed the secret of TPS as being "one-by-one confirmation." One-by-one confirmation, which means one-piece flow, is about doing it right the first time.[107] One-piece flow is the physical manifestation of one-by-one confirmation, and both Dr. Johnson's and Dr. Spear's writings support this thinking in manufacturing. Such a change in thinking will modify how manufacturing systems—machines, processes, systems, support functions, and people's activities—are designed.

Economies of Scale

"Economies of scale" can be defined as costs per unit falling as the speed and volume of output rise.[108] It has become the mantra of industry throughout the twentieth century and continues today.

The economies-of-scale mentality will work as long as output growth is consumed by the market, but as soon as the market slows too much, levels off, or declines, the success gained from scale economies rapidly fails. When this occurs, two undesirable issues occur. The first problem is that managers are not trained to deal with this type of situation, other than applying plant closings, layoffs, and the like. Secondly, manufacturing systems were not designed for such a situation and cannot adjust to deal with markets slowing or shrinking. This is a two-front dilemma with which industry is continuing to struggle. As industry people slowly learn about lean principles, they work to try to adjust their enterprises, but it has been and continues to be an uphill battle.

Most managers, executives, and engineers do not understand the underlying principles of TPS and only pick up the tools and apply them; therefore, when issues occur when applying the tools, they have little or no understanding of what to do to resolve the problem and ultimately fail with implementation.[109] The transformation to the lean enterprise continues to be difficult. What is needed to remedy the struggle for companies to understand the underlying principles of TPS is a much deeper understanding of what lean manufacturing really strives to accomplish and a complete system design to achieve it. Toyota has and continues to properly design the complete system to give customers just what they want exactly when they want it while maintaining superior quality at a minimum price.[110] To only remove waste from the current systems helps and is an improvement, but the more pressing issue is that the entire enterprise system needs to be completely redesigned. Obviously this is not an easy or quick task.

The economies-of-scale mindset leads managers to focus on cost reduction at point locations, not system improvements. As mentioned previously, cost reductions are not the issue—establishing continuously flowing (called one-piece flow) value stream is what must be pursued. The focus on point-location improvements may seem to make sense at the level of micro-department, but it reinstitutes the ever-demanding increase in volume mentality, which is the crux of the economies-of-scale failure.

Batch production is the result of economies of scale. In order to maintain favorable costs, managers push output through their local areas or departments, creating an environment of speedy, increased output. As discussed in the previous section, The Evil of Overhead, such managers need to increase output to allow more product to "absorb" accounting/costing, thus providing the illusion of reduced costs. This mentality can be so ingrained that even if product is being produced in a cellular-value stream-flow operation, the manager is still yelling at his people to bring down costs: "We need more cost-reduction projects!" The demand to produce more and decrease costs creates a vicious cycle, which confuses and deflates operation folks. Dr. Johnson explains such a problem:

> The main cause of overhead cost is kept to a minimum by minimizing the unit costs of output produced in every individual process. In other words, total cost is assumed to be the sum of individual costs in all the parts. Thus, the strategy for achieving minimum total cost is to produce as much output as possible in each and every part of the organization. Minimizing the cost per unit of output from every individual operation presumably ensures the lowest total cost for the products assembled from that output.
>
> An inevitable but usually overlooked consequence of this cost minimization strategy is that it requires a company to produce more output in every period. The usual rationalization for requiring more output to achieve lower unit costs is the concept of scale economies.[111]

The speed and volume mentality creates overproduction. In their Shingo Prize–winning book, *Learning to See*, John Shook and Mike Rother repeat the economies-of-scale definition: "Mass production thinking says that the more and faster you produce the cheaper it is to produce."[112] They confirm that this method of operation inherently creates overproduction. "The most significant source of waste is overproduction, which means producing more, sooner, or faster than is required by the next process."[113] Ohno famously professed that overproduction was the worst of all wastes. He writes of "the waste of overproduction—our worst enemy—because it helps hide other wastes."[114] Ohno states that "this kind of waste is definitely the result of pursuing quantity and speed."[115] Overproduction is simply a manifestation of economies of scale.

Economies of Scale Are Dead

As companies move toward becoming lean, they shed the economies-of-scale mentality, which also destroys the need for overhead and standard cost methods. A discussion of how this affects the manufacturing enterprise will be reviewed. Dr. Johnson states:

> Here is where it is important to begin educating people in the fallacies of scale-economy thinking. It is time to raise awareness of how production systems designed along the lines of Toyota's system turn scale-economy thinking completely on its head, making it possible to build manufacturing capacity on a much smaller scale than ever before thought possible, yet produce at unit costs equal to or lower than in those large-scale facilities now thought necessary for cost-effective operations.[116]

Let the Journey Begin

The premise that all manufactured products should be equal in cost at any volume parallels the concept of "just-in-time" or flow. The ultimate goal of just-in-time is to have zero inventory. The ultimate goal of having no economies of scale is having all parts or components cost the same no matter what their volume. With just-in-time, the companies that are furthest along with the concept, like Toyota, are still not perfect but are getting closer every day. This same journey must be made for the cost of products. Although no one is there yet, the pursuit of perfection—equal cost—must be ventured. In some respects it is being pursued. The concept of rightsizing or right designing pushes companies in this direction.

This is why equal cost is a journey just like lean is. Companies that are taking advantage of just-in-time did not just wake up one morning and decide to go to just-in-time manufacturing, walk into their facilities and demand zero inventory, and continue to operate effectively. The firms that did take this approach (and some do) discovered that this would kill an operation. Manufacturing lines would be shutting down right and left and product would not be going out the door to their customers.

The companies who understood how to implement flow realized that it is a long journey, and the approach to zero inventory is not an action in itself, but a result of other actions and principles that must be implemented. Such actions include SMED (Single Minute Exchange of Dies or quick changeovers), inventory control, U-shaped cells, preventative maintenance, and many others. Just-in-time does not happen because an organization desires it to be so. It happens because of the concerted effort that a manufacturing company makes to properly execute the concepts with an understanding of the underlying philosophy they represent.

Rightsized Equals Right Cost

Why does the concept of economies of scale exist? It exists because equipment, facilities, and personnel (resources) are not designed or utilized properly to manufacture products effectively. Takt time is a concept key to achieving equal cost.[117] It is the initial concept that must be considered. The calculation of takt time sets the standard that a firm's entire operation for a particular product or family of products will be designed around. All machines, operators, and support functions should be established based on takt time. One of the major reasons economies of scale exist is that machines, operators, and support functions are not designed to meet takt. They are usually designed to exceed the takt time, therefore causing the desire for manufacturing more parts to bring down the cost (the economies of scale mentality). In reality, what is happening is that the parts are being manufactured at excessive costs from the start. This was Ohno's point about limited production—design for only what the customer needs and nothing more. The following example illustrates this point.

Right Designing a Machining Line

An engine crankshaft seal needs to be machined at the following volumes per year over a five-year period—204,000, 516,000, 614,000, and 828,000. If rightsizing is applied, the cost of this part should remain constant through all of the volumes. First we will look at the components that make up the cost of the part. They are capital equipment, material, labor (operators), and support. Capital equipment is normally comprised of equipment to manufacture the part or add value to the part. If rightsized/right designed machinery is developed, each piece of equipment will be small and have just enough capacity to accomplish its particular assignment up to the takt time. This equipment will also be arranged in a cellular, one-piece flow configuration. Next, labor will be balanced up to the takt time, which delivers the minimum amount of operators to manufacture the part. One more person would be too many and one less would be too few. This will minimize the labor needed to manufacture the part. Finally, the support function must be rightsized. Support includes utilities workers, supervisors, maintenance people, and engineers, and also includes facilities.

Utilities are items like air, gas, electricity, and water. All of these can be easily monitored to measure the exact usage in manufacturing. Our homes are an excellent example of how this can be accomplished. Everyone who owns or rents a home has meters that allow for the measurement of our electricity, gas, and water usage. The same measurement techniques can be used in a manufacturing facility. The argument is often made that putting meters on each line is expensive. It is widely believed that if all the systems and administration used to monitor and manage overhead and its inaccurate distribution were eliminated there would be significant savings. Also, the maintenance required would be extremely minimal after installation of the metering devices. Think of the last time the meter on a home needed to be fixed or replaced. This concept may seem extreme, but it does drive home the point that is being illustrated. One company researched for this book strongly considered doing this with its manufacturing cells.

Next, consider the supervision needed to manage the manufacturing of this product. Since the supervisor of this product *is* the supervisor of this product, the cost associated with the part for supervision is direct and is easily accounted to the part. There is no indirect cost; the supervisor is a direct cost, or, more appropriately, a resource directly consumed by the value stream. Of course techniques should be used to minimize the supervision needed for manufacturing, but any cost for supervision would be placed directly to the cost of the part. No special cost-tracking or accounting techniques are needed to do this, and no percent allocation is required.

Maintenance can be a more difficult function to rightsize. It is difficult because its needs are based on equipment quantity, reliability, and technology; training and education requirements and timing; and execution procedures. These requirements may be difficult to accurately size because it is normally a judgment. The important point is that it may be difficult, but it is *not* impossible. With time and experience, rightsizing maintenance can be accomplished. Doing this will allow for costs to be aimed directly to the product family either by maintenance personnel being assigned to the product, cell, or focus factory, or by being "contracted" by the supervisor of the product line. Implementing a Total Productive Maintenance (TPM) system is another aspect of maintenance. If TPM is fully utilized by a company, then the operators of the manufacturing line accomplish a large bulk of the maintenance. This will put the cost of the maintenance directly to the part without having any tracking or resources needed to allocate costs.

Engineering should be able to rightsize its requirements toward a product. This feature could be either manufacturing or product engineering. This development would also come from experience with demands needed from a particular project or product. If a product were under development, then most, if not all, of the engineers working on it (both manufacturing and design) would be dedicated to the project. The number of them would determine if the engineering resources would be rightsized. Normally, bringing a product from development to production is a full-time activity involving product engineers, manufacturing engineers, marketing personnel, and operations personnel working simultaneously on the project. This allows the cost of these people to be part of the product directly. Just as with maintenance over time, by gaining experience, one can rightsize/right design the number of people needed and accurately determine the specific time period they are needed.

Finally, facilities should be rightsized. Ideally, if each product or product family could be set in its own facility, then all costs with the facility could be associated with the product. If rightsized, a plant would have just enough floor space, an HVAC unit and air compressor with the right amount of capacity, just the right amount of office space, and so on. It would also be designed to allow for easy expansion if needed to increase demand of the product. To achieve this is not necessarily out of the question. Everything associated with a product is under one rightsized roof. All costs and equipment would produce just what is needed, when it is needed. When larger buildings are constructed for housing multiple unrelated products, much waste is built in with it—waste in facilities, floor space, logistic requirements, and more.

All Parts at an Equal Cost

If we begin to implement the concepts mentioned above, the *journey* to achieving all parts at an equal cost at any volume can become closer to reality. Since the right-sized/right designed world will take a while to achieve as we evolve our equipment, facilities, and resources, the costs of parts per volume will appear as a sawtooth graph and should flatten over time as "perfection" is approached (see Figure 2.6).

Examples of the Sawtooth Graph

The reason the cost per volume graph resembles a saw tooth is that cost will drop slightly as volume goes up. This result is due to typical mass-production economies of scale changes: costing the number of parts produced over the equipment and resources used to manufacture them. But the difference or elimination of economies of scale comes into play due to the implementation of lean production principles, which increase output, or production capacity, in tiny increments based on customer demand.

Rightsizing/right designing is a key concept to successfully implement lean production. As one reviews the graph and the drop in cost as volume increases,

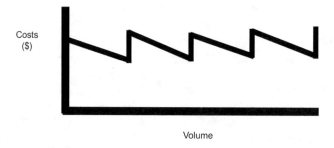

Costs
($)

Volume

Figure 2.6 Sawtooth graph of part costs versus volume output

rightsizing/right designing and other lean principles cause the graph to quickly and sharply return to the original cost. Two main factors contribute to this: equipment and operators. Although other factors, including facilities, utilities, and support functions, can contribute to this, the assumption will be made that they have been properly adjusted or rightsized/right designed as the volume changes. Or they should be rightsized as companies understand and implement lean production!

How People Impact the Sawtooth Graph

In a properly designed and controlled lean environment, operators and material handlers can be adjusted to keep a nearly even productivity level at any volume. The methods used to accomplish this are good cell design and balancing operator workloads to takt time. If production is designed to meet takt time, labor is added or subtracted according to the demand level of production. Figure 2.7 shows how the number of operators should change within a production line to balance it to takt time or customer demand while maintaining equal productivity or equal costs per output.

The adjustment of operators and material handlers can be achieved on any type of line, whether it is a machining, welding, fabrication, or assembly line. If operators and material handlers are loaded and balanced to the takt time, then near equal costs per volume can be achieved.

The Sawtooth Graph Should Flatten

The only issue is that people are integer entities and not fractions. The meaning of this is that when balancing to takt time, it may be necessary to change from four operators to 5.8 operators. Since a 0.8 person does not exist, it would be necessary to man the line with six operators. This contributes to the sawtooth configuration of the cost-per-volume graph. But as a company becomes more skilled and experienced in lean principles, the impact of increasing costs per output becomes greatly diminished. Many

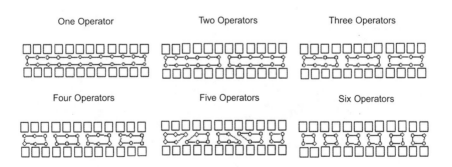

Figure 2.7   Operator balancing for volume changes

techniques exist in lean production that lessen or eliminate this situation. As a result, the path to perfection—defined as equal costs at any volume—becomes closer.

How Equipment Impacts the Sawtooth Graph

The second contributor is capital equipment. Equipment can have the largest impact on the sawtooth graph due to its cost. If implemented properly, lean principles will lessen the cost of machines and equipment (see previous section titled "Rightsized Equals Right Cost"). Precision chip-cutting machines for critical components and assembly conveyor systems for large products like automobiles can cost considerable amounts of capital. The cost obviously has a great impact on the *cost* of the product.

If production lines are designed to lean principles (that is, takt time, U-shaped, rightsized machines, flow, and so on), strategies can be applied to lessen the x-axis length of the "teeth" of the graph. For example, if the volume of a product is projected to increase over time, lines can be added as needed to meet the market demand. Figure 2.8 illustrates that additional machining lines can be added over time as demand increases, therefore maintaining a minimized sawtooth cost-per-volume graph.

The capability of adding only small increments of capacity creates many advantages besides equal costs per volume. Capital equipment costs can now be made in smaller incremental investments. With rightsized/right designed equipment, it becomes much easier to invest capital incrementally with volume increases, instead of one initial capital outlay to cover the projected-estimated final volume, which is hoped for but not always met. With incremental investments in capital equipment due to purchasing rightsized equipment, if increasing volumes are not reached due to changes in the estimated market demand, capital will be saved. Also, if the market demand would not peak at estimated projections and in fact decreases, the amount of capital sunk will be less. Practicing these techniques helps to dissipate the scale-economies mentality.

Mark DeLuzio refers to the same concept of how understanding, developing, and implementing right designed systems and machines allows for the flattening of the sawtooth graph and smooth integration of capacity and capital. He writes:

> Many companies think of manufacturing in terms of buying large increments of capacity. But if you think of lean in a machine design sense, you are purchasing small increments of capacity that is flexible and can be quickly changed over. It can be easily adaptable to new designs, and can be easily movable within your plants so you can add an extra 10 percent of capacity without any problem. Your investment is small—you're not adding another $500,000 machine to add just 10 percent more capacity.[118]

The Journey to the Promised Land: Perfection

If the lean principles and rightsized/right designed equipment are properly applied, the road to equal costs per volume becomes closer to reality than some distant vision.

It is definitely achievable, and one must make the effort to journey toward it. A great thing about it is that the further a firm travels down the path to equal costs per volume, the easier it becomes. Manufacturing companies develop great skills and experience, which allow the journey to become faster, easier, and more fun and exciting. In the end, it will allow for incremental investment of capital for equipment and facilities and incremental increases in operators and support. All incremental increases are per-volume increases—it all should increase by equivalent ratios giving equal costs per volume or destroying the concept of economies of scale. A company also potentially becomes much more deadly to its competitors and much more valuable to the owners.

Are Economies of Scale Dead Yet?

The conclusion is that many different skills are needed to make the best decisions. Knowledge and experience in operations, accounting, marketing, and lean production are essential to moving down the path to perfecting manufacturing. If one has such skills and experience knows how the areas interact, one will be a competitive force to be reckoned with. Also, it is important to understand how and why economies of scale should be dead.

How a manufacturing firm can take advantage of flow and simple information technology to develop and support cost management is the central theme of this book. Dr. Johnson explains how Toyota approaches such a goal:

> Even machinery and capital resources are scaled as much as possible to the amount needed to fill one order at a time, and no more. It is difficult to imagine how one could produce output at any lower cost.
>
> The usual explanations of how Toyota delivers large varieties of high quality output in a short time, and at exceptionally low costs, tend to stress many technique practices at Toyota, such as kanban replenishment, automatic error detection systems, "five S" housekeeping practices, and kaizen training. None stress the point I make here; namely, that Toyota does not view low cost as a consequence of producing more, only as a consequence of consuming just enough to meet each customer's expectations, and no more. In short, Toyota's approach to cost minimization stresses "enough," not more, and it focuses attention on resources consumed, not on output produced.[119]

Economies of Scale in Japan

Another misunderstood point about economies of scale is that being a Japanese company is synonymous with being a lean enterprise. Toyota, their group companies, and a few others are unique. Dr. Michiharu Sakurai examines this point and explains how Japanese industry has struggled with this same issue of scale economies.

According to Dr. Sakurai, from 1961 to 1990 the major goal of most Japanese companies was volume expansion. Japan had high economic growth and developed many new markets. Japanese firms responded through mass production and reducing

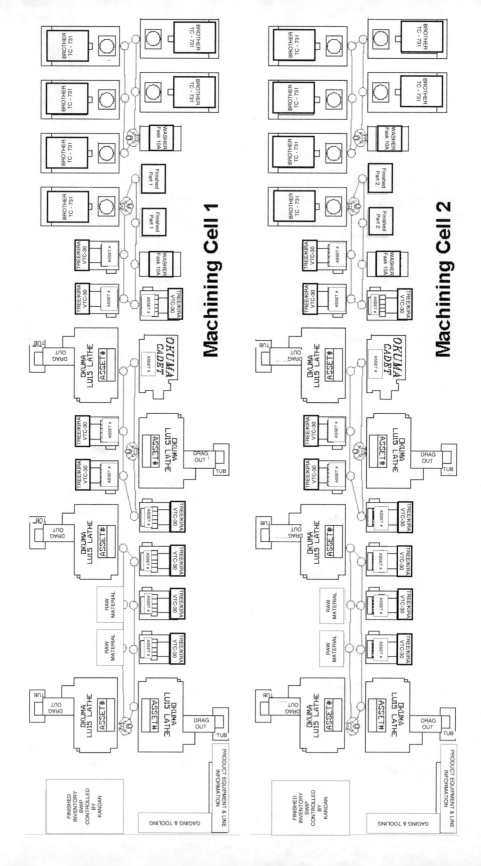

Machining Cell 1

Machining Cell 2

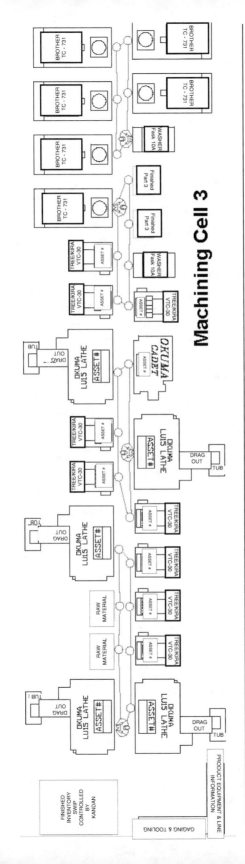

Figure 2.8 Adding manufacturing lines due to volume increases

unit costs by utilizing scale economies. Variable costing was the most common practice and supported the gains received by volume production increases.[120]

A few unique companies (including Toyota) understood that using economies of scale was a potentially dangerous prospect. These companies pursued effective use of resources instead of just volume production. Through practice and understanding, they developed methods (for example, TPS at Toyota), that allowed for success and continued growth even after the burst of the economic bubble in Japan.[121] Most Japanese companies have struggled since the economic bubble burst because they relied strictly on scale economies—volume expansion.

Shook, who spent eleven years working for Toyota while they transplanted to the United States, also relates that Toyota's focus was not economies of scale, but a completely different approach. He writes: "Economies of scale need not be the goal of the production system. You can attain greater overall system efficiency through concerted efforts to eliminate waste thoroughly. Ohno's efforts focused on developing the ability to survive and even thrive in low growth."[122]

NOTES

1. Johnson and Kaplan, "Management by Accounting."
2. Dr. David S. Cochran in his 1994 thesis states this same issue. See Cochran, "The Design and Control of Manufacturing Systems," 199–200.
3. Wells, *Accounting for Common Costs*, 138.
4. Wells, *American Engineers' Contribution*, 2.
5. Taylor, "Accounting for Lean Production," 84.
6. Garner, *Evolution of Cost Accounting to 1925*, 1–26.
7. The remainder of this section is based on Garner, *Evolution of Cost Accounting*; Johnson, "The Role of Accounting History," 444–50; Johnson, "Toward a New Understanding," 510–18; Johnson, "The Decline of Cost Management," 5–12; and Kaplan, "The Evolution of Management Accounting," 390–418.
8. Johnson, "Toward a New Understanding," 512.
9. The market also directly determined labor costs during this time.
10. Johnson, "The Role of Accounting History,"445.
11. In this case, cost means the price that the market would bare.
12. Johnson, "Toward a New Understanding," 510.
13. Johnson, "The Role of Accounting History," 448–49.
14. Wells in his 1978 monograph, *Accounting for Common Costs*, details this very point and on pages 122 to 125 discusses the battle that engineers and accountants waged in developing accounting methods. According to Wells, the engineers won out until 1914. Although after 1914 the engineers' work and development in the accounting arena stopped, the methods used during post 1914 through today are based on the techniques developed by engineers between 1870 and 1914.
15. Johnson, "Toward a New Understanding," 516.

16. Wells, *Accounting for Common Costs*, 67. Wells states this same point in *American Engineers' Contribution*, 2.
17. Wells, *Accounting for Common Costs*, 74.
18. Johnson and Kaplan, *Relevance Lost*, 12.
19. For a review of why university business schools failed to achieve this, see "Why Business Schools Focus on the Wrong Customer," 178–83.
20. Johnson and Kaplan, *Relevance Lost*, 14–15.
21. Ibid., 9.
22. Wells, *Accounting for Common Costs*, 19, 34. Wells summarizes the same issues (of irrelevance) presented by a number of authors and the confusion that results. He also emphasizes the contribution of engineers to the development of accounting methods from 1870 to 1910.
23. Kaplan, "The Evolution of Management Accounting," 407.
24. Wells, *Accounting for Common Costs*, 19.
25. Baggaley, "Costing by Value Stream," 24.
26. Johnson and Kaplan, *Relevance Lost*, 184.
27. Ibid., 187.
28. Brian Maskell, *Making the Numbers Count*, 83.
29. Ibid., 26.
30. Ibid., 76.
31. Noreen, Smith, and Mackey, *The Theory of Constraints*, 16.
32. Johnson and Kaplan, *Relevance Lost*, 230.
33. DeLuzio, "Danaher is a Paragon of Lean Success."
34. Although we tend to pick on accountants, they are by no means the sole culprits. Most manufacturing executives, accountants, and others are filled with excuses on why they cannot do what is needed in the accounting arena.
35. Although this book is not about financial, or external, accounting, reporting methods for financial accounting have also come under fire for reporting misleading information due to poor methods. See Gibbs, "Are Earnings Meaningless?," 37–40.
36. Maskell, *Making the Numbers Count*, 6.
37. Ibid., 14.
38. Dhavale, *Management Accounting Issues*, ix. Dr. Dileep G. Dhavale is an associate professor of accounting in the Graduate School of Management at Clark University in Worcester, Massachusetts. He is a CPA and has a professional certification in production and inventory management. Dr. Dhavale has published extensively in academic and professional journals in accounting, production management, and labor and industrial relations.
39. Ibid., 186–87.
40. In July 2002, Orest "Orry" Fiume retired as vice president of finance and administration at The Wiremold Company. Wiremold's lean journey is one of the case studies presented in Womack and Jones, *Lean Thinking*. Wiremold is

one of the leading companies in North America, which has successfully transformed into a lean enterprise. Mr. Fiume has lectured often through the last ten years about how Wiremold transformed their accounting practices to support their lean transformation.

41. Jean E. Cunningham is the former chief financial officer and vice president of company services for Lantech, Inc. Lantech's lean journey is also one of the case studies presented in the book *Lean Thinking* by Womack and Jones and represents the success that can be achieve through a lean transformation.

42. Fiume and Cunningham, *Real Numbers*, 29.

43. Johnson, "Beyond Product Costing," 15.

44. Johnson and Kaplan, *Relevance Lost*, 1.

45. Ibid., 2.

46. The specific situation was the epicenter of my interest in cost and managerial accounting methods, systems, and history.

47. Johnson, *Relevance Regained*, 48–49.

48. Johnson and Kaplan, *Relevance Lost*, 2.

49. Taiichi Ohno was the operation manager and later the executive vice president at Toyota who developed, implemented, and drove the Toyota Production System (TPS) through Toyota and its supply base.

50. Ohno, *Workplace Management*, 138.

51. I have heard John Y. Shook relate the information about Ohno and the accountants several times since 1998.

52. Shook spent ten years with Toyota helping to transfer its production, engineering, and management systems from Japan to its overseas affiliates and suppliers. He is the coauthor of the Shingo Prize–winning workbook, *Learning to See*, and is an advisor to the Lean Enterprise Institute. John is currently the codirector of the University of Michigan Japan Technology Management Program and continues to help companies to understand and implement lean manufacturing.

53. Shook, e-mail to the author, June 4, 2003.

54. Ohno, *Toyota Production System*, 36. Also, in *Workplace Management*, 76–77, Ohno credits Toyota executives (Eiji Toyoda and Saito Naoichi) for supporting his efforts.

55. Ohno, *Workplace Management*, 18. Ohno also references the misunderstanding of the number-pushers on page 21. Also see his section titled "The Lean Cost Equation" for further detail on Ohno's issues with number-pushers.

56. Ohno, *Workplace Management*, 36.

57. This very point—system, department, and subsystem disconnection—is a major issue and theme discussed in detail in Johnson and Anders Bröms, *Profit beyond Measure*.

58. Ohno, *Workplace Management*, 143.

59. Noreen, Smith, and Mackey, *The Theory of Constraints*, 24.

60. Ford, *My Life and Work*, 176.
61. Johnson and Kaplan, "Management by Accounting," 8.
62. Other poor decisions resulting from this situation are explained in Johnson, "Activity-Based Information: Accounting for Competitive Excellence," 6.
63. Johnson and Kaplan, *Relevance Lost*, 126.
64. Johnson and Kaplan give a detailed explanation of this development in *Relevance Lost*, 129–35.
65. Johnson, "The Decline of Cost Management," 10.
66. In chapter 7 of this book, Church discusses the issues of crossing cost-management accounting and financial accounting.
67. Johnson and Kaplan, *Relevance Lost*, 51.
68. Johnson, "The Decline of Cost Management," 5.
69. Ibid., 5.
70. Cost Management is a term stressed by Uminger in both "Manufacturing Cost Management" and also in his presentation for the 2003 University of Michigan's Lean Manufacturing Conference.
71. Johnson, "The Decline of Cost Management," 5.
72. Ibid., 8.
73. Kaplan, "The Evolution of Management Accounting," 401.
74. Johnson, "The Decline of Cost Management," 6.
75. Ibid., 7.
76. Dr. Cooper was professor of management at the Peter F. Drucker School of Management, Claremont University, before he was faculty at Emory University's Goizueta Business School in 1998. Prior to those positions, he spent ten years on the faculty of the Harvard Business School, Harvard University. His research interests include strategic alignment and strategic cost management. Dr. Cooper has worked extensively with industry implementing activity-based cost systems. He is a fellow of the Institute of Chartered Accountants in England and Wales. He has also authored and coauthored many books and articles on accounting methods in world-class organizations.
77. Cooper, *When Lean Enterprises Collide*, 90–91.
78. Ibid., 12.
79. Fiume and Cunningham, *Real Numbers*, 85–86.
80. Taylor, "A Piece-Rate System," 898.
81. In this book, mass production is not analogous to "batch" production, but to volume production. Batch production is manufacturing large quantities of products without regard to demand or customer requirements, which seemingly reduces the costs of overhead, labor, and equipment by spreading costs over a large amount of product.
82. Johnson and Bröms, *Profit beyond Measure*, 4.
83. Ibid.

84. Ibid., 101–2. Also see Ohno, *Workplace Management*, 30–31. Ohno states, "A philosophy of making things as inexpensively as possible calls for 'limited-volume' management and a 'limited-volume' production system" (30).
85. Mark DeLuzio was a financial executive for the Danaher Corporation— one of the first companies in North America to apply lean manufacturing—who developed the Danaher Business System, which was modeled after TPS. DeLuzio retired from Danaher in 2001 and founded the firm Lean Horizons, which helps traditional companies transform to a lean enterprise. He is also a Certified Management Accountant and has published papers on just-in-time accounting.
86. DeLuzio, "Danaher is a Paragon of Lean Success," 1, 6–12.
87. Huntzinger, "Roots of Lean—Highland Park."
88. Johnson and Bröms brilliantly detail this story in "Lessons from the Rouge," in *Profit beyond Measure*.
89. Managing Directors Eiji Toyoda and Shoichi Saito both visited Ford's River Rouge Plant, Toyota from July and Saito from October 1950. See Toyota Motor Corporation, *Toyota: A History*, 113.
90. Kiichiro Toyoda had been the inspirational leader with a vision of just-in-time manufacturing that led Ohno and Eiji Toyoda to support and develop the principles and methods of the Toyota Production System. Kiichiro's influence is acknowledged by Ohno in his own writings and is detailed in "Founding of Toyota," in *Toyota: A History*. Kiichiro also "pored over Henry Ford's *My Life and Work* and urged everyone around him to read it too" according to Toyota Motor Corporation, *Toyota: A History*, 42.
91. The Toyota Motor Company was established in 1937 (see Toyota Motor Corporation, *Toyota: A History*, 490), although Kiichiro had been working on automotive projects for a number of years prior.
92. Halberstam, *The Reckoning*, 88.
93. Johnson and Bröms, *Profit beyond Measure*, 16. The same point is also described in Johnson, *Relevance Regained*, 35–39.
94. Johnson and Bröms, *Profit beyond Measure*, 17.
95. Ibid.
96. Although this tie between Toyota and the Highland Park plant is usually missed, James P. Womack and Daniel T. Jones do give credit to Highland Park in their studies and reports. See Womack and Jones, "How the World Has Changed." On page 12 they report, "Taiichi Ohno and the other innovators at Toyota therefore really did gain their starting point from Henry Ford, but at Highland Park, and they made a critical leap at the point where Ford took a wrong turn.... Toyota's achievement was truly brilliant, but it rested more firmly on Henry Ford's shoulders at Highland Park than we realized." For further details on lean manufacturing's (and Toyota's) tie to the Highland Park plant, see Huntzinger, "Roots of Lean—Highland Park."

97. If Ford's *My Life and Work,* Ford's and Crowther's *Today and Tomorrow,* and Ohno's *Toyota Production System* and *Workplace Management* are studied, a similar and complementary thinking process is apparent. It is also well known that Ohno studied Ford's writings in great detail.

98. Different thinking is shown to be key to change and success. Womack and Jones's book, *Lean Thinking,* Johnson and Bröms's book, *Profit beyond Measure,* and Spear's dissertation, "The Toyota Production System," all illustrate this very point.

99. Johnson and Bröms, *Profit beyond Measure,* 183.

100. Dr. Jeffrey Liker's background in lean also includes having produced many books and articles on lean; keynote speaking and leadership at lean functions and seminars; having been a principle and senior consultant for Optiprise, Inc., a consultancy dedicated to helping companies get lean; and having received the Shingo Prize several times.

101. Liker, *The Toyota Way,* 8.

102. Johnson, "A Recovering Cost Accountant Reminisces," 3. At the time I received the draft, the article was to be published in fall 2002 *Journal of Innovative Management.*

103. Womack and Jones, *Lean Thinking.* Their fifth step, Perfection, is discussed in "Introduction: Lean Thinking versus *Muda*" and Chapter 5, "Perfection."

104. Liker, *The Toyota Way,* 11.

105. Barclay, *Ford Production Methods.* Mike Rother shared this quote with me.

106. Johnson and Bröms's book, *Profit beyond Measure,* illuminates how TPS behaves like natural living systems, which are both autonomous and interlinked, and emphasizes MBM (excellent execution, meaning a high level of functionality versus dysfunctionality) versus management by results (MBR). Spear, "The Toyota Production System," and Spear and Bowen, "Decoding the DNA of the Toyota Production System," explain how the Five Rules-in-Use promote distinctive organizational features that manifest themselves into the methods and tools outsiders view as TPS.

107. Kitano, "Toyota Production System."

108. Johnson and Bröms, *Profit beyond Measure,* 15.

109. A case in point at the time of this writing is the apparent demise of Ford and GM. Their largest suppliers, Visteon and Delphi, both spin-offs from each auto firm, have filed for bankruptcy and are shedding plants at a rampant pace. Ford and GM continue to lose market share and hundreds of millions of dollars each quarter while selling off other parts of their organizations and closing plants.

110. The minimum price in this case means both an acceptable customer or market price and also a manufacturer cost that supports acceptable margins.

111. Johnson, "A Recovering Cost Accountant Reminisces," 3.

112. Rother and Shook, *Learning to See,* 39.

113. Ibid.

114. Ohno, *Toyota Production System*, 59.
115. Ibid., 109.
116. Johnson, "How the Universe Story and MBM Can Save Business," 18.
117. Takt time is used in manufacturing to tie production to customer demand. It is calculated by dividing the amount of time available per a given time period—that is, a shift—by the rate of the customer demand during that period.
118. DeLuzio, "Danaher is a Paragon of Lean Success," 11.
119. Johnson, "A Recovering Cost Accountant Reminisces," 5. What Johnson is essentially describing is Ohno's "limited production."
120. Sakurai, "Past and Future of Japanese Management Accounting," 23.
121. Ibid., 23–24.
122. Shook, "Bringing the Toyota Production System to the United States," 49.

3

TOYOTA'S SUCCESS:
PROFIT BEYOND MEASURE

Interestingly, even though Toyota is a multibillion-dollar firm and one of the largest companies in the world, their corporate headquarters (see Figure 3.1) remains relatively modest, especially compared to their competitors.

Any company's business will most likely slow when the sales in a particular market drop off. Toyota is no different. In Japan, their sales have slowed during the post-bubble period. But Toyota's financial position has remained significantly more robust than their struggling competitors. Toyota affirms the following:

> In May 1972, TMC [Toyota Motor Corporation] replaced Matsushita Electric Industrial Co., Ltd. as the top company in terms of profits in Japan.
>
> With the help of its high earning potential, TMC inaugurated a policy of financing, in principle, all its plants and equipment investments by internal funds.[1]
>
> In 1978, it redeemed all its outstanding obligations and became totally debt free.[2]

Dr. H. Thomas Johnson and Anders Bröms also report on Toyota's financial success in their book, *Profit beyond Measure*, where they describe how Toyota has achieved results above and beyond the rest of their industry. The success is one of the meanings behind the book's title. They state: "Certainly it is undeniably impressive that Toyota, without ever resorting to layoffs, has not reported an accounting loss in any year since 1960, a record not equaled by any other company in the industry."[3]

Toyota has reported positive, albeit variable, operating profits every year since 1960. Moreover, the company's long-term profitability is among the highest in its industry, with less variation in results from year to year than shown by competitors.[4]

In 2003, Dr. Johnson again expressed Toyota's superior performance and ability: "[The] company for over forty years has far surpassed the performance of all its competitors in the industry in terms of product quality, reliability, design-to-delivery lead times, customer satisfaction, employee morale, productivity and cost, and overall

Figure 3.1 Toyota City, Japan. The former headquarters (August 1960 to February 2005) are pictured on the left and the new headquarters (February 2005 to the present) are shown on the right.
Source: Photo of former headquarters is from Toyota Motor Corporation, *Toyota: A History of the First 50 Years* (Toyota City, Japan: Toyota Motor Corporation, 1988), 448. Photo of the new headquarters is courtesy of the Toyota Motor Corporation, Toyota City, Japan.

financial performance. If there are objectives that automakers seek to fulfill, Toyota has managed to excel at all of them, not just some."[5]

Dr. Jeffrey Liker verifies Toyota's competitive and financial strength in *The Toyota Way*, writing of Toyota's high level of business enterprise:

> Every time Toyota showed an apparent weakness and seemed vulnerable to the competition, Toyota miraculously fixed the problem and came back even stronger.[6]

- Toyota is far more profitable than any other auto manufacturer
- Toyota's annual profit at the end of fiscal year in March 2003 (was) larger than the combined earnings of GM, Chrysler, and Ford, and the biggest annual profit for any auto maker in at least a decade
- Toyota's market capitalization (the total value of the company's stock) was $105 billion as of 2003—higher than the combined market capitalization of Ford, General Motors, and Chrysler
- The company has made a profit every year over the last 25 years and has $20–$30 billion in its cash war chest on a consistent basis
- Camry was the top-selling U.S. passenger car in 2003 and five of the years prior. Corolla was the top selling small car in the world
- Lexus was introduced in 1989 and in 2002 outsold BMW, Cadillac, and Mercedes-Benz in the U.S. for the third year in a row.[7]

According to Yasuhiro Monden, Toyota focuses on utilizing its own financial resources by maintaining a huge amount of retained profits and depreciation expenses in order to fund capital procurement.[8] Monden also emphasizes that in 1981 and 1982, Toyota showed absolutely no external use of capital, which highlights just how little they rely on outside sources of funds. And Monden confirms Toyota's own statements that they have operated under "debt-free management" since 1978.[9]

Monden reveals how Toyota has supported its supply base (Toyota Group Companies) not only with knowledge and personnel resources but also with finances. Toyota has financially invested in its supply base.[10] Toyota itself states that one of the distinctive characteristics of its management is its deep cooperative support and relationship to its suppliers.[11] Toyota's close relationship with its supply base has given rise to the supply-chain management movement over the last several years in North America. Although much effort has been attempted, no company has been able to replicate Toyota's success. Monden confirms this: "When we mine the energetic way in which Toyota has invested in its affiliated companies, we can see that Toyota's management policy has been one of strengthening ties within the Toyota group and furthering the group's development."[12]

Monden finally discusses how Toyota's financial policies support its operational policies and vice versa. This point is key to understanding the tie between excellent operational and financial management and execution. According to Monden:

> Toyota has been conspicuous for its strong aversion to stock-market investments. This conservative approach is seen as part of Toyota's staunch policy of putting its main business before all other considerations.
>
> ...One point worth noting with regard to the relationship between Toyota's financial management system and its production management system is that the latter's success in drastically reducing inventory levels for materials, parts, in-process goods, and products has minimized the need to tie up funds in such inventory assets. This has contributed greatly to the company's financial management.[13]

Toyota becoming debt free and financially independent is simply the *result* of practicing lean, that is, good, management in general and focusing on execution. Dr. Steven Spear corroborates Toyota's success: "Toyota has continued its performance leadership despite sustained effort on the part of its competitors to emulate its practices.... Toyota has maintained the lead in cost and quality."[14]

In 2003, Daniel Jones[15] of the Lean Enterprise Academy also confirms Toyota's financial strength compared to its competitors. "Toyota is making record profits and could buy many of its competitors for cash."[16] Jones continues, affirming one of Toyota's most fundamental differences in management philosophies:

> It is clear that lean is a journey which requires stamina and perseverance. Toyota made the fundamental switch from managing assets to creating flow and pull.... Having made this switch it has been refining its processes ever since.... The changes that are required are in part a physical reconfiguration of our operations.... This can only come by learning by doing, and by working out your own answers for your own situation.[17]

Dr. Liker also reiterates on the success Toyota has accomplished: "Critics often describe Toyota as a 'boring company.' This is the kind of boring I like. Top quality year in and year out. Steadily growing sales. Consistent profitability. High cash reserves. Of course, operational efficiency by itself can be dangerous."[18] Mark DeLuzio simply states, "Toyota and some of their suppliers are the best manufacturing companies in the world."[19]

Toyota accomplishes their success, not by focusing on finance, but by focusing on a long-term philosophy. Their executives value their impact on the company's future and its connection to the company's history. Dr. Liker expresses Toyota's focus in his book, *The Toyota Way*:

> They are working within a long-term philosophical mission to bring the company to the next level. The company is like an organism nurturing itself, constantly protecting and growing its offspring, so that it can continue to grow and stay strong.[20]

Liker continues, noting that "the poignant message is that the company must enhance growth of society or it cannot contribute to its external or internal stakeholders. This is its *reason* for making excellent products."[21] On Toyota' leadership, Liker states that "Toyota leaders truly believe that if they create the right process the results will follow.... *The Right Process Will Produce the Right Results*."[22]

NOTES

1. Toyota Motor Corporation, *Toyota: A History*, 196–97.
2. Ibid., 255.
3. Johnson and Bröms, *Profit beyond Measure*, 217.
4. Ibid., 70.
5. Johnson, "How The Universe Story and MBM Can Save Business," 12.
6. Liker, *The Toyota Way*, 3.
7. Ibid., 4.
8. Monden, *Toyota Management System*, 3.
9. Ibid., 5–6.
10. Ibid., 18.
11. Toyota Motor Corporation, *Toyota: A History*, 406–15. The other two distinctive characteristics are the Toyota Production System (TPS) and Toyota's constant pursuit of creativity and ingenuity, a spirit that can be traced back to Sakichi Toyoda, the company's founder.
12. Monden, *Toyota Management System*, 18.
13. Ibid., 27–28.
14. Spear, "Just-in-Time in Practice at Toyota," 2–3.

15. Daniel Jones is the CEO of the Lean Enterprise Academy in the United Kingdom and is the coauthor of *Lean Thinking* and *The Machine that Changed the World*. He spearheads lean leadership in Europe as a counterpart to James Womack in the United States and they jointly research and educate industry on lean thinking.

16. Jones, "The Beginner's Guide to Lean."

17. Ibid. Please take note that this quote mentions two important topics that will be discussed in detail later in this book. The first is the requirement of physical changes to the operation and the second is the approach of learning by doing.

18. Liker, *The Toyota Way*, 14.

19. DeLuzio, "Danaher is a Paragon of Lean Success," 7–8.

20. Liker, *The Toyota Way*, 72.

21. Ibid., 81.

22. Ibid., 87.

4

EXECUTION

> The mechanism of management must not be mistaken for its essence, or underlying philosophy.... Hundreds of people have already mistaken the mechanism of the system for its essence.[1]
>
> —*Frederick Winslow Taylor, 1911*

Designing the systems properly is key to integrating lean into a business enterprise. Both Dr. H. Thomas Johnson and Dr. Steven Spear articulate the underlying principles of lean or the Toyota Production System (TPS) in their writings. Designing the proper lean systems must manifest itself into the physical operations to achieve a successful transformation. But another key aspect is simple execution. Dr. Steven Spear and H. Kent Bowen explain: "We found that people in companies following the Toyota Production System share a common goal. They have a common sense of what the ideal production system would be, and that shared vision motivates them to make improvements beyond what would be necessary merely to meet the current needs of the customers. This notion is very pervasive, and we believe it is essential to understanding the Toyota Production System."[2]

Appropriate execution is vital in creating the environment described by Dr. Spear and Bowen. In an enterprise, many speak of creating an environment with good discipline. Achieving good discipline is essential, but it must be articulated into superior execution throughout the system, with all people functioning within it. Achieving sound execution actually contrasts with traditional methods, especially methods associated with accounting.

Management by Means versus Management by Results

Traditional companies strive to achieve excellence by setting targets for their managers to attain. These targets are often referred to as stretch goals. Most of the time, these "stretch goals" are, or are based on, financial results, or accounting targets.

Relying on such results is the hallmark of modern management. Recall the department managers' monthly "berating" for not achieving end-of-the-month goals or negative variance results.

In a lean enterprise, the real objectives are completely different than those traditional, educational, or financial organizations typically target. (Again, recall the discussion earlier about lean being a completely different way of thinking about the enterprise—see *Lean Thinking* by James Womack and Daniel Jones.) It has nothing to do with results. It has everything to do with execution or means. Dr. Johnson writes: "The task of managers is to stop treating business results as a target one reaches by aiming better. Instead, business results are an outcome that emerges spontaneously from mastering practices that harmonize with the patterns inherent in the system itself. In other words, manage the *means*, not the results" (original emphasis).[3] Dr. Johnson here stresses the points covered in this chapter: the first is execution, or "mastering practices," and the second is right designing, or "harmoniz[ing] with the patterns inherent in the system itself." If a company focuses on these two objectives, instead of on "results," the organization will prosper and continue to prosper over the long term. Dr. Spear's dissertation stresses the same point. He acknowledges that "the purpose of the specification was not to entrench 'best practice', per se. Rather, it was to use the current best practice as the basis for discovering large and small problems. These, when remediated, contributed to substantial improvements on multiple performance measures. *Solving these individual problems, one-by-one, was the means by which I was learning TPS and we were teaching it to the supplier's workforce*" (emphasis added).[4]

As Spear and Johnson describe above, MBM is a lean manufacturer's key to superbly executing and rightly designing systems. James Womack articulated Toyota's view of this theme at the 2002 Annual Conference of the Association of Manufacturing Excellence: "We get brilliant results from average people managing brilliant processes. We observe that our competitors often get average (or worse) results from brilliant people managing broken processes."[5]

Womack's presentation pinpoints the battle between MBM and MBR and reveals the outcome of choosing MBM. Toyota's record of delivering a high quality product at a competitive price over multiple decades speaks quite loudly. The essence of the difference is that Toyota's focus is on developing people within the system, but their competitors' focus is on hiring "top" people to be "heroes" in a flawed system, resulting in no development of the people hired and no development of the system.

Mark DeLuzio affirms the battle between MBR and MBM in his 2001 interview in the trade journal *Manufacturing News*:

> A lot of managers today are only being measured on results and they are not being measured on creating the business process. People say, "You just delivered a new product in 16 months, that was fantastic." Nobody says to them: "Show me the business process that yielded that result and I want to make sure it's sustainable so we can repeat it again next time."[6]

DeLuzio concludes that "they [executive management] need to really drive process improvement and not just results."[7]

Cost management must be viewed as an aspect of enterprise design, not just an accounting exercise.[8] As Womack's presentation reveals, the design and execution of a lean enterprise, or "managing brilliant processes," excels far beyond the capability of results, or "brilliant people managing broken processes." What Womack means is that MBM greatly outperforms MBR. Traditional companies search for sharp, intelligent, and experienced folks and assume that if these folks are given particular targets or objectives that the systems will perform at a high level. This premise is absolutely false, especially over the long term.

In his book *Let's Fix It!*, Richard Schonberger illustrates very well, in a simple but common scenario, the failure that occurs in operations when companies practice MBR. He describes circumstances in which a senior manager instructs one of his supervisors that the unit costs of his department must be reduced by 5 percent. The supervisor responds in a typical manner by stopping all training, overtime, maintenance, and improvement activities until he meets the goal of the 5 percent reduction. Even though this results in late deliveries, quality issues, machine breakdowns, and a drop in morale, the supervisor is steadfast until he reaches the objectives, or numbers. Schonberger writes: "When the performance of the parts of a system, considered separately, are improved, the performance of the whole may not be (and usually is not) improved. Financial feedback has the same weaknesses, only worse. Financial results are even more remote, aggregated, and manipulable."[9]

Why MBM?

In *Profit beyond Measure,* Dr. H. Thomas Johnson and Anders Bröms demonstrate how Toyota's TPS achieves MBM in both its systems design and in the strict execution of its procedures. They write: "Perform every step according to … takt time; follow standard work procedures; recognize abnormal conditions and stop to correct them … work only in response to a customer order; space varieties over the shift as evenly as possible, and so forth. *Do those things properly, and cost will take care of itself*" (emphasis added).[10]

Also, Dr. Johnson and Bröms make clear that Toyota's MBM methods do not feature any accounting system: "No accounting information compiled during the period can help the managers and workers in the plant achieve, or improve, that outcome."[11] This insight supports the cost-management view articulated in prior chapters of this book. Cost management is not about cost accounting; it is about doing the correct thing in the correct way—MBM. Every worker performs standardized work at the appropriate rhythm because of the traits inherent in the TPS, not because "expert" handlers of abstract quantitative information instruct and cajole everyone to hurry along and meet "the targets."[12]

MBM does not entail that companies ignore financial concerns, but it does mean that a company does not use accounting practices to manage the operation of its systems and processes, particularly for the day-to-day functions and operations. The focus must be customer needs, not financial objectives, according to Dr. Johnson and Bröms. They write: "The system's purpose is to continually meet new customer needs as expeditiously as possible—not to pursue financial, part number, or other scorecard targets. By focusing all design activities on that purpose, the system enhances profitability year in and year out."[13]

An analogy that is commonly used and illustrates this point very well is a football coach coaching a game, calling plays and substituting players, by simply watching the scoreboard. At the end of the game, the scoreboard, of course, shows the results. However, in a real game, the game is not won by the coach watching the scoreboard. The coach watching and making decisions from the playing field achieves a real victory. In a normal situation, the coach understands what occurs on the field and responds accordingly based on the actual actions and the *design* of the game plan. He also relies on the *execution* of his players based on their training and capability.[14]

Another adverse effect of MBR is the degradation of the operational and support systems. By focusing on results, managers will tend to compromise the system by negatively exploiting it, ignoring it, and not investing in it in order to strictly achieve targets. MBM, in contrast, makes managers focus on sticking strictly to the system and immediately fixing the system when and where it breaks down. Managers also continually advance the system to better serve customers' needs. Dr. Johnson and Bröms expand on this: "MBR thinking causes companies during periods of prosperity to sacrifice system and discipline to the pursuit of financial targets. In the inevitable economic slump that follows, advocates of such thinking … have many new MBR strategies—such as activity-based management, reengineering, restoring core competencies, and so forth—pick up the pieces."[15]

Such thinking and strategy in organizations leads managers on a vicious cycle of chasing results and never understanding the how and why of what they are doing; in other words: *"American businesses substitute an obsession with meeting scorecard targets without regard for the means used to do it"* (emphasis added).[16]

Orest Fiume and Jean Cunningham relate an anecdote that illustrates the destructive conclusion of MBR management:

> Experience teaches us that when goals are set, people will do whatever they can to achieve the target, even if it results in dysfunctional behavior. Consider the craze of the 1970s and 80s, MBO or Managing By Objective.[17] All that focus on the *what* part of the equation—the objective—instead of the methods for achieving the objective created loopholes that hurt a lot of business. In the end, MBO often created suboptimization, with managers eagerly optimizing the one little piece of the process over which they had control, without concern for the big picture. It is a kind of natural law that people will try to meet the metrics set by the boss in order to make themselves look good, no matter the consequences.[18]

Fiume and Cunningham further stress that

> this focus on improving the individual elements of the process, by eliminating waste and increasing velocity, has great impact on the bottom line, but only when we are not focused exclusively on that bottom line. The winners will be companies that focus on process first, not results.[19]

Do the Parts Equal the Whole?

Another important theme presented by Dr. Johnson and Bröms in *Profit beyond Measure* is how the whole of a business enterprise does not equal the sum of its parts from a quantitative viewpoint. The reason for this is the interdependence each part of the organization has on the other. In other words, if a change is made in one part of the organization, it changes activities in every other part connected to that changed part. This, in turn, has ramifications on all of the parts connected to the parts connected to the changed part, and so on. Even though all of the independent parts of an organization can act independently, they have direct effects on many other parts of the overall system.

This effect is especially true with costs. A savings in one area very well may have an adverse effect on the cost in another area or, most likely, in multiple areas. This is why savings in one area does not necessarily directly benefit the company's bottom line. Since traditional manufacturing firms are a collection of dysfunctional departments that are striving to meet their own independent results—MBR—they cannot pass cost improvements seamlessly through the other systems and functions that are connected to the source area. Each time the improvement passes through these other connected areas, it changes their activity and impacts the effectiveness of the improvement. So by the time it passes along the organizational path to the bottom line, it simply does not appear as it did in its original form—or as cost savings.

That the sum of the parts is equal to the whole of an organization is a concept taught in most of our educational institutions, as well as the model that serves as a cornerstone of traditional management as it is used throughout industry today.[20] Dr. Johnson and Bröms state: "In other words, change in either revenue or cost simply changes profit by the same magnitude, in the direction indicated by the equation ... [This] seems to frame the way managers think about an organization's affairs, almost inevitably they think about performance improvement in terms of increasing profit either by raising revenue or cutting costs."[21] Such thinking equates a company, according to Dr. Johnson and Bröms, to a collection of "separate parts, and treats each part only as an independent object." And each part is thought to be easily manipulated "through the one-dimensional lens of quantitative measurement."[22]

Dr. Johnson and Bröms's argument is that lean, by its design and function, imitates living systems.[23] Living systems understand and function knowing that what an individual entity does affects the entities around it, whether that entity is a cell in the body, a celestial body, or a living creature. All affect other entities around them with whatever they do. Organizations must function with this understanding in order to survive and evolve effectively and successfully. Therefore, the *means* of an entity's actions and functions are what is important, not the *results* of its behavior. Toyota and other successful lean companies behave with this principle in mind.[24] The implementation of flow along the value stream is a physical manifestation of Dr. Johnson and Bröms's opinion of emulating living systems: "Managers who perceive companies as actual living systems deem it impossible to enhance the overall profit of an organization simply by removing or adding amounts of revenue or cost ... quantitative measures can describe end results, but they cannot penetrate the means—the relationships and patterns—from which results emerge."[25] This very notion is why lean manufacturers focus on the means for establishing flow of products and information along a value stream in response to customer needs and requests.

The 2003 Shingo Prize–winning book *Better Thinking, Better Results* reaffirms Dr. Johnson and Bröms's belief. The authors write: "Conventional management practice focuses on optimizing the individual parts of a business and assumes improvements in each functional area will accrue favorably to the business as a whole. It is easy to set function-specific goals and hold department heads accountable for results. This seems like a reasonable thing to do and just about everyone does it."[26] The writers, just like Dr. Johnson and Bröms, report the folly of conventional management of thinking and how it stifles a lean environment and a lean transformation.

Dr. Jeffrey Liker in *The Toyota Way* also warns of the recklessness of this management thinking style and its contrast with Toyota's management thinking: "Toyota is a true learning organization that has been evolving and learning for most of a century. This investment in its employees should frighten those traditional mass production companies that merely focus on making parts and counting quarterly dollars while changing leaders and organizational structures every few years."[27]

In an episode of CBS's *60 Minutes* in fall 2002, the CEO, president, and cofounder of the SAS Institute,[28] Dr. James Goodnight, reiterated this same view. According to Goodnight, "It's pressure from Wall Street to please share holders by delivering rising quarterly earnings that has poisoned the corporate well."[29] Goodnight goes on to say:

> I am basically my own Board so I don't have to worry about pressure from the Board or being fired if I don't improve earnings.
> ...There's no possible way I can tell you what my earnings [SAS's earnings] are gonna be to the penny each quarter. There is only one way to get there, to the penny, and it's that you have to cook the books.[30]

Goodnight's statements reflect that he does not have to resort to MBR, either by his own actions or by a board of directors, which is a common reality today. He can focus on creating an environment where his employees can concentrate on executing their processes, or MBM. His views are reminiscent of managers and business owners of the period prior to 1925.

The leadership of pre-1925 companies was not driven by financial results, but by the execution of the company and employees to meet customer satisfaction. Goodnight's statements also reveal that the financial targets used by most companies today, especially public companies, are simply a farce. These financial targets cannot create an environment with information that will contribute to valuable or correct decisions for running the operations.

Robert Lutz, the feisty former Chrysler executive, agrees with this charge. He writes: "Wall Street loves companies with tight controls—the tighter the better. Is this because financial analysts are secretly masochists? Or is it because they believe tight controls invariably cut waste? If it's the latter, they're wrong."[31]

Michael Hammer also drives this point home in his 1996 book, *Beyond Reengineering*, while discussing the reason that a business enterprise exists. His point parallels the views of others, including Toyota's TPS. As a method to achieve customer satisfaction, Dr. Johnson and Bröms's proposal of MBM and Dr. Steven Spear's Rules-in-Use connect the purpose of the company to the needs of the customer: "This viewpoint confuses means with ends. While profit, jobs, and all the rest are desirable and worthy objectives, they cannot be approached directly. The road to all these other destinations lies through customer value."[32]

Hammer reiterates what has been a common theme throughout this review of information. MBR cannot establish excellent procedures or superior execution key to achieving an exceptional manufacturing enterprise. In an article for *The Manufacturer*, Rich Weissman expounds on this point: "Directors and other top level management have all not accepted lean, often due to a lack of understanding of its principles and benefits ... directors can be quite removed from day-to-day manufacturing operations. 'Many board members ... are not educated in lean thinking,' said Cote. [Larry Cote, President of Ottawa, Ontario-based Lean Advisors] 'However they are quite tuned into financial results and stock prices.'"[33]

ACCOUNTING AND EXECUTION

Using financial accounting information to control people as well as to plan financial consequences is what present-day accountants refer to as management accounting.[34] Nearly all businesses and educational institutions treat accounting information as the central and main source for any manufacturing company to understand how and what they must do in order to make operational decisions. Contrary to common belief, costing methods, developed between the late 1800s and the early 1900s and based on information from work processes and other operational activities, were not derived from financial accounting information, even though such methods were sometimes reconciled with accounting data. Prior to World War II it was developed to understand cost and margin information to evaluate the performance of companies' operational departments and divisions. This evolution during the turn of the century was a response to understand market price information, which disappeared when companies managed transactions internally.[35]

As Dr. Johnson points out, "financial results emanated from driving workers and business units to 'do the right thing,' not from driving them to do things that would achieve desired overall financial targets."[36] He emphasizes that "top managers in most companies before World War II would have blanched at the idea of using financial accounting information to control operations. They often used it to plan and evaluate results."[37]

As will be discussed in Chapter 17, the plan for cost management presented in this book will also establish a method and philosophy that uses cost information for planning and evaluating decisions for applying resources, not for managing day-to-day operations or deciding how and what should be done to satisfactorily manufacture and deliver a product to the customer. In essence, cost management should have nothing to do with execution of the operation, but it is a helpful and valuable tool for planning and resource deployment. In this understanding of cost management, the manufacturing enterprise will be taken back to the days and methods that brought manufacturing into its own: the time between 1885 to 1925, or the Industrial Revolution.

This idea relates directly to the intimate understanding the nineteenth-century and early twentieth-century managers had of their operations, products, and customers. They did not need, nor did they engage in, some financial melee when discussing operational issues with their subordinates, supply base, or customers. Managers during this period focused on properly executing their operations to satisfy customers. This very simple and straightforward goal manifests itself in today's lean enterprise, which focuses itself on flowing product along a specific value stream directly into the hands of the customer. Dr. Johnson writes: "There was little chance that plant managers would achieve cost savings by cutting corners that might risk quality."[38]

Dr. W. Edwards Deming promoted a very similar message during his work in industry. Dr. Johnson describes Dr. Deming's message and connects it to the focus and methods of the early industrial managers and his own and Bröms's holistic view of the operation enterprise. Dr. Johnson writes: "Processes in a business form a *system of interdependent* (i.e., cooperative, not competitive) components that have an *aim*, which in business is to exceed customer expectation profitability. Management's job is to *optimize the system* by ensuring that its components cooperate, not compete" (original emphasis throughout).[39]

Dr. Johnson goes on to state that Dr. Deming's message is that "a company earns the required long-term rate of return—a condition necessary for survival—by optimizing the system, not by maximizing returns to individual components of the system."[40] Dr. Johnson made this statement eight years prior to his book *Profit beyond Measure*, which put MBM into full perspective. What Dr. Johnson, Bröms, Dr. Deming, and the late nineteenth-century and early twentieth-century industrialists are trying to express is that the goal is not to make money, but to supply customers' expectations via excellent execution of an operational enterprise in order to make money.

Obviously, receiving a profit and maintaining cash flow is necessary for any business, but their point is that the effort *must* be put into customer satisfaction through superior execution—or means—to be successful over the long term. Financial returns will result if this is accomplished. Such a mindset is completely different from what is taught in academia and performed in today's business enterprise.

ACCOUNTING AND EXECUTION AND FAILURE

Dr. Johnson expresses: "Businesses in the past forty years have used financial accounting information not only to plan the extent and financing of the business as a whole and to report to outsiders, but also to manage operations inside the company. Thus, accounting information intended primarily for reporting the financial results of business operations is used to shape decisions and actions that determine those results."[41] Such practices are the blight of MBR. As has been discussed, the focus on results—especially financial results—cannot guide organizations to achieve superior results. A concentration on brilliant execution is the best practice to actually achieve world-class success. Financial results do not "provide the basis for understanding what needs to be changed and how."[42]

AN MBR MOMENT

In a former engineering position, I experienced a very poignant MBR situation. During a meeting for salaried employees at the end of the fiscal year, the company's Chief Operating Officer (who is the company's CEO today) responded to the company's past-year results.

He politely and professionally berated the efforts of the employees based on performance in terms of financial results. Our company had not performed very well that year based on the expected performance.

The prior year, our company had performed very well—in fact, it had been one of the company's best years. Company executives had praised the employees at the previous year's end-of-fiscal-year meeting and had even held a private party at the city's public zoo and given out large bonus checks to both salaried and hourly employees.

The interesting point is that as the COO berated the salaried employees attending the meeting (our efforts did not matter, only the results according to our COO), I looked around at the faces of the salaried employees. Their faces (and the comments afterwards) revealed the MBR moment. Their efforts put forth over the two separate years had been the same. So why would the same effort be wonderful one year (and the employees told to "keep it up!") but poor and unacceptable the next year? Perhaps it was the power of MBR.

The MBR companies of today continue to work hard and push their managers to focus on being efficient. The MBR mindset is amplified by the need to cover costs. The Evil of Overhead section discussed this issue. Instead of developing and executing great processes and procedures, traditional companies relentlessly drive their systems and people to be efficient. Dr. Johnson writes:

> For overhead costs, reporting schemes track the percentage of overhead "covered" or "earned" by units produced. The goals of these reporting schemes is to have all recorded direct labor or machine hours go toward production of standard output and thereby "absorb" or "cover" direct and overhead—a condition referred to as "efficient."[43]

"Efficiency" is the replacement for proper execution in traditionally managed manufacturing businesses. As can be seen, such businesses focus on achieving dictated financial results, not on achieving customer satisfaction. These companies make the critical mistake of assuming that hitting their target efficiency will "result" in customer satisfaction. The continued damage of the MBR efficiency game is exhibited in larger and larger batches, overproduction, more scrap and rework, large amounts of inventory, large and expensive equipment, poor or slow information feedback, and a feast-or-famine production mentality.

Lean manufacturers like Toyota take a completely different approach. They ignore such an efficiency quest and completely focus on executing superior processes (value streams that flow), driving control down to the lowest levels of their operations, and focusing on customers in all levels of the enterprise. Dr. Johnson writes: "Managers of conglomerates who followed such strategies [MBR and efficiency] turned their attention completely *away from internal operating activities and customer satisfaction* and attempted to create value out of thin air by 'acquiring stars,' 'milking cash cows,' and 'divesting dogs'" (emphasis added).[44]

The lean enterprise has brought business thinking back to the original intent of business leaders from the industrial revolution. It creates an environment that allows the entire enterprise to function for the benefit of the customer and not for the benefit of the targeted financial results. Today's cost-accounting methods promote financially driven behavior and, according to Dr. Johnson, have lost relevance:

> Underlying modern management accounting—and the cause of its lost relevance—is the belief businesses can both plan and control their affairs with financial accounting information. This belief was not widespread before the 1950s. Indeed, before World War II companies rarely viewed financial accounting information as anything other than a compilation of results....

> Top managers after the 1950s took a fateful leap that their nineteenth- and twentieth-century predecessors had resisted. They began to use accounting information for a purpose it was not intended to serve.... That practice, more than any other, defines management accounting's lost relevance in recent years.[45]

Therefore, the manufacturing enterprise began with a strict focus on and understanding of its internal operations and how to best execute to achieve customer satisfaction. During the middle and end of the twentieth century, though, manufacturing executives left this practice and understanding behind to embrace MBR's financial objectives as their guiding star. Today's lean manufacturers, exemplified by Toyota and their group companies, have reestablished the vision and understanding of manufacturing's original leaders. Intimacy and understanding of the products, processes, and customers are the key to immediate and long-term success and the underpinning of execution and MBM: "Before World War II … managers of plants and departments were expected to think in terms of customer satisfaction, employee morale, product quality, and adherence to cash budgets—not return on investment (ROI), net income, or unit cost variances."[46]

NOTES

1. Taylor, *The Principles of Scientific Management*, 112.
2. Spear and Bowen, "Decoding the DNA of the Toyota Production System," 105.
3. Johnson, "A Recovering Cost Accountant Reminisces," 3. At the time that I received the draft, the article was to be published in fall 2002 *Journal of Innovative Management*.
4. Spear, "Just-in-Time in Practice at Toyota."
5. Womack, presentation at the AME Annual Conference, 2002.
6. DeLuzio, "Danaher is a Paragon of Lean Success," 8.
7. Ibid., 12.
8. Johnson, "A Former Management Accountant Reflects on His Journey."
9. Richard J. Schonberger, *Let's Fix It!*, 88.
10. Johnson and Bröms, *Profit beyond Measure*, 108.
11. Ibid.
12. Ibid., 99.
13. Ibid., 139.
14. Ibid., x.
15. Ibid., 138.
16. Ibid.
17. MBO can be considered the same as MBR.
18. Fiume and Cunningham, *Real Numbers*, 38.
19. Ibid., 40.
20. Johnson and Bröms, *Profit beyond Measure*, 220.
21. Ibid.
22. Ibid.
23. At the 2003 University of Michigan's Lean Manufacturing Conference, Glenn Uminger acknowledged this same point in his May 6 presentation, "Lean: An Enterprise Wide Perspective." A lean enterprise is a living, evolving, organized system!

24. Johnson and Bröms repeat this throughout *Profit beyond Measure*.
25. Johnson and Bröms, *Profit beyond Measure*, 221.
26. Emiliani, *Better Thinking, Better Results*, 202n1, 227. The authors also point out the failure of universities, which taught incorrect or poor principles that led to the improper thinking of today's managers.
27. Liker, *The Toyota Way*, 13.
28. The SAS Institute is a software and service company headquartered in Cary, North Carolina, and is the largest privately held software company in the world with approximately nine thousand employees.
29. Statement made by Dr. James Goodnight during a *60 Minutes* segment, "The Royal Treatment," which aired October 13, 2002.
30. Goodnight, *60 Minutes*.
31. Lutz, *Guts*, 91.
32. Hammer, *Beyond Reengineering*, 101.
33. Weissman, "Bringing Lean to the Board," 42–43.
34. Johnson, "Managing by Remote Control," 42.
35. Ibid., 42–43.
36. Ibid.
37. Ibid., 48–49.
38. Ibid., 49.
39. Johnson, "Deming's Message for Management Accountants," 34.
40. Ibid., 34.
41. Johnson, "Managing by Remote Control," 56.
42. Ibid.
43. Ibid., 59–60.
44. Ibid., 61.
45. Ibid., 62.
46. Johnson, "Beyond Product Costing," 16.

5

ALEXANDER HAMILTON CHURCH: HIS COST-MANAGEMENT SYSTEM

According to accounting historians Michael Chatfield and Richard Vangermeersch, Alexander Hamilton Church "stands out as an engineer who played a major role in popularizing costing methods. He was a prolific writer and a staunch advocate of allocation procedures that would enable the profit or loss to be established on every item of production."[1] A photograph of Church appears in Figure 5.1.

My introduction to Church came from a study of Ford's Highland Park plant and a reference from 1918: "If the reader wants a more scientific method of cost keeping, a careful study of 'Production Factors,' by A. Hamilton Church, will be found of pronounced value."[2] Alexander Hamilton Church was truly a man ahead of his time. Born on October 11, 1866, in England to American parents, Church was educated in England and began his professional career there as an electrical engineer. He worked for three different companies during his tenure in England and moved permanently to the United States between 1900 and 1905. During this period he became a manufacturing consultant and began writing on management and accounting issues.[3] He presented ideas that have had a direct impact on the accounting practices not only in his own time but also in today's world. His concept of moving all costs to being direct costs ("production factors" in Church's terms) is one of the cornerstones of the methods proposed in this book and will be discussed in detail in Chapter 17.

Church realized and articulated that in order to change the costing structure, organization must change. Ninety-six years before James Womack and Daniel Jones's *Lean Thinking*, Church acknowledged the same declaration: "The real need is to get rid of the system and start over, on a new basis."[4] In Church's 1900 article titled "The Meaning of Commercial Organisation," he notes: "The general effect of leaving this important section out of account is much the same as that of trying to restore life to a dying man by mounting him on a bicycle, instead of building up the decaying tissue first."[5]

69

Figure 5.1 Alexander Hamilton Church
Source: Lyndall F. Urwick (ed., part one) and William B. Wolf (ed., part two), *The Golden Book of Management: A Historical Record of the Life and Work of More Than One Hundred Pioneers* (1956; second ed., New York: American Management Association, 1984), 113.

M. C. Wells of the University of Illinois concluded the same point in 1978 in his monograph, *Accounting for Common Costs*, which is a thorough review of the origins and development of accounting and cost allocation. He writes: "The techniques required for the calculation of unit total costs of production are unnecessary and inappropriate for inclusion in cost-accounting systems. Those techniques include the allocation of overhead, standard costs, and transfer prices. Abandoning them makes it possible to develop a system based upon factual data."[6]

Robert Lutz advises the need for change in accounting and finances in his book *Guts: The Seven Laws of Business that Made Chrysler the World's Hottest Car Company*. Lutz states that he "feel[s] strongly that the function [finances] needs to reinvent itself. As constituted now, it's much too much obsessed with imposing tight controls."[7]

Womack and Jones, Church, Wells, and Lutz reveal that the business enterprise must change at the fundamental level in order to truly institute change in its function and operation. Surface changes are nothing more than that: when they are made the business has not actually changed. The discussion in this book thus far has been about completely changing the methods, techniques, and principles that affect how the manufacturing company functions. MBM replaces MBR. Flow manufacturing replaces batch manufacturing. Economies of scale become a thing of the past. And cost-management accounting disappears, becoming cost management. The cost-management system becomes a reflection of the physical operations and subservient to its needs.

These ideas are the very principles Church articulated around the early part of the twentieth century. His ideas are the views that form the foundation of the cost-management system developed in this book.

A Man Ahead of His Time

Alexander Hamilton Church was one of the most innovative and influential engineers of the period between 1885 and 1925. The process developed in this book is a direct evolution of his ideas and methods. Church, although completely obscure in accounting and industrial history, contributed as much as anyone during the development of accounting thoughts and techniques around the turn of the century. His legacy deserves more credit than it is given—and in most traditional accounting literature, it is given no credit.

Church's ideas interestingly parallel today's principles behind lean production and its methods of management. One such idea is Church's understanding that organizations must change at the fundamental level in order to truly institute real change. These concepts will be reviewed in a context that provides a background of Church's thinking.

CHURCH AND MBM

In 1961, Joseph Litterer of the University of Illinois wrote an outstanding article reviewing not only Church's views and developments in accounting but also his philosophies about industrial management. According to Litterer, and based on his review of Church's original writings, Church understood the importance of how each part of the enterprise interacted with other parts and functions of the business system. Church understood how parts impact the holistic system and how change and implementation must be considered in the context of the entire system. They should be considered not only as point improvements but as impacting the function of the entire system.

Church's view of such a principle is aligned with Dr. H. Thomas Johnson and Anders Bröms's view of how businesses must be managed by means (MBM), not by results (MBR), which they outlined in *Profit beyond Measure*. Although MBM is unique today, it was most likely not unusual in Church's time since, as discussed earlier, managers of businesses prior to 1925 understood all aspects of their businesses. But few of Church's contemporaries articulated this philosophy to the degree that Church did. Perhaps Church foresaw the upcoming movement of management to manage by numbers, MBR.

Litterer writes of Church:

In his writing, Church repeatedly returned to a common theme that, if a management is going to be concerned with the total efficiency of the firm, it cannot be exclusively concerned with the efficiency of the parts.

He goes on further to condemn the practice of looking exclusively at certain operations done on a machine, thereby failing to look at these operations in a larger context.[8]

ACCOUNTING AND ENGINEERING

As mentioned frequently throughout this book, the early developers and innovators of accounting practices were for the most part engineers. As is the case with Alexander Church, being an engineer and having a background in engineering and operations gave management pioneers a huge advantage, which is missing in today's industrial environment. The early engineers had intimate knowledge and experience with products, processes, machine tools, and support functions that gave them the understanding of what needed to evolve and be created in order to move the manufacturing enterprise forward.

Most of what these engineering frontiersmen developed and implemented is either still in use today or is still relevant for today's manufacturing operation. Whether it is accounting, processing, or systems design, the engineers of the 1885 to 1925 period blazed new trails that allowed manufacturing, particularly in the United States, to evolve into its modern day essence and methods.

Industry needs engineers to return to the forefront of these areas of development, especially in accounting, that is, cost management. I agree with Vangermeersch, an accountant, accounting historian, and expert on the work of Church, when he states:

> Engineering input into accounting included many more writers than just Church. It is doubtful that engineers today play anywhere near such a vital role in either management or accounting. After reviewing Church's work, and briefly looking at some of the work done by the engineering pioneers in management, this writer longs for much more engineering input now.... Engineers should not only know and be proud of the early contributions by the pioneers to management and accounting but also should strive to emulate them.*

The famous industrial historian Alfred Chandler Jr. corroborates Vangermeersch's assertion about the early industrial pioneers and their contribution to accounting while being engineers in their trade. He writes:

> The pioneers in cost accounting were, on the other hand, the industrial engineers who developed new techniques as they systematized the factory management and attempted to make it more scientific ... cost accounting innovators were publishing numerous articles in these journals dealing with overhead standard costing, factory burden, and accounting controls.**

---

* Richard Vangermeersch, *Alexander Hamilton Church: A Man of Ideas for All Seasons* (New York, NY: Garland Publishing, Inc., 1988), 101–2.
** Alfred D. Chandler Jr. *The Visible Hand: The Managerial Revolution in American Business* (Cambridge, MS: Belknap Press, 1977), 464–65.

Litterner is emphasizing Church's understanding of how a business enterprise is an interlinked combination of subsystems and individuals where changes in each resonate changes through the entire system. Church also offers a warning about the use of MBR and how it guides decisions blindly with no understanding. He writes: "But these decisions are usually based on financial considerations that have little or nothing to do with manufacturing proper."[9]

CHURCH AND LEAN PRODUCTION

Amazingly, Church seemed to have grasped many principles today associated with lean manufacturing. Although he did understand some of these principles, it does not appear that his respective ideas on cost-management accounting and lean principles were able to join together. In this book the union of the lean production idea and the idea of production factors occurs and will be discussed in Chapter 17. The ability to achieve production factors, resources directly aligned to products without the need for an allocation procedure, is physically manifested when flow is applied to an operation. First, it is necessary to review Church's thoughts and ideas, which relate to today's lean principles.

Church and Flow

Church recognized the importance of moving products rapidly through the production system. This concept of flow production would be given life in Henry Ford's Highland Park plant in Church's lifetime.

Church acknowledges his understanding, stating that "equipment must be arranged so that product, persons and communications follow the path of least effort."[10] By today's standards in manufacturing, flow production is the best operational technique to achieve such a path. Although flow production was actually developed and implemented at Highland Park during the 1910s, it did not appear as a universal approach until after the discovery of the Toyota Production System (TPS). Church had an instinctive understanding of what was achieved at Highland Park during his time and later at Toyota, and his discussions in *Production Factors* clearly state his objective to create an operational environment for flow. Church's understanding seems to have helped prepare him for developing his ideas on management and accounting methods.

Church also understood the impact of a system without sufficient flow production on manufacturing and how such a system could adversely influence finances. He writes: "This demands that the material shall remain in its raw or partly finished state *as short as time as possible*, thus avoiding locking up capital, occupying valuable space, and multiplying the numbers of matters requiring the attention of officials at any one time. The ideal condition from this point of view will be a smooth, rapidly running stream of material passing through the plant into the hands of the customer" (original emphasis).[11]

Church's quote echoes something that Womack and Jones might write today to describe flow production, although Church's statement was written over seventy-five years before their breakthrough book, *The Machine that Changed the World*. Church goes on to write, in *Practical Principles of Rational Management*, about material movement, which "*is not an accumulation but a flow of material*" (original emphasis).[12]

In the same article, Church articulates further on flow and also seems to suggest a simple pull signal: "Generally speaking ... the nearer we keep to making the material do its own signalling or 'dispatching,' the nearer we shall keep to simplicity and, above all, flexibility. That is to say, the fact of completion of a stage or process should be in itself the signal for transfer of the material to the next machine or production center."[13]

Church and Value Streams

In *Practical Principles of Rational Management*, Church describes the most effective method of production: the value stream. He titles this section of his article "Law of Efficient Flow." He writes:

> In considering the question of the flow or stream or work.... Maximum efficiency *as regards flow* is achieved when each machine in the plant is continuously engaged in producing one single component of the product, the output of the various machines being so proportioned that all the components turned out in the shop are assembled as fast as they are produced; also where the supply of raw material is so provided for that the quantity of raw material carried in stock is not more than absolutely necessary to prevent shortage which would stop the stream of production. Further, on the commercial side the flow of work is at its best when the manufactured and assembled product is sold and delivered as fast as it leaves the shop.[14]

In this same article, Church describes three "divisions of effort" that must run together to complete the "streams" of work as they progress through operations. He outlines the streams as follows: "(1) Supply and Movement of Material, (2) Supply and Movement of Instructions, (3) Actual Operations."[15] Again, Church's description is conspicuously similar to another one of Toyota's methods, value-stream mapping. Mike Rother and John Shook's book *Learning to See* provides a detailed description of this methodology, creating the same three items Church expresses as one value stream.

Church, as emphasized in stream two, also realized the importance of information and how it must be available to the shop floor in a timely manner in order to retain its value. For shop managers, the design and use of cost information systems are key to achieving quick, accurate turnaround. This is reminiscent of information flows in today's lean value streams:

> Another cause of trouble is that the design of a cost system may be approached from two opposite viewpoints—that of the commercial accountant, who thinks in ledger accounts, and that of the shop staff, who think in

terms of hours, men and materials. The accountant thinks of details as troublesome necessity; the shop staff know that detail is the life-blood of cost system provided it is available at the right time and in the right place.[16]

Church and *Jidoka*

Church's manufacturing model emphasizes the flow of material and information. He also expresses another Toyota principle—*jidoka*—or he at least recognizes the need for such a response mechanism to maintain control in an erratic environment.[17] Manufacturing can be unpredictable and must have means for feedback and control in place to respond quickly to customer demands and maintain order. Toyota accomplished this with *jidoka* and Church states the same need: "The co-ordination of these different classes of effort must be arranged in such a manner that changes in plan, cancellation or urging forward of orders, spoilt work, and the innumerable troubles of every-day factory experience are easily and instantly responded to by the persons concerned, without the 'system' getting into tangles or requiring heroic struggles."[18]

Church and Design for Manufacturing

In a number of writings, Church stresses techniques for designing for manufacturing, or DFM. He underscores the importance of DFM as a cost-reducing practice and a method for allowing effective manufacturing. He writes:

> Good design is, however, evidently the basis of the pyramid; no high efficiency in other departments can hope to recover the waste of effort forced by poor design.
>
> Design has two sharply defined sides—design for technical excellence of use, and subsequent scrutiny and possible modification of such design with a view to manufacture. These two should, but very frequently do not, go hand in hand.[19]

Church continues with his point:

> The designing of work ought not to be divorced from machining considerations, but should proceed hand in hand with them. There seems to be no escape from this position. To do otherwise is almost inevitably to get away from the closest line of profit.[20]

Church's comprehension of the critical aspect of DFM illustrates his intimate knowledge of manufacturing. His insight is key to knowing how operational methods affect costs. Church's understanding plays a key role in the development of his "production factors" concept. It illuminates the point that physical operations must be reflected by the costing system or, in this book's case, the cost-management system.

Vangermeersch—who, as an accountant and accounting historian, has studied the work and writings of Church more than anyone—reinforces Church's focus and knowledge of manufacturing and his effort to develop ideas that support the factory. He writes: "Despite stressing the theoretical impact of Church's ideas upon contemporary business structures, this writer does not neglect the very practical implications of Church's work. Church geared his writings toward the working man in industry, not the scholar. In short, Church's writings sprang from his work experiences and, in turn, he strove to better the common man's work day."[21]

Church offers his version of cost management and its essential tie between engineering and manufacturing—called "constructive accounting"—and indicates that its purpose is not controlling but planning, which is the purpose proposed in this book. Church writes: "Constructive Accounting frames and plans.... And successful constructive accounting is usually the result of an alliance between engineering and manufacturing experience and that of highly trained professional accountant."[22]

Church and the Pursuit of Perfection

Church explains that "the most skillful organizer will be he who gets with the means at his disposal the nearest approximation to this continuous stream of production that his conditions will allow."[23] Church parallels an attitude of continuous improvement and the pursuit of operational excellence by creating efficient flow: "The nearer any business can approach these ideal conditions the nearer it will be to absolute efficiency, regarded from the point of view of the flow of work."[24]

Church, throughout many of his writings, discusses the importance of striving to develop an enterprise-wide system that functions as effectively as possible. He raises this idea in regard to a variety of industrial functions, such as personnel, equipment, management systems, measurement methods, accounting, control functions, and product design. Without a doubt, Church held a vision of a holistic approach and worked to progress toward developing the entire business enterprise. His view is similar to Dr. Johnson and Bröms's in *Profit beyond Measure*—that all parts of the business must be viewed and understood in the context of all of the other parts and functions of the organization. Church states, "If design is inefficient all the operative efficiency in the world will not help. Excellent equipment service may exist alongside poor operation. All three of these functions may be excellently run, and yet inefficiency in control will not thereby be remedied."[25]

Church's view of the continual development of a more effective company is parallel to Womack and Jones's fifth principle of a lean enterprise, presented in their landmark book *Lean Thinking*: perfection.[26] Church pursued such an idea diligently throughout his career in both his writings and work. Church opined:

> I will go further, and say that the whole object and end of organization should be to create the right kind and degree of habit in everyone of the persons engaged in production, from the president down to the shop sweeper.
>
> It is not enough for the workman to be so instructed that he forms good habit. Every living link in the chain of production requires equally to be so trained that his acquired habit is harmonious with the rest.[27]

Church spent his career working and thinking about new ideas and methods, seeking to drive all aspects of industry to more efficient levels. He continually worked to evolve his own—and others'—contributions:

> It [a manufacturing firm] will not claim if it is wise, that it has a machine that cannot possibly be improved on.... Machine design has no finality.
>
> The more that people come to discover that there are other methods of doing things than their own time-honored ones, the better for eventual perfection.[28]

Church here appears to be discussing concepts of a lean production system with the same thoughts and ideas that exist currently. The roots of TPS were being formulated at Henry Ford's Highland Park plant during the time of Church's writings. But what is important when reflecting on these discussions about Church and some lean principles is his thinking process. His thinking—unique in his own time, as well as in our own—is critical to understanding the context in which he develops his principles. Thinking in a different way is key to developing, implementing, and understanding a lean enterprise. Church accomplished such thinking in many respects.

Even the name of Womack and Jones's 1996 book is *Lean Thinking*. Womack and Jones chose this name because TPS is about *thinking* differently. In fact, such different thinking is exactly what Church accomplished during the early part of the twentieth century.

CHURCH AND SCIENTIFIC MANAGEMENT

Church also took to task his contemporaries' ideas about how management principles and methods should be developed to create the most effective business. He even verbally sparred with Frederick Taylor in a series of articles and put forth his own view on scientific management. Church, forever reaching for better ideas and conclusions, understood the efforts of Taylor and used his principles to drive even further toward concepts of perfect management. He writes: "The essential features of scientific management, then, consist of principles and not systems or methods.... In brief, it is the application of accurate thinking, accurate planning, and accurate doing, so as to increase output, reduce cost, and by consequence render available a larger margin of surplus for division between employer and employee."[29]

Taylor, in his own writings, concurred with Church. Taylor viewed management as a philosophy and not a set of methods. Even though Taylor did develop many methods that, like Church, contributed to the progression of industry, Taylor strongly believed that the foundation of excellent management was principles, like the ideas of TPS put forth by Taiichi Ohno and underscored by Dr. Steven Spear's research.

Unfortunately Taylor is remembered for his techniques instead of his philosophies, which, like the work of Church, defined present-day management philosophies. Taylor is remembered by most in industry and academia for his work with a stopwatch and development of time study methods, and he is often—even today—demonized for this work. Not only does Taylor's work—overall as well as in his time studies—contain philosophies *and* methods for today's manufacturing firms that are excellent methods, but he also developed and pushed strong management principles that parallel many of today's lean principles and philosophies, as well as those of his contemporary, Church. Regrettably, most people in industry and academia have not studied Taylor's work in enough detail to understand this misinterpretation:

> The mechanisms of management must not be mistaken for its essence, or underlying philosophy.... The same mechanism which will produce the finest results when made to serve the underlying principles of scientific management, will lead to failure and disaster if accompanied by the wrong spirit in those who are using it.[30]

Taylor continues:

> Scientific management, in its essence, consists of a certain philosophy, which results, as before stated, in combination of the four great underlying principles of management.
>
> When, however, the elements of this mechanism, such as time study, functional foremanship, etc., are used without being accomplished by the true philosophy of management, the results are in many cases disastrous.[31]

Taylor's warnings are prophetic and predict the failure of companies that do not understand what they are really trying to accomplish. His same counsel is every bit as true for today's firms trying to implement lean. Without understanding the underlying principles of lean and instead merely focusing on its tools and methods, companies will end up in failure, as many firms currently have.

CHURCH'S PREMISE: ACCURATE COSTS

In his book *Alexander Hamilton Church: A Man of Ideas for All Seasons*, Vangermeersch's description of Church's writings reaffirms Church's straightforward, matter-of-fact ideology. He also confirms Church's preoccupation with the methods of overhead distribution. Vangermeersch describes Church as having a "succinct and matter-of-fact style carried over to his overall philosophy on the correct application of manufacturing overhead. Throughout his writings, he remained extremely concerned about an application of a constant percent of overhead for each job."[32] Vangermeersch notes that

> applying an arbitrary increment or percentage equally on all, will produce not any approach to facts, but merely a fancy figure, which will be not even constant in its error. It is, in fact, a guess, and not the less so because based on figures. Arrangements of this kind probably originated the unkind saying that figures will prove anything, "except facts."[33]

Church was passionate about methods that would deliver facts or accurate information. He provides many examples illustrating how using an average rate for distributing overhead fails to give the proper cost picture of the operations. Church also warns of using a simple system to develop the overhead structure. These simple systems—based on academia's use of a simple system taught at today's universities— were the foundation of many present-day allocation systems. Since industry between 1885 and 1925 progressed beyond the single product-process environment, the manufacturing enterprise has since moved well beyond the ability for a simple management system to successfully handle a firm's cost information. Church cautions, "The snare of the 'simple system' must therefore be avoided."[34]

Church viewed the use of these simple methods as an unacceptable distortion of the actual product cost, or a misrepresentation of the "facts" of cost. Such a situation was completely intolerable to Church, and his method of production factors was a direct assault meant to remedy this problem. As TV's Joe Friday famously would say, "Just the facts."[35] Church was the Joe Friday of cost accounting. He was *only* interested in the facts. He writes:

My own view is that it is the business of organization to regulate production, and the business of costs to represent facts and nothing but facts.

This statement may seem to be a truism, but unfortunately many people believe that costs may be usefully manipulated and twisted and averaged so that they cease to represent what actually happen and come to represent what are in the opinions of their manipulator ought to have happen.[36]

The last part of Church's statement is eerily in tune with Dr. Johnson and Bröms's views of the use of MBR.

Church was not the only one concerned with cost information being accurate and useful. Jonathan Harris wrote an article in 1936 detailing a new concept, direct costing. In this article, Harris details his idea for new accounting and allocation methods. But more importantly, his concern is for cost information being correct and helpful to managers; he, like Church, worked to put his ideas into action. In his 1960 doctoral dissertation, *The Theory and Application of Direct Costing*, Phillip Fess[37] reveals Harris's concern: "It is quite obvious from even a cursory reading of this original article on direct costing that Mr. Harris was vitally concerned with the inadequacy of accounting data being supplied to management. Harris held high hopes that direct costing would become that management tool which would satisfy the desires of management for more useful financial data."[38]

CHURCH AND THE EVIL OF OVERHEAD

Church directed assaults at the use of the simple overhead allocation based on direct labor dollars and hours. He understood that during the early twentieth century direct labor was a small and shrinking contributor to the overall cost of manufactured products. Church realized this situation and wrote extensively about it, emphasizing the fact that while overhead was growing, direct labor costs were dwindling.[39] Many today view this issue as more of a present-day concern, but the reality is that manufacturers during the turn of the century were dealing with this same issue.

Church, according to Mariann Jelinek in her 1980 article, "Toward Systematic Management: Alexander Hamilton Church," viewed overhead differently than even his contemporaries. She writes:

> Unlike others of his time, who saw overhead as "unnecessary" expense to be reduced or eliminated where possible, Church saw clearly that such expenditures were legitimate adjuncts to actual operation: "Every legitimate expense in a machine shop is incurred for the purpose of getting the work up to, under, or away from the tool point, in one way or another."[40]

Church's stance, as stated by Jelinek, reflects his strong view of developing and understanding exactly what resources are consumed by the product and its particular process. This opinion again reflects Church's desire to collect accurate cost information for management purposes—cost management.

In a 1987 article by Dr. Johnson on the history of twentieth-century developments in cost accounting, he reveals Church's stance on how costs should be treated and applied to products. Dr. Johnson discloses Church's movement toward the concept of viewing all costs as direct costs. He writes: "Church believed that overhead cost, ultimately, should consist only of an irreducible residual of costs that cannot be traced to individual products. He suggested that accountants and managers abandon the distinction between direct and indirect expenses of a product and focus attention on 'the *real* incidence (of expense) on particular jobs'—the differences in rates at which products consume resources."[41]

Church fully divulges his production factors concept in his 1910 book, *Production Factors in Cost Accounting and Works Management*. He also explains this concept as early as 1901 in a series of articles for *The Engineering Magazine* illustrating his method for formulating direct costs for a variety of typically allocated overhead costs.[42]

As mentioned in Church and the Evil of Overhead, Church loathed the method of equally distributed overhead across products. He even expressed that practicing such overhead allocation was inferior to having no system at all. He writes: "It is not too much to say that any system of accounts which lumps both classes of charge together and averages them all round is entirely worthless ... [and can] be positively dangerous and worse than no system at all."[43]

Vangermeersch substantiates Church's belief while reviewing his writings on production factors. He also reveals a clue to how Church's concept of production factors can relate to present-day manufacturing cells: "Church wrote that the cost of a process on a single part becomes a perfectly definite and tangible thing and can be recorded as such. The tendency to regard burden or indirect expense as something that should be averaged, manipulated or juggled with, disappears."[44] Church's aforementioned view of the ability to focus tangible costs dovetails nicely with the ability of cellular manufacturing when it is properly designed and managed. This point will be addressed in detail in Chapter 17.

Church disparaged the industrial executives of his day. He viewed them very much as many in today's lean arena view executives and their failure to understand lean principles. Church's most pronounced problem with executives hinged on his view of overhead allocation. He writes:

> If 19 out of 20 executives were to be suddenly asked, "Overhead is the cost of—what?" they would probably frame the definition in terms of product, thus: "Overhead is that part of the cost of product which is neither direct wages nor direct material."
>
> A definition of this kind does not explain the nature of overhead, nor does it give a true picture of the natural relation of overhead to the cost of a product. Under the popular methods of overhead distribution there is, in fact, no real relation between burden and cost. Although a ratio has been struck, it is both accidental and temporary. Nothing has resulted but an arbitrary and misleading mathematical trick. No clear picture is forthcoming as to the effectiveness of overhead expenditures or their impingement on processes.[45]

Based on my experience as both a practitioner and consultant in lean manufacturing, I would express the same sentiment if executives were asked such a question today. I have experienced the very results that Church predicted result from general allocation methods being used: incorrect cost information. Again, Church states his opinions on the use of overhead very strongly.

Church, Overhead, and Labor

Church recognized the significant problems with using direct labor as the base for allocating overhead to product costs. Even in his era, labor was a decreasing portion of the resources consumed by manufacturing products. According to him, the use of direct labor was just another misguided method that inaccurately distributed cost over products. As is the case today, equipment costs for Church were normally the largest costs associated directly with production. Again, Church was only interested in factual information and creating systems that would deliver such information. He writes: "From the earliest days of manufacturing there has grown up a custom of considering labor as the main and only direct item in production, and of expressing all other expenditure in more or less vague percentages of wage cost. The fact is, however, that labor, while always important, tends to become less important relatively to other items as the progress of organized manufacture develops and the use of specialized and expensive mechanical equipment increases."[46] This situation was as strange to Church as it is for many today. Why is overhead allocated based on such a smaller percentage of consumed resource cost?

Church absolutely believed in using accurate and correct information. To him, production cost must strictly follow this line; otherwise, the cost information is useless. To Church, production costs were definitely not a catch-all for other costs associated with a manufacturing firm's business. According to Church, "Costing should be registration of production—events that have actually happened—it should be nothing else."[47]

Church railed against using an averaging allocation overhead method with a firm that manufactured a diverse product line. Church understood clearly that the production of a wide variety of products and product line that developed during the latter part of the nineteenth century consumed factory resources at greatly varying rates.[48] As stated previously, Church believed that unless the results from efforts revealed accurate information it made no sense to exercise a practice and it would lead to misinformation and poor decisions. Church believed that information about a product's cost should reveal the real resources used to make the product.[49] The method developed and explained in later sections of this book will follow Church's same premise. He writes:

> We find that as against $100 direct wages on order, we have an indirect expenditure of $59, or in other terms, our shop establishment charges are 59 percent of direct wages in that shop for the period in question. This is, of course, very simple. It is also as usually worked very inexact. It is true that as regards the output of the shop as a whole a fair idea is obtained of the general cost of the work.... And in the case of a shop with machines all of a size and kind, performing practically identical operations by means of a fairly average wage rate, it is not alarmingly incorrect.
>
> If, however, we apply this method to a shop in which large and small machines, highly paid and cheap labour, heavy castings and small parts, are all in operation together, then the result, unless measures are taken to supplement it, is no longer trustworthy.[50]

Church's example directly explains the failure of averaging overhead burden across products to develop accurate and useful information. He also asserts his opinion that overhead "as a guide to actual profitableness of particular classes of work ... is valueless and even dangerous."[51] Church continues to explain how dropping the concept of direct and indirect expenses contributes to accomplishing the ability to put forth a real picture of what products consume which resources. In *Relevance Lost*, Johnson and Kaplan explain that "he suggested that the distinction between direct and indirect expenses of a product ought to be abandoned in order that accountants and managers focus attention on 'the real incidence [of expense] on particular jobs'—the differences in rates at which products consume resources."[52]

Church and His "Modern" Contemporaries

In *Relevance Lost*, H. Thomas Johnson and Robert Kaplan explain how the engineer "cost accountants" of Church's period—mainly from the metal-working industries—

promoted developments in product costing, although Church innovated the most highly developed method.[53] These engineers wrote much literature explaining their ideas, which stressed their desire to develop more accurate product-costing methods for estimating, pricing, and planning. They did not have any intrinsic interest in accounting per se, just systems and methods to achieve good product costing information for internal use.[54]

Dr. Johnson and Kaplan point to this same idea, emphasizing how the use of this cost information leads to poor or even incorrect decisions. The results are due to the use of traditional methodology, which Church worked to discourage over ninety years ago. Johnson and Kaplan express that

collecting costs into traditional financial accounting categories, like labor, material, overhead, selling, distribution, and administrative, will conceal the underlying cost structure of products. It will lead firms to make critical decisions such as price and distribution based on average costs that incorporate cross subsidies and distortions. Misguided decisions leave the company vulnerable to attacks by focused competitors or by competitors who know their costs well. These competitors can price aggressively in high-volume segments where the company has priced its output too high because of inaccurate information from its cost system.[55]

The same point was articulated by Michael Porter, the famous Harvard Business School professor, in 1985 when he stated that "indirect activities are also frequently grouped together into 'overhead' or 'burden' accounts, obscuring their cost and contribution to differentiation."[56] Porter also expresses the notion—similar to Dr. Johnson and Bröms's key to MBM—that all parts of the firm are interlinked and interdependent. Porter writes: "The value chain is not a collection of independent activities but a system of interdependent activities."[57] Porter continues by discussing the importance of "linkages" between value activities that connect the activities and play the key role in performance and costs.[58] Interestingly enough, Spear's Rules-in-Use also focus on the critical importance that the linkages—or in Spear's term, connections[59]—play in creating the most effective operational environment and how they are significant to the success of TPS.

Porter also makes the connection between misunderstanding the importance of such linkages with lack of ability to develop a useable cost system. He agrees with Church, Dr. Johnson, and Bröms that "cost systems categorize costs in line items—such as direct labor, indirect labor, and burden—that may obscure the underlying activities a firm performs."[60] Porter emphasizes how the absence of a usable cost system in a firm forms many of the issues undermining reasonable decision making.

The alternative to traditional methods, which Church developed and promoted and Dr. Johnson and Kaplan allude to, is the creation of an environment that moves indirect costs and allocation into direct costs. This change is achieved by implementing physical changes or one-piece flow in the form of cellular manufacturing of value streams. Managers of the manufacturing enterprise must understand what changes must be made and where they must be made in order to be successful. Church explains:

> It is true that the broad results of a half-year's work can be read in unmistakable figures in the balance sheet. But the mischief[61] is not only done by that time, but in the absence of proper shop accounts, it cannot be ascertained where is the element at fault. To introduce reform one must first know where reform is necessary.... A modern system of organization is a high class machine tool. It can be done without, but not economically. That is all there is to it. The wise man will make his own choice.[62]

CHURCH, OVERHEAD, AND PRODUCT COSTING

As reviewed in the three previous sections, overhead allocation—especially using averaging techniques—creates unusable and useless information, in many cases information that may lead to poor or misguided decisions. Creating an operation and information system that directs resource consumption directly—to which products or product lines that consume the resource can be traced—is the crux of Church's proposal. This concept is the point this book develops and describes to be contained within any information system for product costing.

Church stresses the importance of obtaining correct information and how traditional methods fail to achieve this. He puts forth a solid method to develop usable and correct facts about product costs for operational planning and decisions. He writes:

> All valuation is an attempt to represent certain facts. The facts are indubitably these: the charges incident on a variety of articles as truly represent part of the cost of such articles as the actual direct wages paid on them. And these charges are rarely, it would be safe to say never, identical in their incidence on different classes of articles nor are they constant from period to period. Therefore an attempt to represent their value either by ignoring this factor of production or by applying an arbitrary increment or percentage equally on all, will produce not any approach to facts, but merely a fancy figure, which will be not even constant in its error. It is, in fact, a guess, and not the less so because based on figures. Arrangement of this kind probably originated the unkind saying that figures will prove anything, "except facts."[63]

CHURCH'S PRODUCTION FACTORS: DIRECT COSTS[64]

To create an information system, Church proposes establishing what he calls "production factors." Reviewing his definition of a production factor allows for better understanding his proposal:

> A Production Factor may be defined as any expense that has a *definite* relation to cost of production. It is not pretended that each and every item of

expense can be reduced to production factors, but it will be seen that a very large and important number of them can be so reduced. The principle of "Organization by Production Factors" is to keep things in sight that are generally covered up, disguised and lost to view, and to observe the facts and phenomena of product along nature lines, as distinct from arbitrary and artificial lines. [original emphasis][65]

Church's opinion of the purpose of costs drove his need to develop his production factors methodology. He devised a way to present in a logical manner how and what resources were consumed by production or, more specifically, by products flowing through the shop floor. He states that "the object of organization [the manufacturing firm] is to determine the ways and means of efficient production"[66] or, in particular, to determine the physical techniques in which products will be assembled, machined, fabricated, or whatever method of production must be undertaken in order to achieve the most effective results. Church continues by stating: "The object of cost accounts is to register and record every stage and step of production as it actually happens."[67] Church's production-factors method accomplished his intentions.

Church and Rightsizing Processes

Church states, "It will be seen that the cost of a process on a single part becomes a perfectly definite and tangible thing and can be recorded as such."[68] Church understood the importance of the ability to focus on a particular product and the ability to attach information to it. This understanding distinguished Church from most of his contemporaries. As discussed in the section "Church and Lean Production," Church's production-factors method is known today as a value stream. He knew in a fundamental sense that using basic concepts of flow and cells and connecting production factors to a product's manufacture would be greatly simplified and create the ability to track costs directly to products. Although his views were not completely in tune with cellular manufacturing under the methods and concepts of lean, he did express their principles in nearly all of his writings on this subject.

Church discusses the issues resulting from improperly proportioned processes: inefficiencies result from employing equipment not properly sized for a particular operation, which serves as a negative impact on costs. He did acknowledge that even if an improperly sized process is used to manufacturer a product, its cost must be carried by the product to maintain the accuracy of the cost-information system.[69] He writes: "Charging the normal rate instead of the actual in the costs would be a very dangerous proceeding."[70] Church emphasizes his view of rightsizing equipment, stating, "The large tools might be sold and replaced by others better adapted to the work."[71] Wrongly sizing machines, equipment, and processes directly impacts costs.

Direct Costs: Production Factors

Church again underscores the need to create direct costs for resources consumed and the drive for a cost system that reports accuracy:

> In the method of organization by production factors it is sought to isolate as many as possible of the special functions exercised by the manufacturer, to determine their steady and regular rent-value, by foreseeing their fluctuations, and to charge these rents as regular production factors of perfectly determinable value.
>
> The answer is that the production factor method isolates direct production costs from the confusing influence of a number of other expenditures, and enable the true facts of production to be much more clearly realized than before.[72]

He also articulates another of his unique ideas, rental-style production charges. He uses the analogy of a property owner and a renter to establish a method to tie production or products to an accurate cost of production. Church uses the rental technique for a number of production factors. Figure 5.2 shows these production factors, which are applied by Church as rental charges. As he states in the caption for this diagram, the rent or "service" charges are, in fact, his method for changing the overhead "glob" to definitive resources consumed by the production of products. According to Church:

> It will be seen that some of these are incident on the floor space and others directly on production centres, which may be a machine or bench, or a plain

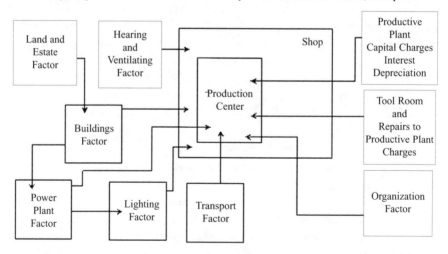

Figure 5.2 Diagram of Church's production factors
Source: Adapted from A. Hamilton Church, *Production Factors in Cost Accounting and Works Management* (1910; repr., NY: Arno Press, 1976), 54.

floor area in an erecting shop or foundry. Those incident on floor space are reduced to a charge per square foot and enter in that form into the production-centre rate (machine rate). It will be noticed that each of these factors represents a special kind of "service" rendered to production, reduced in each case to a unit-value. The indefinite nature of a large number of "indirect charges" is thus replaced by a limited number of definite "rent charges," called herein "production factors."[73]

Church's method parallels what in a lean-operational environment would be aligning products along their value stream. Although Church is not doing it in the same physical context, he is achieving it from a resource assignment or consumption perspective. What he does accomplish is moving production resources or "production factors" out of the nebulous realm of overhead and directly attaching it to the resource that consumes it. This action is key to his view on costs and key to the method developed in this book.

In *Production Factors in Cost Accounting and Works Management*, Church provides detailed explanations of how each of the production factors are developed and directly assigned to the production of products. His methodology allows resources other than material and labor to be assigned to the product, which consumes it during the production process.[74] Church's basic technique will be used to accomplish the same in the lean-manufacturing environment.

Church believed that any work must be directly applied to the product itself, which is similar to a view found in TPS. In his example, he uses the tool point[75] as the focus of where "all expenditures converge."[76] By this, he is expressing the importance of focusing on the activities associated with making a product conform to the customer requirements: Church states that such costing activities must be subservient to the tool's operation on the work. If either of these situations does not exist, the activity is a wasted expenditure[77] or, in lean terms, a waste or a non-value-adding activity.

In *Production Factors in Cost Accounting and Works Management*, Church provides a schedule of production factors, which is illustrated in Figure 5.3. The schedule is basically a spreadsheet of cost information, or production factors, and is very similar to, or even a basic version of, the spreadsheet developed for the method proposed in this book and discussed in detail in later sections.

In his 1974 book, *Evolution of Cost Accounting to 1925*, S. Paul Garner recognizes the significant development of product costing that Church makes with his production factors. Garner emphasizes that Church is able to "narrow down" costs to associate the proper cost with its specific area of consumption:[78] "The first interesting feature of Church's new technique was concerned with the proper incidence of shop charges. It was his idea that these could be narrowed down in large part to six or seven 'factors,' such as, for example, land, building, or power. That is to say a large proportion of indirect charges were not as general as it is commonly believed. In fact, Garner would subdivide practically all these charges, leaving only a relatively small amount to be divided on a strictly arbitrary basis."[79] The ability to tie actual resources

Schedule of ___	Shop Factors & Machine Rates							Shop Totals per Annum
1. Description								
2. Machine No.								
3. Space Occupied								
4. Power Absorbed								
5. Capital Value								
6. Depreciation Rate								
7. Buildings Factor								
8. Power Factor								
9. Lighting Factor								
10. Heating Factor								
11. Stores-Transport Factor								
12. Supervision Factor								
13. Organization Factor								
14. Interest, Depc'n, & Ins'ce								
15. Repairs & Mt'ce								
16. Oil & Allowance								
17. Tool Room Charge								
18. Yearly Total for 2700 Hrs.								
19. Hourly Rate								

Figure 5.3 Schedule of production factors
Source: Church, Production Factors in Cost Accounting, 128.

to products is crucial for facilitating the ability to create direct costs. Garner recognizes this in Church's work.

In 1913, Church continued to develop his view of the role of production factors. Again, it is clear that his innovation is synonymous with the theme of this book. Just as the roots of lean manufacturing are tied directly to the early part of the twentieth century,[80] the roots of cost-management are as well. Church affirms that

> the method of "production factors," is designed to give, among other things, due expression to the influence on costs of the USE of capital in manufacturing operations. This applies not merely to the capital involved in productive machines and tools, but also to that involved in auxiliary factors of production such as land-building factor, the power, heating and lighting factors, the stores-transport factor, etc. Each of these factors represents a definite kind of expense, having a particular and definite bearing on the manufacturing processes. The cost of each factor is separately assessed against the productive machines making use of the services involved in, of course, exact proportion to the extent of the service.[81]

In summary of Church's production factors concept, Dr. Johnson discusses Church's literature on the subject. Johnson, like Vangermeersch and Garner, acknowledges the effort Church made to tie as many production activities as possible to products or to processes that manufacture products with the goal of developing direct and accurate product-cost information. Dr. Johnson discloses that Church "devoted a great deal of attention"[82] to developing his production-factors concept, which changes indirect costs to direct ones. Dr. Johnson writes that Church argued that indirect resources can be traced to specific products, therefore creating the ability to make a proportionate correlation between the cost and the correct product. Johnson adds :

> Church believed that overhead cost, ultimately, should consist only of an irreducible residual of costs that cannot be traced to individual products. He suggested that accountants and managers abandon the distinction between direct and indirect expenses of a product and focus attention on 'the *real* incidence [of expense] on particular jobs'—the difference in rates at which products consume resources.[83]

Church and Factory Design

Dr. Johnson elaborates on cost's impact on the development of the operation. He writes: "The cost of a process is the aggregate of direct labor costs plus the cost of the various indirect 'services' to production [or production-factors] which are necessitated by the form of the organization."[84]

Church emphasizes the role of the design of the manufacturing system. As will be discussed in the next sections, the manufacturing system design (in today's case, a lean or one-piece flow design) is integral to achieving Church's original intentions. The design aspect that is unfortunately missing for Church is the implementation of a lean or one-piece flow operation, which is the precursor for achieving a Church-style cost management system. Although flow was missing from the manufacturing repertoire at the time,[85] Church did discuss the basic concepts of flow (see the section "Church and Lean Production") in many of his writings. But it does not appear that he was able to apply his costing concepts directly in such an environment.

CHURCH AND CELLULAR MANUFACTURING

Operational design is one of the foundations in achieving use of the cost-management method proposed in this book. A significant amount of this book will discuss the design, design principles, and performance methods that allow such a cost-management method to achieve its goal.

As operational design becomes key to realizing Church's concepts by allowing for directly aligning costs, the design of the lean enterprise builds the ability to establish Church's system in today's environment. The link between Church's system and operational design has been recognized by prior examinations. Wells affirms that "Church's system was closely linked to a carefully designed organizational structure."[86] This link constitutes two of the three principles, moving to flow manufacturing and aligning resources directly, which the cost-management method developed and proposed in this book rests upon. Wells, in his 1978 *Accounting for Common Costs*, reiterates Church's idea of product costs being the actual facts representing what has actually happened in the operations instead of allocated costs.[87]

Church and His Little Shops

Another one of Church's innovative ideas was using a production center to create a focusing effort, which would help guide the ability to direct resource costs to the product or process that consumed it. His product-center concept is synonymous to the concept proposed in this book and to the implementation of manufacturing cells and focus factories in today's lean environments. Church's production-center concept is another tie of his thought process to the themes investigated and developed in the later sections of this book.

Church refers to his production centers as "little shops" and uses the analogy of each little shop being its own separate business enterprise with its own specific needs and resource consumption. These tiny businesses within a business allow for the focus and ability to point costs directly to the products being manufactured within the little shop or production center. Johnson and Kaplan explain that

> Church argued that overhead, ideally, was the cost of countless factors of production, each of which should be traced separately to products. For practical purposes, however, he advocated dividing the factory into a series of "production centers" through which overheads should be loaded onto products.[88]

Both Garner and Vangermeersch acknowledge the connection Church made between his production factors and production centers. Vangermeersch reports: "A significant part of Church's designing of an approach to account for manufacturing overhead was a proposal for cost collection by production centers."[89] Garner goes on to state: "This narrowing down was to be carried only so far as was profitable, and each firm would have to decide that for itself. After the 'factors' had been determined, the plant was to be divided into what he called 'production centers.' These were not necessarily departments in the ordinary interpretation of the term; they might be a series of machines or workbenches."[90]

Church uses the production-center approach to enhance the ability to eliminate the averaging effect of spreading overhead. By creating the little shops throughout a firm's operations, Church creates direct costing, or production factors, by the physical design of manufacturing. Church explains:

> A production center is, of course, either a machine or bench at which a hand craftsman works. Each of these is in the position of a little shop carrying on one little special industry, paying rent for the floor space occupied, interest for the capital involved, depreciation for the wear and tear, and so on, *quite independently of what may be paid by other production centers* in the same shop.… Unlike the averaging methods, almost any actual working conditions can be faithfully represented on this system. This is because each production center is virtually independent of any other, and therefore complexity is indifferent to it.[91]

The analogy Church makes with his little shops is an interesting and innovative concept. It provides the physical environment to achieve his idea of directing costs to each product as the little shop consumes each product. The difference between Church's little shops and today's lean manufacturing cells is the magnitude in which part flow and process or machine location is derived. Church's production center seems to be one process or a small series of bench-top processes operated by an individual operator. Today's manufacturing cells tie together all possible processes needed to manufacture a particular product or component.

As was discussed in an earlier section, Church did understand the fundamental concepts of a value stream, but he did not seem to ever be able to tie it completely to today's concept of a one-piece continuously flowing manufacturing cell. Regardless of Church's simpler version of a production center, Church's concept of identifying costs directly with the production center is a valid and important model.

In a May 25, 1911, article in the *American Machinist* magazine, Church provides an example of an analogy of the little shop, how it envelops everything needed for the production of its product, and how it simply and easily traces its costs. He emphasizes the need to maintain separate information for each production factor to enable the ability to compare and contrast the costs of each factor. Church explains that "if three production factors[92] so far introduced are kept entirely distinct, intelligent comparison becomes at once possible."[93] This concept will be part of the method developed and proposed in this book.

Garner, in *Evolution of Cost Accounting to 1925*, also emphasizes the ability of Church's production-center concept "to localize the overhead as much as possible."[94] This would allow for the ability to develop and understand the direct costs of resources used in the manufacturing process. Garner also regards Church's system as "the best that had been proposed up to that time" and states that "it served as a model for a great number of cost authorities in later years."[95]

Both Wells and Dr. Johnson underscore the ability of Church's concept of little shops to develop accurate cost information by alleviating the averaging of overhead, placing it directly with the product or process. According to Johnson: "For practical purposes [Church] advocated tracing indirect costs to their causes by dividing the factory into a series of production centers, through which expenditure of all classes should be traced to items of output."[96] Wells notes that "the control [Church] envisaged was to be achieved by dividing the factory into a series of little shops and charging to each the costs for which the foreman was accountable, plus a fair proportion of the general factory overhead."[97]

From Church to the Focus Factory

Church's little-shop or production-center concept is a vital innovation for today's lean operation. Although Church was not quite able to evolve his production center method to ensnare a value stream as it is viewed today in the lean enterprise, it remains a sound idea and can be expanded further when combined with value-stream management. The next step in this idea is combining the "little shop" and the value stream into the cost-management theme of this book. Using Church's idea and applying it to a value stream or a one-piece continuous flow cell, a more practical advance in Church's production center is achieved.

This concept for cost management can be taken a step further. Assuming that the manufacturer manufactures a reasonably complex product, a broadened concept of what Church called "focus factories" can in turn be developed. A focus factory is a collection of component value streams that produce products, which are combined into a final assembly.

CHURCH AND THE PURPOSE OF COST INFORMATION

Alexander Hamilton Church was truly a man ahead of his time: he uniquely understood cost-management accounting's role in manufacturing. He was driven to continually bring ideas in both management and accounting methods to more innovative levels. He also understood how management and accounting work together for the benefit of the overall business enterprise.

Very much in the nature of Dr. Johnson and Bröms's MBM and the belief that a cost-management system must be reflective and supportive of the manufacturing system, Church provides his vision of the purpose and use of a firm's cost system. He writes: "The best system of costs cannot do more than give results *severely conditioned by the form of the organization*. No existing system of costs is worth anything by itself; the data it provides must be read in connection with a knowledge of the form of the organization" (emphasis added).[98] This "form of the organization" is embodied in concepts of the lean enterprise, that is, focus factories and cellular manufacturing.[99]

NOTES

1. Chatfield and Vangermeersch, eds., *The History of Accounting*, 228.
2. Knoeppel, *Installing Efficiency Methods*, 239. This quote is what introduced me to Alexander Hamilton Church in 2000.
3. Urwick (ed., part one) and Wolf (ed., part two), *The Golden Book of Management*, 113–17.
4. Womack and Jones, *Lean Thinking*, 52.
5. Vangermeersch, *Alexander Hamilton Church*, 5. The book includes Church, "The Meaning of Commercial Organisation," *Engineering Magazine* 20 (1900): 393. The same point is reviewed in Jelinek, "Toward Systematic Management," 72.
6. Wells, *Accounting for Common Costs*, 151.
7. Lutz, *Guts*, 91.
8. Litterer, "Alexander Hamilton Church and the Development of Modern Management," 222. Litterer is referencing Church, "Practical Principles of Rational Management," *Engineering Magazine* 45 (February 1913), 674–75.
9. Litterer, "Alexander Hamilton Church and the Development of Modern Management," 217. Litterer is referencing Church, *The Science and Practice of Management*, 73.
10. Vangermeersch, *Alexander Hamilton Church*, 67. Referencing Church, *The Science and Practice of Management*, 321.
11. Church, "Practical Principles of Rational Management," 895.
12. Ibid., 900.
13. Ibid., 901.
14. Ibid., 902.
15. Ibid., 895
16. Vangermeersch, *Alexander Hamilton Church*, 71. Referencing Church, September 9, 1915, "What is a Cost System?" 455.
17. *Jidoka* is the ability of an operating system to detect an abnormality and stop before moving to the next process. It is manifested in both human activity and equipment operation.

18. Church, "Practical Principles of Rational Management," 895. Litterer also recites this point (not about *jidoka*, but about a quick self-correcting system for operations) about Church in his 1961 article, "Alexander Hamilton Church and the Development of Modern Management," 219.
19. Church, "Practical Principles of Rational Management," 490.
20. Ibid., 897.
21. Vangermeersch, *Alexander Hamilton Church*, 2.
22. Church, "Practical Principles of Rational Management," 167.
23. Ibid., 902
24. Ibid.
25. Vangermeersch, ed., *The Contributions of Alexander Hamilton*, 151. Referenced from Church, "Industrial Management," 465.
26. In *Lean Thinking*, Womack and Jones present five principles to developing and implementing a lean business enterprise: 1) Specify value, 2) identify the value stream, 3) implement flow, 4) pull when you can't flow, and 5) continually pursue perfection.
27. Vangermeersch, ed., *The Contributions of Alexander Hamilton Church*, 48. Referenced from Church, "Comments," 1158.
28. Ibid., 101–2. Referenced from Church, "Machine Design and the Design of Systems," 61–62.
29. Vangermeersch, ed., *The Contributions of Alexander Hamilton Church*, 20. Referenced from Church, "The Meaning of Scientific Management," 100.
30. Taylor, *The Principles of Scientific Management*, 112.
31. Ibid., 113.
32. Vangermeersch, *Alexander Hamilton Church*, 19.
33. Ibid., 20. Referenced from Church, *The Proper Distribution of Expense Burden*, 22–23.
34. Vangermeersch, *Alexander Hamilton Church*, 22. Referenced from Church, *The Proper Distribution of Expense Burden*, 114–15.
35. Joe Friday was a detective character made famous for his straightforward, matter-of-fact approach and demeanor in the (1951–1959 and 1967–1970) television series *Dragnet*.
36. Church, *Production Factors*, 34–35.
37. Dr. Phillip Eugene Fess is the Arthur Anderson & Co. Alumni Professor of Accountancy Emeritus at the University of Illinois and has authored accounting textbooks for over twenty-five years, two of which are listed in the bibliography of this book and used for reference.
38. Fess, "The Theory and Application of Direct Costing," 122.
39. Ibid., 29. Church also stated this point in his February 1913 article, "Practical Principles of Rational Management," 679.
40. Jelinek, "Toward Systematic Management," 75.
41. Johnson, "The Decline of Cost Management," 6–7.

42. Church, "The Proper Distribution of Establishment Charges," 508–517, 725–34, 904–12, 31–40, 231–40, and 367–76. The explanation of Church's method for placing resources used in manufacturing as direct costs appears on pages 32 through 34.

43. Church, "The Proper Distribution of Establishment Charges," 374.

44. Vangermeersch, *Alexander Hamilton Church*, 30.

45. Vangermeersch, *The Contributions of Alexander Hamilton Church*, 48. Referenced from Church, "Overhead," 38.

46. Church, *Production Factors*, 9–10. Church makes the same point in "Practical Principles of Rational Management," 679.

47. Church, *Production Factors*, 36.

48. Johnson and Kaplan, *Relevance Lost*, 53.

49. Ibid., 55.

50. Ibid., 55. As referenced from Church, *The Proper Distribution of Expense Burden*, 24. Also, Church, on page 726 of his 1901 *The Proper Distribution of Establishment Charges* originally gave the same example using English pounds instead of dollars. Church's example is also reviewed and discussed in Kaplan, "The Evolution of Management Accounting," 395.

51. Church, *Production Factors,* 170.

52. Johnson and Kaplan, *Relevance Lost*, 55.

53. Ibid., 55–56.

54. Ibid., 138.

55. Ibid., 247.

56. Porter, *Competitive Advantage*, 44.

57. Ibid., 48.

58. Ibid., 48–49.

59. As discussed in Chapter 2, Spear emphasizes in his Rules-in-Use that the "connections" must be direct, binary, and self-diagnostic, and that they attach "flow-paths" that must be simple, prespecified, and self-diagnostic.

60. Porter, *Competitive Advantage*, 62–63.

61. What Church means is the lack of usable information to manage operations—in Dr. Johnson and Kaplan terms, "relevance lost."

62. Vangermeersch, *Alexander Hamilton Church*, 19. Referenced from Church, *The Proper Distribution of Expense Burden*, 14–15.

63. Church, "The Proper Distribution of Establishment Charges," 515.

64. According to Phillip Fess in his doctoral thesis, Jonathan N. Harris introduced the term "direct cost" in "What Did We Earn Last Month?," 501–26. Fess writes: "It took the depression years of the 1930's to give the needed impetus to the introduction of a costing concept which ran contrary to this conventional costing—direct costing." Fess, "The Theory and Application of Direct Costing," 8.

65. Church, *Production Factors*, 15.

66. Ibid., 36.

67. Ibid., 36.

68. Ibid., 40.

69. Ibid., 42–43.

70. Ibid., 43.

71. Ibid., 43.

72. Ibid., 48.

73. Ibid., 54.

74. Church provides a list of the incidents associated with each production factor on page 116 in *Production Factors*.

75. The tool-point example is a reminder that much of the work done in the area of costing between 1885 and 1925 period was in the metal-working industries.

76. Church, *Production Factors*, 115.

77. Ibid.

78. Garner, *Evolution of Cost Accounting to 1925*, 187.

79. Ibid., 187. This information is also quoted and discussed in Vangermeersch, *Alexander Hamilton Church*, 22.

80. For details about the roots of lean manufacturing and its early developments, see Huntzinger, "Roots of Lean—Training Within Industry: The Origin of Japanese Management and Kaizen," "Roots of Lean—Training Within Industry: The Origin of Kaizen," and "Roots of Lean—Highland Park.

81. Vangermeersch, *The Contributions of Alexander Hamilton Church to Accounting and Management*, 62–63. Referenced from Church, "On the Inclusion of Interest in Manufacturing Costs," *The Journal of Accountancy*, April 1913.

82. Johnson, "The Decline of Cost Management," 6.

83. Ibid., 7–8.

84. Ibid., 40.

85. Flow manufacturing was developed and implemented by the Ford Motor Company between 1913 and 1925 at their Highland Park plant.

86. Wells, *Accounting for Common Costs*, 80.

87. Ibid., 79–87.

88. Johnson and Kaplan, *Relevance Lost*, 55.

89. Vangermeersch, *Alexander Hamilton Church*, 21.

90. Garner, *Evolution of Cost Accounting to 1925*, 187. This information is also quoted and reviewed in Vangermeersch, *Alexander Hamilton Church*, 22.

91. Vangermeersch, *Alexander Hamilton Church*, 21. Referenced from Church, *The Proper Distribution of Expense Burden*, 44–45.

92. In his example, Church focuses on time, rent, and power as the specific production factors.

93. Vangermeersch, *The Contributions of Alexander Hamilton Church to Accounting and Management*, 26. Referenced from Church, "Distribution of the Expense Burden," *American Machinist,* May 25, 1911, 992.

94. Garner, *Evolution of Cost Accounting to 1925*, 249.
95. Ibid., 250.
96. Johnson, "The Decline of Cost Management: A Reinterpretation of 20th-Century Cost Accounting History," 6.
97. Wells, *Accounting for Common Costs*, 80–81.
98. Church, *Production Factors*, 11.
99. Anytime the term cellular manufacturing is used in this book, the assumption is made that one-piece, continuous flow within the principles of takt time are being strictly utilized. For excellent discussions and examples of true flow manufacturing, see Rother and Shook, *Learning To See* and Rother and Harris, *Creating Continuous Flow*. Another excellent reference on this subject is Rother, "Crossroads."

6

THE FOCUS FACTORY

To illustrate the methods developed for cost management, a model company will be used in this book to explain in detail the concepts and principles. The company will engineer and manufacture a small, air-cooled, single-cylinder, internal combustion engine. Operations will include machining, assembly, and some fabrication. Further details will be discussed as needed to explain the concepts and methods throughout the rest of the chapter and book.

FOCUS FACTORY ATTRIBUTES

First, the bond between cost information and physical operations needs to be discussed. The basic philosophy for the connection is simply the ideas Alexander Hamilton Church proposed, which have been discussed in detail in previous chapters. Cost information is needed to allow for good decision making and planning. In keeping with Church, unless it is accurate and timely cost information, it is not worth the effort, and it very well may be damaging information if used. Therefore, accuracy and timeliness are absolutes for the system proposed. The other necessary attribute is that the information and system—which gathers, traces, or tracks physical and informational transactions—must be simple both in the ability to track, trace, or gather and in the ability to tie the information to a particular production factor, to use Church's term.

COST INFORMATION IN THE VALUE STREAM

Dr. H. Thomas Johnson and Robert Kaplan confirm Church's vision of how product-costing methods reflect information from a specific product or product line. This view parallels the establishment of value streams along products or product lines and allows appropriate information flow to correspond to the product production flow of the value streams. In 1987 Johnson and Kaplan explained that "as Alexander Hamilton Church intimated over eighty years ago, a good product cost system will accumulate costs, by product and product line, across the entire value chain so that the company will know its total cost of producing each good and service."[1]

James Womack's Lean Enterprise Institute also proposes that "the prerequisite to implementing a lean accounting system is having a lean value stream."[2] This point is critical to the theme of this book, which is that by establishing the physical layout of the processing of a product or product family in a cellular fashion via its value stream—one-piece flow according to takt time—cost information may be established and gathered simply and directly. Direct costs become the larger percentage of costs, where in a traditional accounting system the larger percentage of cost is in the allocated, overhead portion. As stated by the Lean Enterprise Institute: "The team gathered data on costs consumed in the value stream directly related to manpower, equipment, material outside costs, facility costs, and any other costs—such as supplies, soft tooling, and MRO parts consumed in the value stream. *These costs were charged directly to the value stream*" (emphasis added).[3]

Jamie Flinchbaugh,[4] in his 1998 master's thesis, provides an enlightening analogy for value stream management and function. He writes:

> The group leader … act[s] as the president of a mini-company, with the upstream line segment [in vehicle assembly] as the supplier and the downstream line segment as the customer.
>
> These mini-companies need the same support for their operations as any company, particularly material supply and maintenance. An additional goal of the factory design is to decentralize essential activities, moving them closer to where the decisions are being made.[5]

IS PRODUCT COST THE COST OF A PRODUCT?

An important point to establish at this time is defining what is meant by product cost. In this book, product cost is referred to quite frequently and is one of the major objectives of the proposed methods. But when product cost or the cost of product is referenced, discussed, or developed in these pages, it is referring to a product family or product line, not to an individual product. For an example, consider the crankshaft machining cell, which is used in Chapter 17 of this book and is used in the example of part of the model factory also used in this book. When the product costs are developed for crankshaft machining, or more specifically the cost of a crankshaft, cost is actually developed from the line (or cell) in the context of the product line. The results of the cost-management system proposed here, the product costing, is *not* for (or capable of) revealing the cost of crankshaft part number X machined on some "specific" date and shift. The purpose of the product costing system is to give accurate costs of the product line—in this example, crankshafts machined and supplied to the engine assembly line in the model engine factory.

The appreciation of this point is critical in understanding the purpose and capability of the cost-management system proposed. Since lean enterprise is also the focus of this book, product line or product family examples are in line with product value streams.[6] Dr. Robin Cooper verifies this point: "I encountered a system that could not report individual product costs although it could report product line costs."[7] Dr. Cooper explains further:

> The view that product lines should be complete[8] reduces the need for accurate individual product costs. As long as the product line is relatively accurately costed, then major decisions (such as where to source a product line, whether to try to increase sales volumes, or whether to drop the line) are adequately supported. Indeed, some firms have recognized that so many decisions are taken at the product line level and so few at the product level that their product costing systems report only the costs of product lines, not products. These systems are less expensive to maintain because they do not have to report product costs.[9]

Dr. Cooper confirms the basic method used for developing product-cost information. He stresses the important point discussed above, that product cost information does not come from an individual product standpoint but from the cost of the product family or a manufacturing cell of a product's value stream. Dr. Cooper also reveals the purpose of product cost information, which is planning activities, not operational control.

Whenever product cost is mentioned in this book, it is referring to product line costs, not individual product costs.

WHY COST INFORMATION IS NEEDED

Cost information, as discussed in earlier sections, takes on a different role from its use in traditional cost-management accounting. Traditionally and presently, cost-management accounting is used to control operations. In this book, cost information, or cost management, shifts from controlling manufacturing to a planning function for operations. And, as stressed by A. H. Church, it must be accurate and timely information to be of *any* use.

Many—or maybe most—operational business decisions are based on cost information. Cost information is not the only information used for a manufacturing business decision, but it usually does play the largest role when firms make decisions. Therefore, a simple conclusion can be made that any cost information used—whether gathered or tracked—must be correct and accurate in order to be useful or valid in the decision-making process. H. Thomas Johnson explains:

> In running a business, managers need information about the financial consequences of intended actions. As a guide for planning, and to choose among alternatives, managers need profitability information. They especially need reliable cost information. Cost information serves in many planning and decision support roles, such as estimating profit margins of products and product lines, evaluating decisions to make or buy components,

preparing departmental cost budgets, and charging administrative services to production departments.[10]

Dr. Johnson confirms the point stressed by Church in much of his work. Cost information is needed for managers to make planning decisions—and it must be reliable. Cost-management information must reflect products and product lines. As was mentioned previously, the value stream provides the means to easily develop accurate product cost information. Dr. Cooper and Kaplan corroborate the views of Johnson and Church as well. They write: "Decisions about pricing, marketing, product design, and mix are among the most important ones managers make. None of them can be made effectively without accurate knowledge of product costs."[11]

Product cost information plays an important role for manufacturing managers, but its limits must be understood to use it in its fullest extent. Cost-management information provides needed information for planning and decision making. Its intention is not to control operational functions; such a use is the reason for its lost relevance. The reason for this is simple. Cost information does not have the capability to inform managers how to link work and information and create flow; where and when manufacturing issues happen; how to resolve manufacturing issues; how resources are or should be consumed; or whether customers are being satisfied. Knowledge of such things comes from information about customers and manufacturing activities, not product costs.[12] Johnson states that "before World War II, top managers in most large U.S. industrial firms would have blanched at the idea of controlling operations with accounting numbers that had been 'rolled down' from planning budgets.... Managers of plants and departments were expected to think in terms of customer satisfaction, employee morale, product quality, and adherence to cash budgets—not return on investment (ROI), net income, or unit cost variances."[13] A current-day analogy of such a scenario is the coach of a sports team calling plays by strictly watching the scoreboard instead of watching the players on the field or court as mentioned previously.

COST SYSTEMS AND THEIR FUNCTIONS

As put forth by Kaplan, cost systems generally have three basic functions. Their purpose is to (1) develop inventory valuation for financial accounting, (2) control operations by providing feedback to department and production managers, and (3) develop product costs.[14]

The focus of this book is on cost-management accounting, not financial accounting. Therefore, inventory valuation is not broached here.[15] Kaplan's second function, control operations, will be used in Chapters 10, 11, 12 and 13 to demonstrate that using any accounting methods is unnecessary. Physical attributes and measures in the lean enterprise enable firms to control their operation significantly more effectively. Brian Maskell affirms, "Lean creates operational control and the tracking[16] is no longer necessary."[17] The third function, product costs, is the purpose of the cost system or cost-management system developed and proposed here. According to Kaplan, "No single system can adequately cover all three functions. The demands of each differ."[18]

The major roadblock to achieving superior functioning systems is executive management's insistence on using a single system. Developing and using a single system creates compromises for each of the functional needs, but the usual case is that inventory valuation for financial reporting wins out. Unfortunately, the financial accounting focus neglects the other two functions (product costs and operational control) and forces them into the realm of financial accounting.[19] This situation, as reported earlier in this chapter, is the reason why Dr. Johnson and Kaplan contend accounting has lost relevance.

With the focus here on product costs, the cost information developed by implementing value streams has specific purposes; operational control, Kaplan's third function, is not it. Planning and guidance will be the purpose of the cost-management system. Kaplan repeats this point. He writes: "Without knowledge of product costs, the new freedom to quote prices and to enter or leave markets could have been disastrous."[20] Kaplan, as has been previously stated numerous times, reiterates the failure of traditional cost-management accounting methods (the same failure that Church describes in his writings). Kaplan writes:

> Traditional standard cost systems in manufacturing companies are designed not to measure product costs accurately but to value inventory. The standard costs usually bear no relation to the resources consumed to design, produce, market, and deliver the product. I have seen cases where a more accurate system revealed that products yielding healthy profits according to the standard cost system—with indicated margins of more than 45%—were actually losing money.
>
> Seriously distorted product costs can lead managers to choose a losing competitive strategy by de-emphasizing and overpricing products that are highly profitable and by expanding commitments to complex, unprofitable lines.[21]

THE FOCUS ON PRODUCT COST: YESTERDAY TO TODAY

The misguided focus of today's accounting procedures due to the inaccurate allocating of overhead, as discussed earlier in this chapter and also in Chapter 5, is the key to the loss of cost-managerial accounting relevance between the post–World War II period and the present. Manufacturers did not have much concern for product costing prior to 1885. Prior to 1885, product costs—or values for unsold and unfinished inventories—were still mostly determined by market prices, not by any need for financial reporting. Between 1885 and 1925, many engineers were developing methods to determine product costs, not for financial reporting, but for determining internal costs for manufacturing products as industry continued to internalize processes and products. This product-cost information was used strictly for understanding the costs of these internal processes and component products as operational consolidation increased in industry.[22]

The reason engineers between 1885 and 1925 developed methods for product costing was to better understand and exploit operational execution, *not* to obtain better financial results. Prior to this period, engineers were not even focused on product costs but concentrated on working on the factories' conversion costs, again a focus on execution, not results.[23] Early engineers were practicing MBM, not MBR.

Between 1885 and 1925, engineers began to show an interest in methods for understanding product costs. This period was a critical time because innovative techniques grew out of their concern. Johnson explains this further:

> In the second phase, between 1885 and World War I, managers in some industries showed enormous interest in the issue of product costing. However, this interest did not reflect any desire to compile product cost information for financial reporting. Rather, the interest reflected a need for information to evaluate prices and profitabilities of diverse, often custom-made products made in complex metalworking shops. Facing diverse lines of products that consumed resources at widely varying rates, managers in those firms sought accurate product costs and profitability information, primarily to help them bid on customer orders.[24]

As Johnson describes above, some of the techniques of this period are the foundation for the methods that deliver accurate product costs used in decision-making, not for operational control. Accurate product cost is the purpose of these methods, and businesses today should have the same purpose for the methods and information as business managers did from 1885 to 1925. In their essence, the methods have not changed in purpose and process. They support today's lean-manufacturing enterprise even more effectively than they supported the manufacturers of the late nineteenth and early twentieth century. This is another example of how solid and robust methods can withstand the test of time. According to Roy Harmon, who worked on introducing new techniques during the late 1970s and 1980s, "reported results [involve] an archaic set of procedures ... that have no chance of either representing real product costs or providing a sound basis for decision making that is based on the assumption that the numbers are or will be accurate reflections of reality."[25] Harmon continues by explaining that even though significant changes in manufacturing have occurred, accounting has not had any significant changes. Also, no one is currently proposing noteworthy changes in accounting practices.

PRODUCT COSTS: REFLECTING REALITY

Harmon states, "Management accounting's failure to alert American manufacturers to impending change in the competitive environment after World War II may be due to its failure to distinguish between information for planning and information for control."[26] Dr. Johnson's point is particularly poignant. Today, most companies—even many working on a lean transformation—have a blurred understanding of the purposes of their cost systems. Again, this blurred vision is a result of cost-managerial accounting's lost relevance, which is the focus and trickle-down effect of financial accounting into cost-management accounting. This misunderstanding has also led to little or no development in the area of cost-management accounting in the manufacturing field.

What Harmon reported in 1992—that the progress toward inventing imaginative new cost systems has been shockingly limited[27]—has remained true even today, fifteen years later. Dr. Johnson and Kaplan echo the same dilemma in *Relevance Lost*. They write: "So little innovation has occurred during the past half-century."[28] They state that manufacturing firms "must attempt to design entirely new manufacturing accounting systems."[29] The purpose of this book is to develop and propose a "new manufacturing accounting system" based on some original ideas and concepts of Church.

Breaking Down the Barrier

Dr. Theeuwes of Technische Universiteit Eindhoven in the Netherlands explains, "Most of the criticism on traditional management accounting systems concerns product-costing methods (more specific cost allocation practices)."[30] The ability to deliver reliable product cost information has always been a quandary for any cost-management accounting system. Unfortunately, most companies see the choice as binary: either they use methods for product costing that were developed for an entirely different purpose—external reporting, or inventory valuation—or they conclude that using another type of method is not cost effective. Ronald Clements and Charlene Spoede, in an article for *Management Accounting*, state: "In the past, considerable time and effort had been devoted to achieving *precise* labor and overhead costs. We decided that the time and resources devoted to achieving this previous degree of precision was not cost-benefit effective and, in fact, encouraged a misguided level of confidence in the final numbers."[31]

Such a scenario is all too common. The potential error of this thinking is that time and resources will be consumed beyond a cost benefit. With traditional manufacturing practices, the statement is absolutely correct, but in a lean manufacturing environment and using the methods proposed here, it can be achieved easily and accomplished cost effectively. As discussed in previous chapters, physical transformation to a lean enterprise is the biggest key to achieving an excellent cost-management system.

Implementing flow manufacturing delivers a means for tracking and calculating accurate costs of products and product families. It will deliver this capability without the consumption of costly resources. It provides manufacturers a cost-effective option to track and understand their product cost information without increasing resources and while actually reducing the consumption of resources.

Dr. H. Thomas Johnson and Anders Bröms, in *Profit beyond Measure*, also implicate executive management's unabridged use of accounting information not only to assess results externally but also to measure internal activities and control. Johnson and Bröms explain: "They fail to see the flaw in this position. Accounting information can measure and keep track of an organization's results at a system-wide level, but it offers no insight into the particular inner relationships that determine those results."[32]

Basically, Dr. Johnson and Bröms are reporting that the view of the whole gives no indication of the makeup of its parts. The cost-management system discussed here is simply an effective tool that reveals information in an accurate and timely manner about the costs of manufactured components. It is for planning and guidance purposes for managers, not a control mechanism for managing and directing daily operations as, unfortunately, is the use of traditional accounting methods.

An interesting and insightful example listed by Dr. Johnson and Bröms is Toyota and Scania.[33] They report that both companies do not use any accounting information in the control and direction of their operations. The information used in their operations is simply provided by the work itself.[34] What Dr. Johnson and Bröms are inferring is that the design and execution of the manufacturing system itself is the very information and method that drives the work itself. This type of system tacitly achieves this. Such a concept is key: the physical operation determines the ability (or reflection) of the information system or cost-management system to gather and inform usable product cost information in a simple and timely way. Dr. Johnson and Bröms reflect: "Neither company [Toyota or Scania] uses accounting targets to direct or control the work of the people who ultimately produce those results."[35]

Crossing the Barrier

Moving away from traditional accounting methods is extremely difficult for most companies and their managers. Completely dropping existing management accounting methods and systems has proven to be impossible for nearly every manufacturing firm. A tiny number have done this, but for most—even firms that recognize the failures of traditional accounting—it remains too forbidding of a prospect. The reasons for this situation are many, but a couple major roadblocks stand out.

First, most managers have been educated in their undergraduate and graduate curriculum in traditional accounting methods and principles. This creates business managers on the broad scale that are completely unfamiliar with conceiving of or using alternatives. Also, how much faith are industry managers going to put in undeveloped accounting systems when the entire academic system has been teaching existing standards for nearly fifty years? They would have to believe that a major portion of the entire higher education system is *wrong*, which is not an ideal situation for new accounting methods to gain the support of manufacturing management troops.[36]

Second, whether managers have had formal education in accounting or not, they have been completely indoctrinated in the methods of traditional accounting by their employment at any manufacturing enterprise. Since nearly all companies use traditional accounting in some form or another, the only methods managers have exposure to and experience with are traditional accounting systems and techniques. Such a situation creates an environment in which managers, whether they like the methods or not, know no other system, have experience in no other system, most likely cannot conceive of any other system, and do not have any support structure with which to think of, develop, or implement any other type of accounting system. Even beyond this environment, managers are most often measured by traditional accounting systems. Therefore, they are reined in by the system, never able to break free of its constraints. So how do manufacturing companies move beyond traditional accounting? The task is not easy or common. Like the implementation process of lean manufacturing, changing from traditional cost-management accounting to a cost-management system supporting the lean enterprise takes a "leap of faith."[37] Believing an improved system can be developed and attained, managers must move forward with new and innovative ideas. Maskell reflects on this notion and draws conclusions similar to Dr. Johnson and Bröms's focus on execution and MBM. He writes: "If you want to save cost, have your people become committed to process improvement, 100 percent quality, and customer satisfaction. The step of faith is that you take care of the right things the costs will take care of themselves. I am not saying that costs should be ignored—but they should be placed in the correct perspective in relation to quality and customer service."[38] Maskell also continues by quoting Dr. Johnson about how business performance would improve drastically if manufacturing executives dropped the use of all management-accounting methods and systems and changed the operations to focus on execution to achieve customer satisfaction.[39]

Crossing to Direct Costs

If manufacturing executives and managers choose to take the leap of faith,[40] they can begin to implement lean manufacturing, which in turn will allow for the implementation of a lean cost-management system. As has been reviewed, the move to one-piece flow in the manufacturing operation allows the consumption of resources to easily be recognized as direct costs. Resources become intimately and physically tied to a product or product family and visibly associated with a product's manufacturing line or cell. Maskell confirms that "as a company moves into cellular manufacturing and begins to gather costs by production cell or group of production cells, the number of cost centers is dramatically reduced."[41] And the gathering of cost information must provide the decision-making information and be the servant of the operations and needs of managers.[42]

What Maskell is reporting is that by implementing flow lines—or cells with one-piece flow—the points of information gathering are significantly decreased, creating less information needed to be traced and tracked. This activity will be discussed in detail in Chapter 14.

According to Johnson and Kaplan, "the cost tracing process starts not at the product level, but at the component level."[43] What Dr. Johnson is describing is the need to understand costs of components, as has been discussed already in this chapter. In the example used as a model manufacturing plant in this book, a small engine is manufactured. The engine manufacturing operation consists of the machining and fabrication of engine components, the assembly of subassemblies, and the assembly of the final product: a small single-cylinder engine. The operation must know the costs of the components in order to know the cost of the final product: the engine. This is the point that Dr.

Johnson is making when he writes: "For many production processes, the product does not appear until the final assembly stage."[44]

Another important point Dr. Johnson discusses is actually a point made by Peter Drucker in 1963. Johnson writes, "Drucker warned of the dysfunctional consequences from following a full-line marketing strategy with cost systems that do not accurately trace the costs of individual products."[45] Dr. Johnson's and Drucker's points tie back to both the lost relevance of accounting and the ability to understand and develop the accurate product costs noted by Church—the ability to create a manufacturing operation where most (ideally all) costs can be recognized as direct costs. As reviewed in earlier sections, this was Church's concept. Implementing flow manufacturing can achieve this: an environment of mostly direct costs.

PRODUCT COSTS: DIRECT COSTS

Dr. Johnson and Bröms note, "In other words, no cost system traces or calculates the flow of those items inside the plant."[46] Dr. Johnson and Bröms are referring to Toyota's Georgetown, Kentucky, assembly plant. They state that, unlike nearly every other manufacturer, no standard cost accounting-style system is used to manage, control, or track product flow or costs in its operations. The interesting point shared by Dr. Johnson and Bröms is that Toyota does use a cost system seemingly similar to the cost-management system proposed in this book. It traces actual costs and is used for planning purposes. Dr. Johnson and Bröms express that "Toyota does maintain cost systems for pricing and project purposes, but never to drive operations. In any event, the cost systems maintained reflect actual, not standard, costs, and they compile costs only as needed."[47]

Maskell presents an excellent discussion of what direct costs[48] involve and, in the end, how to eliminate overhead by making it a direct or actual cost:

> An actual costing system collects the actual costs incurred during the production process and reports them directly. These costs may include actual material costs, actual labor costs, actual machine costs, and actual outside processing costs. As with direct costing, making as many as possible of the currently indirect costs into direct cost centers is advantageous.
>
> Actual costs can be reported each day on each shift in total or in terms of actual cost per unit produced.... The direct costs can be expressed in terms of the financial contribution obtained from selling the products manufactured that day.
>
> Actual costing is easy to use and understand and provides a clear-cut and directly relevant method of communicating productivity information to the people on the shop floor.[49]

As Maskell describes, shifting from indirect to direct costs provides a host of advantages. One of the major advantages is the ease of developing direct cost information. This is due to the physical design of a lean operation. Dr. Dhavale concurs:

"The record-keeping needs are much simpler for CM [cellular manufacturing] because all activities take place within a cell, thus eliminating job tracking."[50] This important point will be discussed in detail in the later section on Coase's theory. It stresses the strong advantage of operational design, not only for excellent flow operations, but also for the ability to create an environment for simple, straightforward cost information and direct costs.

In the book *Management Accounting Issues in Cellular Manufacturing and Focused-Factory Systems*, Dileep Dhavale emphasizes the ability of cellular operations to simplify and accurately collect products costs. Dhavale underscores how "*many costs become direct cell costs.*"[51] He confirms Maskell's point about the movement of indirect costs to direct costs. Dhavale writes: "In focused factories even more resources are directly traceable, so there is less need for resource drivers. Because traceable costs do not involve allocation, they provide higher product-costing accuracy."[52] Interestingly enough, Dhavale is stressing the same points as Church did about costs in the early twentieth century for both directness and accuracy.

Kaplan and Dr. Cooper even more place stress on how organizational cost information ("other corporate overhead", according to Kaplan and Dr. Cooper) can be directed to the actual points that consume them. This is another key philosophy in the development of an accurate cost-management system. Kaplan and Cooper explain that "virtually all organizational costs, not just factory overhead and marketing expenses, can and should be traced to the activities for which these resources are used, and then to the divisions, channels, and product lines that consume them."[53] Much of their point is manifested in the cost-management system developed for this book and in the spreadsheet and methodology discussed in Chapter 17.

As may be recalled, the original reason for developing product costs took place during between 1885 and 1925. As manufacturing organizations became more diverse in both product lines and processes, they needed information on product costs for internal decision making. In fact, engineers and managers from this time period who developed the methods even warned about improper use of this information. This information was spawned from the desire for the capability to make good internal decisions and not for any financial reporting. Dr. Johnson explains:

> Rather, the interest reflected a need for information to evaluate prices and profitabilities of diverse, often custom-made products made in complex metalworking shops. Facing diverse lines of products that consumed resources at widely varying rates, managers in those firms sought accurate product cost and profitability information, primarily to help them bid on customer orders.... Epitomized by the writings of A. H. Church, a contemporary of Frederick W. Taylor, they advocated meticulously tracing resources.[54]

Dr. Johnson confirms what both Maskell and Dhavale have stated that managers must have information to make reasonable management decisions. Cost information, as in product cost information, is a key to having the capability of making planning decisions. Estimating profits of products or product lines, evaluating whether to make or to buy components, and many other management decisions must be based on correct or accurate information.[55] Unless accurate product cost information is available, poor or even incorrect decisions will result.

Dr. Johnson also relates this message back to the ideas of Church. He writes: "Church believed that overhead cost, ultimately, should consist only of an irreducible residual of costs that cannot be traced to individual products."[56] Dr. Johnson goes on to reveal that Church suggests that firms must "abandon the distinction between direct and indirect expenses of a product and focus on 'the *real* incidence [of expense] on particular jobs'—the differences in rates at which products consume resources."[57]

The statements by Dr. Cooper, Dr. Kaplan, Dr. Dhavale, Dr. Johnson, and Church reveal the same message about product costs. In order to develop accurate product cost information, the information must be developed from direct costs, or, as Maskell refers to them, actual costs. Cost information must derive from the point of actual consumption of the resource by the product being manufactured. The only way to achieve consuming and identifying direct costs is to change the physical operation so that the resources *are* direct costs or directly consumed resources.

One final point to reiterate is the reason for, or use of, product cost information. It is for planning purposes as stated previously in this chapter and must not be used for operational control. Understanding and implementing lean techniques and philosophies will provide the manufacturing means to operate the most effective production and support functions. But it must also be understood that even accurate product cost information "does not tell managers how to link work, resource consumption, and customer satisfaction to achieve competitiveness and sustained profitability."[58] That is where the physical lean operation comes into play. According to Johnson, "If you think your traditional financial product costing system tells you what your products cost think again!"[59]

DIRECT COSTING IN JAPAN

In Japan, a very similar scenario to the one proposed in these pages has been unfolding for a number of years. In his 1996 book *Integrated Cost Management: A Companywide Prescription for Higher Profits and Lower Costs*, Dr. Michiharu Sakurai discusses such a situation in Japan. A growing number of Japanese companies are developing and practicing what Dr. Sakurai calls DCOPLS, or direct charge of overhead to product line system. DCOPLS is a method that moves traditionally allocated overhead charges into direct charges to production departments.[60]

The other point Sakurai presents was also presented by Dr. Cooper in the section "Is Product Cost the Cost of a Product"? The cost object of the direct cost is actually not a specific product or specific part number, but the product line,[61] or value stream flow cell, or product family, in the terms of this book. By moving costs information from allocation to direct costs, Japanese companies are able to reduce overhead to only 4.5 to 5 percent of "full production" costs.[62]

Japanese companies are able to practice the DCOPLS method by working to change the costing of previously allocated resources—for example, tooling, depreciation, maintenance, material handling, and the like. In doing so, these companies have also—according to Dr. Sakurai—abolished standard costing. It has become unnecessary under such circumstances, direct alignment of resources to the incidence of consumption, as the focus of operation controls has changed.[63]

As Dr. Sakurai reports, there are two reasons that these Japanese companies have chosen to pursue the DCOPLS method. He writes: "The first is because they treat many overheads as direct costs to product lines, resulting in indirect costs that are small in number and amount. The second reason is that even if you try to allocate as accurately as possible allocation's arbitrary nature is inescapable."[64]

In Dr. Robert Hall's 1983 classic book *Zero Inventories*, he observes finding a similar situation to that reported by Dr. Sakurai. Interestingly, though, Dr. Sakurai comments that the methods on direct costing had only materialized ten years previous to his book's publication in 1996. Hall's observations occurred approximately three years earlier than Dr. Sakurai's reported time frame. Hall observed that "results are measured by the costs as based on end-of-month cumulative totals, incorporating all the costs of the department."[65] Hall also discloses that the monthly costs are given as unit costs.[66] It is remarkable how much this activity in Japan parallels the methods and the reasons behind the methods discussed and developed in this book. Toshiro Hiromoto explains the contrast between manufacturers in the United Stars and Japan: "Like their U.S. counterparts, Japanese companies must value inventory for tax purposes and financial statements. But Japanese don't let these accounting procedures determine how they measure and control organizational activities."[67]

NOTES

1. Johnson and Kaplan, *Relevance Lost*, 247.
2. Lean Enterprise Institute, "Creating the Course and Tools for a Lean Accounting System," 2.
3. Ibid., 4.
4. Jamie Flinchbaugh is a founder and partner of the Lean Learning Center and brings successful and varied experiences of lean transformation as both a practitioner and facilitator. He was part of the development, training, and implementation of the Chrysler Operating System. Flinchbaugh is a graduate fellow of the Leaders for Manufacturing Program at the Massachusetts Institute of Technology, where he received an MBA from the Sloan School of Management and a master's degree in engineering. His research thesis was "Implementing Lean Manufacturing through Factory Design." He also received a master's degree in engineering from the University of Michigan and holds BS in Engineering from Lehigh University in Bethlehem, PA.
5. Flinchbaugh, "Implementing Lean Manufacturing," 55.
6. In this book, product line, product family, and product value stream are all the same concepts.

7. Cooper, *When Lean Enterprises Collide*, 92.
8. Cooper is referencing value streams utilizing flow in the form of manufacturing cells.
9. Cooper, *When Lean Enterprises Collide*, 210.
10. Johnson, "Managing by Remote Control," 56–57.
11. Cooper and Kaplan, "Measure Costs Right," 97.
12. Johnson, "Beyond Product Costing," 15.
13. Ibid., 16.
14. Kaplan, "One Cost System Isn't Enough," 61.
15. Although inventory valuation is not investigated or developed by the methods proposed in this book, the possibility of using the methods and techniques discussed for this purpose is a valid one and has been used in one example known to the author.
16. Tracking, in this case, refers to the tracking of transactions of labor and material associated with traditional cost-managerial accounting procedures.
17. Maskell, "Lean Accounting Executive Briefing," slide 26.
18. Kaplan, "One Cost System Isn't Enough," 62.
19. Ibid., 61–62.
20. Ibid., 64.
21. Ibid., 64.
22. Johnson, "Managing by Remote Control," 54–55.
23. Ibid., 54.
24. Ibid., p. 54.
25. Harmon, *Reinventing the Factory II*, 17.
26. Johnson, "Activity-Based Information," 8.
27. Harmon, *Reinventing the Factory II*, 255.
28. Johnson and Kaplan, *Relevance Lost*, xii.
29. Ibid., xiii.
30. Theeuwes, "Shortcomings of Traditional Accounting," 511.
31. Clements and Spoede, "Trane's SOUP Accounting," 47.
32. Johnson and Bröms, *Profit beyond Measure*, 142.
33. Johnson and Bröms use Toyota and Scania as their case studies in the book *Profit beyond Measure*. Scania is a Swedish-based manufacturer of heavy trucks, buses, and diesel engines. Scania developed a process for designing trucks individually tailored to meet specific customer's needs. Scania's story is detailed on pages 115 to 140 of *Profit beyond Measure*.
34. Johnson and Bröms, *Profit beyond Measure*, 141.
35. Ibid.
36. Johnson, in his books and many of his articles, reviews and discusses the history behind how the educational system has evolved in the wrong direction. See preface in *Relevance Lost*, pages 54 through 62 of *Profit beyond Measure*, and Chapter 10 of *Relevance Regained*, 175–96.

37. Richard Campbell, who was an engineer and upper-level manager for Delco Remy for over thirty years, advised me that "it takes an extreme dissatisfaction with the current system, which provides faulty information for management decisions" to get people to possibly take the leap of faith. He had to work with these dysfunctional systems his entire career and recognized their limitations and faults early on.
38. Maskell, *Making the Numbers Count*, 85.
39. Ibid., 86.
40. Richard Campbell pointed out to me his dislike of the phrase, "leap of faith." He opines that "it sounds like a gamble or wishful thinking when in reality it's merely recognizing the well demonstrated success of lean manufacturing." I absolutely agree with Mr. Campbell, but unfortunately, the majority of managers I have encountered do not achieve the level of understanding Mr. Campbell has in which they can articulate the true reason for the needed change. Therefore, quite often change may require these managers to take a "leap of faith." Many, though, are simply not able to make such a change on faith alone.
41. Maskell, *Making the Numbers Count*, 76.
42. Ibid.
43. Johnson and Kaplan, *Relevance Lost*, 238.
44. Ibid.
45. Ibid., 242.
46. Johnson and Bröms, *Profit beyond Measure*, 107.
47. Ibid., 240n35.
48. Maskell refers to direct costs as actual costs, which may be a more descriptive term.
49. Maskell, *Performance Measurement for World Class Manufacturing*, 365.
50. Dhavale, *Management Accounting Issues*, 29.
51. Ibid., 96.
52. Ibid., 105.
53. Cooper and Kaplan, "Measure Costs Right," 101.
54. Johnson "Managing by Remote Control," 54.
55. Ibid., 56–57.
56. Johnson, "The Decline of Cost Management," 6–7.
57. Ibid., 7. Johnson is quoting Church, "Organization by Production Factors," 77–88.
58. Johnson, "Beyond Product Costing," 15.
59. Johnson, "Activity-Based Information." See the Figure on page 7 of this article.
60. Sakurai, *Integrated Cost Management*, 77.
61. Ibid.
62. Ibid.
63. Ibid., 78–79.

64. Ibid., 79–80.
65. Hall, *Zero Inventories*, 253.
66. Ibid., 253–254.
67. Hiromoto, "Another Hidden Edge," 22.

CHURCH AND EXCESS CAPACITY

Another important and interesting point worth reviewing is excess capacity. In traditional accounting methods, excess capacity is simply part of the overhead, which is allocated across products. Two issues arise from using this philosophy. One is the difficulty of distributing costs evenly to product lines, which consume resources at different rates. This practice will not develop accurate cost information. The other issue is excess capacity, which in most cases has nothing to do with costs or resources consumed by individual product lines, even though traditional methods charge each product line for their existence.

Adding the costs of excess capacity to a product line can greatly distort actual costs, leading to inaccurate information and, in turn, poor decision making. Whether excess capacity exists or not should have nothing to do with the costs of individual product lines. In the scope of the manufacturing enterprise as a whole, excess capacity must be understood and accounted for, but charging it to individual products is misleading and inaccurate.

It must be noted that excess capacity in the terms of this discussion is not process capacity, which is intermittently used because of particular customer requirements for specific product numbers. One example of such a situation is an extra machine used for a product that receives a special operation, only used a few days per month. The excess capacity covered in question is along the lines of extra factory floor space, groups of extra machine tools, and the like. This type of capacity may result when a product line is lost, but its manufacturing equipment is retained but sitting idly, requiring the use of production floor space Traditionally, the rest of the product lines, creating distorted cost information, absorb this extra capacity. The firm must account for this extra capacity in the aggregate, but imposing it on a single product line must be avoided.

Alexander Hamilton Church recognized such a situation and proposed a solution or, at least, a methodology to deal with it properly. Church explains:

> This circumstance, however, *does not affect the value of those services to the production still going on*. They remain as before. The production centers

actually working take up no more room, do not consume more or less power, and require the same amount of supervision whether the others are idle or working. It seems obvious, therefore, that though in one sense and looking at the shop as a whole the cost of the whole volume of production is actually higher (and the percentage of indirect expenses to labor on the old averaging methods would rise in proportion to the idleness of machines), yet the cost of the work that is being actually done really consists of two entirely distinct portions, viz., (1) the normal cost, due to the call on services at the tool point, and (2) another portion that simply represents waste. This latter item really represents, in fact, *the incidence of indirect charges on work that was* NOT *done.*[1]

Church refers to this excess capacity as the supplementary rate. The supplementary rate was very much in line with his view of maintaining product information accuracy. Church continues: "However carefully the incidence of the various services at the tool point may be determined, it is an absolutely necessary element of accurate representation of the facts of production that some provisions be made for keeping the cost of wasted time and resources separate from normal costs."[2]

Church continues with the discussion of how the supplementary rate must be maintained for management purposes of the firm as a whole, but also describes how employing it back into the costs of products using an averaging method distorts the facts. He writes:

Strictly speaking it [excess capacity] is no part of such cost. If for example only half the machines in a shop are working, half the resources of the shop, roughly speaking, are being wasted. Under any percentage system the incidence of indirect charges on the work actually going through would be roughly doubled. On the production-factor plan, the incidence at the tool point, on the work actually going through, would remain unchanged; but the balance of wasted resources would be known as a separate amount and expressed as a *separate* percentage of the normal cost, if desired. Which of the two plans is the most truthful, and which is the most useful![3]

Church's point is simple. Excess capacity, or the supplementary rate, has nothing to do with individual product lines and must not be allocated to any of them. It must be kept separate. The cost of excess capacity is understood and accurate product costs are available by the supplementary rate being separated. In doing this, accurate information is available for the decision-making process of management. As Church puts it: "It is not in itself a cost at all, but merely the *ratio of wasted capacity to utilized capacity.*"[4]

Others gave similar thought to the issue of excess capacity and Church's opinion and idea of handling the cost of excess capacity. Robert Kaplan reflects on his own thoughts and those of Donaldson Brown:

The solution is not to apply the cost of excess or idle capacity to the products that were produced—in effect, a cost of products that were *not* produced—and have it appear as a line item in the department income/expense statement.

Managers have a variety of actions they can take with respect to idle or excess capacity. I cannot, however, discover any useful purpose served by allocating the idle-capacity costs to items actually produced. This is not a new insight. Donaldson Brown, for one, implemented a system of charging for capacity resources over a standard (80%) measure of utilization more than 60 years ago at General Motors.[5]

Donaldson Brown, who came to General Motors from the Du Pont company (which was Du Pont Powder company at the time), was the architect of the universally used financial measurement Return on Investment (ROI).[6]

NOTES

1. Church, 1976 reprint (originally published in 1910), *Production Factors in Cost Accounting and Works Management*, 120. As has been previously mentioned, Church's discussion of the "tool point" references the work done in the metalworking industries. Church also uses the tool point as an analogy for value-added activity, similar to the manner in which value-added is referenced today: any activity that makes a product conform to customer requirements.
2. Church, *Production Factors*, 120–21.
3. Ibid., 121.
4. Ibid., 122.
5. Kaplan, "Limitations of Cost Accounting in Advanced Manufacturing Environments," in *Measures for Manufacturing Excellence*, 33.
6. Johnson and Kaplan, *Relevance Lost*, 86–87. An interesting note about Brown is that he was an electrical engineer by education. Most of the innovators of accounting methods from 1885 to 1925 were engineers.

THE PHYSICAL OPERATION

Yasuhiro Monden comments: "The standard cost control system no longer has the importance it once had in cost control because, under the JIT production system, more emphasis is placed on physically oriented target control systems implemented in the workplace."[1]

An important distinction between the past and future of cost-management accounting is that the situation has changed completely. Yesterday's and today's traditionally managed manufacturing companies focus on making points of operations "efficient." Lean enterprises are not concerned with points of efficiency but with creating an effective operation, which allows entire value streams to flow smoothly and efficiently. This situation translates to creating a physical operation that manifests in smoothly flowing value streams of products and product families.

Mark DeLuzio supports this suggestion when he states that "many, if not all of these changes to the MAS [management accounting system] cannot occur unless the organization changes."[2]

If the purpose of accounting is to satisfy manufacturing's needs, then it must perform a task that manufacturing can effectively use.[3] From an accounting perspective, the cost-management information systems must support and reflect this physical operation for manufacturing products. Traditional cost-managerial accounting methods do not and cannot accomplish this need. Ahlstrom and Karlsson explain:

> The present management accounting systems were designed for environments dissimilar to those that face today's companies. Lean production principles are different from those that were pending when traditional management accounting systems were developed. Thus, the implementation of lean production requires changes in the management accounting system.... Many live with systems that are inappropriately designed to support the progress currently taking place within manufacturing.... Not much work has been done on how these systems interact with and affect an attempt to implement a complex production strategy.[4]

119

In their 1996 article, Par Ahlstrom and Christer Karlsson supported the contention that the cost-management system in a lean environment must be more reflective of the physical operation. It must not be confined to monetary measures but must also include nonfinancial measures, such as quality and throughput times.[5] As will be discussed in detail in Chapter 11, the change in physical manufacturing methods that takes place when implementing lean principles impacts the transactions of both the production of products and the information that supports production, part of this information being cost information.

In developing and implementing lean production methods, the application of product costs changes. The amount of costs that can be directly applied to a product increases. The total of all related costs is applied to the *day's production*, not *individual jobs and tasks*.[6]

THE THREE FACTORS OF THE LEAN COST-MANAGEMENT SYSTEM

In this book, three key factors will be used as the foundation of the cost-management system proposed for a lean enterprise. The following three actions are needed for implementing the cost-management system::

1. Changing all costs into direct costs (which was advocated by Alexander Hamilton Church)
2. Developing and implementing flow production (or true one-piece flow via the Toyota Production System [TPS])
3. Utilizing desktop hardware and software (which is simple and inexpensive)

The first factor of changing all costs into direct costs has been discussed in detail throughout the book. Up to this point, the discussion has been devoted to the reasons, history, and context to support changing over to direct costs.

The second factor is the development and implementation of lean manufacturing, or true one-piece flow production. As the first factor creates a context for this book's proposition, the second creates the environment in which the proposition has the capability to be fulfilled. Most of the following sections will cover this aspect, discussing what the physical lean enterprise looks like and what it does to enable the first factor.

The third factor, desktop hardware and software, finalizes the proposition proposed. Discussion of the third factor will focus on the creation of a spreadsheet that gathers the information used for cost-management purposes. The model engine factory developed for this book will be used as an example for the cost-management information system. Its use and function will be discussed and reviewed in detail also.

THE PHYSICAL OPERATION IS COST MANAGEMENT

Dr. H. Thomas Johnson and Robert Kaplan explain the difference in focus between engineers and auditors in gathering cost information. They write: "The difference in accuracy between the engineer's product costing and the auditor's inventory costing procedures arose from the allocation of indirect, or overhead, costs. The engineers took care, often at great cost, to trace indirect costs to the specific activities that caused the cost; in other words, they tried to trace *all* costs of the firm as direct costs of the product. That clearly was Church's intent."[7]

As reviewed in previous sections, Church and other more contemporary writers emphasized the practice of creating an environment where resources consumed become direct costs. By developing and implementing lean manufacturing, the ability to achieve direct costs can be moved forward greatly because of the very nature of a flow environment. Ahlstrom and Karlsson explain: "All costs that were allocated to the flow-lines were to be split up evenly between the number of products manufactured. This would be possible since the installation of flow-lines made it easier to trace costs, and because each flow-line would produce family like products."[8]

Mark DeLuzio agrees that costs are directly traceable and that this ability exists because of the design of the physical system:

> In a JIT environment, many support costs, which were previously centralized in a traditional setting, are now directly associated with a manufacturing cell. Because of this direct association, these costs can now be traced directly to the particular products of that cell. Product costing is in fact more accurate than ever before. Please note, however, that the driving force behind these changes in overhead allocations are not due to changes in the accounting systems, but they are due to changes in the organizational structure brought on by JIT.[9]

Not only are costs easier to trace, but in fact they are direct costs because of the design of the manufacturing lines in a lean or flow-line environment. In turn, many costs or resources, which had to be traced or tracked in the past, now do not need to be. They are a physical part of the value stream, cell, or manufacturing line. In the traditional manufacturing environment—the batch production or scale-economies environment—the ability to effectively trace resource consumption can be quite daunting and most likely inaccurate upon its conclusion; this was the bane of Church.

To create the ability to change costs into direct costs, the physical implementation of lean manufacturing is necessary. Great understanding of skills, techniques, methodology, philosophy, leadership, and the implementation process must precede the implementation of the lean cost-management system. Since the lean cost-management system is a reflection of the lean enterprise, it is the next step in the process after some physical change takes place. According to Ahlstrom and Karlsson: "the process was such that the physical and organizational changes had to produce effects that reached a certain threshold before changes in the management accounting system was [sic] conceivable."[10]

So how must the enterprise proceed in order to achieve the physical lean environment? The following sections will discuss an overview of what must take place.[11]

FIRST FLOW, THEN PULL

Lean principles are the underlying structure that will create success of cellular manufacturing implementation. The most fundamental technique in lean is to create flow. Flow is accomplished by implementing cellular arrangements of machines and passing parts immediately to the next process at the rate of *takt time*. Everyone must understand and be aware of takt time. Figure 8.1 illustrates a manufacturing cell or flow line utilizing one-piece flow.

TAKT TIME

Takt time is the "guiding star" to ensure the operations produce and function to meet customer demand. Any cost-management system must, as stated in Chapter 1, reflect the manufacturing system and serve its customers, operating managers, and personnel. Takt time is the starting point for this cost-management system simply because it is also the starting point for the designing of a flow or lean-manufacturing enterprise. The system is designed to meet takt time. Howell, Shank, Soucy, and, Fisher explain:

> A new accounting system[12] must first satisfy the … customers: the manufacturing managers. Manufacturing managers wanted information on a "real-time" basis to provide immediate feedback and to make corrections.
>
> Provide information as needed to those … who can truly affect the operation; do not do accounting to satisfy the needs of the accountants.[13]

Recall Dr. H. Thomas Johnson and Anders Bröms's emphasis on MBM: tying MBM to takt time creates many of the techniques popularized by lean systems. Takt

Figure 8.1   One-piece flow manufacturing cell

time is the guiding star: it basically ties the firm to the market or the customer needs. If MBM is used conceptually to manage the execution of the enterprise to meet customer needs via takt time, flow operations follow suit. The lean techniques that are used to achieve such a situation, or support flow, in turn become the physical design of the operation and the activities that support flow (see Figure 2.5). Items like standard operations, *jidoka*, *kaizen*, and many other methods materialize to contribute to the MBM of the flow.

STANDARD OPERATIONS

If MBM is prepared to be achieved by the lean system, recall that Dr. Steven Spear in his dissertation develops the Five Rules-in-Use. In the first three rules, Dr. Spear specifies that each guides the "design and performance/operation" of "connections" and "flow," which must be "structured," "direct," and "prespecified."[14]

Dr. Spear confirms Dr. Johnson and Bröms's MBM concepts and enforces the need for the proper design of the system. His Rules-in-Use are focused on the underlying means (Dr. Spear calls them guiding principles) by which TPS works to achieve customer satisfaction. The later statements of his first three rules—which describe the system as structured, direct, and prespecified—emphasize the fortitude of TPS or its repeatability and robustness as a system. This repeatability and robustness is most soundly manifested in TPS's standard operations. Toyota's own internal TPS manual states that "standardized work is a tool for maintaining productivity, quality, and safety at high levels. It provides a consistent framework for performing work at the designated takt time and for illuminating opportunities for making improvements in work procedures."[15]

History of Standard Operations

To really understand the importance of standard operations, it is beneficial to understand how they evolved and from where they came. A brief review of the history of standard operations leads back to the first two decades of the twentieth century. Frederick Taylor's management philosophy and Henry Ford's Highland Park plant hold the two main keys to today's standard operations.

Taylor and Highland Park

Taylor's management philosophy, which is not widely understood, used standard operations as a key tool. Taylor's *Principles of Scientific Management* has a broad scope of ideas and thought about management and its function. His use of the stopwatch and his developing "the one best way" through time study has influenced industry since his experiments and publication in 1911. Ever since that time companies have been using stopwatches and careful observation to develop their standards to develop standard operations for a lean environment.

Henry Ford's Highland Park plant is the source of modern manufacturing techniques. Although many manufacturers influenced industry in the United States, Highland Park brought together a variety of key lessons—flow manufacturing, continuous improvement, plant design, cash flow management, and material handling—which converged to create modern manufacturing methods for mass production. In this case, mass production is not analogous to "batch" production, but to volume production. The three principles that were applied to Highland Park were interchangeable parts, interchangeable workforce, and a simple, robust, or manufacturable design. These three principles were crucial for allowing Ford's production engineers to develop flow manufacturing, made famous by the moving assembly line. In order to achieve flow manufacturing, standard operations had to be developed and implemented to allow flow to happen. The standard operations at Highland Park combined with these three principles allowed workers to attain a repeatable and robust process, which contributed to the ever-dropping cost and price of the Model T.

Toyota and TWI

Toyota eventually used the standard operations technique implemented at Highland Park to support their relentless pursuit of flow manufacturing. Toyota was also heavily influenced by Training Within Industry (TWI) methods during the post–World War II Allied occupation of Japan. TWI was a set of techniques developed in the United States because of the huge production increase to support the war effort and the large influx of untrained workers into industry when so many men went overseas to fight. TWI focused on the convergent point of the supervisor and operator. (More about TWI will be explained in the "TWI and Standard Operations" section of this chapter.) Toyota used the TWI methods to develop and strengthen their development of standard operations to support their implementation of flow manufacturing.

More under the Surface

Standard operations are more than just a set of procedures that an operator uses to do his or her work. Standard operations for a lean manufacturer include several strong support mechanisms of a manufacturing infrastructure: work instructions, flow support, mistake proofing, and quality. Standard operations are, of course, work instructions. They are instructions that operators are taught and follow to make (machine, fabricate, assemble, and so on) whatever they are supposed to make. Work instructions is the most well-known idea in standard operations. Standard operations also create a repeatable process. This is necessary for flow to happen. A repeatable process—which must be repeated by an operator each time a product goes by, as well as repeated to build products, which are interchangeable—is what Ford and his engineers developed. Having standard operations is, in fact, a type of making something mistake proof. This is especially true at Toyota. By following consistently good standard operations, the product being manufactured should be built correctly or be of high quality, the fourth point of standard operations. Therefore, standard operations are a means—mistake proofing—to an end—high quality. Toyota effectively utilizes the concept that Henry Ford did at Highland Park.

TWI and Standard Operations

TWI was introduced to Toyota during the Allied occupation of Japan after WWII. TWI was meant to apply a democratic or humanistic mentality to Japanese industry. The methodology fit very well into Toyota as a whole; they applied it vigorously to their own system. As previously mentioned, TWI was purposely designed to create a solid and comfortable relationship between front-line supervisors and their employees. Its three points of focus were instructing employees and improving work methods and employee relations. Toyota emphasizes the same relationship today as a result of applying these methods to their daily operations. Standard operations are the convergence point of the front-line supervisors (the term "supervisor" includes team leader, foreman, or any other name used to describe the person responsible for hourly employees) and their employees. This convergence point is critical as it is the point where value is added or created for the product being manufactured. This is why TWI chose to focus on it and later Toyota focused on it as they still do today. Toyota uses standard operations as a springboard for their *kaizen* process, or continuous improvement. Their procedure is simple: teach the workers the standard operations so that the workers can develop better ideas (*kaizen* or improvements) to incorporate into the existing standard operations via their supervisor. Therefore, the relationship between supervisor and worker is critical for this to be a continual and smooth function.

The "J" Programs

Toyota's methods for standard operations are exactly what TWI developed during WWII: job instruction, job methods, and job relations. The three "J" programs, as TWI called them, were based on a four-step process developed by Charles Allen during WWI. The four-step methodology was used to develop all three programs and is the basis of developing standard operations and *kaizen* (see Figure 8.2).

STEPS	TWI			KAIZEN
	Job Instruction	Job Methods	Job Relations	
1	Prepare	Breakdown	Get the Facts	Observe and Time Current Process
2	Present	Question	Weigh and Decide	Analyze Current Process
3	Try Out	Develop	Take Action	Implement and Test New Process
4	Follow Up	Apply	Check Results	Document New Standard

Figure 8.2 Comparison of steps

This methodology is the same for Toyota or any lean company using it today to develop standard operations and *kaizen*.

The Purpose of the Three "J" Programs

Job Instruction focused on instructing employees rather than on "letting them learn." The objective of Job Methods training was to give supervisors a technique to achieve obvious improvements in the work area using a practical approach instead of a technical approach. The Job Relations program was implemented mainly due to supervisors needing a great deal of help in human relations, the art of handling people. Although the shop floor interaction was that of human relations between supervisors and their subordinates, the program used the word "job" so that program would be related to the job, as all the "J" programs were. With this emphasis on human relationships in mind, the ideas that in production "poor relationships caused poor results" and "good relations lead to good results"[16] would become the objective of the job relations procedures.

Standard Operations and Flow

As mentioned above, standard operations are necessary to implement flow. This is true today just as much as it was during operations at Henry Ford's Highland Park plant. Standard operations are part of good cell design and operation. This section is focused on what standard operations are and how to develop them. Standard operations are part of developing, implementing, and operating a manufacturing cell. Cell design and standard operations go hand in hand. These two techniques support flow.

Standard operations are key to achieving continuous improvement, or *kaizen*. Without standard operations, there can be no improvement. This statement is common at Toyota and at any lean company. Even Henry Ford understood this important point: "If you think of 'standardization' as the best that you know today, but which is to be improved tomorrow—you get somewhere. But if you think of standardization as confining, then progress stops."[17]

Standard Work: The Basis for *Kaizen*

Toyota associates standard operations with *kaizen*. Standardized work is a tool for maintaining productivity, quality, and safety at high levels. It provides a consistent framework for performing work at the designated takt time and for illuminating opportunities for making improvements in work procedures. Standardized work provides detailed, step-by-step guidelines for every job in TPS. Team leaders determine the most efficient working sequence. They make improvements in conjunction with their team members, which is a point reinforcing the aims of TWI.[18] *Kaizen* creates the dynamism of continuous improvement and the very human motivation of encouraging individuals to take part in designing and managing their own jobs. *Kaizen* improvements in standardized work help maximize productivity at every worksite.[19]

The Starship Captain Analogy

One important point that is commonly missed with the development of standard operations and *kaizen* is who is responsible and who has authority. At Toyota, the team leader (supervisor) and workers *both* have the responsibility to develop ideas for standard operations and *kaizen*, but only the team leader has the authority to implement the changes and improvements. It is not an absolute consensus situation. For any *Star Trek* fan, it is similar to the relationship between a starship captain and his crew. The captain has complete authority to make decisions, but he must be dependent on the capability of his crew—who are many times delegated authority by the captain—to handle their positions and tasks. The relationship between the team leader and worker at Toyota is exactly the same. As mentioned above, this is what the TWI programs successfully accomplished.

Standard operations are a key foundation to a successful lean enterprise and must be mastered to be able to utilize a lean cost-management system. As Dr. Johnson and Bröms and Dr. Spear have discussed, standard operations are an underpinning to execute a repeatable and robust flow environment. Standard operations become an integral aspect of cellular manufacturing.

CELLULAR MANUFACTURING

For the lean enterprise, implementing cellular manufacturing physically creates an environment that directly aligns costs to the resources that consume them. Ahlstrom and Karlsson point out: "The operations included in the flow lines are no longer separated, but treated as a whole. The next step that has been proposed is to take all costs that are allocated to the flow line and split them evenly between the number of products manufactured."[20]

Cellular manufacturing is a physical manifestation of the themes put forth by Dr. Spear and Dr. Johnson and Bröms. Cells or manufacturing lines that operate with one-piece flow within the rules of takt time exhibit and enable Dr. Spear's Five Rules-in-Use and Dr. Johnson and Bröms's MBM philosophies and principles.

As previously mentioned, Dr. Spear's first three Rules-in-Use reveal TPS's underlying focus on design, performance, operation, and flow, which are elements that must also be structured, direct, and prespecified. Dr. Johnson and Bröms's MBM concepts focus on executing systems of superior design. From a fundamental and holistic viewpoint, the Rules-in-Use and MBM can be considered as one. From a lean-enterprise standpoint, flow manufacturing, or cellular manufacturing, accomplishes many of the Rules-in-Use and MBM philosophies and principles.

Material, or parts, and people move within the flow line under the repeatability and robustness created by standard operation. But the physical design of the cell must be able to achieve these principles in the daily operation. Machine tools, assembly lines, part placement, fixtures, part design, and shop floor hierarchy design are all involved in the functionality of achieving excellent lean execution. The design and execution of these same details are also enabling factors in creating a lean cost-management system. This is why understanding, developing, and implementing one-piece flow is so critical to lean or TPS and enabling the lean accounting principles discussed in this book. This rolls back to one-piece flow according to the guidelines of takt time.

Using cellular manufacturing will inherently allow for much simpler cost tracking. The reason for using cellular manufacturing is to create flow, which is often referred to as just-in-time (JIT) production. JIT production supports the manufacturing philosophy to produce exactly what is needed when it is needed and in the exact quantity required. In its most fundamental essence, it is one-piece flow or the manufacturing of a batch of one. JIT production will be considered in these writings to be implementation of flow production.

Cells are a physical implementation of flow or an alignment of the value stream. Putting processes (operations and equipment) in sequence and locating them physically next to each other creates flow or manufacturing a batch of one, which satisfies just-in-time.

Some situations may prevent the entire value stream of a product or product family from being completely cellularized. Such situations may be caused by machines being unable to be dedicated to a value stream, like large presses, or caused by many component cells being separated from an assembly line due to too many machines with different products feeding one final line. In such a case, pull systems help buffer the break in flow.

PULL SYSTEMS

If You Can't Flow, Then Pull

If flow cannot be implemented due to technology or machine quantity constraints, then pull systems must be implemented. Pull systems help create a situations similar to flow by implementing the controlled flow of small batches. The smaller the batch size, the better the pull system and the closer to true flow that is obtained. Quick changeovers are the critical measure for reducing batch sizes. Pull systems keep inventory levels to a minimum and under very tight control, which means minimum fluctuations in the amount of inventory (see Figure 8.3 for an example).

Monden explains the methods and principles that support a pull system as the following:

- Production leveling
- Job standardization
- Reduction of setup time
- Implementation of improvement activities

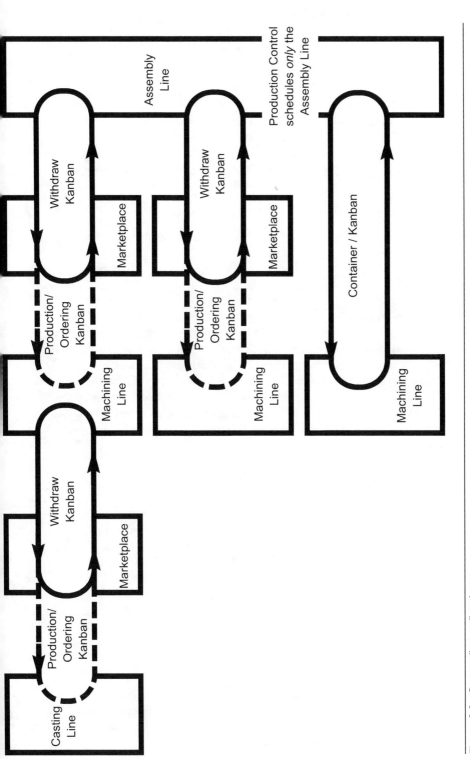

Figure 8.3 Cascading pull systems

- Improvement of machine layout
- Autonomation (*jidoka*)

In short, the kanban system [pull system[21]] is an information system to control the production quantities in and between processes. Unless the various prerequisites of this system are implemented perfectly (process design, standard operations, production leveling, and so on), just-in-time will be achieved with difficulty, even with the introduction of the kanban system.[22]

FLOW, PULL, AND COST

Implementing flow, or cells, and pull, or kanban, creates simplified and improved cost tracking by utilizing containment. Costs are contained, becoming direct costs, because these techniques dedicate or self-allocate equipment, material, people, and activities directly to products. The guessing game of how much, what percent, or how to evenly spread the costs does not exist. The physical attachment of costs—equipment, material, people, and activities—exists, meaning all items become direct costs.

Measurements for lean are no longer in dollars; they are physical attributes, such as number of people, output per operator, throughput time, inventory reduction, and equipment uptime. The traditional methods of cost-managerial accounting in the way of variances, overhead allocation, labor, and machine standards disappear completely. Brian Maskell firmly reiterates this point about traditional accounting methods, calling it "[a] fruitless, futile, time-wasting task. In a world class manufacturing environment it is pointless and misleading and should be immediately abandoned."[23] So how should lean be measured?

NOTES

1. Monden, *Cost Management*, 78.
2. Mark DeLuzio, "Management Accounting in a Just-In-Time Environment" (unpublished article, circa 1992), 12. A copy of this article was sent to me by DeLuzio on May 30, 2003. The published version of DeLuzio's article is "Management Accounting in a Just-in-Time Environment," 6–15.
3. Turk, "Management Accounting Revitalized," 34.
4. Ahlstrom and Karlsson, "Change Processes Towards Lean Production," 11.
5. Ibid., 12.
6. Ibid., 13.
7. Johnson and Kaplan, *Relevance Lost*, 132.
8. Ahlstrom and Karlsson, "Change Processes Towards Lean Production," 15.
9. DeLuzio, "Management Accounting in a Just-In-Time Environment," 13.
10. Ahlstrom and Karlsson, "Change Processes Towards Lean Production," 16.
11. Many excellent books are available that discuss lean implementation in detail. See the bibliography for a list of them.

12. In this case, a new accounting system can be equated to a cost management system as described in this book
13. Howell, Shank, Soucy, and Fisher, *Cost Management for Tomorrow*, 82.
14. Spear, "The Toyota Production System," 4–5.
15. Toyota Motor Corporation, *The Toyota Production System*, 32.
16. These two statements are repeated and emphasized throughout the Job Relations training. See War Production Board, *Job Relations*.
17. Ford and Crowther, *Today and Tomorrow*, 82.
18. Toyota Motor Corporation, *The Toyota Production System*, 32.
19. Ibid., 34.
20. Ahlstrom and Karlsson, "Change Processes Towards Lean Production," 17.
21. At Toyota, pull systems are commonly referred to as kanban systems. The name comes from Toyota's extensive use of cards (kanban is the Japanese word for card) to manage their pull systems. Although cards/kanban are used widely at Toyota, their group companies, and many companies worldwide implementing lean manufacturing/TPS, pull system is a more general and inclusive name for this type of inventory management and control system, and that is why the term is used in this book.
22. Monden, *Cost Management in the New Manufacturing Age*, 54. This same point and further details are also given in Monden, *Toyota Production System*, 6 and in detail in Chapters 2, 3, 18, 19, and 21.
23. Maskell, *Making the Numbers Count*, 76.

LEAN MEASUREMENTS: MEASURING THE BUSINESS

Dr. Dileep Dhavale states: "Excessive and total reliance on financial measures may promote dysfunctional behavior."[1] If traditional accounting performance measurements are no longer the available for use, what is the alternative for the lean enterprise? The manufacturing shop still needs performance measures in order to maintain operational excellence and understand where steps must be taken to sustain flow, delivery, quality, and a robust factory—or ensure customer satisfaction. Within the lean enterprise there are measurements that allow for feedback to managers and operators that guides their progress and work. According to Maskell: "Tom Johnson has pointed out that 'business performance would improve dramatically if top management eliminated all existing management accounting control systems and started people talking about customer satisfaction being everyone's job.' This is truly a revolution."[2]

The measurements used are simple, straightforward, and easily understood by all participants in the operation. This is something that traditional accounting measures cannot claim. Orry Fiume explains that "unlike the traditional metrics that are focused on results, most metrics in the Lean environment should focus on the process."[3] Process, focused on flow, has been central to the discussion throughout this book, and it is no different when it comes to measuring the business. As Jean Cunningham and Orry Fiume point out, "the goal of performance measurements should be to manage processes, not results."[4]

Much discussion has been spent reviewing the efforts and methods of the late nineteenth and early twentieth centuries. In previous chapters, managing concepts have been presented that today's lean enterprise would benefit from—the same techniques and thought patterns used by these early industrial pioneers. As financial measures were not only not in use during this early period but also purposely avoided in many cases, these turn-of-the-century managers intimately understood physical operation and what made it function. Their innovations and ideas were extracted from the close contact and physical changes happening while the process and products grew more diverse. Today's lean firms must reach back to the use of nonfinancial measures. Dr. H. Thomas Johnson and Robert Kaplan write: "In an important sense, a call for more extensive use of nonfinancial indicators is a call for a return to the operations-based measures that were the origin of management accounting systems. The initial goal of management accounting systems in the nineteenth-century ... provided easy-to-understand targets for operations managers and valuable product cost information for business managers. These measures were designed to help management, not to prepare financial statements."[5]

Brian Maskell agrees with Dr. Johnson and Kaplan's need. He writes:

> If production personnel, supervisors, and managers are to use performance measures to help achieve the manufacturing strategy, the performance measures must directly inform them of success or failure. Reports must present the results of their efforts in terms that are relevant to their work and must not be disguised in financial figures.[6]

Maskell continues:

> Most people in a factory do not think in terms of the financial aspects of their work; they concentrate on such issues as production rates, yield quantities, on-time deliveries, reject rates, schedule changes, and stock-outs.[7]

Another important aspect of using and understanding the right performance measures relates back to proper execution and MBM. The use of lean-performance measures, which tie into the physical attributes of the manufacturing system or process, guides and motivates people to improve the operation or, more specifically, the flow of material and information. These measurements must be relevant and understandable. Traditional performance measurement methods rising from cost-management accounting methods and even attitudes toward these measurements are focused on cutting cost. Although reducing and removing costs are important—even for a lean company—such a focus has created a mindset that needs to change. The state of mind that a lean firm takes is not one focused on cost cutting, but is instead focused on improvement in execution, that is, flow. If the focus is on improvement in execution, or MBM, then cost reduction and waste removal will happen at an unprecedented rate. Unfortunately, most managers do not understand this, including many working in firms trying to develop lean enterprises. Dr. Johnson explains: "They view improvement as cutting costs, not as continuously discovering and creating opportunities."[8]

Dhavale draws a very interesting and poignant analogy with measurements, comparing financial measures to physical attributes. He writes: "The linkage problem is exacerbated by financial measures because they fail to measure the operational and production variables adequately. It is the same as asking someone's height and then insisting that the question be answered in dollars and cents."[9]

WHAT TO MEASURE

In his thesis, "Performance Measures for Lean Manufacturing," David Stec cites Dr. W. Edwards Deming's prolific statement on MBR: *"Management by numeric goal is an attempt to manage without the knowledge of what to do."*[10] Hiromoto continues this point:

> Business metrics are different in a lean operation. Traditional measures become obsolete. Lean measurements are simple and focused on the shop floor. The metrics are developed and must be understood equally by management and shop floor employees
>
> Like their U.S. counterparts, Japanese companies must value inventory for tax purposes and financial statements. But the Japanese don't let these accounting procedures determine how they measure and control organizational activities.[11]

Fiume then points out that "most of your measurements ought to be quantity-based measurements, not dollar-based measurements."[12]

As explained throughout this book, control of a manufacturing enterprise must not be accomplished by financials or "results" (MBR) but by understanding and managing the actual activities that create value or the processes that manufacture and support manufacturing. This is the practice of MBM. Dr. Johnson explains:

> Financial information is important to a company's overall health. However, it must not be used for controlling operations, but for planning and reviewing activities: "Nor does Company J appear to use any other accounting cost information to control operations, even though company accountants keep the usual double-entry books for external reporting purposes. In short, Company J's management information seems to focus on the control of activities that determine competitiveness, not on the financial results of being competitive. It does not ignore the financial results (indeed, Company J has an enviable record of long-run profitability)."[13]

Johnson also points out that "they will do these things to plan and to monitor, not to control, results."[14]

The basic parameters that performance measures must reflect for excellence operation feedback are given below. The list is based on several references and the author's own experience.[15]

- Focusing on improvement and promoting flow
- Sustaining standards
- Maintaining the schedule and takt time
- Maintaining and controlling inventory
- Maintaining quality
- Developing the workforce

- Maintaining safety
- Using simple and straightforward measures
- Providing immediate feedback

Most of the parameters listed cross-support each other, which in turn contributes to the robustness of the lean system. For example, by following the standard operations (sustaining standards) set for a manufacturing cell through the course of a shift, takt time is maintained, and when operators follow standard operations, the scheduled output is achieved and the proper inventory is maintained.

Although there are many measures used by lean firms or companies transforming to lean, this section will discuss several of the main or most fundamental performance measures.

PRODUCTIVITY

Productivity is a key measure because it reflects a number of targets. It is measured by output per operator.

Number of Units/Operator

Productivity is used at the cell or value-stream level. With properly designed cells or value streams, productivity should remain relatively equal regardless of the customer demand or takt time. This productivity measure reflects improvement based on *kaizen*, which is fundamental in the elimination of waste (*muda*) and in turn improves flow. The measure also indicates consistency of productivity if customer demand—and therefore takt time—changes. The other important target of this measure is that it is product or product-family specific since it is measured at the cell level, or value-stream level. Orest Fiume explains this point:

> If we get more output with the same level of input we have a productivity gain. Therefore, measuring productivity gains focuses on quantities, not dollars.
>
> In our education and experience we are trained to focus on measuring things in dollars, but productivity cannot improve through financial engineering. Only physical change can influence the relationship between quantities of output and quantities of input. Therefore, these metrics should be quantity-based and maintained where the work is done.[16]

This productivity performance measure can also contribute to another measure, revenue per operator. In a lean environment, costs are more directly associated to parts or part families; therefore, there are no standard costs and substantially less cost associated with allocation, which is a central theme in this book. This enables much more accurate costs to be determined for each product or product line. Knowing the actual cost of parts allows for the ability to determine revenue per operator.

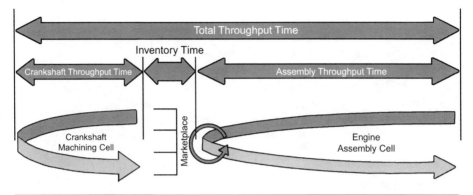

Figure 9.1   Throughput time

THROUGHPUT TIME

Throughput time is simply the physical time within the operations that it takes for raw material to be processed to a shippable product. It is an important measure because it is a direct reflection of how well the operation *flows*. It can be determined from the information developed for value stream maps. Throughput time can also be broken down on a per-cell basis or across cells that are all part of the same value stream; an example is the throughput time for the engine factory used as a model in this book (see Figure 9.1).

It is important to understand that throughput time is different from lead time. Lead time is the time from the receipt of a customer order to the shipping or delivery of the finished product. Lead time can be nearly instantaneous if finished inventories are kept. So the lead-time measure alone may be deceiving, although it is positive from the customer's viewpoint regarding delivery. True cost saving is achieved only by decreasing the throughput time, and it is therefore a key measure that must be tracked.

EQUIPMENT UPTIME

The uptime of equipment is critical in a lean environment and must be available so flow will not be disrupted. Since timing is significant due to flow, takt time, and delivery, the lean manufacturing line cannot afford unscheduled downtime. Equipment uptime must be maintained at a high level and tracked to show where improvement must be targeted. Equipment uptime is why the principle of Total Productive Maintenance (TPM)[17] is so important to the lean operation. It can be used for each machine and each cell. It is a simple measure: it tracks the actual time operating per scheduled time to operate:

Actual Operating Time/Scheduled Operation Time

QUALITY

Product quality is an obvious measure that must be a part of any lean performance measurement. A variety of measurements are available to measure quality in a lean operation. Although quality measures are a must in the lean enterprise—as they are for any manufacturer—specific measures will not be discussed in any detail. Instead, major targets will be reviewed.

The first target is defective parts manufactured. Defective products may be scrap or rework parts. They may be finished products, components, or subassemblies. Obviously, catching defects at the component level or subassembly level is much preferred to the finished level or, even worse, the customer level. Proper measures must be established within any system. It must be noted that other measures mentioned—for example, standard operations and TPM—can play a critical role in preventing defects.

Zero defects, a philosophy pioneered and promoted by Shigeo Shingo, combines principles and a variety of techniques and methods that ultimately enable the operating system to never produce a defective product. If a company were to pursue a high-level quality system—that is, zero defects—Shingo's ideas would be the foundation for achieving it.[18]

Dr. H. Thomas Johnson and Anders Bröms, in *Profit beyond Measure*, reveal a very interesting point that may very well underscore Shingo's zero-defects philosophies and methods. In a footnote, they reveal how Toyota no longer uses statistical process control (SPC) to maintain their world-class quality level:

> Toyota has nearly dispensed with the statistical information gathering required to maintain statistical process control (SPC) systems.... Today it maintains virtually all its processes in control without explicit use of SPC. But Toyota achieved this level of process sophistication only through decades of disciplined attention to mastering standards and creating fail-safe processes.[19]

Capability of equipment, machine tools, processes, and systems is another measure to consider. The six sigma statistical measure (not the methodology with its roots from Motorola) of products is the expected norm in today's industrial environment. With this requirement, capability is an important role for the manufacturing system, although it may be that Toyota has been able to move beyond this need and measure.

KAIZEN: CONTINUOUS IMPROVEMENT FOR THE BETTER

Kaizen activities can be tracked in a variety of ways: number of *kaizen* ideas per employee, number of *kaizen* implemented, target *kaizens* such as safety or TPM, or *kaizen* workshops, to name a few. The most important aspect of *kaizen* is that it happens in a structured manner. Companies should use whatever method or methods function best for implementing and sustaining flow. It is imperative that *kaizen*, or waste elimination, *is* part of the key measures that are used for the business metrics. It should be remembered that the first parameter listed in the "What to Measure" section focused on improvement, which will and should affect the other parameters listed. For a history of how the *kaizen* methodology developed at Toyota, see the paper "Roots of Lean—Training Within Industry: The Origin of Japanese Management and Kaizen," listed in the bibliography.

INVENTORY REDUCTION: WORK IN PROCESS (WIP)

Measuring inventory is a reflection of throughput time and simply how much waste or *muda* are remaining in the operations. It also represents where flow manufacturing has not yet been established. Waste, such as changeover time, equipment uptime, and time given to reaction to abnormalities are the largest contributors to inventory levels. Measuring the percent reduction of inventory reflects the *kaizen* activities within a cell or throughout a value stream. The measurement is simply the amount of inventory from a time period over the amount of inventory from a subsequent time period. Consider the following example:

Work-in-Process (WIP) Inventory Quantity for
Part X for March/WIP Inventory

Quantity for Part X for April

Another aspect of inventory that is just as important is work-in-process (WIP) stability. Whatever parameters are set for a marketplace (WIP inventory or finished good inventory)—such as maximum level, minimum level, and kanban quantity—must be robust and sustained on a regular—daily or shift—basis. The stability of these parameters is a reflection of other attributes of the lean system—for example, machine uptime or building-to-takt time. This again demonstrates that the measures and attributes of a lean operational system cosupport one another.

STANDARD OPERATIONS

Adherence to standard operations is critical to the ability of the system to maintain the continued and repeatable output required by manufacturing that uses flow and meets takt time.

Recalling Dr. Stephen Spear's Rules-in-Use, four of the five rules specify the system being structured or prespecified. Structure and prespecification can be considered the essence of standard operations. Standard operation itself may not be a performance measure, but it is the main *enabler* for achieving the needs of a lean system or flow. While takt time may be the "guiding star" to a lean enterprise, standard operations could be considered the lifeblood of the system. Both these principles support flow, the essence of the system, which in turn satisfies the customer, or the purpose of the system. (This statement by no means excludes the necessity of people in any firm.)

Simply put from a measurement standpoint, the crucial question is: Are standard operations being followed or not?

CAPACITY

Although capacity is not a measure focused on daily operations of the factory, it is an important measure for decision-making purposes, especially as new business and demand increases. Measuring capacity in a lean environment provides exact information on the capacity of cells and equipment down to the minute. The capacity table, one of the standard operations tools, is information that must be maintained as part of the manufacturing line and focus factory and allows for accurate understanding of their capacity and potential bottlenecks.

THE FIVE S'S

Although the Five S's are not a front-line performance measure, they are an activity and measure that greatly contributes to the lean implementation process. Unfortunately, the role the Five S's play in the lean enterprise is misunderstood. A review of the purpose of the Five S's is needed. Figure 9.2 illustrates the Five S's.

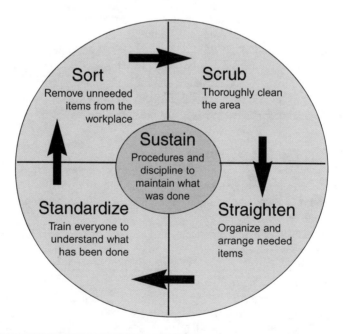

Figure 9.2 The Five S's

The Role of the Five S's

Many companies working on a lean transformation use the Five S's as a foundation. Obviously, implementation of the Five S's is needed; they play an important role in lean enterprise. The problem is that firms apply the Five S's for the sake of the Five S's themselves. They become the purpose and objective of the lean transformation. This is *not* the correct use of the Five S's. The Five S's, like many of the lean techniques, are just another of the many enablers that help *support* the lean transformation. Again, see Figure 2.5. Transitioning to lean is all about *flow* and the ability to deliver customer satisfaction by solving problems. Developing and implementing flow to achieve absolute customer satisfaction must be the focus; anything less than that will achieve a partial lean implementation or will not achieve it at all.

I have visited many firms working to transform into lean enterprises. These visits have included many to companies featuring a broad range of progress along the journey. I have visited a few firms that have focused on the Five S's and have developed incredibly clean and organized work environments. The shop floors of these firms would be the envy of any manufacturing operation, and these companies deserve kudos for their efforts and accomplishments. However, their flow is nonexistent and there is not a concerted effort to achieve it. In the end, the company has a very clean and pleasant work environment but has not reduced costs or lead times.

Other firms I visited have put an absolute focus on implementing flow. In doing this they have had to accomplish cleaning and organization activities. A true lean or flow transformation accepts nothing less than a clean and organized environment, but the main effort has been on implementing and developing flow. Their results have been dramatic reductions in costs and lead time. They have also reduced WIP and many other visible attributes of the shop floor. These firms have used the Five S's, but they have used them as an enabler to achieve their major focus—flow.[20]

The Five S's play an important role in a lean enterprise. Their importance must not be underestimated, but their role must be clear. The key is to develop and implement true one-piece flow and create a clean and organized operation to support the flow effort. An excellent example illustrating this point is Aisin Seiki, a Toyota Group Company and one of Toyota's largest first-tier suppliers.

Aisin Seiki: Example of the Five S's and Flow

Aisin Seiki exemplifies lean, or the Toyota Production System (TPS), and the use of the Five S's to support flow. Aisin uses one-piece flow cells to manufacturer a large variety of products. The photos in Figures 9.3 and 9.4 were taken during the author's visit to Aisin's Nishio City plants in 1995. The factory in the photos is a very large machine shop that machined a wide variety of engine components. The photo in Figure 9.3 was taken in the main center aisle of the shop, and the photo in Figure 9.4 is a view down an auxiliary aisle between manufacturing cells.

Figure 9.3 Main aisle of the engine component machine shop at the Nishio plant of Aisin Seiki

Figure 9.4 Auxiliary aisle of the engine component machine shop at the Nishio plant of Aisin Seiki

It should be noted that the photos were taken during a typical work day, not during a special tour. The machine shop contained approximately twenty-five to thirty machining lines or cells and most consisted of as many as twenty to forty machines, many of which were large CNC (Computer Numerical Control) equipment.

Aisin achieves superb product flow and superior Five S's, a combination that few other companies have demonstrated. The photos reveal Aisin's capacity to maintain a highly organized and clean factory in an environment in which it is generally considered difficult to maintain cleanliness: a machine shop that uses cutting fluids in most processes and machining metal chips in all processes. Aisin's machine shop illustrates that the Five S's are a very important enabler of one-piece flow—but just one of the many means to such an end. It is also an important part of achieving customer satisfaction.

The Five S's Measurement

The Five S's are an important measure for the lean enterprise. The specific measure for the Five S's can be varied according to the needs of the manufacturing operations. It is very important that all five are monitored and followed but even more important that they are understood in their supportive role for the lean enterprise.

The role of the Five S's dates back to the beginning of flow manufacturing in Henry Ford's Highland Park facility. Ford himself stressed the role and importance of a clean and orderly plant and conditions to support any manufacturing operation. He writes, "That is another of our absolute rules—every operation must be cleanly performed."[21]

On equipment and operators Ford stresses that one must

Put all machinery in the best possible condition, keep it that way, and insist upon absolute cleanliness everywhere in order that a man may learn to respect his tools, his surroundings, and himself.[22]

According to Ford, "Cleanliness is an integral part of our plan."[23] Ford continues:

Good work is difficult excepting with good tools used in clean surroundings.

These are not unimportant points; they are fundamental. They make for the working spirit. They are as important as the wages. The work would not be retuned for the wages were not the conditions so arranged that the work is possible.[24]

Taiichi Ohno, Toyota's renowned developer and the driving force behind TPS, reiterated Ford's insistence about creating an organized and clean work environment:

Organization involves disposing of things you don't need and orderliness means always having access to things you need…. Workplace management demands organization and order.[25]

Ohno continues:

If one is not careful, cleaning up and cleanliness may amount to nothing more than a lot of paint. What is really needed is to make things clean—not pretty—just clean. In a machine shop, this includes having to sweep up cuttings and dust.[26]

Ford's and Ohno's messages are just as true for today's lean enterprise.

THE NEW LEAN MEASUREMENT OPERATION

The performance measures discussed throughout this chapter are not meant to be an all-inclusive list, but they are the most fundamental ones. The lean enterprise may use others, but it must be known that too many measures can be as disruptive as too few. The use of the wrong measures can be disruptive as well. Also, different industries may need to use other or unique measures depending on their needs, processes, or type of products. The important thing to remember is to use measures that are physical attributes and that either give immediate feedback to support flow or improve it. Keeping this simple philosophy in mind will help one to find and implement right and useful measures.

As Dr. Jeffrey Liker reports, Toyota applies only a few basic metrics that focus on the "means" of their operation, not the results:

> To their [companies desiring to learn about Toyota's measurements] inevitable disappointment, they learn that Toyota is not particularly strong at developing sophisticated and common metrics across the company. Toyota measures processes everywhere on the factory floor, but prefers simple metrics and does not use many of them at the company or plant level.[27]

Dr. Liker explains further:

> We discovered the top management in the companies with vital [continuous improvement] programs had a process orientation, while the unsuccessful companies had results-oriented managers.[28]

This phenomenon is the result of MBM being chosen over MBR. The vast majority of managers of today's firms are always asking about the immediate return they will receive from the implementation, not the longer-term functional benefit that the organization will receive. According to Liker:

> The results-oriented managers immediately wanted to measure the bottom-line results of the continuous improvement program. The process-oriented managers were more patient, believing that an investment in the people and the process would lead to the results they desired.

In short, developing standard, global metrics is not a high priority at Toyota.[29]

A final fundamental point on performance measures is that they *are* the replacement of traditional management-accounting control measures. Thus far, much of the book has discussing how and why traditional accounting fails: how it has become irrelevant and counterproductive. Using lean measures in combination with physically designing an excellent flow operation completely replaces the measures of traditional management accounting. The new lean environment, lean measures, and flow production support the lean cost-management system and methods proposed in these pages.

Mark DeLuzio provides a very nontraditional view of return on investment (ROI), perhaps the most common and widely used measurement. DeLuzio asserts his view in the context of transforming to a lean enterprise. He writes: "A measure I consider non-actionable is return on investment. We don't calculate it. We don't report it. We believe that if you pay attention to all the basic things, ROI will end up improving."[30]

DeLuzio's argument for not using ROI poignantly demonstrates the need for complete understanding, implementation, and execution of lean philosophies and techniques. Without a "total picture," difficulty can prevail, but with this complete understanding, dramatic changes and new abilities develop.

CAUTION! IF YOU WANT SOMETHING DONE, MEASURE IT

Because there is a critical connection between measurements and system design, it *must* be understood how the two are tied together and how most companies make a crucial error. (A similar mistake is made when developing a sense of teamwork and empowering people. This topic will be discussed in a later section.) Companies— actually, people—mistakenly think that if the right measurements are put in place, then the right results will happen. Again, this is an example of MBM versus MBR, although this common error could more specifically be considered an example of MBR embedded in an MBM environment.

The title of this section—Caution! If You Want Something Done, Measure It—is an old adage common in business. The axiom can and does create a dangerous environment because it is incorrect.[31]

Managers of companies must use the right measurements to help manage and guide their operation and to give employees at all levels useful information to make adjustments and changes. Many of these basic performance measures were described throughout this chapter. They must be present and useful for the lean enterprise. But even the right measurements will *not* always yield the right results, that is, actions. They will motivate the right intentions, but they will not result in the right actions.

The reason that the right measurements do not guarantee the right results is that people simply do not know what right actions they must engage in to change the result in the correct direction. Most people in manufacturing, no matter what their position, experience, or education, do not have knowledge or experience in lean principles, tools, methods, or philosophy. Measuring the right results *cannot* change this. What must become part of the lean enterprise is the focus on training and learning to create the knowledge base in people to understand what is the correct action to take, teaching to execute. This is the very reason why Toyota emphasizes that they focus on developing people.

Before the right measurements can guide a firm to lean success, people within any firm must know how to execute activities properly—or in a lean manner. Simply put, before a manufacturer can execute, the people within a company must learn *how* to execute. Only then will the desired measures or results happen, supporting and guiding the lean enterprise or company going through a lean transformation. In other words, it is important to learn how to perform MBM in order to perform MBM. The old proverb must be updated to if you want something done, learn how to properly do it, then measure it.

In the book *Better Thinking, Better Results*, this point is stressed in a discussion concerning the mistaken belief that if the parts, or departments, of a manufacturing business get measured for the right results, then the right results—particularly financial—will occur and make their way to the bottom line or transpose directly onto the aggregate result. Emiliani et al. tell us, "The phrase 'what gets measured gets managed' (or 'what gets measured gets done') is invariably stated as an axiom—a statement that is accepted as true without formal proof. This statement is false when tested using mathematical logic. That is, the phrase 'what gets measured gets managed' can be true in some cases but it is not true in all cases."[32]

NOTES

1. Dhavale, *Management Accounting Issues*, 246.
2. Maskell, *Making the Numbers Count*, 83.
3. Fiume and Cunningham, "Lean Accounting and Finance," 8.
4. Fiume and Cunningham, *Real Numbers*.
5. Johnson and Kaplan, *Relevance Lost*, 259.
6. Maskell, *Performance Measurement for World Class Manufacturing*, 23.
7. Ibid., 48.
8. Johnson, *Relevance Regained*, 159.
9. Dhavale, *Management Accounting Issues*, 259.
10. Stec, "Performance Measures for Lean Manufacturing," 49. This statement is from Dr. Deming's 1982 book, *Out of the Crisis*.
11. Hiromoto, "Another Hidden Edge," 22.
12. Ohno, "Overcoming the Obstacle of Accounting," 1.
13. Johnson, "Performance Measurement for Competitive Excellence," in *Measures for Manufacturing Excellence*, ed. Robert S. Kaplan, 86.
14. Ibid., 85.
15. Although a number of resources were referenced, the primary ones were Hall, *Zero Inventories*, 254–56; Imai, *Gemba Kaizen*, 128–40; Dhavale, *Management Accounting Issues*, 264–66; Stec, "Performance Measures for Lean Manufacturing," 56–58; and Maskell, *Performance Measurement for World Class Manufacturing*, 19–40.
16. Fiume and Cunningham, "Lean Accounting and Finance," 7.
17. TPM can be defined as an innovative approach to maintenance that optimizes equipment effectiveness, eliminates breakdowns, and promotes autonomous

operator maintenance through day-to-day activities involving the total workforce. This definition is taken from Nakajima, *Introduction to TPM*.

18. For details on Shingo's zero-defects philosophies, principles, and methods, see Shingo, *Zero Quality Control*.

19. Johnson and Bröms, *Profit beyond Measure*, 240n33.

20. Two companies that the author has visited that illustrate this point are Chrome Craft in the United States and Daihatsu in Japan.

21. Ford and Crowther, *Today and Tomorrow*, 47.

22. Ibid., 199.

23. Ibid., 200.

24. Ibid., 201.

25. Ohno, *Workplace Management*, 117.

26. Ibid., 118.

27. Liker, *The Toyota Way*, 260.

28. Ibid., 261.

29. Ibid., 261.

30. Ohno, "Overcoming the Obstacle of Accounting," 3.

31. Emiliani, "The False Promise of 'What Gets Measured Gets Managed'," 612–15. In the article, the axiom "what gets measured gets managed" is mathematically proven false.

32. Emiliani, Stec, Grasso, and Strodder, *Better Thinking, Better Results*, 227n2.

10

DESIGNING FOR THE LEAN
ENTERPRISE: RIGHT DESIGNING

A system can only deliver what a system is designed to achieve.
—*Dr. W. Edwards Deming*[1]

The best way to eliminate *muda* is not create it in the first place.
—*Glenn Uminger*[2]

It may be recalled from Chapter 8 that the second factor in the lean cost-management system is developing and implementing flow production, that is, the utilization of one-piece flow. In order to meet this fundamental objective, firms must understand and know how to design or redesign the operational system. This section will discuss exactly what it means to design the enterprise to become a lean enterprise.

In his doctoral dissertation, Dr. David Cochran[3] emphasizes the importance of the manufacturing system design having the ability to properly support functional needs and control:

> There are certain system characteristics that cannot be controlled or improved unless the manufacturing system design is changed or redesigned. Therefore, system design preceded system control and is an enabler of control. The system measurables are the functional requirements of the manufacturing system design and effect system design and subsequent system controllability. When a system is not designed according to the functional requirements or objectives of the system, the risk is that there may be a limited capability to exercise control of that system.[4]

Dr. Cochran is saying that the system design must precede the measurement if significant changes are desired. Dr. H. Thomas Johnson emphasizes the same point as

Dr. Deming, Uminger, and Dr. Cochran and dismisses the need for any type of targets or financial controls:

> Production costs are low and quality and variety of output are high because of the way the operating system itself is designed, not because people are responding to top-down quantitative targets.[5]

Dr, Johnson emphasizes that "we don't create or control the results, the system does."[6]

In an earlier section, Mike Kitano, former president of Toyota Motor Manufacturing North America, explained the Toyota Production System (TPS) as a one-by-one confirmation process or one-piece flow, which produces products one at a time and makes it right the first time as well. This concept is key to the design of the system. It also confirms the call of Dr. Steven Spear's Rules-in-Use for the ability to be "self-diagnostic," which means the confirmation that the product is being made correctly by the standard operations. The system *must* be designed to achieve this. Dr. Johnson describes this ability by stating that Toyota's production facilities are "designed to provide economies of proximity, not economies of scale, by integrating material transformation and machining with final assembly in the same plant."[7] The model plant for engine manufacturing used in this book does exactly this. Dr. Johnson also states that "TPS achieves this without having to increase the scale of facilities or the volume of output,"[8] which supports the section "All Parts at an Equal Cost," Figure 2.6, and the death of economies of scale.

Glenn Uminger, manager of production control for Toyota Motor Manufacturing North America, confirms this point about flow. He writes: "The linked process flows are the foundation for executing the management philosophy."[9] Uminger also acknowledges one of the points presented: that cost-managerial accounting has little to do with accounting but is actually structured around designing and implementing a right designed, or lean, system and executing its operation properly while continually improving it for better flow and function.[10]

Since takt time is the focal point of system design, it guides the system to match output exactly to demand. Takt time is the design feature that comes after knowing what product will be manufactured, which should be based on customer demand. Takt time can only be calculated after a product and its quantity from the customer are known. The system design is developed from the required takt time and designed to meet this critical requirement. Brian Maskell illuminates this point:

> The world class manufacturer approach is opposite of the traditional approach. The capacity to manufacture is made available just in time, in the same way that materials are made available. When a new product is launched, new machines are bought with enough capacity to meet immediate needs for six to 12 months. This approach may require machines that are smaller and, perhaps, slower than before. The machines chosen will be flexible so that, in the event of the new product failing to meet planned sales, the

equipment can be diverted to another use. When product takes off, additional machines can be purchased to meet the increasing demand.[11]

LEAN ENGINEERING

Jamie Flinchbaugh of the Lean Learning Center, in his thesis on lean factory design, suggests that "support functions, such as Advance Manufacturing Engineering or Product Engineering, are producing products and processes that are not consistent with the direction the plant is trying to head, namely towards lean manufacturing."[12]

Engineering is the front line in creating, designing, and implementing a lean enterprise. Unfortunately, it is not usually the primary target for companies going through a transformation. Engineers design the products and the processes, but if they are not knowledgeable in lean requirements, methods, techniques, philosophies, and principles and armed with experience, the change process will be greatly diminished if it does not actually result in failure. As Shigeo Shingo states, "It is important for engineers to take pride in the fact that they know better than anyone how to manufacture your plant's products."[13]

PRODUCT DESIGN IS PROCESS DESIGN

It is widely recognized that the design of the product is where most cost-reducing activity can and must take place. Dr. Robin Cooper reports that "the Japanese recognized that the most efficient way to keep costs down was to design them out of the products, not to try to reduce costs after products entered production."[14] Manufacturing engineers take the specifications of products to guide them for process requirements. Product and manufacturing engineers must work together to develop products that will satisfy the needs of the customer and that are capable of being manufactured at low cost and high quality.

Uminger poses three "critical cost control points" that impact the life cycle of manufacturing costs of a product:

- Product design
- Process design
- Manufacturing operations[15]

Although, as stated, the product design portion of the critical cost-control points is the main contributor to the ultimate product costs, this book focuses on the second two cost control points: process design and manufacturing operations. Uminger acknowledges that all three cost points must overlap and be interactive. This observation is very important in understanding and developing a strong and functional lean system and will be discussed in a later section on system evolution. Uminger notes: "Each cost control point requires a special focus supported by a systematic process. The three cost control points should be interactive, with each providing input and receiving feedback. They represent an endless step-by-step generational flow. Learning,

PRODUCT AND PROCESS

Toyota is well known for the ability to design a manufacturable product. This ability is one of their many advantages in delivering a high-quality and low-cost product. But little is known about their history of developing the ability to achieve this. Their production system, TPS, is well known, but how operations impact product design is not so well known.

In a presentation at the 2003 University of Michigan's Lean Manufacturing Conference, John Shook revealed the story behind Toyota's tie between operational processing and product design. He stated:

> The development of Toyota's product development system is far less well-known, but it is no less interesting or important. And the development system had its own headstrong, visionary curmudgeon, every bit Ohno's equal. Kenya Nakamura was assigned to lead the development of Toyota's first, from the ground up passenger vehicle. That assignment was made to the great dismay of most members of the company. Nakamura was considered by many to be—while a genius—too hard to work with, too demanding. But his work as Chief Engineer was documented to become a template for the company's "Chief Engineer (Shusa) System". Interestingly, keeping in mind Al Ward's definition above,[*] Nakamura was not a product engineer—*he was a process engineer*. He was known—in addition to being famous for his eccentricities—for his abilities to overcome process engineering problems. The Toyoda family recognized that the company needed to be able to actually manufacture whenever product design was created. Therefore, they asked their best processing engineer to lead their most important development project. I believe this set the tone for Toyota's product development process that continues to this day. It is a tone that places manufacturing operations firmly in the center of the corporate concerns, far more than any simple Design For Manufacturability program. It is a tone that fits precisely Al Ward's definition [emphasis added].[**]

John's story and thoughts put in perspective Toyota's attitude that explains their manufacturing prowess and how it permeates their entire business structure. It is truly a lean enterprise.

---

[*]   Al Ward's definition of product development cited by Shook is: "The aim of the product development process is the creation of profitable value streams." John Shook, "The Lean Enterprise," *Ninth Annual Lean Manufacturing Conference* (Ypsilanti, MI: Japan Technology Management Program at the University of Michigan, Ann Arbor, MI, May 6, 2003).

[**] Shook, "The Lean Enterprise."

development, and improvement should take place at each step in each generation. When you consider that most new products are variations or improvements to some existing product, this generational approach is easy to understand."[16]

Uminger confirms: "Manufacturability, for example, is directly affected by design, which affects costs."[17] Product and manufacturing engineers must develop products and processes, or systems, in a joint manner to enable the best lean system to evolve.

Engineers must be knowledgeable of each other's requirements, the customer's requirements, and lean principles and techniques. This is no simple task, and it takes a strong effort to develop the standards and procedures to make it not only a reality but also a quick, repeatable, and ever-improving process. Hiromoto explains, "Japanese companies have long recognized that the design stage holds the greatest promise for supporting low-cost production.... They don't simply design products to make better use of technologies and work flows; they design and build products that will meet the price required for market success—whether or not that price is supported by current manufacturing practices."[18]

Manufacturing engineers must develop the knowledge and experience to conceptualize, design, implement, and operate rightsized and right designed equipment and systems to manufacture the products they jointly developed with product engineers.

The importance of superior design is nothing new to industry. Alexander Hamilton Church stressed this point in 1913: "Good design is, however, evidently the basis of the pyramid; *no high efficiency in other departments can hope to recover the waste of effort forced by poor design.*"[19] Church ties the importance of product design into the ability to design outstanding manufacturing capabilities. He writes:

> "as has already been shown, design really has two independent aspects—design for use, and design for economical manufacture.... But in a general way much good will come of an attempt by the designers to keep the method of manufacture steadily in view whilst the shape and material of the piece are germinating in his mind.... It is or should be the duty of the designer to picture to himself, not only the finished component, but the same component at all its intermediate stages of manufacture.[20]

In Church's lifetime, the product engineer was also the manufacturing engineer. Today, the two functions are most often performed by different people—usually in separate departments—but the merging of the engineering disciplines must remain as strong today as it was during Church's period. Although design for manufacturing (DFM) has been recognized since the early twentieth century, it has yet to manifest itself in most firms' product-process development procedures. It is an absolute necessity for the lean enterprise.

Perhaps Shingo summarized the need best: "'Know-how' alone isn't enough! You need 'Know-why'!"[21]

MANUFACTURING ENGINEERING
AND DESIGNING THE LEAN OPERATION

Dr. H. Thomas Johnson and Anders Bröms state: "Few American or European business leaders have ever recognized that Toyota's strategy of *conserving resources* by incorporating every step into a balanced continuous flow is not the same thing as *cutting costs* by eliminating 'nonvalue activity.'"[22] What Dr. Johnson and Bröms are saying is that Toyota strives to minimize the amount of waste designed into the system in the first place. Recall in Chapter 3 the section "Flow versus Economies of Scale," where Taiichi Ohno's "limited" production system was discussed. Of course, Toyota is constantly and relentlessly working to eliminate waste in their operation, but they also relentlessly strive to design the system with as little waste as possible from the start of its design. In this sense, Toyota continues to design its systems utilizing Ohno's concept of limited production.

Dr. Johnson and Bröms indicate that companies trying to emulate Toyota miss the point. They state, "The latter idea is central to recently popular process improvement initiatives such as 'activity-based management,' 'business process reengineering,' and 'lean manufacturing,' none of which really captures the essential point of conserving resources by avoiding—not eliminating—waste."[23]

Toyota learned this lesson from the Ford Motor Company's Highland Park plant and applied the lesson to their situation. Johnson and Bröms confirm that "by the early 1980s, Toyota's system produced output at just the rate needed to satisfy current demand, as Henry Ford's system had done in 1925, but Toyota now produced that output in varieties."[24]

With all of the attention focused on improvement on the shop floor, everyone misses the effort and planning of the system design that Toyota does before any product is ever manufactured. Johnson and Bröms reveal that "their continuously linked system featured much smaller machines than those used in American Big Three plants, and each step operated at a slower rate. Indeed, virtually every step operated at just the rate needed to complete the requirements for one customer's order at a time."[25]

Simply put, this was their situation and they had little choice but to do it or face bankruptcy. Therefore, Toyota combined the lessons learned from Ford with Ohno's concept of limited production. According to Johnson and Bröms, "The steps in Toyota's system were designed 'to carry small loads and make frequent trips,' like the fabled water beetle in Japanese mythology. And each trip had to matter. Therefore, Toyota's employees always attempted to do things right the first time."[26]

This strategy was reinforced at Toyota when "W. Edwards Deming taught in his famous presentations to Japanese manufacturing executives during the summer of 1951."[27] This combination of function and thought secured Toyota's direction as they developed their business model based on their needs and circumstances.

The points Dr. Johnson and Bröms make above stress the need for and understanding of designing manufacturing systems and support functions that do not contain waste—at least not at the level of traditional operation systems—so that the system can function in a smoothly flowing manner. This is not to say that improvements or waste removal does not happen; such things must happen, but improvement efforts can then focus on improvement instead of on system redesign. This task must be accomplished by manufacturing engineers, which means that a huge change in knowledge must take place. Dr. Johnson tell us that "manufacturing engineers at Toyota in the 1950s set out to design a system that could achieve the benefits of specialization and division of labor in a continuously flowing system, yet produce variety without waste."[28]

Toyota and any firm transforming into a truly lean enterprise will use the engineers as their front line in deploying lean-manufacturing systems. Companies going through the transformation must journey through the learning process for their engineering staff. Toyota and its group companies have such an inherent knowledge base in their engineering staffs that many times the engineers have difficulty discussing the systems they are designing and deploying. For them it is simply the way they do things,[29] not any lean effort per se. It has become much like standard operations for their own systems design.

It was discussed that the deployment of a lean system is about developing and implementing flow and *not* about focused cost-cutting projects. By designing the system for flow, continually improving it, and correcting interruptions in flow, cost reduction will result. Again, a focus on the means, or MBM—and proper system design is a large part of MBM—will yield excellent results, outperforming MBR. The leaders of delivering a system with this ability are engineers. Dr. Cooper emphasizes this point: "It is not sufficient to simply launch cost reduction programs. Without the right organizational context, these programs will not work."[30]

LEAN ENGINEERING HORSEPOWER

Another failure many companies have applied in their effort to become more efficient is slashing their engineering and technical staffs, the very source that leads to the creation of lean systems, methods, and processes. As discussed, the manufacturing engineers (and other technical staff) are those who must understand, develop, implement, and evolve the concepts of lean that create functional systems. (It may be noted that these people are the ones who developed the cost-accounting management systems between 1885 and 1925—as previously mentioned—and were the brainpower behind and implementers of the Highland Park plant's manufacturing system, the cradle of flow.)

So many companies that have misused these technical people to "cut costs" end up cutting the engineers themselves in an effort to cut costs. So much engineering and technical cost cutting occurs that most manufacturing companies cannot even come close to supporting operational problems, let alone developing and evolving their manufacturing systems into lean enterprises. Perhaps this is one of the reasons that so many companies, managers, and engineers try for the "homerun" project. They simply do not have the time to think, develop, implement, and nurture an excellent system, which is fundamental in the transformation to a truly lean enterprise. Also, perhaps this is the reason that most companies incorrectly rely on their operators and frontline supervisors to develop and implement their lean systems and major improvements. This mistake will be discussed in detail in Chapter 12 on teamwork. Tom DeMarco offers a description of the culture that results after personnel cuts. He writes: "Anyone who's not overworked (sweating, staying late, racing from one task to the next, working Saturdays, unable to squeeze time for even the briefest meeting till two weeks after next) is looked on with suspicion." [31] This damaging situation causes a flurry of work that is more focused on getting the work or a project complete than getting it done properly or learning its lesson deeply so that it can be better applied in the future. What this creates is "a dangerous corporate delusion: the idea that organizations are effective only to the extent that all of their workers are totally and eternally busy." [32]

Basically, traditional manufacturing firms have an innate belief that getting something done is more important than getting something done correctly. This point is an offspring of the MBR attitude. James Womack shares Toyota's view toward managing perfection: "We get brilliant results from average people managing brilliant processes." The reality is that if the priority is to get something done rather than to get something done correctly, it has simply not gotten done.

If engineering staffs are so thin that they scramble from one project to the next or one operational issue to the next, they do not have time for countermeasures, only Band-Aids, which are usually not real solutions. They do not have the time to nurture countermeasures and evolve methods that, in time, may permanently resolve issues and contribute to a better understanding of how to better design manufacturing systems. They apply poor process designs and do not have time to receive needed feedback that would further evolve their knowledge of excellent lean-system design, which is discussed in Chapter 13, System Evolution. They are simply scrambling to complete a project in order to jump into the next project, which is most likely already in progress. DeMarco suggests the frenzied workplace is so common today that it has been elevated to a cultural expectation. He writes: "An increasingly common bit of our organizational folklore holds that pressure improves performance and that maximum performance can occur only in the presence of maximum pressure." [33]

Of course, a company taking its time is also not the manner in which it will succeed in becoming a lean enterprise. A firm must move rapidly through the process if its situation necessitates such a course. But a critical part of the transformation process is gaining and applying knowledge about a lean manufacturer's behavior and how to change to become a lean manufacturer. The knowledge of how to change includes everyone in the organization, but it is the engineers who should lead the system-design change process.

George Koenigsaecker,[34] who intimately knows the process of changing into a lean enterprise and the requirements for such a change, clearly spells out the dilemma most manufacturers have placed upon themselves. He writes:

> On top of all this change, most U.S. manufacturing operations are wholly understaffed in the technical areas.... These technical skill areas are the ones we have traditionally reduced when we had to "cut costs." Over time, these

cuts have culminated in a situation in which we are barely able to keep the plant running, let alone improve its operations.

For example, Honda has noted that 80 percent of its nonproduction members focus on making improvements. This includes product design and process design, both major and minor (*kaizen*). They have also noted that 80 percent of their nonproduction members are technical in background. They have a lot of improvement horsepower.... By adding to technical staff [at the Jacobs Brake Company] as we reduced costs, and allowing for nontechnical attrition, we were able to increase this proportion to almost 60 percent over four years. This gave us the horsepower to drive improvement at a fast pace.[35]

Koenigsaecker acknowledges the stripping of intellectual technical knowledge at most manufacturing firms, including both traditional batch manufacturers and companies working toward a lean transformation. Many companies have only one or two engineers for an operation that has well over one hundred operators and dozens of processes, most of which are not stable or reliable and must be constantly monitored, adjusted, and repaired. This situation leaves no time for learning, understanding, developing, and implementing lean changes. Even if the overstretched engineers did not have to spend 100 percent of their time with the existing operation, they may still be too few in number to develop and implement the complete system redesign and change required for a lean transformation. According to DeMarco, "Change represents investment. You invest in a change by paying for its two key components: conceptualization (or design) and implementation."[36]

DeMarco, in his book *Slack: Getting Past Burnout, Busywork, and the Myth of Total Efficiency*, explains how slack is the key to a company's ability to change.[37] DeMarco corroborates Koenigsaecker's analysis of the loss of technical horsepower: "What I call bankruptcy of inventiveness is often the result of a failure to set aside the resources necessary to let invention happen. The principle resource needed for invention is slack. When companies can't invent, it's usually because their people are too damn busy."[38]

MATERIAL AND INFORMATION FLOW

Another critical design parameter for a lean operation is its absorption of the support function for information flow. In the lean operation, material and information merge together. The system is designed to accomplish such a merger. Traditional production systems starkly contrast this notion. They create completely separate information systems that manage and control the manufacturing system. These separate entities include cost-management accounting systems (to which this book has particularly objected), giant computer systems such as MRP (material requirements planning) and ERP (enterprise resource planning), and other MBR functions that manipulate the flow of material and activities of shop personnel and create the chaos that is the norm in most manufacturing environments. Johnson and Bröms clarify this:

An "external" customer order is the only information introduced from outside the work process, from start to finish. Anything that any worker does on an order after the process begins is initiated and directed by information arising from within the work process itself.[39]

Johnson and Bröms continue, noting that "the two associated flows, customer information and material transformation, are always linked, never separated, in every step of the process."[40]

This is critical to implementing a good flow process. The material is the information and the information is the material. Instituting this type of situation obviously contributes greatly to enabling flow. If the information is the material, then no need for hunting or waiting for information—that is, instructions—is necessary to carry on with the work. Unfortunately, this concept is very difficult for many manufacturing managers to comprehend because they are so accustomed to the "hunt and wait" mode for information and instructions. Johnson and Bröms tell us that "people resist hearing that TMM-K[41] does not need computer information systems to provide instructions or targets to guide work. People do not accept the idea that Toyota must supply workers very little information other than that which flows automatically with the work, 'real time.'"[42]

Computerized systems that manage almost every aspect of the operation for most manufacturers is absent from the TMM-K operation: "TMM-K does not have the standard-cost systems … MRP … or the shopfloor computer systems that almost every manufacturing organization in the world … considers to be indispensable. These systems are not necessary in Toyota's continuous flow setting because *every employee's mastery of TPS practices insures that results are immanent in the work*."[43]

Another point from Johnson and Bröms' statement above is Toyota's emphasis on MBM instead of MBR. Recalling Dr. Deming's quote on lean designing at the beginning of this chapter, the lean enterprise reaps benefits from its uniquely and properly designed system. Dr. Johnson and Bröms stress that "variety at high quality and low cost is a spontaneous result of the careful attention Toyota pays to the way work is organized."[44]

Standard operations and adherence to them forms the lifeblood of the system. Tying the parts of the system together, standard operations are the major connecting mechanism that allows the system—and all persons and function of the system—to connect and nourish the system based on the customer's needs. The construct of the system is the focus of, not the results of, the system, although the results are expected based on the design of the system and its proper execution. Dr. Johnson and Bröms state, "Every worker performs standardized work at the appropriate rhythm because of the traits inherent in the TPS, not because 'expert' handlers of abstract quantitative information instruct and cajole everyone to hurry along and meet 'the targets.'"[45]

Unfortunately, most companies fail not only to achieve the physical link between information and material but also to understand its importance. Shook confirms this point when he notes companies' "failure to mesh together in seamless fashion the various sub-systems … the flow of material and information (JIT and Kanban remain woefully misunderstood)."[46]

WORK IN PROCESS

The traditional connection between cost-management or physical work-in-process (WIP) and financial WIP is one of the greatest sources of confusion. In financial accounting, WIP inventory was developed simply as a method to capture production costs. It is not specific, nor does it give an actual level of WIP. It is a simple method developed during the early part of the twentieth century to capture cost information to be used for external reporting. It was not developed or used for operational controls. And since most traditional manufacturing companies have such a constant fluctuation of inventory levels, the number captured for reporting is only good at the exact moment it is captured, but even that is not guaranteed. According to Dr. Schwarz, "this structure in our present cost accounting—where we identify Work-in-Process (WIP) as an inventory account—has created the greatest confusion in modern teaching of cost accounting."[47]

A company that is truly operating under lean principles and methods will have a constant and reasonably accurate level of inventory throughout the operation. This situation has a three-fold advantage. First, the result of practicing a lean operation sets a standard of consistent and level amounts of inventory where it is needed to maintain operations. Operating to demand or takt time and applying *heijunka*[48] levels the fluctuating effects of production in a traditional manufacturer. Tying a value stream and its processes and equipment to takt time creates a leveling and equalizing effect on production. How this works is explained in detail in Chapter 8.

The second advantage results from the implementation of one-piece flow through product-family value streams. One-piece flow in cellular manufacturing lines removes huge quantities of WIP that exists under traditional methods. One-piece flow, by its nature, removes WIP between process flows, equipment, and machines. Most companies using lean techniques commonly reduce their quantities of WIP by 50 to 99 percent—generally, the number is closer to 99 percent.

The third advantage is a result of the first two advantages. If operations are producing to demand and flowing through the value stream in a one-by-one production methodology, the result in the value stream is drastically reduced inventory stores, or marketplaces. Simply put, if the operations are producing to a leveled schedule based on the demand of takt-time production and flow one piece at a time wherever possible, the necessity of a large amount of inventory in stores between nonflowing processes does not exist. Inventory stores or marketplaces are small, tightly controlled, and vary only slightly in quantity (there is a small variation between the maximum and minimum levels).

RIGHT DESIGN AND IMPROVE

The design of the system—or even the correctly manufactured final product— *should* determine its proper function. Designing and operating the lean system properly will enable resources to be used for improving flow design and correcting flow interruption instead of to insure that the poorly designed system does what it should be doing by design—making the correct product in the correct order at the correct time.

Resources should instead be focused on improving the system—in flow and self-correcting flow interruptions (*jidoka*). Such a method of operation would be possible if the system were designed correctly from its inception. Is it any wonder most operations never seem to improve? Personnel spend most of the time just working to get the system to work.

Such a failure also contributes to companies trying to get the big "home run hit" type of project instead of continually improving their current system. This may be why so many companies continue to do major *kaizen* blitzes—because the systems were never designed correctly from the beginning (this is even the case for many companies going through a lean transformation). Unfortunately, such *kaizen* blitzes result in most operators spending their time trying to completely redesign the system in which they are working. Instead, these companies should be making smaller, incremental improvements (true *kaizen* —not *kaikaku*[49]) while the engineers are actually designing and deploying better flowing systems and continual feedback from operators for the smaller but powerful improvements that contribute to making the system more operator friendly and smoothly flowing.

Such a division of "design labor"—in which engineers design and operators incrementally improve and give feedback—may be the key to properly organizing, utilizing, and communicating information. The division would continually improve already well-designed, functioning systems instead of requiring radical attempts to redesign systems that have already been deployed. Nearly all of the manufacturing industry today lives with the painful daily trudge of trying to manufacture products with ill-designed systems.

RIGHT DESIGNING

The concept of, and reasons for, system design have been stressed. For excellent lean companies—Toyota is probably the best example—this is the way of doing business. But most companies must go through a learning process to develop their engineers and management and to nurture the necessary experience, knowledge, and principles. What does right designing mean from a more practical, engineering level? The answer is discussed below.

Rightsizing to Flow

As has been discussed, flow is the most fundamental aspect of lean. A key element to achieving flow in creating and designing cells is to rightsize machines. Without rightsized machines, flow can be difficult to accomplish. The lack of rightsized equipment for some manufacturing is one of the reasons for implementing pull systems. Therefore, when implementing flow or lean manufacturing, companies should rightsize the tools and equipment used in manufacturing operations. Understanding rightsizing is another critical step in lean implementation.

The Right Designed Goal

The ultimate goal of equipment involved in lean manufacturing is to design and build it as absolutely compact as possible, as inexpensively as possible, and so that it will operate exactly to the takt time and be dedicated to only one part or part family. There should be no end to the pursuit of a rightsized piece of equipment. This philosophy parallels the pursuit of perfection, which is the philosophy of lean thinking as put forth by James Womack and Daniel Jones.

Parameters for Right Designing

Womack and Jones in *Lean Thinking* defined a right designed piece of equipment as the following: "A design, scheduling, or production device that can be fitted directly into the flow of products within a product family so that production no longer requires unnecessary transport and waiting."[50] For further explanation, consider a machine or system that conforms to the following standards:

- Is physically compact
- Utilizes one-piece flow, or manufactures one piece at a time
- Operates mixed model production or can be changed over in less than ten minutes
- Can be moved as one contained unit instead of as separate units (such as machine base, hydraulic unit, electrical panel, and so on)
- Operates within the designated takt time
- Is simple to repair, maintain, and operate
- Has autonomation built in to it[51]
- Has *chaku-chaku* and one-touch start[52]
- Exemplifies the 5 Five S's
- Features flexibility and future flexibility—it may be used for the next product generation[53]

If these parameters can be understood, the concept of right designed machines and systems can begin to take shape. These concepts are critical in applying lean manufacturing or lean thinking.

Right Designing for Means

Results

Although, as mentioned above, many valuable reasons exist to right design equipment to promote easier implementation of lean production, a view of the fundamental principle of lean production should be reviewed. Lean production is, as stated in Yasuhiro Monden's book *Toyota Production System*, a profit-making venture. Monden writes: "The Toyota Production System is a viable method for making products because it is an effective tool for producing the ultimate goal—profit. To achieve this purpose, the primary goal of the Toyota Production System is cost reduction, or improvement of productivity. Cost reduction and productivity improvement are attained through the elimination of various wastes such as excess inventory and excessive work force."[54]

One reason for right designed equipment is to dedicate it to the production of one part or a family of parts. This creates a situation in which cost tracking becomes extremely simple, as previously discussed. Since the right designed machine now produces this *one* product, that product carries all costs associated with this machine, which include, for example, initial capital cost, repairs to the machine, maintenance, electricity, air, coolant, lubricants, tooling, and so on. This allows a very large portion of overhead in the cell to be eliminated. All such costs can be directly associated to the one part and therefore become direct costs. This ultimately means that administrative costs are no longer needed to distribute the overhead into inaccurate allocations.

Transactions[55]

If a piece of equipment is wrongly designed, extra costs are associated with it. Such extra costs include tracking, moving, and storing parts that must be processed through the machine. This means that if a machine has extra capacity and a company feels motivated to use that extra capacity to justify its capital expense by pushing as many parts as possible through it to bring down the cost per part—in other words, scale of economies thinking—then people and resources must be utilized to move and manage the different parts that are processed through the machine.

Companies must find and use floor space—which is ideally close to the machine—to store parts waiting to be processed. People and systems are also used to track, store, and manage the material movement and make adjustments to the inventory levels of these parts. If a machine is right designed, it is dedicated to the product or product line and is located in a production cell; therefore, it completely eliminates the need for all of the people and resources needed for material movement. This reduces costs.

An anecdote from the Harley-Davidson Motor Company illustrates very clearly the absurdity of activities that must be tracked as a result of nonflow manufacturing and how they are transformed in a traditional accounting system. William Turk writes:

> For each manufactured part and operation, an industrial engineer must establish a labor hours standard. Cost accounting then converts the labor hours standards to a standard direct labor cost by operation.
>
> Employees record their times and pieces produced for each part-number operation on which they work. Thus, if an employee works on ten different part numbers each day, ten labor tickets have to be recorded. Cost accounting takes these ten labor tickets and calculates the direct labor inventory input. Assuming an average of ten labor tickets and 500 employees, this works out to 5,000 labor tickets per day, 25,000 labor tickets per week, and 100,000

labor tickets per month. Accounting must ensure that the 100,000 labor transactions are all accurate—a hopeless task.

For overhead absorption, the accountants add an additional 400 percent on top of the direct labor input to inventory, which produces the manufacturing absorption credit. If an employee's work does not constitute direct labor, it must be classified as indirect labor or diverted direct labor, both of which are thought of as "bad labor." That is, direct labor employees should be producing direct labor ("good labor").[56]

This situation was not unique to Harley-Davidson but typical of most manufacturing companies. Maskell reiterates the futility of this point: "In order to keep track of the overall situation, it is necessary to maintain thorough and careful records of the status of each job—and this is a time-consuming and wasteful task."[57]

At Toyota (or any well-executed lean manufacturer), inventory levels are so low and controlled so well that any need to count inventory is very limited or nonexistent. Recall the physical inventory activity that most traditional or batch manufacturers must continually go through. Toyota's inventory is so controlled, or standardized, that physical counting is unnecessary: the amounts of inventory are already known. If a physical count is needed, it takes only minutes instead of hours or days, which are lengths of time typical for any batch-style manufacturer.[58]

Part Numbers and Containers

Two other costly side effects of equipment being wrongly designed are part-number changes and containers. If machinery is wrongly designed and batches are moved from machine to machine or department to department, then many times companies will change the part number to track the part as it changes its configuration due to being machined, fabricated, shot blasted, painted, assembled, heat treated, and so on. This again adds unnecessary time and resources to track, assign, change, and store the data involved with multiple part numbers for one product. If machines are right designed so parts can be processed in a cell using one-piece flow, then all the above transactions and activity are eliminated.

Containers also have a similar situation. In the machine-to-machine or department-to-department scenario, extra containers must be purchased and maintained. They also must be tracked and managed through the system using time and resources, therefore adding costs. Extra labor must be used to load and unload all the containers many times as the parts move in batches through the many different departments or machines. Also, different sizes and configurations of containers often have to be used. For example, if the parts must be heat treated and the customer is requiring plastic returnable containers, then extra metal containers must be purchased and used so that they will not melt. Again, unnecessary costs are incurred.

Washer Example

Another area for savings when implementing right designed equipment is the elimination of the big batch machines, such as washers, paint booths, and heat-treatment equipment. Sometimes the requirements of these processes—such as the time required for heat treating—can make right designing difficult, but solutions exist to resolve many of these issues.

Washers will be used to illustrate this point. Presently, many companies purchase large washers to wash a large variety and volume of parts. The parts are either dipped into large tanks in large baskets or are flowed though the washer in large baskets. This may appear to be cost effective since one machine can handle nearly all or all the parts in the facility that need washing, but is it the most cost-effective way? If many small right designed washers are purchased for each component that needs a washing operation, the washing operation becomes less expensive for several reasons.

First, the right designed washer will fit directly into the manufacturing cell, facilitating one-piece flow and eliminating the logistics of material handling. The capital cost is directly associated with the product or product line. The largest impact is that even though manufacturing will now have many washers instead of only one, the total capital outlay for several right designed washers will be less than that for one giant washer. Also, an added benefit is that right designed washers will clean parts much better because they are designed to wash a particular part and should do it one at a time. Operators and processes that follow in the value stream will greatly appreciate the cleaning improvement of the part. Finally, these smaller, right sized machines will take up less floor space than the giant batch-style machine.

Simplification

Another cost advantage for using right designed equipment is that it is simpler. Since right designed machines are smaller, they generally cost less and are also simpler in design and construction. This means fewer and simpler machine components are needed and less complicated systems (for example hydraulic, lubrication, controls, and so on) are required. Simpler equipment is much easier to troubleshoot, repair, and maintain. All this substantially decreases costs over the life of the machine. Improved uptime is easier to maintain with the equipment running better and being easier to diagnose and repair.

Capital Expense

The final cost advantage is incremental investments. With right designed equipment, it becomes much easier to invest capital incrementally with volume increases instead of investing one initial capital outlay to cover the projected—but not always met—final volume. With incremental investments in capital equipment allowed by purchasing right designed equipment, if increasing volumes are not reached due to changes in the estimated market demand, capital is saved. Also, if the market demand does not peak at estimated projections, the amount of capital sunk will be less.

ARE COMPANIES RIGHT DESIGNING?

Although many more firms are interested in or working on a lean transformation, most companies thus far do not understand what it really means to implement lean manufacturing. And many manufacturing companies have yet to do anything with lean manufacturing.

The firms that have implemented some aspects of lean manufacturing have made some excellent changes for the better. Their business has indeed improved. But they remain only at the beginning of a true lean transformation and most do not realize the dramatic changes that have yet to be made. This point was explained in the section that discussed the Five S's. Figure 10.1 illustrates where companies are with their transformation. Most either do not realize or do not understand just how far the change must evolve.

Figure 10.1 reveals that most companies currently do not view the changes in their firm beyond the lean techniques. Most struggle to see beyond the lean "hinterland." The "hinterland" is the gap between lean methods and true understanding of lean philosophy. It is the rare company that travels beyond the "hinterland" to a level where they develop capabilities and techniques to take them to new levels.

Who Is Responsible?

Many times, the level of understanding beyond just the techniques is the result of the company's executives retaining the focus on results—or the MBR mentality—even though they do support lean changes. They view lean as simply a set of methods that improve the business, that is, introduce results: they expect "the numbers," or the bottom line, to be met or their support of the lean transformation wanes. They must see results via the financial statements or they think something must be wrong. Many times—in fact most times—the lean implementation may not hit the bottom line immediately. According to Koenigsaecker, "The reality is that very few Chief Executive Officers today fully realize what the potential of a long-term lean conversation can be."[59]

The critical issues and pitfalls that most companies discover on their journey toward lean prevent them from reaching the far right of Figure 10.1. Thus far, most companies have not fully implemented lean manufacturing. The lack of ability to implement lean is the real issue that should be addressed and that this book addresses.

Mark DeLuzio, a veteran lean executive, substantiates the lack of companies successfully transforming to a true lean enterprise in an interview:

> **Q:** Do you believe that only 1 percent of all manufacturers have adopted a lean strategy to grow their businesses?
>
> **DeLuzio**: I agree on the numbers because lean exposes problems and is a pain in the butt to do. You have to be prepared to deal with big problems. Not a lot of companies even think in the right frame of mind to be able to go and deal with the problems in a fact-based manner.[60]

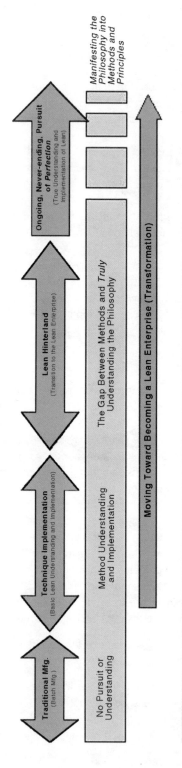

Figure 10.1 Path to lean transformation

Rick Harris[61] concurs with DeLuzio: "30 percent to 40 percent of all manufacturers in the United States claim to be implementing lean principles. 'However, only 5 percent are truly implementing lean manufacturing.'"[62]

In an interview with Dr. Jeffrey Liker, Gary Vasilash, editor-in-chief of *Automotive Design & Production* magazine, reveals the magnitude of poor progress achieved so far in the North American journey toward lean manufacturing. Vasilash states: "Two percent. Not very much in any estimation of the number of facilities doing something. Two out of 100. Almost trivial. Two percent. That's the number of plants that Jeff Liker thinks can be defined as 'lean.'"[63]

In the article, Dr. Liker goes on to explain that part of the difficulty with becoming lean is the time frame for implementation. It may take up to ten years. He also explains that other priorities tend to get in the way and that too many companies focus on random specific actions—a focus known as cherry picking—instead of taking action focused on a holistic aim. Nearly three years later in his book *The Toyota Way*, Dr. Liker expresses even more dismally how few companies have been able to replicate Toyota's system: "What percent of companies outside of Toyota and their close knit group of suppliers get an A or even a B+ on Lean? I cannot say precisely but it is far less than 1%."[64] Liker continues: "The problem, I believe, is that U.S. companies have embraced lean tools but do not understand what makes them work together in a system."[65]

Liker suggests that "most attempts to implement lean have been fairly superficial. The reason is that most companies have focused too heavily on tools such as 5S and just-in-time, without understanding lean as an entire system that must permeate an organization's culture."[66]

In Dr. Liker's book *Becoming Lean: Inside Stories of U.S. Manufacturers*, Mike Rother contributes a chapter that explains five common pitfalls companies fall into when trying to implement lean:[67]

1. Confusing techniques with lean objectives
2. Expecting employee training to make lean manufacturing happen
3. Saying "That's not lean manufacturing, that's a program!"
4. Relying solely on *kaizen* workshops
5. Quitting after failures[68]

Automotive Industries magazine has a five-part series by Ron Harbour[69] on the difficulty of becoming lean.[70] In the article, Harbour emphasizes the lack of understanding between company management and their desire for the quick fix, which does not exist within lean manufacturing. He places the burden on company management, writing, "Leaders are responsible for lean."[71] Orest Fiume agrees: "You have to look at everything you do in the business to see if it is consistent with the Lean philosophy. And if it's not, senior management has to change it."[72]

Senior management of any firm holds the ultimate responsibility as to whether or not a company will transform into a lean enterprise. Many executives want to see the bottom-line savings before they will fully commit to supporting changes to become a lean enterprise. This creates a situation where many potential change agents scramble to figure out how to capture the lean changes and show the financial results from them to these skeptical executives.

If senior management wants to see the financial results of transforming to lean, they do not understand the lean enterprise or what it takes for a lean transformation. Whether or not one is able to see the results of lean is not the issue. The executives' lack of understanding is the problem and is where the focus of the effort must take place. Orest Fiume and Jean Cunningham point out this very issue: "All senior leaders must adopt lean as a business strategy and not a manufacturing tactic."[73] Fiume and Cunningham continue:

> Don't establish a task force to spend six months studying lean and come up with a traditional economic (e.g., ROI) justification for it. Our strong recommendation is, simply, this: *Lean works, so just accept it and get started* [emphasis added].[74]

John Shook confirms the lack of progress in companies and explains why companies have not been able to successfully make the transformation to a lean enterprise. He writes: "For 20 years much of the world auto industry has tried to copy Toyota's success. *It has largely failed*. Why? A common assessment would be to say that companies have not 'properly, or fully, understood' Toyota's system" (emphasis added).[75]

Harbour, Fiume, Cunningham, and Shook verify exactly what Ohno revealed about what companies must do to implement lean and who has the ultimate responsibility. Changes in thinking—which have been stressed throughout these chapters—and a clear understanding are two of the main ingredients in transformation to lean, according to Ohno. Ohno writes: "Top management must change its way of thinking and make a commitment to reverse the conventional flow of production, transfer, and delivery. This will meet lots of resistance and requires courage. The greater the commitment, however, the more successful will be the implementation of the Toyota production system."[76]

Ohno also discusses the personal impact on him and the direct support he received from Toyota's top executive during his development and implementation period. He writes:

> During this period, Toyota's top manager was a man [Eiji Toyoda] of great vision who, without a word, left the entire operation entirely to me. When I was—rather forcefully—urging foremen in the production plant to understand kanban, my boss received a considerable number of complaints. They voiced feeling that this fellow Ohno was doing something utterly ridiculous and should be stopped. This must have put the top manager in a difficult position at times, but even then he must have trusted me. I was not told to stop and for this I am grateful.[77]

Wrongly Designed Manufacturing Cells

As stated in the previous section, many pitfalls occur as companies work to implement lean and transform their business. Rother opines, "It is surprising to see how little true continuous material flow actually exists in practice."[78] He continues, "Almost any grouping of machines that performs processing steps in a sequence is labeled a cell. But in most cells we see no continuous flow, which is really what makes a cell a cell."[79] As Rother clearly indicates, firms working to implement lean commonly misunderstand what it really means to establish flow. The physical components of manufacturing cells are usually not designed to establish flow. And true flow— one-piece flow—is absolutely fundamental to transforming to a lean enterprise.

The ability, skill, and experience to right design cells must be fully understood in order to implement flow. Although engineers must take the lead and have this skill set, the entire organization must understand the reasons for and methods of right designing cells, which must be applied to the manufacturing structure and support function. Management must also give the correct support for the system to change and thrive.

The Bottom Line

Another failure on management's part is the inability to understand how lean implementation affects the bottom line. Unfortunately, nearly all managers remain products of MBR. They demand that lean implementation must affect the bottom line. Improving the profitability of any company is important and must be pursued. But most managers, being students of MBR, do not understand how, or how quickly, the change process impacts financials. And as stated, the focus should not be the financials, but the means. Managers should be asking whether the firm is creating right designed flow.

As Dr. Johnson and Bröms explained, the focus of companies must be on the means or how the parts of the system interact with each other. Dr. Spear also discusses this same point in his Rules-in-Use when he stresses "connection of activities." Flinchbaugh points out that the Rules-in-Use "have many purposes, but most simply, they provide the organization guidance when designing or improving systems."[80] Fiume discusses in detail why many managers miss the potential of a lean transformation: they follow the numbers instead of understanding and focusing on flow implementation. He writes: "Very few companies understand that Lean is a business strategy, not a manufacturing tactic, and are unable, or unwilling, to address changing the other aspects of the business."[81]

Fiume reveals the financial scenario in which so many companies miss the impact of their lean transformation. When companies begin the change process they remove large amounts of WIP inventory from their operational systems by implementing flow manufacturing. If the firm's managers are watching "the numbers"—as they usually are—they will see gross profit drop. This drop will send them reeling. And their lean support will also reel.

What managers do not understand is that large amounts of inventory were removed from operations due to flow implementation. Inventory contributes to cost of goods sold, and therefore, gross profit is initially reduced as the excess inventory is purged from the system. Although gross profits are initially reduced, cash flow is greatly improved because the money previously tied up in inventory is now free for other uses.[82]

NOTES

1. A similar quote by Deming is given on page 2 of Johnson and Bröms, *Profit beyond Measure*. Deming writes: "If you have a stable system, then there is no use to specify a goal. You will get whatever the system will deliver. A goal beyond the capability of the system will not be reached. If you have not a stable system, then there is ... no point in setting a goal. There is no way to know what the system will produce: it has no capability."
2. This statement was made by Glenn Uminger during his presentation at the 2003 University of Michigan's Lean Manufacturing Conference. Uminger is referencing the ability of designing a manufacturing system correctly or without waste in it in the first place.
3. Dr. David S. Cochran founded System Design, LLC, in 2003. He was on the Mechanical Engineering faculty at MIT from 1995 to 2003. He established the Production System Design (PSD) Laboratory at MIT in 1995 and at his company to advance the science of system design and integrated-performance measurement, which provides a roadmap for advancement beyond the success of lean and the Toyota Production System (TPS). He is a two-time recipient of the prestigious Shingo Prize (2002 and 1989) for manufacturing excellence for his work in the design of lean systems. He received the Dudley Prize in 2000 for best paper from the International Journal of Production Research for his work to integrate system-design theory.
4. Cochran, "The Design and Control of Manufacturing Systems," 46.
5. Johnson, "How The Universe Story and MBM Can Save Business," 14.
6. Ibid, 10.
7. Johnson and Bröms, *Profit beyond Measure*, 87.
8. Ibid., 88.
9. Uminger, "Lean," Slide 33.
10. Uminger discussed his ideas with the author during several conversations at the 2003 University of Michigan's Lean Manufacturing Conference and correspondence after the conference.
11. Maskell, *Performance Measurement for World Class Manufacturing*, 59–60.
12. Flinchbaugh, "Implementing Lean Manufacturing" 29.
13. Shingo, *Non-Stock Production*, 111.
14. Cooper, *When Lean Enterprises Collide*, 91.
15. Uminger, "Manufacturing Cost Management," 37.
16. Ibid., 39.
17. Ibid., 40.
18. Hiromoto, "Another Hidden Edge," 23.
19. Church, "Practical Principles of Rational Management," 490.
20. Ibid., 406–7.
21. Shingo, *Non-Stock Production*, 68.

22. Johnson and Bröms, *Profit beyond Measure*, 32.
23. Ibid.
24. Ibid.
25. Ibid.
26. Ibid.
27. Ibid.
28. Johnson, *Relevance Regained*, 40.
29. Toyota recently began using "The Toyota Way" to describe their business system instead of Toyota Production System (TPS).
30. Cooper, *When Lean Enterprises Collide*, 111.
31. DeMarco, *Slack*, 3.
32. Ibid.
33. Ibid., 47.
34. George Koenigsaecker led the Danaher's Jacobs Vehicle Equipment Company's lean conversion in the late 1980s, which was highlighted in the book *Lean Thinking*. He also authored the original version of the Danaher Business System, which was credited for the company's success. He went on to lead The HON Company's successful lean conversion, which doubled productivity and tripled revenues. Currently, Koenigsaecker is president of Lean Investments, LLC, a company that acquires manufacturing firms and leads their lean-enterprise conversions. He is also the chairman of the Shingo Prize board and is on the board of directors of several companies.
35. Koenigsaecker, "Lean Production," 466–67.
36. DeMarco, *Slack*, 34–35.
37. According to DeMarco, "slack" is defined as a prescription for building a capacity to change into the modern enterprise (*Slack*, xi). Slack is the extra knowledge capacity, derived from people and their time, that a superior company maintains for both innovative change and periodic surges in resource requirements, that is, the requirement for more people. Companies that do not maintain this *slack* are actually in decline, as they lose ground since they do not and cannot dynamically change as the market demands.
38. DeMarco, *Slack*, 41–42.
39. Johnson and Bröms, *Profit beyond Measure*, 83.
40. Ibid., 84.
41. TMM-K, Toyota Motors Manufacturing, Kentucky, is Toyota's assembly plant and complex in Georgetown, Kentucky.
42. Johnson and Bröms, *Profit beyond Measure*, 105.
43. Ibid.
44. Ibid., 97.
45. Ibid., 99.
46. Shook, "The Lean Enterprise," 2.

47. Schwarz, *Internal Accounting*, 117.
48. Heijunka is the overall leveling in the production schedule of the volume and variety of items produced in given time periods. See glossary.
49. Kaikaku approximately translates as rapid or radical improvement.
50. Womack and Jones, *Lean Thinking*, 309.
51. Autonomation is automation with the human touch, which allows a machine to automatically stop when an abnormality is detected.
52. *Chaku-chaku* is literally translated as "load-load." It means that a part is cleared from a fixture automatically so that an operator can load the next part without having to manually remove the previous part from the fixture.
53. This parameter is discussed in detail in Uminger, "Manufacturing Cost Management," 42–43.
54. Monden, *Toyota Production System*, 1.
55. Chapter 14 will discuss in detail the theory and results of lean manufacturing on operational transactions.
56. Turk, "Management Accounting Revitalized," 33.
57. Maskell, *Performance Measurement for World Class Manufacturing*, 157.
58. The information about Toyota's inventory was given by Uminger in his presentation at the 2003 University of Michigan's Lean Manufacturing Conference.
59. Koenigsaecker, "The Cost Benefits of Going Lean."
60. DeLuzio, "Danaher is a Paragon of Lean Success," 7.
61. Rick Harris is the president of Harris Systems and does manufacturing consulting and training for a variety of companies. He is a Shingo Prize winner and coauthor of the book *Creating Continuous Flow*. He is a former manager of final assembly at Toyota's Georgetown, Kentucky, facility.
62. Weber, "Lean Machines."
63. Vasilash, "Lean Lessons," 60.
64. Liker, *The Toyota Way*, 10.
65. Ibid., 12.
66. Ibid., 7.
67. Mike Rother teaches with the Center for Professional Development at the University of Michigan and is a manufacturing consultant based in Ann Arbor, Michigan. He coauthored the *Learning to See* workbook, which introduced the value-stream mapping tool, and its sequel, *Creating Continuous Flow*, which explains how to create true flow at a pacemaker process. He is also the recipient of two Shingo Prizes for *Learning to See* and *Creating Continuous Flow*.
68. Rother, "Crossroads," 477–95.
69. Ron Harbour is the president of Harbour and Associates, a manufacturing consultant firm and provider of automotive reviews that appear in publications such as *The Harbour Report*.
70. Harbour, "Opinions & Analysis" (November 2001), 14; Harbour, "Opinions & Analysis" (December 2001), 10; Harbour, "Opinions & Analysis" (January

2002), 8; Harbour, "Opinions & Analysis" (February 2002), 16; and Harbour, "Opinions & Analysis" (March 2002), 16.

71. Harbour, "Opinions & Analysis" (December 2001), 10.

72. Emiliani, Stec, Grasso, and Strodder, *Better Thinking, Better Results*, 208.

73. Fiume and Cunningham, *Real Numbers*, 159.

74. Ibid., 161.

75. Shook, "The Lean Enterprise," 1.

76. Ohno, *Toyota Production System*, 30.

77. Ibid., 36.

78. Rother, "Do You Really Have Continuous Flow in Assembly?," 1.

79. Ibid.

80. Flinchbaugh, "Connecting Lean and Organizational Learning," 6.

81. Fiume, "Lean Accounting and Finance," 6.

82. Ibid., 10–12. The same point is illustrated in Taninecz, "Cost Accounting Undercuts Lean," 73–74.

11

LEAN IMPLEMENTATION CREATES LEAN COST MANAGEMENT

Cells create the situation where nearly all costs can be directly associated with each cell or product. Cells are essentially a micro version combining lean-implementation principles and focus-factory concepts (see Figure 11.1). This combination creates a focal point of flow and simple cost tracking. The reason for cost management is to help the company's managers understand costs for planning purposes and provide guidance so they can improve the business;[1] cellular manufacturing and focus factories physically accommodate simple and accurate methods for tracking costs.

The crankshaft machining line example reveals a view of the operator and part flow within the cell and shows how information is a part of the one-piece flow line. As discussed in the Material and Information Flow section, product, operator, and information flow are one and the same. Operators are tied directly to a product family. Right designed machine tools and equipment are also directly tied to the product family. As was discussed in Chapter 2, cost items like utilities, floor space, and tooling are also directly tied to the manufacturing line and therefore tied to the product. This situation reinforces the ability of lean manufacturing, and particularly flow cells of a value stream, to physically link most costs directly to a product family, which makes them direct costs.

LEAN COST MANAGEMENT AND THE FLOW CELL

A cell is a collection of processes for a product or product family that has an established flow and is designed to meet takt time. A cell is a focused value stream of a product or product family; therefore, by design, it allows for the direct assignment of costs components. This situation will move product cost from the nebulous category of overhead to simple and understandable direct costs. Cascades of benefits stem from the development and implementation of cells and focus factory concepts.

STANDARD WORK SHEET

SCOPE OF OPERATIONS	FROM RAW CRANK CASTING	DATE:
	TO FINISHED CRANK ASSY	11/20/93

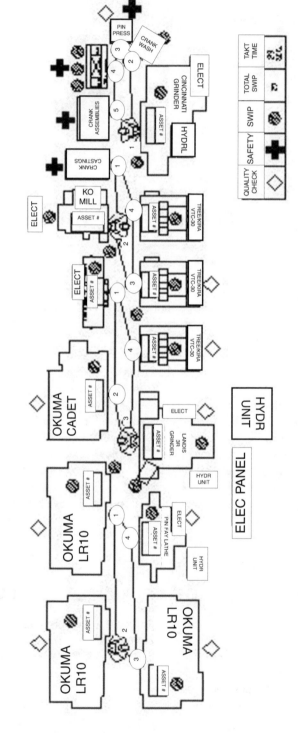

QUALITY CHECK	SAFETY	SWIP	TOTAL SWIP	TAKT TIME

Figure 11.1 Crankshaft machining line, one-piece flow cell

In traditional manufacturing, parts are processed in departments that are responsible for manufacturing. Consider the example of machining crankshafts. All crankshafts for all models are machined in one department. The department contains all equipment, personnel, tools, coolant, operators, setup personnel, and so on. Since much equipment and tooling, and all personnel, can be shared between all parts from all of the models, tracking information associated with the manufacturing is cumbersome and inaccurate. As a result, cost information for each part is questionable; however, it is still used for decision making and monthly operational reviews. Administrative resources have to track, update, and monitor information for each operation at both a department and divisional level. Even the cost of these physical administrative activities is not possible to collect accurately.

Changing the crankshaft-machining department from the traditional batch manufacturing to cells dedicated to machining crankshaft models allows for focused and accurate information to be easily tracked. The new information, not previously available, includes the following:

- Known and accurate product costs
- Monthly adjustments to target product costs and cost components (this is a potential capability, not a requirement)
- Accurate and simple cost comparisons for outsourcing
- Cost information understandable to shop personnel (dollars per part instead of dollars per machine hour)
- Comparison between part costs (considering the crankshaft example: model A crankshaft versus model B crankshaft)
- Significant reduction or elimination of work-in-process (WIP) and material handling logistics (which would reduce or eliminate the need for tracking).

Cost tracking now becomes a user-friendly method for planning purposes. Both accountants and shop personnel can understand what the information means (dollar per part), where it comes from (for example, the number of operators), and how to capture it (for example, one hundred drills used at $1.25 per drill). This information will be discussed in detail in Chapter 17 on the cost management spreadsheets. The administrative activities at the department level are eliminated and extremely minimized at the divisional level but also simplified and accurate. Tracking production information and the record of operators' and setup personnel's number of hours worked are completely eliminated. Figure 11.2 illustrates a basic spreadsheet for tracking. Due to the physical design and operation of flow cells, the majority of costs become direct costs and only a small percentage become allocated costs.

Correct management and cost-accounting methods are a critical step to becoming a lean enterprise and changing to a cost-management system. The requirement is that a company must implement physical lean changes to be able to fully utilize lean methods of management and cost accounting, that is, cost management. But the positive result is that implementing lean accounting methods puts in place critical support

Value Stream (Part Family)	Cost Tracking System (Cost Management)			— Generated on a per part (M1A, M2A, ...) basis						
	Overhead Glob			Direct Costs						
	Corporate Overhead	Division (Engine) Overhead	Focus Factory Overhead (General Factory)	Machines (Dep reciation)	Operators	Maintenance and Repair	Tooling (Perishable and permanent)	Coolant	Utilities (Air) (Elect) (Etc.)	etc.
M1A										
M2A										
M3A										
M4A										
M5A										
M1B										
M2B										
M3B										
M4B										
M5B										
M1C										
M2C										
etc.										

Figure 11.2 Sample cost-management spreadsheet

for continuing onto the highest levels of lean. It also provides immediate and accurate information for business decisions. For most companies, this would be the first time in their history that such information was available.

With cellular manufacturing, accurate and focused information becomes the normal method of business because the information is simply a reflection of the operation's physical attributes—that is, number of operators, floor space, WIP, inventory (raw material and finished parts), tools/tooling, capital equipment, setup time, utilities, scrap/rework, supervision, and so on. Focus factories and cells by nature focus affiliated activities, information, and physical production, which allows for accurate and straightforward cost tracking. Considering the engine manufacturing factory model as an example will illustrate these points.

As shown in Figure 11.3, each cell—including the assembly line—is designated as a department. The differences between traditional departments and "lean" departments are significant. First, one-piece flow manufacturing is utilized in each cell and

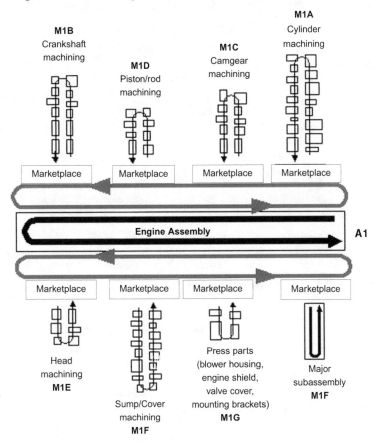

Figure 11.3 Engine manufacturing factory

is balanced to takt time. Second, all activities are contained within the cell; therefore, tracking cost is directly associated to each cell (each part or part family) and is easy and straightforward. The spreadsheet shown in Figure 11.2 is used to capture the costs associated with each cell. Tracking can now be easily done on a daily, weekly, monthly, and yearly basis.

COST COMPARISONS

Important decisions are made from the cost information of parts or products. Having accurate cost information is the best method for doing comparisons of products for internal and external manufacturing decisions. One of the main factors involved in a "make or buy" or a "continue to make or buy" decision-making situation is the cost of the part or product family. Accurate costs are essential to be able to make the proper decision. Traditional cost-accounting methods simply fail to give accurate costs for manufactured products. The lean methods deliver this information accurately, easily, and understandably. Dr. Dhavale states:

> Information about manufacturing costs of products is very useful but that information, generally speaking, has been rather inaccurate and unreliable. The inaccuracy in product cost information is due to the fact that only some costs (i.e., direct costs) of making a unit can be relatively easily identified with the unit. Others, indirect manufacturing costs, cannot be traced easily to units yet somehow must be allocated to units to find the cost of manufacturing. Although various procedures have been devised, allocation can be arbitrary and subjective, so the accuracy of manufacturing costs that include this arbitrarily assigned component is questionable.[2]

Internal cost comparisons can also help manufacturers make good decisions. Having accurate information on cost components like tooling, for example, helps managers and engineers discover improvements on processes and support functions. For instance, being able to compare the tooling costs and performance of machining an engine piston provides managers and engineers the information they need to implement improvements in the best manner.

Not only does this type of cost information contribute to good decision making but it also provides a straightforward language that all employees can understand. With the new methods, operators can know, for example, that the tooling they use to machine the piston, described here, costs seven cents per piston as opposed to eleven cents. This information is accurate and tangible to the operators involved. Having understandable information of this nature is important in training shop employees to help drive the improvements forward. Dr. Dileep Dhavale also references many of the management uses of accurate cost information:

> In competitive markets, market forces determine prices. Nonetheless, cost information is useful in determining product profitability margins and various tactical and strategic options.

Knowledge of manufacturing costs is essential to estimate future cash flows from a new investment.

Favorable or unfavorable cost impact of decisions regarding whether to make or buy, continue or discontinue production, sell or process further.

Knowledge of manufacturing cost is necessary to determine whether a company can, with its existing cost structure, manufacture a product and obtain the necessary return on investment.[3]

KAIZEN BY ACCOUNTING

In *Harvard Business Review*, Toshiro Hiromoto states: "A central principle that seems to guide management accounting in Japan [is] that accounting policies should be subservient to corporate strategy, not independent of it."[4]

Since cost and management accounting's purpose is to help managers control and improve the business or operation, using the lean methods described in this section produces accurate and simple information about the cost of products. This information becomes a powerful and useful tool for targeting improvements or *kaizen*. Dr. Cooper states:

By reporting product costs, product costing systems identify products that are either unprofitable or at risk of becoming unprofitable. Once these products are identified, *kaizen* costing is put into action ... *Kaizen costing* is continuous improvement applied to cost reduction in the manufacturing stage of a product's life. While it is through *kaizen* costing that the costs of existing products are reduced, *kaizen* systems do more than just reduce costs, they also increase the quality of products and the safety of production processes.[5]

Kaizen costing does not concern itself with product design, focusing instead on the production process related either to a given product or to the processes in general.[6]

Kaizen is key to creating flow and maintaining the pursuit of perfection.[7] All employees play a role in discovering and implementing *kaizen*. Dr. Yasuhiro Monden emphasizes this point by noting that "people in every level of the plant are involved in attaining the kaizen cost target. Thus, *people involvement* is very important in Japanese companies for executing target costing as well as kaizen costing."[8]

With the above methods for cost and managerial accounting, prioritization of *kaizen* activities can be improved. Resources are always an issue for companies when they deploy allocations for improvement activities. Knowing where the most effective impact is located will allow for the best deployment of resources against the highest impact from a cost or a change-in-cost standpoint. Improvements are almost always evident, especially in a company practicing lean principles. Knowing which of the improvements are the most critical to the company's cost is important in targeting and prioritizing the best cost-reduction activities. Even Toyota's *kaizen* efforts are targets for cost reduction. The model Toyota uses (see Figure 11.4) to represent their Toyota Production System (TPS) is best quality, lowest cost, and shortest lead

Figure 11.4 Model for the Toyota Production System (TPS)

time through shortening the production flow by eliminating waste through cost reduction. This aim of TPS is supported by the physical operation, just-in-time (JIT) production (or flow), and *jidoka* and is set up on a foundation of operational stability.

According to Monden, the TPS uses *kaizen* to continually pursue and implement the physical attributes exemplified by the system model in Figure 11.4. *Kaizen* improves and institutes these features and methods and *kaizen* costing ties the improvements to cost targets. Dr. Monden opines:

> This system requires small lot sizes for certain parts—in other words, small-lot or one-piece flow production and corresponding small-lot or one-piece conveyance. However, a factory cannot carry out small-lot production unless it first manages to shorten changeover (retooling) times, nor can it achieve one-piece flow production without multi-process handling by each operator.
>
> By combining standard operations appropriately, all work required to produce one product unit can be made to fit within the product's takt time.... JIT production also depends upon 100 percent nondefective production. The method for achieving zero defects is called "autonomation" (a method for automatically handling abnormalities).[9]

Kaizen and cost information are used in tandem in order to drive improvement. Although most of the *kaizen* objectives are based on physical attributes (throughput time, productivity, and so on), the lean firm must have a grasp on its cost in order to understand the cost-reduction level obtained by the improvement activity. This information is key for planning purposes and resource deployment. Monden emphasizes the tie between the physical lean operation and *kaizen* cost improvements:

> The kaizen cost target is achieved by daily kaizen activities. The JIT production system also intends to reduce various wastes in the plant by these daily activities. Therefore, kaizen costing and the JIT production system closely related with each other.[10]

> Managers at each organizational level determines polices and means to attain the kaizen cost target in their department. Their policies and means are mostly non-monetary measures, but the purpose is to realize the kaizen cost targets.[11]

COSTING: *KAIZEN* AND TARGET

Although target costing is out of the scope of this book, it will be briefly discussed to contribute to developing the context in which *kaizen* costing is used. Monden continues: "Target costing is the system to support the cost reduction process in the development and design phase of an entirely new model, a full model change, or a minor model change."[12] And in order to understand the motive for target costing, the price-cost equation will be reviewed; in the case of this book, it is referred to as the *lean cost equation.*

The Lean Cost Equation

According to Charles Sorensen, in his book *My Forty Years with Ford*, the method Henry Ford used to set prices for the Model T is an interesting comparison to the target-costing practice acclaimed by Toyota. In the book *Kanban: Just-In-Time at Toyota*, an explanation of Toyota's philosophy on price and cost is given by the following equation:

$$\text{Profit} = \text{Selling Price} - \text{Cost}$$

The market sets the selling price and is not controlled by the manufacturing company. The cost is subtracted from the selling price and what is left over is the profit. The manufacturing company has control over the cost and not the selling price; therefore, the company must work to reduce costs, or eliminate waste, in order to improve profits.

This philosophy directly contrasts with the typical approach given in the following equation:

$$\text{Selling Price} = \text{Cost} + \text{Profit}$$

In this equation, the selling price is determined by taking a company's cost and adding the "desired" profit.[13]

Kanban: Just-In-Time at Toyota also includes the "Sayings of Ohno," which reinforce the points given in the book. The "Sayings of Ohno" include the following:

- Don't confuse "value" with "price."
- When a consumer buys a product, he does so because that product has a certain value to him.
- The cost is up, so you raise your prices! Don't take such an easy way out. It cannot be done. If you raise your price but the value remains the same, you will quickly lose your customer.[14]

Toyota sets a target price that the market will support and then drives their cost to meet that target through design, tooling, and production: right designing.

Shigeo Shingo also confirms and discusses the purpose of the lean cost equation approach.[15] Understanding this approach to cost is key to successful implementation of lean methods and philosophy. This is why both Ohno and Shingo stressed it and spent time discussing it in the context of their writings.

Henry Ford's Cost-Price Equation

According to Charles Sorensen, Henry Ford used nearly the same philosophy to set prices that Toyota uses today.[16] Sorensen writes:

[Henry] Ford held that if the price is right the cost will take care of itself. Price first, then cost, was a paradox. It ran counter to prevailing business practice, but Ford made it work.

We first reduced the price to a point where we thought the most sales would result; then we went ahead and tried to meet that price. What use is it to know the cost if it says you cannot manufacture at a price which the article can be sold?[17]

The traditional cost equation, Selling Price = Cost + Profit, fails to address "*how* to raise revenue and *how* to cut cost," according to Dr. H. Thomas Johnson and Anders Bröms. They write:[18]

The problem caused by using accounting profit and loss information to direct and control a natural living system is evident if one examines the behavior implied by the conventional accounting equation for profit.[19]

Johnson and Bröms continue:

Managerial thinking that accepts this conventional accounting equation sees the company as consisting of separate parts, and treats each part only as an independent object … addition and subtraction signs alone are used to connect parts of this system. No other relationships are acknowledged.[20]

This view of the price-cost equation is typical of the lean enterprise and is the very belief Henry Ford and the Ford Motor Company held in the days of Highland Park and the Model T. There is an important connection that can be made between Dr. Johnson and Bröms's theme and the action undertaken by Ford's engineers at

Highland Park. Dr. Johnson and Bröms tell us that "managers who perceive companies as actual living systems deem it impossible to enhance the overall profit of an organization simply by removing or adding amounts of revenue or cost."[21] Ford's engineers innovated, developed, and implemented flow manufacturing, a system that linked all discreet processes that make up manufacturing; rapidly processed and moved components from raw materials to final products to meet the ever-growing customer demand; and drastically reduced costs to meet the ever-falling price.[22] The early Ford Motor Company did exactly what Dr. Johnson and Bröms describe—they emulated a living system, just as the TPS was to do.

The Cost-Price Equation Today and Yesterday

Orest Fiume agrees with the obsolescence of the traditional cost-price equation: "Target costing recognizes the reality that the old cost-plus method of pricing died many decades ago. The market sets the price. Instead of Cost + Profit = Selling Price, the current reality is Selling Price − Cost = Profit."[23] Many recognize Fiume and Toyota's notion as a new view of the cost-price equation, or at least a modern industrial viewpoint, but, in fact, this is not the case.

Charles Knoeppel, one of the early twentieth-century engineering and management thinkers and developers and a contemporary of Alexander Hamilton Church, recognized the importance of the market—not a company's cost—in determining price. He writes: "In the last analysis cost does not govern price. Cost is merely an expression of outlay. What one can get for his product in the open market is distinctly another matter. The formula, cost plus profit equals price, many times becomes price plus loss equals cost. Competition has a real voice in saying what the price will be."[24]

Brian Maskell continues Knoeppel's point fifty-eight years later:

> The reason for this is that world-wide competition has made the prices of a wider range of products more market-driven than cost-driven. Few companies have the luxury of setting prices according to an acceptable margin above product costs.
>
> For the majority of manufacturers, prices are established by market decision rather than by analysis of costs.... The trend is to establish acceptable manufacturing costs based on the required market price.[25]

In his 1960 thesis, Phillip Fess reviews the role of cost in setting prices. In his writing, it is obvious that this issue with the cost-price equation has been an ongoing struggle for industry throughout the years:

> There is great disagreement among economists and other businessmen as to the role of cost in this area of establishing selling price. Some argued that cost has an affect on the selling price; some have even stated the reverse proposition that selling price affects cost; while others have set forth the notion that costs have little effect on selling price.[26]

Fess continues:

> The point of intersection of the two forces of supply and demand determines the market price for a product. The individual firm, then, does not determine selling price because selling price is determined by the total forces of supply and demand.[27]

In addition, Fess stresses that "the going concern must concentrate on making the maximum profit at the selling price as determined by the market forces of supply and demand."[28]

It also becomes obvious that the approach to the cost-price equation is key in determining how a firm views its method of using cost information and the methods that support and develop this information. It is about *thinking* and *understanding*.

The Cost-Price Equation and Lean Thinking

As shown in the previous section, the cost-price equation is—like most ideas and concepts proposed and presented in this book—about a different way of *thinking*. Many times these unique views are not new; in fact, many were developed at the same time several of today's traditional business thought processes were originally developed. Taiichi Ohno writes:

> At Toyota, as in all manufacturing industries, profit can be obtained only by reducing costs. When we apply the cost principle *selling price = profit + actual cost*, we make the consumer responsible for every cost. This principle has no place in today's competitive automobile industry.
>
> Our products are scrutinized by cool-headed consumers in free, competitive markets where the manufacturing cost of a product is of no consequence.[29]

Ohno points out that a key to successfully achieving the cost-price equation proposed by Toyota—and in this book—is that a firm must execute a (limited) production system following the guideline, "Make only what you can sell."[30]

Cost and Price

In the end, obtaining a different view of the cost-price equation leads a firm to a different way of thinking, which, in turn, changes its actions. From a leadership perspective, Ohno's and Ford's views of the cost-price equation directed their firms in a very customer-focused way.

This change in thinking clearly guided Toyota and the early Ford Motor Company in a unique direction that allowed them to drive costs out of their products. This concept is the best way to guide a firm to achieve superior prices (low and competitive via their costs) in the open market.

Many dynamics play a role in pricing in a free market and this discussion is beyond the scope of this book. But cost can be one of the many factors that impact market prices. Its level of impact will vary greatly—again, depending on many factors and dynamics within the marketplace. Perhaps Fess in his 1960 thesis states this factor best and illustrates how the cost-price equation is a dynamic factor itself. He writes: "Costs influence prices but do not control them.... Goods sell for what buyers think they are worth."[31]

Target Costing

Target costing targets are developed by establishing a target selling price based on what the market will accept. The firm specifies a target profit margin based on their own strategic plans and projections. The difference between the target selling price and target margin is the target cost. The target cost is then used to drive all engineers and departments involved with the design phase. Much interaction and feedback must happen during this cycle to ensure that the target cost of each component is reached and the final product meets the goal.[32] What target costing focuses on is the reduction of product costs during the design stage in order to meet target margins using a selling price determined by the market. It is strictly a process of the design procedure.[33]

Another interesting point about target costing is that although it is part of the cost-management system it has nothing to do with accounting in the traditional sense. Fiume restates Michiharu Sakuri's view of target costing as "a cost-planning tool used for controlling design specifications and production techniques. Therefore it is oriented much more towards management and engineering rather than accounting."[34] Monden points out: "Target costing and kaizen costing, when linked together, constitute the total cost management system of Japanese companies. 'Total' cost management in this context implies cost management in all phases of product life. The concept of total cost management also comes from total involvement of all people in all departments companywide."[35]

Kaizen Costing

Kaizen costing is focused on the production stage of the product and targets— maintaining costs or preferably further reducing costs. Although *kaizen* costing is meant to maintain and reduce costs, it is targeted toward improving the physical attributes of the operation. These attributes encompass a firm's factory floor–level *kaizen* activities.[36] These shop-floor activities are centered on establishing flow, improving flow, reducing WIP, and increasing productivity. Any improvement in lean methods and techniques supports *kaizen* and the *kaizen* costing process (see Figure 2.5).

Kaizen costing is, in a sense, a continuation of the cost-management system, which starts with target costing during the design phase and continues with *kaizen* costing during the production phase. *Kaizen* costing, which is manifested in *kaizen* activities, continually reduces product costs in manufacturing. Not only does *kaizen* reduce costs but it is also a method that ensures MBM. It is focused on improving the means by which products are manufactured. Therefore, the MBM of the *MBM* process reinforces Dr. Steven Spear's Rules-in-Use and, in turn, reduces product cost.

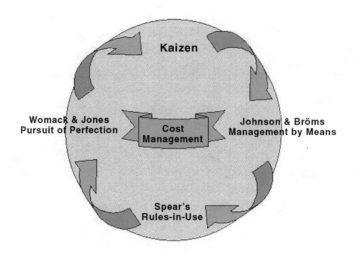

Figure 11.5 Continually and mutually supporting cycle

This mutually supporting process is never ending in a lean enterprise and in turn supports James Womack and Daniel Jones's pursuit of perfection. This continually and mutually supporting cycle is illustrated in Figure 11.5. Cost management supplies information to support the cycle.

COST MANAGEMENT AND STRATEGY

In the New World of lean accounting, traditional cost and managerial accounting vanishes and cost management rises to support operations. Managers will view it in a favorable manner. Operation managers and supervisors loathe traditional methods because of the monthly verbal beatings they receive due to variances. Not only is the information inaccurate and misleading but the managers are also expected to justify each variance. Such a monthly ritual is debilitating because in most cases they have no idea what causes variances. The situation has led to operational managers manipulating information and figures to keep the monthly beatings to a minimum.[37]

The unfortunate conclusion to this situation is a loss of the purpose, or relevance, of cost and management accounting, which should be to help control and improve the business or operation and, it might be added, to do it in an easy and understandable manner. Using lean cost-management methods creates a simplified and straightforward method, which not only is easy and understandable to the managers and supervisors but is also easy and understandable to all employees. Lean cost-management methods create a condition where all employees contribute to, understand, and use the same information to drive their activities for the operations. Maskell supports this view and states, "It is vital that everyone throughout the company is using the same information, derived directly from the operational data."[38] This unified effort is incredibly powerful, especially when companies are always attempting to get employees working toward the same high-level goals. Alignment of direction is critical to establishing a world-class company in today's value-focused and customer-driven market. According to Monden:

> The logic behind this approach to existing products is simple: If all of the company's existing products can be turned into moneymakers, then the company as a whole will surely be profitable.
>
> The rule of thumb for kaizen of existing products is also simple: Clarify the various causes of poor profitability and then make improvements to eliminate the causes.[39]

Figure 11.6 illustrates the purpose of a company's mission statement: aligning all employees toward a common goal. A mission statement's purpose is to create a guideline to achieving a common goal.

More important than having a mission statement is having a system or structure that allows and even directs all employees to function in a manner in keeping with a common goal or goals. This system or structure becomes the company's infrastructure and/or culture. It includes the development of procedures and methods that must be followed very strictly. The advantage of this strategic procedure is the use of *kaizen* to constantly develop and implement improved standard procedures. According to Dr. Steven Spear and H. Kent Bowen, that is the "paradox of the system ... that activities, connections, and production flows in a Toyota factory are rigidly scripted, yet at the same time Toyota's operations are enormously flexible and adaptable."[40]

Maskell observes: "If the strategy is right and the production personnel are continuously achieving and improving upon clearly defined goals, then the financial aspects will take care of themselves."[41] Maskell's observation is shared by many

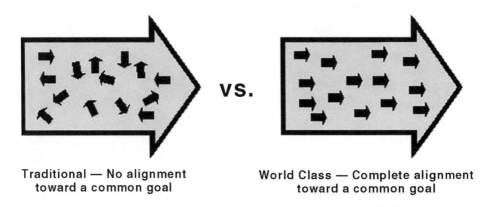

Traditional — No alignment
toward a common goal

World Class — Complete alignment
toward a common goal

Figure 11.6 Tactical and strategic alignment

observers of Toyota, like Dr. Johnson, Dr. Liker, and Dr. Womack, as well as the leadership within Toyota.

Having a cost and managerial accounting system that contributes to improvements and standard procedures is important. It must be simple, accurate, and understandable to everyone. The lean cost-management system accomplishes this because of its straightforward information that provides the same usable information to everyone in the company. Richard Schonberger notes: "No measurement system is worth much unless it ties closely to overall business success."[42]

Dr. Johnson invokes the axiom that what a company measures is what will drive its employees to achieve. He also goes on to say that implementing new measures will not develop new systems and functions, which, as described in this chapter, are essential to creating and establishing a lean enterprise.[43] People must be prepared with the knowledge, skills, and experience to design, implement, and drive the lean system throughout their firms. This must include people at every level of the enterprise. It must become more than using the right measures, more than creating the right strategy, and even more than using the right tools and methods. It must be everything working together and supporting each aspect, phase, principle, and method. People are the central figure in creating and achieving this enterprise. As Dr. Johnson observes, only leadership can nurture the necessary spirit to change. He writes: "A company first must be filled with the spirit of employee-driven customer service. That spirit comes from forceful leadership, not from tinkering with performance measures or management accounting information."[44]

NOTES

1. Maskell, *Making the Numbers Count*, 14.
2. Dhavale, *Management Accounting Issues*, 185.
3. Ibid., 186.
4. Hiromoto, "Another Hidden Edge," 26.
5. Cooper, *When Lean Enterprises Collide*, 239.
6. Ibid., 240.
7. Perfection is the fifth principle in Womack and Jones's book *Lean Thinking*.
8. Monden, *Toyota Management System*, 51.
9. Monden, *Cost Reduction Systems*, 311, 313.
10. Monden, *Toyota Management System*, 47.
11. Ibid., 48.
12. Monden, *Toyota Management System*, 30.
13. Japan Management Association, ed., *Kanban*, 4–7.
14. Ibid., 5.
15. Shingo, *Non-Stock Production*, 25–26; and Shingo, *A Study of the Toyota Production System*, 75–76.
16. Charles Sorensen became Henry Ford's main "production man" or, by today's

terms, head production engineer. He met Henry Ford in 1901, went to work for Ford as a pattern maker in 1905, and resigned from the Ford Motor Company in 1944. See Sorensen, *My Forty Years with Ford*, inside of back book cover.

17. Ibid., 143.
18. Johnson and Bröms, 2000, *Profit beyond Measure*, 220.
19. Ibid., 219.
20. Ibid., 220.
21. Ibid., 221.
22. The Model T was introduced in 1908 at a price of eight hundred and fifty dollars (Ford began manufacturing the Model T in the Piquette Avenue plant prior to the Highland Park plant) and by 1916 it was selling for a price of three hundred and sixty dollars. Nevins and Hill, *Ford*, 646–47.
23. Fiume, "Lean Accounting and Finance," 9.
24. Knoeppel, *Profit Engineering*, 195.
25. Maskell, *Performance Measurement*, 48–49.
26. Fess, "The Theory and Application of Direct Costing," 126.
27. Ibid., 127.
28. Ibid., 128.
29. Ohno, *Toyota Production System*, 8–9. Ohno also provides a detailed explanation of what the three versions of the cost-price equation mean in Ohno, "Arithmetic's Blind Spot," 20–24.
30. Ohno, "Arithmetic's Blind Spot," 30.
31. Fess, "The Theory and Application of Direct Costing," 204. Fess is quoting Geer, "Cost Factors in Price-Making—Part I," 45. Fess continues the discussion on page 204 and 205 of his thesis.
32. Hiromoto, "Another Hidden Edge," 24.
33. Cooper, *When Lean Enterprises Collide*, 135–37.
34. Fiume, "Lean Accounting and Finance," 9.
35. Monden, *Toyota Management System*, 30.
36. Monden, *Cost Reduction Systems*, 289.
37. Maskell, *Making the Numbers Count*, 23.
38. Maskell and Baggaley, "Lean Management Accounting."
39. Monden, *Cost Reduction Systems*, 327.
40. Spear and Bowen, "Decoding the DNA of the Toyota Production System," 97.
41. Maskell, *Performance Measurement*, 24.
42. Schonberger, *Let's Fix It!*, 89.
43. Johnson, *Relevance Regained*, 105.
44. Ibid.

12

TEAMWORK

A major area of misunderstanding in the lean enterprise is teamwork. The vast majority of companies working on a lean transformation completely misstep and misconstrue the design and implementation of teamwork. Teamwork relates to the design element of a lean enterprise because it is a key element in becoming a successful lean manufacturer, but it is actually more of a result of lean implementation than it is a supporter of lean. Most companies use "teams" as a method of constructing or designing a lean enterprise. Implementing teams is not the best route to become lean. Although this statement may seem to go completely against common lean thought, its reasoning will be discussed in detail as it is the most misinterpreted concept of the lean enterprise.

A TEAM TO RULE ALL

Teamwork is not directly designed in a successful lean environment. It is a result of other aspects of a well-designed lean manufacturer. Most companies spend much or most of their lean-implementation time establishing teams: teams for manufacturing lines, teams for projects, team for decisions, teams for anything and everything.

Team empowerment in most companies too often can be defined as "if you don't know where you are going you will probably get there." The message and reality is that companies want the team to decide on the direction a company will go how it will get there. This is a grave mistake. This version of empowerment is unfortunately the standard, but it does virtually nothing to move a firm to become lean. Everyone feels warm and fuzzy, but feeling warm and fuzzy and having complete control of the direction of a company and how it gets there get a team nowhere. Unless nowhere is where a company would like to get, this is a dangerous route. The warm and fuzzy empowerment mode is actually a deceptive stepchild of MBR. This is because a firm is simply telling the team, "We want you to achieve the result, now you figure out how to achieve it." This is MBR.

To move a team into a management-by-means (MBM), successful lean environment, a firm must have the team's focus on the customer needs (which is the direction), and it must enforce the use of basic methods (how the team will get there). Now it is up to the team to develop and implement the details.

To further understand this situation, consider the following example: the team is responsible for developing and implementing a manufacturing line or cell to machine crankshafts. The customer needs are manifested in the part drawing and volume requirements. (This is assuming the given product, a crankshaft, exists and has a specific customer demand.) The direction is the specific crankshaft specifications (per the part drawing) and the takt time. The team does not decide on this information—the customer does. Other constraints exist for the team in a true lean environment. The manufacturing line must maintain one-piece flow and meet the other requirements for a right designed machine tool or process (see Chapter 10). The team is restricted to these requirements and constraints, but the details of deciding how the they will reach their destination is where they use their ideas, knowledge, and experience to put the manufacturing line together. Teams are not a freewheeling entity that has the power to decide everything or even most things. Teams must have specific purposes and specific constraints to be successful in the lean enterprise.

Another issue present when firms are beginning their lean transformation is that the people on the team have little or no experience in lean design, methods, techniques, or principles. This adds to the misdirection. Not only do the teams have no—or not enough—design constraints placed on them (the management mentality is that they are the team and can decide what is best) but they also do not have the knowledge or experience to guide them to correctly design a lean attribute—a cell, pull system, or whatever. These are the reasons so many companies cannot design good and robust cells, marketplaces, or material-handling systems and why they ultimately do not design and develop true flow manufacturing. Jamie Flinchbaugh of the Lean Learning Center confirms this. He writes: "The biggest problem is when people are given the authority to make decisions without any guidance or skills in *how* to make them."[1]

TEAMS AND THE SUPERVISOR AT TOYOTA

In Dr. Jeffrey Liker's book *The Toyota Way*, Sam Heltman,[2] senior vice president of administration for Toyota Motor Manufacturing North America, states that "respect for people means respect for the mind and capability."[3] Mr. Heltman continues: "Americans think teamwork is about you liking me and I liking you. Mutual respect and trust means I trust and respect that you will do your job so that we are successful as a company. It does not mean we just love each other."[4] Liker explains the statement:

> The lesson was clear: don't implement work teams before you do the hard work of implementing the system and culture to support them."[5]

"Empowering" employees too quickly when setting up the facility can be premature. Until individuals and teams really understand the Toyota Way and TPS, they are not in a position to be empowered.[6]

Even today at Toyota, empowerment manifests itself in the leadership of the supervisor (team or group leader at Toyota), and standard work is the essence of their work, as stated in their self-published booklet on the Toyota Production System (TPS). In the booklet, *kaizen* is referenced as "the lifeblood of standardized work":

> Standardized work is *a tool for maintaining productivity, quality, and safety* at high levels. It provides a consistent framework for performing work at the designated takt time and for illuminating opportunities for making improvements in work procedures.
>
> Standardized work provides details, step-by-step guidelines for every job in the Toyota Production System. Team Leaders determine the most efficient working sequence. With team members, they make continuing improvements kaizen—in that sequence. Kaizen thus begets new patterns of standardized work.[7]
>
> Kaizen furnishes the dynamism of continuing improvement and very human motivation of encouraging individuals to take part in designing and managing their own jobs. Kaizen improvements in standardized work help maximize productivity at every worksite.[8]

And where did the practice method come from that led to this action? Conceptually it came from Kiichiro Toyoda, but as an applicable method it came from Training Within Industry (TWI). The original Job Methods training manual, which was deployed at Toyota after World War II, declares that "improved job methods give good work—because production is increased by eliminating unnecessary parts of the job—and making the necessary parts easier and safer to do."[9] It also urges the reader to "remember there will always a better way. Keep searching for further improvements."[10]

The supervisor is the cornerstone to their teamwork system and the standard work that leverages employees as a fulfillment to their "respect for people." The supervisor is put squarely in charge of the team and has responsibility to fulfill the needs that are the critical interface of management and employee. The Japan Management Association states:

> There are several necessary conditions for performing the task of supervisor adequately.
>
> The first is always to *observe what is going on in the workplace*. If a supervisor does not visit the line and shows no interest in what is going on out there, that alone marks him as a failure; with this he is saying that he cannot check the standards which he himself has established. Of course, he will not be able to differentiate between what is normal and what is abnormal. How can he be expected to engage in improvement activities?

The second is to *control and guide his subordinates well*. This means to let them do what he wants them to do and train them toward that end. It is not to make the subordinates feel good, or even to defer to them. That is not a good way to establish a good human relationship. One of the subordinates will one day become his successor as supervisor. He must teach them, train them and in the end make them worthy of becoming supervisor. Only in this way can the present supervisor become the true "father" to all.

The supervisor must be able to tell his subordinates when to stop and when to start. That ability to guide and control is an essential part of being a supervisor.

The third necessary condition is to *have a broad perspective and render judgment beneficial to the company as a whole*. No matter how effective a step may be in improving one's process, if that step is going to affect the preceding process or the subsequent process adversely, or to necessitate sending difficult work to outside contractors, then it cannot be considered a step toward improvement.

Every supervisor of a line must consider himself the manager of the line. He must have a broad perspective, ready to think in terms of the company's overall benefit.

After having done standardization and improvement, a supervisor who can say "please pull me out of this job" is by far the best supervisor. He has "trained" the line so it can move without him.[11]

LEARNING TO SEE THE TEAM

Mike Rother, author of *Learning to See* and *Creating Continuous Flow*, has written some vital observations about companies misusing the concept of teams in their lean efforts. He notes: "Just trying to establish teams is unlikely to do much for introducing lean manufacturing."[12] Rother stresses the point made in the section "Teams and the Supervisor at Toyota": teams are not the key to transforming to a lean enterprise. Good flow design and right designing are the key to successful transformation. And by implementing good flow design and techniques, teams are enabled to function to help support the flow environment. Rother notes the following:

> Good teamwork on the shop floor does take training and development, but it is the act of developing a lean material flow, moving away from batch-and-push production, that creates both a need and an environment for teams. A lean flow couples islands of work together and creates internal customer/ supplier relationships. Continuous flow makes individual processing steps dependent on one another. Producing only to customer requirements takes out buffers and demands attention to making production and delivering high quality. These types of changes lay the groundwork for individuals to become part of groups.[13]

Rother continues his analysis by taking the issue a step further. He points out that even training teams will not lead to a lean implementation because the change in system design is so much more fundamental. What must be done is a breaking down and redesigning of the operational system or the business itself: a breaking down of traditional thinking, or thinking in terms of batch production. This is the responsibility of management and engineering. Rother asserts:

> There is an implicit belief floating around that if we train our shop floor operators and supervisors in lean concepts and practices they will get excited about them and the concepts and practices will be adopted. This thinking is probably related to the attractive notion of "self-directed work teams" who drive change from the bottom up. It is pure bunk.
>
> Communication will not result in the adoption of lean manufacturing. The problems with mass production are fundamental, and shop-floor operators and supervisors are simply not in a position to change them. Shop-floor personnel have a perspective that naturally emphasizes their own work area, while lean manufacturing concerns itself with the entire production flow, or the "production system." Operators are also busy, making a new part every 60 seconds or so. Asking operators to improve when the system is the problem generally just causes people to work harder, faster, and longer, which is even encouraged by our tradition of rewarding overproduction. Expecting the shop-floor personnel to lead the lean charge results in suboptimization at best. More likely, you'll achieve little change but lots of resentment.
>
> Shop-floor personnel work within the prevailing production system and it is management's responsibility to understand and improve that system.[14]

Rother, in a more recent article, also reflects on the lack of "direction" in most organizations and their lack of applying resources to their lean efforts. He correlates this issue with MBR as well:[15]

> Having just a few people in the organization involved in making improvements will not be sufficient for reaching the ideal state. The whole organization needs to be working on that. Yet, on the other hand, just "setting goals and getting out of the way" (MBO) will not get us to the ideal state either. Traditional, late 20th century western concepts of "employee empowerment" and "Self Directed Work Teams" do not result in much improvement, and there is too little direction.[16]

TEAMS AND CELL DESIGN

Teams in the manufacturing operation for a lean enterprise normally revolve around a value stream or, more specifically, around a manufacturing cell. The team members are generally the operators that run the line or cell and their immediate frontline supervisors (in many lean environments the person in the frontline supervisory role may called a variety of things, such as team leader, group leader, facilitator, cell leader, and so on). Again, the role of operators and the frontline supervisor is usually misinterpreted and misapplied by most companies going through a lean transformation.

The role of any team—the group of operators and their frontline supervisor—in this situation must be reviewed in detail in order to understand how this team functions as part of the lean operation. As previously discussed, most companies misapply and misunderstand the manufacturing team's role and function in daily operation as well as in transformation. Recall, in Chapter 10 on right designing, the emphasis on and discussion of the role of engineers and management in the design and implementation of the physical lean operation. As Rother noted, the operators are, and should be, busy trying to manufacture product via standard operations and within the customer-based takt time.

Many companies going through a lean transformation stress the importance of having operators and their frontline supervisor taking part and having "buy-in" for the new cell. This buy-in and input is important in achievement of cooperation and success as the physical transformation moves forward, but again, recall the points made by Rother and the section "A Team to Rule All" in this chapter. Designing the manufacturing cell and the processes is not the role of the manufacturing team. This statement goes against the common view of lean transformations. The manufacturing team plays a significant role and has input into the design and function, but this is not their primary role. The engineering staff must become experienced and skilled in this role or redesigning and reengineering will continue perpetually.

Most companies are so strapped for engineering resources and are also completely unwilling to take the time actually needed to go through the lean transformation that they shove the manufacturing team into the role of manufacturing engineers, which is a role they are unprepared and untrained for. The unwillingness and misunderstanding of most companies to allow for a reasonable amount of time to move through a lean transformation is most likely one of the main reasons why companies are never able to move past the lean hinterlands (see Figure 10.1).

Companies are typically interested in "getting things done," not getting things done correctly. This attitude is a result of MBR. Most companies going through a lean transformation get a lot done but never actually get anything accomplished, nor do they establish true one-piece flow and robust supporting functions. Companies must focus on MBM, drop MBR, and accomplished things correctly. Rother emphasizes this in his article "Do You Really Have Continuous Flow in Assembly?" Rother writes the following:

> A fake painting looks genuine to the untrained eye, but it is usually worth very little. It is exactly the same with fake flow in your assembly processes.
>   When we see this pattern, we know that the benefits of cellular manufacturing are not being achieved. Almost any grouping of machines that performs processing steps in a sequence is labeled a cell. But in most cells we see no continuous flow, which is really what makes a cell a cell.[17]

The scenario Rother describes often results when a manufacturing team has control of the design of the flow cell. The team does not understand what true lean flow is, and it is not the role of the team to design a manufacturing line to accomplish flow. Over time, however, a team can understand true flow and contribute strongly and positively to its implementation.

TEAMS AND DAILY OPERATIONS

If the team's role is not designing manufacturing cells, what is its role and function? If books and articles about Toyota are examined, they will refer to the importance of teamwork. Teamwork is an important aspect of the lean operation. Even Taiichi Ohno stressed the importance of teamwork, but he also explains how design plays its role within the team. Ohno uses a sports team analogy to explain: "Managers and supervisors in a manufacturing plant are like the team manager and the batting, base, and field coaches. A strong baseball team has mastered the plays; the players can meet any situation with coordinated action. In manufacturing, the production team that has mastered the just-in-time system is exactly like a baseball team that plays well together."[18]

Ohno's analogy refers to the managers and supervisors as the system decision makers, and the production team features the players who execute the activities. The production team must master the skills and standard operations and apply them to the operation. The production team learns the methods needed to operate the system while the managers and supervisors direct the function of the system. The production team executes their skills as a function of the design of the system. That is, the system is designed with specific standard operations to fulfill its requirements. This is also the point that Dr. Steven Spear illustrates in his Rules-in-Use discussed in Chapter 4.

The Bucket Brigade

To further illustrate the relationship between the design of the system and teamwork, a bucket brigade analogy will be used. Often it happens that flooding occurs in cities and towns along major waterways. When this type of event occurs, the TV news will often show townsfolk setting up bucket brigades to move and stack sandbags as temporary levees to prevent the water entering areas that contain houses and building structures that the rising water would damage.

As the citizens of the threatened town line up to form the bucket brigade and deposit sand bags, they begin a continuous flow of sandbags—passing one at a time (one-piece flow) in a smooth, flowing manner until the bag reaches the person who stacks the bag on the growing levee. This activity moves the product (sandbags) quickly and smoothly. The townsfolk become an efficient, smoothly flowing operation—an effective team. Excellent teamwork is created by this situation, and if they work well enough, they prevent much of the potential damage the flood may bring.

The point of this example is that the people did, in fact, create a very effective team. But they achieved this not by any desire for teamwork even though they all did have a strong unifying motivation to build the levee: saving their town. More importantly, they accomplish their task simply because by design the bucket brigade would tolerate nothing less in order to function. By its design, the bucket brigade allowed the citizens to move sandbags quickly and efficiently to build the levee. Teamwork was the result of the properly designed bucket brigade. Just like the bucket brigade, a lean operation *by its design* will lead to an effective teamwork environment. The means (lean design) is the path to the results (teamwork); it is not the case that creating teams will result in a lean operation. As can be seen by the bucket brigade example, the flow line created the effective teamwork environment.

After the bucket brigade completes its task—building the levee—and achieves its higher-level goal—saving the town from flood damage—the townsfolk will be shown again on TV jubilantly congratulating each other on their team effort, which saved the town. They obviously have every right to celebrate their success. They will emphasize how everyone came together and worked hard as a team to save the town. These people deserve admiration. But their teamwork is not the true story of their success. To actually understand their success, the total details of the situation must be uncovered and understood. Their jubilation and teamwork, although very visible, is a result of the other aspects of their situation. The means and success to their triumph was a unified drive to save their town by working together using a well-designed method to complete their task. These two aspects allowed the townsfolk to achieve their goal via means, regardless of whether or not they were friendly neighbors, whether or not they voted for the same candidates for town officials, or whether or not they attended the same church. Teamwork in the lean enterprise must be the same, a result of a right designed system executed effectively. The warm and fuzzy feelings arrived later, as their success resulted through the actual design and function of their bucket brigade.

In the lean enterprise, the same situation should exist as the bucket brigade. The design of the operation or system will tolerate nothing less than properly functioning teamwork. In order for a right designed manufacturing cell to function, the correct product must be delivered at the correct time in the correct amount. A right designed cell enables teamwork to operate efficiently and effectively. Teamwork becomes the result of the design of the cell.

The History of Lean Teamwork

At Toyota or any right designed lean firm, the system or cell is designed not only so that teamwork must be used but also teamwork is reinforced by developing and training the team to understand how to apply good teamwork skills, or, in other words, people skills. This double-reinforced method creates the environment that Dr. Spear acknowledges in his Rules-in-Use. The TPS company designs their system to function properly and to focus on execution, MBM. The following are his rules:

[Focus on Design:]

- Rule 1 states: guides the design and performance of all individual activities.

- Rule 2 states: guides the design and operation of connections between activities.
- Rule 3 states: guides the design and operation of flow-paths.

[Focus on People Skills:]

- Rule 4 states: guides the improvement of individual value-adding activities.
- Rule 5 states: guides the improvement of connections between activities and of flow-paths.[19]

The first three rules are focused on the system design. The lean enterprise will design its operation or, more specifically, a manufacturing cell, by establishing an effective flowing system (or line) that has predetermined (or predesigned) parameters (function and operations, including product, information, and people flow). Such a method is the antithesis of most companies' methods, in which they setup production teams (operators) to do this.

Dr. Spear notes the following:

Certainly, the US-trained managers may not have learned how to look at activities, connections, and flow-paths and from these observations draw conclusions about the production system, the organization, and the organization's managers. Not knowing how to look at an organization as a system made up of components and interfaces, the US-trained managers may not have been capable of looking at the work being done to detect the Rules by which the organization and its parts were designed, operated, and improved.[20]

The forth and fifth rules are generally focused on the interface between the frontline supervisor and the operators or the team. The fourth rule focuses on training. Spear suggests: "Assign each person with a specific, capable teacher to supply training," and "train to improve though solving problems, primarily."[21] The fifth rule expands further the training aspect given in the fourth:

Rule-5 defines another role for people in supervisory positions, beyond that defined by Rule-4. By Rule-4, one critical role of a person in the managerial hierarchy is to teach those at the level immediately below them. By Rule-5, they are also responsible for managing the "interfaces" between the people immediately below them in the hierarchy and for managing and improving the flow-paths over which their group produces, delivers goods, services, and information. In this way, Rule-5 has a significant impact on the structure and dynamics of TPS organization. Rule-5 is the source of the "nested" aspect of a TPS organization's nested, modular structure.[22]

What is striking about the fourth and fifth rules is that they appear to be the evolution of what was known as the TWI program. TWI was deployed in Japan during the occupation of the Allied Forces after World War II. The program, which had been a huge success in the United States during the war effort, was brought to Japanese industry to help rebuild its industrial infrastructure and establish a democratic mindset within its industry. It was manifested in three programs called the "J" programs.[23]

If Dr. Spear's statement above is closely reviewed, the result of the three "J" programs from TWI is apparent. The "J" programs include Job Instruction, Job Relations, and Job Methods. All three were specifically targeted for the interface between the supervisor and operator. Job Instruction was focused on training the operator "to teach those at the level immediately below them." Job Relations were focused on the personal relationship between the supervisor and operator—"managing the 'interfaces' between the people immediately below them." And Job Methods focused on operational improvement—"managing and improving the flow-paths."[24] Dr. Spear reveals: "At Toyota's plants, I observed that the pathway for assistance was specified for each line-worker and extended through the hierarchical levels of the team leader, group leader, assistant manager, area manager, and production manager."[25]

To further understand the possible relationship between Dr. Spear's discovery of the Rules-in-Use and TWI, consider the following definition of each of the "J" programs:

1. *Job Instruction*—Teaching operators (and actually everyone at all levels) how to follow the current standard procedure (standard operations, again at all levels) exactly as designed and specified.

2. *Job Methods*—Focusing on improvement at the lowest level and close to the time, location, and person when the problem (or potential improvement) occurred.

3. *Job Relations*—Applying the "no-blame" resolution and focusing on finding the root-cause of the problem.[26]

Another strong link between Dr. Spear's Rules-in-Use and TWI is that both stress learning by doing. Throughout his writing, Dr. Spear emphasizes how Toyota underscores the learn-by-doing methodology by using it to teach other training needs.[27] Dr. Spear notes that "this guidance [for training process improvement] is largely experimental—putting trainees in a position to experience what they need to know rather than showing or explaining it."[28] He emphasizes that "problem solving ... was deliberately structured to foster skill development primarily, and process gains, secondarily."[29]

Dr. Spear continues:

> If individual learning to acquire a task-skill occurs through frequent practice that allows for repeated failure (or shortfalls) as intermediate steps to acquiring mastery of a subject or skill, then group learning on delegating responsibility and coordinating efforts must also be done through repeated practice that allows for repeated failures or shortfalls. However, if people conduct delegation and coordination experiments in isolation, then their own attempts to learn will create noise for those with whom they are connected.[30]

This practice was also a vital part of TWI: "One of the 'four essentials' upon which the training programs were built was: 'It must be built on the principle of demonstration and practice of "learning by doing," rather than on theory. (*The Training Within Industry Report: 1940–1945*, September 1945, 32)"[31]

How strongly has Toyota's teamwork and team interface remained linked with TWI? Concluding their "J" program training, supervisors were given small pocket-sized cards to carry. The cards listed the main principles and procedures deployed during the training sessions. Figure 12.1 shows a comparison between the original Job-Instruction cards given in 1944 and the Job-Instruction cards presently used at Toyota's Georgetown, Kentucky, operation.

The similarity of the cards is stunning. They are virtually identical. This is a testament to the impact TWI has had on teamwork in the lean enterprise as well as how a solid, robust methodology remains intact. Toyota's Georgetown operation also uses its own version of a Job Instruction training manual. Although their manual is scaled down from the original Job Instruction manuals in total content, it applies the same methodology and techniques.

In his article "Decoding the DNA of the Toyota Production System,"[32] Dr. Spear states that the TPS is simultaneously rigid and flexible. This observation of rigidity and flexibility is the result created by the application of the Rules-in-Use. TWI supports this capacity and appears to be the underlying foundation to the Rules-in-Use. In a general sense, the following statement by Dr. Steven Spear and H. Kent Bowen may sum up this observation: "Any supervisor [in a non-TPS company] can answer any call for help because a specific person has not been assigned. The disadvantage of that approach, as Toyota recognizes, is that when something is everyone's problem it becomes no one's problem."[33]

This statement also echoes the initial misunderstanding and misuse of teamwork by most companies going through a lean transformation. Teamwork does not have everyone jumping on board to help out or everyone empowered to develop the design of the lean system. It does designate specific roles and functions so that everyone can contribute to specific aspects of the system, so that the system develops and improves along specific objectives through specific routes and methods. This is lean's true manifestation in an empowered team.

Teamwork in the Lean Enterprise

Glenn Uminger substantiates the points discussed in the previous section, "The History of Lean Teamwork," of teamwork in the lean enterprise. He writes: "When consensus takes too long, the leader pushes it forward." Uminger is referring to leadership and teamwork at all levels within Toyota."[34] The leader has the final decision. To further understand the use of teamwork in the lean enterprise, recall the *Star Trek* analogy from Chapter 8 in the section on standard operations, titled "Standard Work: the Basis for Kaizen." Robbins and Finley explain how this works: "Members participate in decisions affecting the team, but understand their leader must make a final ruling whenever the team cannot decide, or an emergency exists. Positive results, not conformity, is the goal."[35]

Job Instruction How to get ready to instruct	HOW TO GET READY TO INSTRUCT

1. Have a Planning Time Table
  • How much skill you expect him/her to have by what date
2. Break down the job
  • List major steps
  • Pick out the key points (Safety is always a key point)
3. Have Everything ready
  • The right equipment, materials and supplies
4. Have the workplace properly arranged
  • Just as the team member will be expected to keep it
 	
TOYOTA
	Have a Time Table—
	How much skill you expect him to have by what date
	Break Down the Job—
	List major steps
	Pick out the key points (Safety is always a key point)
	Have Everything Ready—
	The right equipment, materials and supplies
	Have the Workplace Properly Arranged—
	Just as the team member will be expected to keep it
	
	Job Instruction Training
	TRAINING WITHIN INDUSTRY
	Bureau of Training
	War Manpower Commission
	KEEP THIS CARD HANDY

Toyota, 2003   **Front Side of Cards**   TWI, 1944

How To Instruct	HOW TO INSTRUCT
STEP 1: PREPARE TEAM MEMBER • Put team member at ease • State the job • Find out what team member already knows about it • Get team member interested in learning the job • Place team member in correct position **STEP 2: PRESENT OPERATION** • Tell, show and illustrate each Major Step one at a time • State each Key Point • Explain reasons • Instruct clearly, completely, and patiently • Present no more that team member can master (Do you have any questions?) **STEP 3: TRY OUT PERFORMANCE** • Have team member do the job; correct errors • Have team member explain Major Steps as the job is done again • Have team member explain each Key Point as job is done again • Have team member explain reasons for key points as job is done again **STEP 4: FOLLOW UP** • Put team member on own • Designate to whom to go for help and where • Check frequently • Encourage questions • Give any necessary extra coaching and taper off the follow up **If the MEMBER hasn't learned, the INSTRUCTOR hasn't taught.**	*STEP 1— Prepare the Worker* Put him at ease State the job and find out what he already knows about it Get him interested in learning job Place in correct position *STEP 2—Present the Operation* Tell, show and illustrate one IMPORTANT Step one at a time Stress each KEY POINT Instruct clearly, completely, and patiently, but no more than he can master *STEP 3—Try out Performance* Have him do the job--correct errors Have him explain each KEY POINT to you as he does the job again Make sure he understands Continue until YOU know HE knows *STEP 4— Follow Up* Put him on his own Check frequently. Encourage questions Taper off extra coaching and close follow up *If the MEMBER hasn't learned, the INSTRUCTOR hasn't taught.*

Toyota, 2003   **Back Side of Cards**   TWI, 1944

Figure 12.1 Job-Instruction cards

Source: The original Job-Instruction card is from the 1944 Job-Instruction training manual. The Toyota Job-Instruction card is courtesy of the Toyota Motor Corporation, Toyota Motors Manufacturing, Kentucky, TMM-K.

Everyone in the lean enterprise—and, more specifically, the shop personnel and the operator-frontline supervisor interface—contribute to developing and improving the system. But the improvement and development evolves in a hierarchical structure, not in an ad hoc manner, which is generally characteristic of most companies going through the transformation process. In a true TPS environment, the structure is carefully and specifically designed to achieve and incorporate everyone's ideas and contributions.

This explains in a general sense how a team works in a lean enterprise. Rother provides a specific example of how teams work on the shop floor at Toyota: "The way it often works is that the Team Leader observes a problem in his or her area (eg: 'That operator has to bend over too much') and then, during a break or scheduled meeting, asks his/her team or operators to analyze this and propose how to improve this. When a good idea is arrived at—typically through several back-and-forth cycles of discussion & critique with the Team Leader—it is finally submitted as a suggestion."[36]

John Shook also provides significant insight on how the lean firm (Toyota specifically) uses teamwork or employee empowerment. Shook's intimate understanding provides a view that again is very different from the generally accepted assumptions that most companies use and apply.

Empowerment is incorporated into lean systems as a natural part of the work system design. When John Shook joined Toyota, he expected to find a bottom-up management system, but it soon became clear that people at Toyota were not free to set their own agendas. His next thought was that Toyota must be a top-down management system, but soon realized that no one told him what to do. What he learned was the system had well-defined processes, and individual responsibility was nearly always clear. Authority was rarely an issue and the emphasis in the system was doing the right thing, not establishing one's authority.

Shook, when speaking about the TPS, describes three basic leadership styles and how they affect empowerment, teams, and operations. The dictatorial, "do-it-my-way" style has the boss telling everyone what to do. This style results in no transfer of responsibility or empowerment. The second style, which evolved during the 1980s and 1990s and is prevalent today in companies transitioning to lean, is the "do-it-your-way," absolute-empowerment style. Managers will set goals and then let the team set the agenda on how to best achieve the objectives. Shook calls this style the "leader as social worker" approach and says it causes loss of company focus, direction, and control. The third style, or what he found at Toyota (the lean approach), is a "follow-me" approach. With this style, managers tell their people, "I know what to do and where we are going." They will lead "by example," "by questioning," by "understanding the details," "by teaching and influence," and "by being knowledgeable."[37]

In a number of discussions with Shook, it was discussed how the TWI "J" programs were a strong influence on teamwork and team evolution at Toyota. Although a number of issues contributed to the methods and principles of Toyota's team, teamwork, and empowerment environment, according to Shook, TWI did play a major role Toyota's activities. This influence is shown in Figure 12.1. According to Shook, "The notion that there should be a standard and improvements should be based on that standard are, I think, key components of JM [the Job-Methods program] that formed the basis of Toyota's Standardized Work and Kaizen."[38] Shook also believes, based on his own involvement and work with transferring Toyota's systems overseas, "that the JR [the Job-Relations program] course influenced Toyota's team process and the role of the Team Leader."[39]

The conclusion of this chapter's discussion is that many factors influence and play key roles in teamwork at Toyota and at any truly lean firm. These factors are different than many of the generally accepted thoughts and practices about teamwork and empowerment. But, as with most lean principles, many methods lend support to each lean technique and the design of the system is critical in achieving each method, technique, and principle.

To review the points listed throughout this chapter, a number of themes can be highlighted. Dr. Spear emphasizes driving improvement down to the smallest group; in Toyota's manufacturing operation, this is the team leader and team members (or frontline supervisor and operators). The interface between the two groups is critical to the successful function, which is why TWI focused on this and continues to significantly influence operations Toyota. The design of the team's function and teamwork must be specific in order to achieve better and continually improving success; Dr. Spear concurs with this along with Rother and Shook. All of these functional points discussed emphasize the focus on small units of people and their importance to the system. Robbins and Finley tell us:

> Some people think that the larger the team, the better the team. Wrong.
>
> There is a trend in some companies to think of their entire organization as a team. This is an interesting expression, but not a useful one. Teams by their very nature can't be big. At some point they stop being teams and become mobs.
>
> Team size is important. Smaller is much better than large.[40]

This point is a guiding principle at Toyota and at any firm practicing a right designed lean system. Again, a lean system must be designed properly so supporting functions have the ability to function and give the proper support—cost management. Robbins and Finley opine, "The more goals and objectives a team is handed, the worse their performance will be."[41] In other words, they are speaking about MBM versus MBR.

BACK TO CHURCH

Of course, teamwork is very beneficial to the personnel needs and health of employees; the mental health of employees contributes to any manufacturing system. As Toyota emphasizes, teamwork is a result of a well-designed or right designed lean system.

Alexander Hamilton Church provides perhaps the best description of how teamwork is established (through system design) and its benefits to a firm's employees.

He writes:

> The principle regards the human organism in relation to its reaction to the environment, and no psychological principle is better established both theoretically and practically. Hence arises the necessity for ensuring that the environment is as satisfactory as it can possibly be made, having in view the nature of the work to be done.[42]

Church continues:

> [When an organization desires teamwork, it is created] with the formation of esprit de corps. This is not the same thing as team work, though it sometimes includes it. The nearest English equivalent to the phrase may be found in "group pride." The man who believes in his group will exert himself for its welfare beyond the strict letter of his bond. Belief in the purpose for which the group exists is the first essential, and in industrial affairs this means belief in the firm, in its products, in its superiority to other firms in the same line. Naturally, this condition of mind cannot be brought about by any mechanism. It must grow out of the environment, out of a sense of confidence in the justice meted out to all and sundry, out of fairness and pleasant relations with all the individuals to be associated with.... Neither can cooperation be considered as an equivalent to esprit de corps. It is sometimes claimed that this or that system of management gives rise to a spirit of cooperation. But to speak of a spirit of cooperation is something of a misnomer. Cooperation is not an end of itself; *it is a result of something* [emphasis added]. Men will not cooperate for the sake of cooperating, or because they are told it is a fine thing to do. They will coöperate if their attention is focused on a definite end, and this end may be an indefinite and intangible one, like the honor of the regiment or the credit of the plant. In fact, the more intangible the end, so long as it contains a definite principle, the better. This, however, is esprit de corps—a larger issue that controls the will of men unconsciously. Wherever it can be developed it is an asset of the highest level.[43]

In the successfully implemented lean system, the system must demand teamwork, or "group pride," *not* pride demanded by the company or the management. Both Church and Toyota assert this point through the design and operation of their manufacturing systems. Basically, Toyota does two things to support a teamwork environment: it designs a system in which teamwork has no alternative but to function[44] and trains its supervisors—thus, TWI. See Figure 11.4, which is a model of the TPS and shows the house-like structure surrounding its people.

The following lists give the basic characteristics of the two support columns that sustain and focus the supervisor-operator interface (See Figure 12.2).

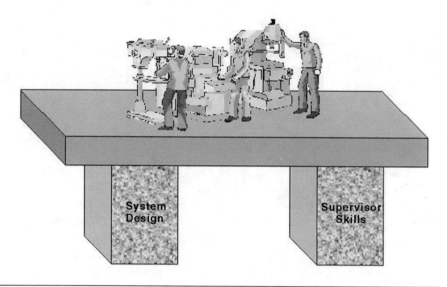

Figure 12.2 Lean teamwork structure

Supervisor skills:

- Training/instructing (or Job Instruction)
- Flow and flow disruption improvements (Job Methods)
- People, material, and information flow
- People's relationships (Job Relations)
- Standard work
- Problem solving/troubleshooting/countermeasures
- Feedback to engineering

System design:

- Flow and flow-disruption improvements
- Standard operations
- People, material, and information flow
- Right designed equipment and processes
- Robust and capable processes and equipment
- Feedback from operations, operators, and supervisors for design improvements

It is important to realize how much the two aspects overlap. The significant overlap is important and intentional. According to Shook, this appears to have happened over time as Toyota worked to improve and focus on the operator–frontline supervisor interface. This interface is one of the most critical components of TPS, and Toyota has put much effort into it and continues to focus on this lean system epicenter.

Teamwork: By Design, Not by Bliss

As has been stressed in this section, teamwork is a result of a well-designed and right designed lean system. The lean manufacturer must understand this point and act accordingly. Teamwork by design, not by designation, seems to go against "traditional" lean thinking but in fact is viable if Toyota is studied in detail.

One reason why most misinterpret the team environment is that in their study of the surface of this phase of TPS, they view only the results. The results are a well-functioning, interacting, cooperative, and blissful (from an industrial standpoint) environment with team members having been empowered. The details under the surface must be uncovered to really understand how it actually does function. Teamwork at Toyota and in a truly lean enterprise is an implicit aspect of the system.[45] Toyota has been able to create a unique working environment where teamwork abounds explicitly, but implicitly the reasons why it exists and functions are very difficult to see and understand.

Today's firms going through a lean transformation search and struggle to reach this blissful and cooperative work environment. Many times, these firms do achieve such a workplace, but it fails to deliver the effective flow of material, information, and people. Joanne Ciulla, in her book *The Working Life*, discusses this point: "Spontaneous sociability might be what management theorists have been trying to orchestrate and engineer since the beginning of the century. Spontaneous sociability is operating when people work as a team, but because they trust each other and agree to work together toward a common goal."[46]

This is what the lean enterprise should accomplish by design. Perhaps Dr. H. Thomas Johnson and Anders Bröms state the situation best when they emphasize the relationship of learning to the organization by MBM to MBM. They write: "Every person ... must participate in ... knowing and doing. 'Knowing' implies ... detailed awareness of both customer needs and company processes. 'Doing' implies detailed knowledge of how to conduct design, production, and logistical procedures. Linking knowing and doing means ... bosses will ... visit and participate in shop floor activities, and workers will ... offer ideas for changing designs and processes."[47]

NOTES

1. Flinchbaugh, "Beyond Lean," 14.
2. According to Dr. Jeffrey Liker, Sam Heltman was one of the first five Americans hired by Toyota, Georgetown.
3. Liker, *The Toyota Way*, 184.
4. Ibid.
5. Ibid., 185.
6. Ibid., 186.
7. Toyota Motor Corporation, *The Toyota Production System*, 32.
8. Ibid., 34.

9. War Production Board, *Job Methods*, 12.
10. Ibid., 33.
11. Japan Management Association, *Kanban*, 157–58.
12. Rother, "Crossroads," 487.
13. Ibid.
14. Ibid., 489–90.
15. In his article, Mike Rother uses management by objectives (MBO), which correlates with MBR.
16. Rother, "Some Current Thoughts on the Management Side of Lean Manufacturing." Mike Rother sent a copy of this unpublished article to the author.
17. Rother, "Do You Really Have Continuous Flow in Assembly?"
18. Ohno, *Toyota Production System*, 8.
19. Spear, "The Toyota Production System," 4–5.
20. Ibid., 156.
21. Ibid., 85. Note: Both Rules 4 and 5 are not totally focused toward what is given in this book. Each rule contains a broader coverage but does cover the specifics reviewed in this chapter.
22. Ibid., 97.
23. To understand the history and impact of TWI on Japanese industry, see two papers by Jim Huntzinger listed in the bibliography, *Roots of Lean—Training Within Industry: The Origin of Japanese Management and Kaizen* and *Roots of Lean—Training Within Industry: The Origin of Kaizen*.
24. Job Methods is the forefather of today's *kaizen* methods and philosophies.
25. Spear, "Just-in-Time in Practice at Toyota," 13–14.
26. The themes of the "J" programs were both explicitly and implicitly described in all of Dr. Spear's work. See the bibliography for reference to his work. For work specific to job instruction, see Spear, "Just-in-Time in Practice at Toyota," 23, and Spear, "Building Process Improvement Capacity," 1, 4, 12. For work specific to job methods, see Spear, "Building Process Improvement Capacity," 29–30. For work specific to job relations, see Spear, "Building Process Improvement Capacity," 26, 36, 39, and Spear, "The Toyota Production System," 222–23. The listings here are just examples relating to each "J" program; again, these themes were expressed throughout Spear's work.
27. The learn-by-doing methodology is discussed and stressed in Spear and Bowen, "Decoding the DNA of the Toyota Production System," and in Spear's working papers. According to Spear, it is key to Toyota's learning process.
28. Spear, "Building Process Improvement Capacity," 30.
29. Ibid., 36.
30. Spear, "Just-in-Time in Practice at Toyota," 22–23. Another interesting point made in the last sentence of this quote by Spear connects with Johnson and Bröms's organizations as a living system discussion.
31. Huntzinger, "Roots of Lean—Training Within Industry: The Origin of Japanese Management and Kaizen," 33.

32. This article was based on the information collected, and conclusions reached, by Spear during his research for his thesis.
33. Spear and Bowen, "Decoding the DNA of the Toyota Production System," 101.
34. Uminger, "Lean."
35. Robbins and Finley, *Why Teams Don't Work*, 111.
36. Mike Rother, "Some Current Thoughts on the Management Side of Lean Manufacturing."
37. These two paragraphs were based on many conversations and correspondences with John Shook, as well as from his lectures, particularly from May 2001 and November 2002. Also, Chet Marchwinski of the Lean Enterprise Institute, Brookline, Massachusetts, posted a good summary of Shook's thoughts on the Lean Enterprise Institute Web site (http://www.lean.org).
38. John Shook, Co-Director of the Japan Technology Management Program at the University of Michigan, 5 January 2003, Subject: TWI, E-mail to the author.
39. Ibid.
40. Robbins and Finley, *Why Teams Don't Work*, 183.
41. Ibid., 34.
42. Vangermeersch, *The Contributions of Alexander Hamilton Church*, 154, quoting Church, "Industrial Management," 465.
43. Vangermeersch, *The Contributions of Alexander Hamilton Church*, 155–56, quoting Church, "Industrial Management," 469–70.
44. This point will be further discussed in the section on how a TPS company is designed to function like a gear train, as explained by Dennis Butt.
45. Shook has a unique and critical insight into this aspect of Toyota. It can be difficult to see and, therefore, difficult to understand. As Shook has explained in his lectures, it even took him a while to realize and understand these features and he was actually working for Toyota.
46. Ciulla, *The Working Life*, 154.
47. Johnson and Bröms, *Profit beyond Measure*, 175.

13

SYSTEM EVOLUTION

Developing a superior designed and functioning operation and business enterprise is achieved by a deep and long-term understanding and strategy—not by a series of workshop events, lack of monthly variances, or series of excellent quarters on the financial statements. Ron Harbour explains the following:

> A plant is going to reflect all of the planning [design] and execution that went into it. The best plants, and the best manufacturers, understand all of the factors that impact a plant's performance. They work hard to carefully put all of these pieces together.
>
> And when it's done right, it's a piece of art.[1]

A need that lean enterprises must develop is the ability to maintain continued system evolution. Toyota exemplifies this notion, which is proven in their continual output of successful vehicles, continued growth of their markets, and continued profitability. According to James Womack:

> In the mid-1990s, Toyota set a goal of a 10% market share in the global motor vehicle market by 2000 and in 2000 Toyota's share was 10.01%. Last year Toyota announced a new vision to achieve a global motor vehicle market share of 15% by 2010, which will push Toyota past GM and Ford as the global market share leader.
>
> This is not being done at the expense of profits, which have been rising steadily in step with growing market share. In the 2003 fiscal year ended March 31, Toyota will report profits of about $10 billion US on about $125 billion in sales. With a return on sales of nearly 8%, Toyota is now the most profitable car company excepting Porsche (with a 17% ROS this past year), a company one twenty-fifth the size of Toyota which has transformed its business using Toyota methods, as Dan and I reported in Chapter 9 of our book *Lean Thinking*.[2]

Evolving the lean enterprise-wide system involves everyone within a company and even those outside a firm. This includes customers and suppliers. For the purpose of this chapter, the focus here will be on the two groups presented in the previous section: engineers, system designers, and implementers, and operators and supervisors in the shop. These two groups of people have the most direct impact on the development and evolution of the operation system and support systems. Such systems include the manufacturing system and the manufacturing support systems such as the cost-management system, although other systems of the business are not necessarily excluded.

As explained in Chapter 12, shop teams and engineers each have specific roles. It is important to recognize that both these groups overlap heavily in the area of both system deployment and system evolution. Figure 13.1 illustrates their roles and their impact on a system's evolution.

THE SHOP FLOOR FEEDBACK LOOP

The first feedback loop focuses on the role of the shop floor as the interface between supervisor and operator.[3] The role of the shop floor is threefold. First, the shop floor performs, develops, and implements improvements. These improvements focus on problems and issues that inhibit or interrupt the application of standard operations. These improvements are termed *jidoka kaizen*, as shown in Figure 13.1.

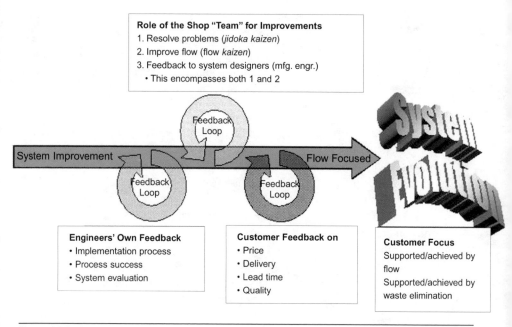

Figure 13.1 Lean system evolution

Jamie Flinchbaugh describes this purpose of the operator's role in systems development and design. He writes: "Not every team member will be required to deeply understand how the process fits into the strategy of lean manufacturing or how to redesign the process using information technology. They do need, however, to know how to relate it to the rest of their job so that they can give effective feedback to others based on what is and is not working."[4]

The second role of the shop floor is developing and implementing improvements in flow of material, operators, and information. Many times, these improvements (or *kaizen*) are the traditionally recognized *kaizens*, like improved fixture or tool designs, improved placement of materials, or better positioning of equipment ideas. Figure 13.1 labels these improvements "flow *kaizen*." It should also be noted that these first two improvement targets, flow interruptions and local flow improvements, overlap in their content and purpose and that although the shop floor can cover improvements on a broader scale, these two areas are the major focus.

The third role of the shop floor is to proactively provide feedback to the engineers and systems designers so that the improvements made are understood and incorporated into the next evolution of system design—design evolution. Also, any ideas and improvements that are applicable to other areas in the operations should be distributed and employed. Of course, as with most of the lean system, multiple supports are in place. The other two feedback loops will be discussed in the rest of this chapter: the ideas, improvements, and communication of all three loops continually overlap to guarantee the capture and dispersion of information throughout the current system in operation and future systems under development. Glenn Uminger explains that "production workers are motivated to control and improve their own workplace supported by management, quality circles, suggestion systems, and so on.... The production workers must feel secure in their role to identify problems and ask for help without fear. They must know they will be completely supported."[5]

THE ENGINEERING FEEDBACK LOOP

The second feedback loop focuses on the role of the engineers, those who design and deploy the lean systems. The engineers and managers that have a thorough understanding of and experience with lean systems use multiple methods to evolve and improve operations and support systems. The first area of their focus in improving the systems is the implementation process itself. The ability of the system to be deployed and ramp up to production demand according to the specific timeline demonstrates both how well the system was designed and how well it followed its design specifications. If many problems exist—or at least problems that hamper the ability of the system to deliver its requirements, as all large projects have issues that must be dealt with throughout their deployment—then the system design, as well as the deployment procedure, must be thoroughly reviewed. The ability to achieve excellent project or program deployment has been highlighted by Toyota, as well as Honda, in their ability to continually decrease their program timelines while continuing to evolve and enhance their lean operational system—especially in Toyota's case.

Upon completion of any deployment of a project, the next test is how well the system delivers the primary attributes: delivery, cost, quality, and demand estimates (whether customers want the product). In the end, was the process a success? Does it deliver lean attributes? Reviewing these attributes and how well the project timeline proceeded provides excellent feedback to indicate what changes and improvements must be made to the next iteration of the lean system evolution.

THE CUSTOMER FEEDBACK LOOP

The third feedback loop focuses on the role of the customer. The customer ultimately decides the success of the lean system and should definitely give feedback to the system designers. Obviously, the customer provides feedback to many entities involved with any business enterprise—lean or not. However, system designers especially must understand the ability of their current lean system to satisfy the customer for future systems. What changes, modifications, and improvements must be made to both current and future lean systems to not only keep up with but actually stay ahead of customer demands and requirements?

Again, it must be stated that all three of these feedback loops can and should overlap in information, methods, and communication. The feedback loops must function hand-in-hand to be most effective (see Figure 13.2).

CUSTOMER FOCUS

All three feedback loops must be focused on the customer. In the end, the lean enterprise system must satisfy the customer. This is accomplished in the lean enterprise via flow. Many discussions about lean or the Toyota Production System (TPS) focus on waste elimination. Waste elimination is key to establishing a lean system, but what is missing from the waste elimination discussion is a direction or focus for the elimination of waste. This focus is flow. It is the flow of products and information to the customer and efforts to satisfy the customer that are crucial. Waste elimination must be focused on establishing flow or removing obstacles from the system's ability to flow products and information. See the box "Customer Focus" in Figure 13.1. This point of customer focus underscores the drive for lean system evolution. Glenn Uminger explains: "The most important aspect of the manufacturing operations cost control point is to establish and nurture an environment that places responsibility and expectations in the hands of the people doing the work and provides feedback to them at the point of action."[6]

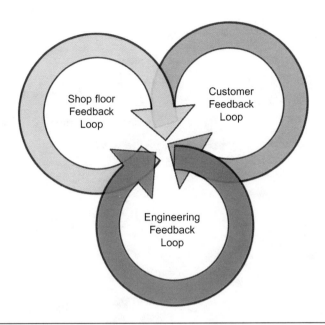

Figure 13.2 Overlapping lean system feedback loops

NOTES

1. Harbour, "Opinions & Analysis: Good Plants, Like Art, Don't Just Happen," 16.
2. Womack, *Here's to Toyota*.
3. It is important to understand that although the focus of this loop is the shop floor personnel, engineering works with the shop floor to help enhance their work and ideas and to give technical support as needed.
4. Flinchbaugh, "Implementing Lean Manufacturing," 95.
5. Uminger, "Manufacturing Cost Management," 45.
6. Ibid., 44.

14

TRANSACTIONS AND LEAN

In any manufacturing firm, transactions take place. In an operation, transactions are primarily the exchange of material and information: these are the two sets of transactions that Mike Rother and John Shook's value-stream mapping technique maps in their book *Learning to See*. The transactions of material and information are directly "attacked" by developing and implementing lean manufacturing. Lean manufacturing converts the enterprise into a transaction eliminating, consolidating, and simplifying entity. This phenomenon is crucial in creating an environment for effective cost management; it is also the reason behind lean's ability to drastically reduce costs and lead time and improve quality. Orest Fiume tells us: "One of the things that you need to do when you convert to Lean is focus on the amount of transaction processing that goes on. They are non–value added, and as you get into a Lean environment you can start eliminating a lot of those transactions."[1]

COASE'S THEOREM

In 1937, an article was published that changed the thinking about companies: "The Nature of the Firm" by Ronald Coase.[2] It gave answers to two fundamental questions that had been inadequately resolved up to that point: the question of why firms are formed and the question of why firms are a certain size.

These two questions concern some of the very activities that Alexander Hamilton Church and his contemporaries were trying to resolve for internal information purposes when they developed their solutions for growing internal processing and product proliferation between 1885 and 1925. Coase concluded that a firm represents an alternative to organizing production through market transactions.[3] Put more simply, firms grow to the point where it is more cost effective for them to have transactions accomplished internally than transactions made externally, or out in the market. Coase writes the following:

> Why is such organization necessary? Why are there these "islands of conscious power"? Outside the firm, price movements direct production, which

is co-ordinated through a series of exchange transactions on the market. Within a firm, these market transactions are eliminated and in place of the complicated market structure with exchange transactions is substituted the entrepreneur-co-ordinator, who directs production. Yet, having regard to the fact that if production is regulated by price movements, production could be carried on without any organisation at all, well might we ask, why is there any organisation?[4]

Coase is describing the very dynamics that affected and drove Church and his peers between 1885 and 1925. These market dynamics were reshaping the industrial structure, or as Coase terms it, "the nature of the firm." As will be shown in the next section of this chapter, a very similar phenomenon occurs within a firm when it goes through a lean transformation. Church's focus on production factors and developing a firm's ability to collect and understand accurate product costs is reiterated in Coase's theory. Although Coase was trying to understand why these transactions develop into a collection—or firm—Church was trying to understand what these transactions cost, or the product costs. Coase states the following:

> The main reason why it is profitable to establish a firm would seem to be that there is a cost of using the price mechanism. The most obvious cost of "organising" production through the price mechanism is that of discovering what the relevant prices are.... The costs of negotiating and concluding a separate contract for each exchange transaction which takes place on a market must be taken into account.... It is true that contracts are not eliminated when there is a firm but they are greatly reduced.[5]
>
> And by forming an organisation and allowing some authority (an "entrepreneur") to direct the resources, certain marketing costs are saved. The entrepreneur has to carry out his function at less cost, taking into account the fact that he may get factors of production at a lower price than the market transactions which he supersedes, because it is always possible to revert to the open market if he fails to do this.[6]

The lean enterprise implicates both Coase's and Church's purposes. The lean firm eliminates, condenses, and simplifies transactions (Coase's theory) and also, through its physical implementation, allows for simple, straightforward product focus that aligns cost activities around product families (Church's principles). Coase concluded that what limits the size of a firm is the cost of transactions. He writes: "First, as a firm gets larger, there may be decreasing returns to the entrepreneur function, that is, the costs of organising additional transactions within the firm may rise. Naturally, a point must be reached where the costs of organising an extra transaction within the firm are equal to the costs involved in carrying out the transaction in the open market."[7]

COASE'S THEOREM AT WORK IN TODAY'S OPERATIONS

Lean significantly reduces internal transactions of a firm (although this book focuses on internal transactions, the same could be accomplished for external transactions).[8] As a company transforms into a lean enterprises, it eliminates and streamlines transactions at all levels and functions. For this reason, much of this book focuses on systems design: the implementation of a physical lean system creates an environment where most material and information transactions are removed and the few that remain are simplified and concentrated within a product's value stream. This situation creates Church's ideal manufacturing company. His development of production factors and his method for tracing them to products to enable accurate product cost information becomes a reality in this scenario.

The ability to trace costs directly to the product that consumes them exemplifies the intersection of Coase and Church and the ability of a lean system to capture cost information for an effective and simple cost-management system. As Coase's theory asserts, firms grow to the size at which internal transactions become equal to transactions in the market. The other side of this theory is that if a company can eliminate and simplify transactions, then it can significantly improve its margins or profits and/or reduce its price and gain market share (think of Toyota). Recall what H. Thomas Johnson and Anders Bröms said in *Profit beyond Measure: Extraordinary Results through Attention to Work and People*: A lean firm can also—as many have successfully done—bring in more business by reassuming manufacturing products that had been farmed out; they can also manufacture products that they have never produced before and develop new products and markets because they have new resources. Or, as Coase contends, the firm will grow. The lean firm can grow in size because it has significantly reduced internal transaction costs below the costs of transactions in the marketplace. And by using Church's production factors method (the one proposed in this book), lean manufacturers will have cost information that will give them the knowledge (actual product costs) and guidance (planning capability) to grow as Coase asserts they would. The lean enterprise can answer the question proposed by Coase: "The question always is, will it pay to bring an extra exchange transaction under the organising authority?"[9] And for the lean enterprise, the answer is "yes."

The lean operation, as discussed in Chapters 8 and 10 on physical operational design and right designing, creates an environment of flow, which alleviates most of the tracking and scheduling transactions that happen in a traditional (or batch) manufacturer. As Dr. Dileep Dhavale reveals, this is due to the "very nature" or design of the lean operation. Dhavale writes: "One of the biggest headaches faced by managers of functional-layout shops is the scheduling, dispatching, and tracking of jobs as they move from department to department. This problem is simplified by the very nature of focused factories. Each focused factory schedules it own jobs, which remain within that factory."[10]

The insanity of the amount of transactions that take place under traditional accounting procedures must be recognized. The resources consumed to manage these transactions are significant in cost, time, and physical activity. All of these will disappear in the lean environment. Recall the Harley-Davidson story in the Results section of the Right Designing chapter and how the implementation of flow would drastically decrease the number of transactions necessary, or resource consumption. William Turk describes the situation at Harley-Davidson:

> Employees record their times and pieces produced for each part-number operation on which they work. Thus, if an employee works on ten different parts a day, ten labor tickets have to be recorded. Cost accounting takes these ten labor tickets and calculates the direct labor inventory input. Assuming an average of ten labor tickets and 500 employees, this works out to 5,000 labor tickets per day, 25,000 labor tickets per week, and 100,000 labor tickets per month. Accounting must ensure that the 100,000 labor transactions are all accurate—a hopeless task.[11]

Coase, Church, and Cost

Coase's theory impacts the cost-management system for the lean firm because, as discussed in previous sections, the physical implementation of lean enables transactions either to disappear or to become greatly simplified. It also, as Church emphasized, ties activities directly to products or product families. Church states what Coase discovered during his 1930s Nobel Prize study: "[A manufacturer] does from necessity, others he does from choice, or because he sees a distinct economies advantage in doing them for himself."[12] These activities are items that generate cost in an operation. As Dr. Dhavale states, this enables "a number of reasons why product costing is simpler and more accurate in cellular manufacturing [or focus factories, or the lean enterprise]."[13]

- "Many costs become direct costs" (think of Church)
- "Cells make homogenous products" (think of the value stream)
- "Costs are current in the cell environment" (think MBM)
- Labor is part of the cell and driven by takt time and standard operations (think of the sawtooth graph: economies of scale is dead)[14]

Coase, Church, Cost, and an Example

Figure 14.1 shows the machining cell for crankshafts from the Engine Model Focus Factory. Within the machining cell, fifteen operations exist to fully machine the crankshaft from a casting to a finished crankshaft ready to be assembled in the engine on the assembly line. Also, the introduction of raw material, the crankshaft casting, and withdrawal of the finished component—a finished crankshaft—are part of the manufacturing line. In total, seventeen operations exist within this manufacturing cell. In a traditional, or batch manufacturing, operation, a minimum of seventeen transactions would take place. As was shown in the Harley-Davidson example, the transactions in a traditional operation involve physical activities to track, trace, and input information and move material.

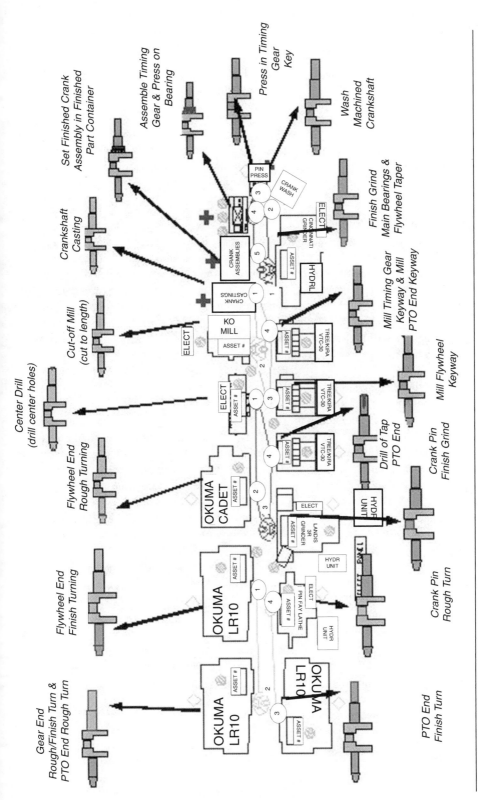

Figure 14.1 Crankshaft machining line from the Engine Model Focus Factory

Many times, each transaction between each process in a traditional operation may actually consist of more than one transactional activity. Take the following list of transactions for example:

- Moving work in process (WIP) out from the preceding process
- Putting the WIP into storage
- Searching for the WIP when the proceeding process is ready for it
- Moving the WIP to the proceeding process

Each of the above physical transactions may need an informational transaction to track it within some information system. Assuming every activity above functions without a hitch, each transaction of taking WIP from a preceding process to the next process may, in fact, total eight transactions. Since this one manufacturing line or product has a total of seventeen operations, in a traditional manufacturer the number of transactions would total one hundred and thirty-six, and this is assuming that everything operated smoothly, which, as most in manufacturing know, usually does not occur. When the entire engine focus factory is viewed, it is not difficult to imagine the beastly magnitude of transactions—both physical and informational—that must take place, which consume time and resources.

As one can see in Figure 14.1, the transactions needed for a properly designed manufacturing line, such as the crankshaft-machining cell, drops from one hundred and thirty-six to four. The four transactions are moving the full raw material—castings in this case—container in; moving the empty raw material container out; moving the finished crankshaft container in; and moving an empty finished crankshaft container out. Since in a lean environment the material itself is the information, no information system transactions are necessary. The magnitude of transactions is nearly eliminated, and the four that are remaining are simplified; the material flow *is* the information flow.

The elimination or simplification of these transactions is a result of, as Mike Kitano says, "confirming processes one-by-one, step-by-step, and not proceeding with the next step until requested."[15] Kitano is referring to flow. The crankshaft machining cell in Figure 14.1 is a physical implementation of flow or, as Kitano puts it, one-by-one confirmation. Flow in the lean enterprise is key to applying Coase's theory and consuming transactions. Flow enables transactions to decrease in cost in both internal and external exchanges.

Dr. H. Thomas Johnson describes how Coase's theory and Church's principles impact today's manufacturing enterprise, and, as this chapter describes and promotes, how Coase and Church influence cost management today. Without a cost-management system in place, any manufacturing firm is in a very poor position to make decisions about alternatives both internally (resource allocation) and externally (in the marketplace). Dr. Johnson writes the following:

> Cost management exists in organizations in which profit-seeking personnel manage economic exchange. All economic exchange is not managed, of

course; most economic activity in our society is conducted through nonmanaged exchange in the marketplace. Whether business-people choose the market or managed enterprise to direct economic activity depends on the cost and quality of opportunities for exchange in the two. That choice requires information about the relative worth of what is given up and what is received in an exchange. In markets, price provides the information to choose among alternative uses of resources. In a managed business enterprise, cost information helps managers select among alternative opportunities for using resources.

Cost management information helps managers judge whether opportunities for economic exchange within their enterprise are as profitable as they might be in another enterprise or in the market. It makes no sense to commit resources to a business unless they are expected to earn more in that setting, for the same risk, than in any other. Managers use cost management information to evaluate how efficiently and effectively an enterprise converts scarce input (resources) into useful output (value to the customer).[16]

As discussed in Chapter 11, the enterprise that designs, implements, and executes a true lean system should easily be able to establish a sound cost-management system and accomplish the very points that Dr. Johnson describes.

Transactions Today

Dr. H. Thomas Johnson and Robert S. Kaplan explain: "We need to start understanding the causes of overhead costs, a goal that virtually all existing systems fail miserably to achieve. The primary cost drivers for manufacturing overhead are not physical volume of production, but transactions—transactions involving exchange of materials or exchange of information."[17]

A significant theme of this book is the need for manufacturers to eliminate the use of overhead and instead to make all costs direct costs. But in order to do this it must be understood—as Johnson and Kaplan emphasize—where and why overhead exists. Understanding current transactions holds the key to achieving this task. Understanding lean manufacturing will guide businesses to understanding traditional transactions that are present in all batch manufacturers—transactions of material and information. In the book *Learning to See*, Rother and Shook's objective is for the users to understand their current state and to design a future state. The contrast between the current state and the future state highlights the elimination, reduction, and simplification of transactions that can occur in a manufacturing operation. James Womack and Daniel Jones's *Seeing the Whole: Mapping the Extended Value Stream* guides the reader to accomplish the same at a broader level. In both cases, it is about *seeing* the transactions that currently take place and *eliminating* and *reducing* them in the future.

Over ten years prior to the value-stream mapping books published by the Lean Enterprise Institute, Dr. Johnson and Kaplan emphasized the tracing of transactions down to the component level, recognizing that for many products, processes and transactions begin prior to some assembly process.[18] The implementation of one-piece flow is the process of eliminating transactions at the lowest level in a manufacturing operation. Dr. Johnson and Kaplan state: "We must work with the basic unit of production at each stage, which will usually be raw material or purchased components and subassemblies."[19]

Dr. Johnson and Kaplan took their thoughts about transactions and their effects on cost through overhead from a 1985 article by Jeffrey Miller and Thomas Vollmann called "The Hidden Factory." The Hidden Factory, according to Miller and Vollmann, is made of transactions. Transactions drive the melee of overhead that in turn distorts costs, which is a concept presented in Chapters 2, 4, 6, 8, and 11. Miller and Vollmann categorize transactions into four basic types—logistical, balancing, quality, and change—that drive the bulk of overhead costs involved in "exchanges of the material/information necessary to move production along, but do not directly result in physical products."[20] They write:

> The doing and undoing of logistical, balancing, and quality transactions that result from change transactions lead companies to incur overhead costs twice, three times, or more, depending on the stability of their manufacturing environments.
>
> If, as we believe, transactions are responsible for most overhead costs in the hidden factory, then the key to managing overheads is to control the transactions that drive them. By *managing transactions*, we mean thinking consciously and carefully about which transactions are appropriate and which are not and about how to do the important transactions most effectively.[21]

Miller and Vollmann contend that transactions contribute greatly to costs—overhead costs in their case—and companies must focus on the activities that direct them. This focus may be transactional elimination or improvement.[22] The same is true in a lean transformation. Miller and Vollmann explain that "this is what the Japanese have done with their 'just-in-time' philosophy of process design, which 'pulls' work through the factory only as needed by operations downstream. This approach eliminates much of the need for elaborate and time-consuming WIP-tracking or shop-floor control systems."[23]

Miller and Vollmann also reveal the mistake most manufacturers make when trying to improve the amount of transactions that take place in a batch-style manufacturing operation. Instead of eliminating transactions of material and information—as can be accomplished with lean manufacturing (that is, one-piece flow and pull systems—companies simply automate the "monstrous" task with a computer system. And as Miller and Vollmann explain, "a second and perhaps more serious problem occurs when manufacturers automate transactions that are not really necessary in the first place."[24] Figure 14.2 illustrates the difference between transactions in a lean enterprise and transactions in a traditional manufacturing enterprise—transactions in a lean enterprise are fewer and therefore cost less.

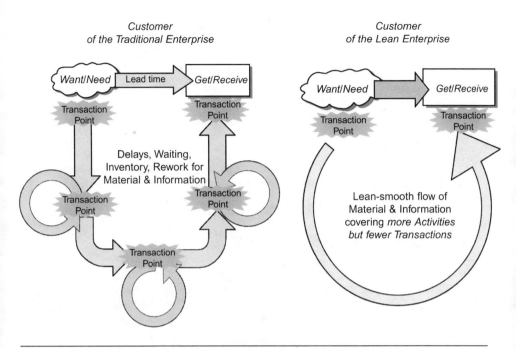

Figure 14.2 Internal transactions of manufacturing firms

Transactions and Lean

Lean implementation becomes the method for transaction elimination. Brian Maskell states: "Transactions are to lean accounting as inventory is to lean manufacturing."[25] Orest Fiume supports Maskell's statement: "As you move into lean, it actually makes everything a lot easier. You end up eliminating a lot of transactions."[26] In the previous section, the review of transactions focused on processing products and how the movement of products in and out of processing and inventory creates a massive amount of transactions. But many other operational activities create excess transactions and "many of the savings that arise from transactions [are] not taken."[27] These other activities that create excess physical and information transactions are items like setup or changeovers, quality checks, rework, scrap, and the like. Not only do these activities create physical transactions—the process of doing them—but they also create informational transaction—tracking systems and activities to trace the physical transactions. And, unfortunately, most of the activities and transactions in a traditional manufacturer fall into the gross overhead allocation.

One function worth reviewing is setup or changeovers. For the lean manufacturer, changeover may very well increase in frequency. If the lean operation is truly lean, then the changeovers will require a fraction of the time of those in a batch-manufacturing environment. Ideally, any changeover will either be eliminated or, at least, reduced to less than ten minutes, which is known as single minute change of die (SMED) capability.

Even though changeovers will most likely increase in frequency in the lean environment, they are very quick and standardized. Changeovers are also automatic—not automatic in the sense of automation but in the sense that flow is established and pull systems let operators know directly what part to make, how many parts to make, and when to make these parts. As stated in Chapter 11, in the lean operation, information flow and material flow are one in the same. Operators know what to do and when to do it as material arrives as it is needed. Information for when to change over and what part number to change over to is included and standard procedures are always established with operators well trained in them. It may be recalled that Dr. Spear's Rules-in-Use support these exact functions and procedures.

COASE AND INDUSTRIAL HISTORY

The very reasons behind Coase's theory were in full action during the mid-1800s through the 1920s. Chapter 2 in this book discussed cost management aspects of this period. What Coase describes in his article "The Nature of the Firm" are the actions and decisions entrepreneurs were making during the period of rapid industrial growth.[28] Dr. Johnson describes what happened: "Although organizations had carried out trading activities for centuries, the idea of internalizing market activity and managing it inside a company was new in the late eighteenth century."[29] Dr. Johnson continues:

> Financial management accounting tools developed from 1800 to the early 1920s largely in response to one force—the transfer of economic exchange from market settings into managed business settings. Before the early 1800s, market prices in "arm's length" transactions between individuals guided virtually all economic exchange outside the household. Then around 1800 people began to "internalize" economic activity and manage it in a business.[30]

Dr. Johnson reveals:

> As these businesses soon discovered, managing economic activity inside a company destroys price signals that people take for granted when they exchange in the marketplace. Without those signals, managers are at a loss to evaluate the profit consequences of choices in order to plan. The development of financial management information between the early 1800s and the early 1920s reflects efforts by companies to simulate market price information and to judge whether their economic activity is conducted as profitably as it might be in another company or in the marketplace[31]

Dr. Johnson's passage suggests that Coase's and Church's work and ideas go hand in hand to support a useful cost-management system. The same situation is true for today's lean enterprise but it has a great advantage over its earlier counterpart. The lean firm has nearly every activity aligned along value streams; therefore, it can create an environment that focuses cost information on accurate and simple cost management for superior planning and guidance purposes, much as described by Glenn Uminger in his overview of how Toyota uses cost information titled "Manufacturing Cost Management: A Practical Life-Cycle Cost Perspective" from the book *New Management Accounting.*

These unique needs for cost-price information motivated the actions of Church and his peers to develop and implement new methods for understanding the new industrial environment. This situation was unprecedented in history and had to be addressed. Dr. Johnson explains: "The vertically integrated industrial firm is quite unlike a mid-nineteenth century firm. The vertically integrated industrial combined into one centrally managed enterprise each specialized activity formerly carried out separately by independent firms. However, in order to control and coordinate these combined activities, the vertically integrated industrial firm had to develop new organizational methods."[32]

The surprise today is that the lean enterprise is in a similar situation. Methods that have been developed for cost-managerial accounting purposes do not work and do not support the lean manufacturer. They are old, outdated, and disruptive to today's manufacturing operation. New methods must be developed and implemented in order to move industry—and particularly the lean firm—forward. Fortunately, many of the ideas, methods, and concepts that support the lean manufacturing enterprise's cost-management system today were developed from many of the needs early manufacturers addressed. These methods and concepts must only be slightly modified to complement and support the needs of today's lean enterprise.

Fiume brings the requirements of these methods directly to the point: "Many of the transactions ... can be eliminated. A simple principle to keep in mind is that transactions that exist in the factory should serve an operational purpose. They should not exist just for accounting."[33]

LEAN ACHIEVES COASE'S THEORY

Larry Downes and Chunka Mui, in their book *Unleashing the Killer App: Digital Strategies for Market Dominance*, describe Coase's conclusion about why businesses grow. They write: "Firms are created, Coase concluded, because the additional cost of organizing and maintaining them is cheaper than the transaction costs involved when individuals conduct business with each other using the market."[34]

A manufacturing business grows as long as it is cost effective to expand out across transactions. Lean achieves this by both eliminating transactions and by greatly simplifying the ones that currently exist. Recall the crankshaft machining cell example: in the standardized-part handoff (a single transaction) in flow lines (or manufacturing cells) versus traditional batch manufacturing departments (make-move-store-move-repeat, which are multiple transactions), value only comes from the "make" operation.

The decrease in the number of transactions results in doing more with less, creating the physical changes necessary for a lean implementation, which eliminates transactions and simplifies the ones that remain. Or, as Coase's theory implies, the firm can grow because with lean manufacturing it reduces transaction costs (both transactions of information activities and physical activities) and expands outward to consume more transactions as a result of their elimination and simplification—both internally and externally.

In the area of cost-managerial accounting, the same is true—transactions are eliminated and reduced. Due to the changes in the physical operation and processing of products, the needs and uses of traditional accounting methods disappear, as does their misinformation and misguidedness. The outdated and ineffective accounting systems and methods can be completely eliminated and replaced with functional and supportive cost-management systems. This change eliminates the layers of excess transactions that do not support operations and are for accounting purposes only and replaces them with simple and accurate information parts of the operation instead of a cumbersome separate information system.

NOTES

1. Emiliani, Stec, Grasso, and Strodder, *Better Thinking, Better Results*, 208. This quote is from Orest Fiume.
2. Ronald Coase, while a graduate student at the University of London, came to the United States on the Cassel Traveling Scholarship from 1931 to 1932. The future economist came to the United States to study the closest thing he could find to a nonmarket economy. Growing U.S. firms such as U.S. Steel, General Motors, and the like gave him his opportunity. Coase wanted to learn why firms exist and why they grow to a particular size. His conclusions were presented in his 1937 article "The Nature of the Firm," and won him the Alfred Nobel Memorial Prize in Economic Sciences in 1991, fifty years later.
3. Coase, "The Problem of Social Cost," 16.
4. Coase, "The Nature of the Firm," 388.
5. Ibid., 390–91.
6. Ibid., 392.
7. Ibid., 394.
8. For a practical lean technique to accomplish this tactic, see Womack and Jones, *Seeing the Whole*.
9. Coase, "The Nature of the Firm," 404.
10. Dhavale, *Management Accounting Issues*, 29.
11. Turk, "Management Accounting Revitalized," 33.
12. Vangermeersch, *The Contributions of Alexander Hamilton Church*, 25, quoting Church, "Proper Distribution of the Expense Burden" 991.
13. Dhavale, *Management Accounting*, 96.

14. Ibid., 96–97. These bullets are a combination of the author's and Dhavale's.
15. Kitano, "Toyota Production System."
16. Johnson, "The Decline of Cost Management," 5–6.
17. Johnson and Kaplan, *Relevance Lost*, 237.
18. Ibid.
19. Ibid.
20. Miller and Vollmann, "The Hidden Factory," 144.
21. Ibid., 145.
22. Ibid., 145–46.
23. Ibid., 146.
24. Ibid., 149.
25. Ohno, "Overcoming the Obstacle of Accounting," 3. Brian Maskell asserts this same point in most of his writings.
26. Ibid., 4.
27. Kaplan, "Yesterday's Accounting Undermines Production," 97.
28. For a full and interesting report on this period and how industry evolved and changed read Chandler, *The Visible Hand*. Chandler recounts this history in great detail.
29. Johnson, "Managing by Remote Control," 45.
30. Ibid.
31. Ibid., 46.
32. Johnson, "The Role of Accounting History," 445.
33. Fiume and Cunningham, "Lean Accounting and Finance," 7.
34. Downes and Mui, *Unleashing the Killer App*, 39.

LEAN: LIKE A GEAR TRAIN

Lean production is often compared to a chain because of a chain's interlocking links. The concept of a tightly linked chain (see Figure 15.1) is a good analogy for lean manufacturing as it illustrates that a break in the chain quickly raises the need for the development and implementation of a countermeasure. However, while a tightly linked chain[1] is perhaps the most common description, a better analogy would be that of a gear train.

Figure 15.1 Lean manufacturing as a linked chain
Source: Based on a slide from Glenn Uminger's presentation at the 2003 University of Michigan's Lean Manufacturing Conference.

From Chain to Gear Train

A gear train analogy better describes a lean operation because it illustrates the same idea that the linked chain does—that of a tightly linked chain with no apparent problems—but additionally shows the multidimensional situation that exists in a manufacturing operation. The gear train also demonstrates connections such as subassemblies and component lines, as well as different velocities (or takt times) of components or operations that are a "two-per," three-per," or some other quantity that is different from the final product based on the bill of materials callout.

Also, any movement of the gear train or movement of one tooth represents takt time. Every subassembly line or component-manufacturing cell must move accordingly. This link through the value stream can be shown by simply moving across gears in the gear train down the supplying manufacturing line, cell, or process. Any breakdown can potentially stop the system (see Figure 15.2).

The movement of the teeth in the gear train can also represent flow or one-piece flow. Dennis Butt[2] introduced this analogy during a presentation[3] he gave on the Toyota Production System (TPS).

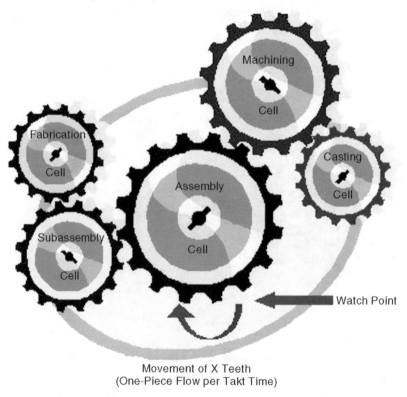

Movement of X Teeth
(One-Piece Flow per Takt Time)

Figure 15.2 Lean manufacturing as a gear train

Butt proposed that TPS,[4] or, more specifically, just-in-time (JIT) flow and Toyota's pull system (the *kanban* system), are actually like a conveyor or gear-train system. He writes: "As noted by the Toyota people ... this formula is a description of a driven conveyor. It also describes a gear train."[5]

Butt expands the formula given by Toyota[6] through a series of derivations (Ohno's formula, Little's formula, Morgan's formula, and finally Morgan's expansion, all of which describe the function of customer demand within a stable system), and arrives at a new formula and a series of spreadsheets, Morgan's expansion, which connect the production processes "to the customer so that the customer can be the direct driver." In his essay Dennis Butt explains:[7]

These equations predict specifically that if flow time or WIP inventory or both are variables then so will output be a variable. They predict more profoundly, that if flow time or WIP inventory or both are random variables, then so will output be a random variable. One implication of these equations is that if flow time or WIP inventory or both are random variables, it will be impossible to tell the customers when their orders will be shipped.

Both WIP Inventory (number of partial or completed units) and Flow Time (hours) must be constant if Output/hour is to be constant. Further, "flexibility" is a meaningless notion in an unpredictable environment. The equations of Little and Ohno tell us that in order for unit output per hour to be predictable, WIP Inventory units and Flow Time hours must be predictable. The Kanban system, for practical purposes, makes WIP Inventory a constant, or predictable and can, given Jidoka, have the same effect on Flow Time.

The Toyota Production System focuses on making both Flow Time and WIP Inventory either constants, predictable or both. This makes it possible to tell customers when their orders will be shipped. Making WIP Inventory either predictable, constant or both, will result in a reduction of WIP Inventory.[8]

Although Butt's work is very interesting and worth reviewing, it is beyond the scope of this book. It is presented here briefly, however, because of its suggestion that lean manufacturing is a kind of a gear train.[9] The concept of the system as a gear train is how the production system (ideally the entire business system) links information and materials between the manufacturer and customer via flow and pull systems. In their *Harvard Business Review* article, Dr. Steven Spear and Kent Bowen reveal: "The point is that when production lines are designed in accordance with rule 3,[10] goods and services do not flow to the next available person or machine but to a *specific* person or machine. If for some reason that person or machine is not available, Toyota will see it as a problem that might require the line to be redesigned."[11]

Spear and Bowen confirm also how the system is designed to function like a gear train. It moves material and information piece by piece, one by one, just like a gear train rotates tooth by tooth and any failure of the lean system to do so results in the redesigning of the system.

FROM GEAR TRAIN TO CHURCH

As the gear train analogy suggests, the lean production system links all processes, cells, or manufacturing lines to the customer's demand. Takt time sets the pace or velocity that the system or gear train moves tooth by tooth or part by part, one-piece flow. Standard operations set how people within the system will function at a pace also based on takt time. And as Chapter 13 on teamwork explained and Dr. Spear's Rules-in-Use supports, specific procedures (countermeasures under the umbrella of *jidoka*) are in place to address and resolve (issues that interrupt the system (see Figure 15.1).

By right designing the system to emulate a gear train, a lean firm can, as Dr. Spear and Bowen suggest, operate with both rigidity and flexibility, by following standard operations consistently and improving them via *kaizen* efforts, to deliver product to the customer—the right part at the right time in the right amount at the right price.

By designing a system in this manner, the opportunity to apply Alexander Hamilton Church's principles—to change activities into direct costs associated with component value streams—becomes simple and straightforward. It is a result of the physical system itself. In Figure 15.2 each gear represents a component manufacturing line or cell whose activities can be tracked. This analogy can be further represented by Figure 15.3. The model engine factory is overlaid with a gear train. If the model engine factory is right designed with lean principles, it will function like the gear train, operating synchronously to the customer demand rate—takt time.

Activities, materials, people, and equipment connected with each cell (or each gear in Figure 15.3) are both separate and linked to the overall system. From a customer and flow standpoint, each cell is linked to each other manufacturing line and also to the customer, as Butt and Toyota recognize with their formulas, which are based on Little's Law, via flow and pull. Each manufacturing cell is also separated by the physical design, which is explained in detail in the section on right designing. Each cell is a component value stream that manufactures (machines, fabricates, or assembles) its own unique product, such as crankshafts, connecting rods, or engine cylinders, and delivers the parts to the engine assembly line as needed or as pulled. All such activities are set to the rhythm of takt time. This is key to the success of the cost-management system for a lean firm.

FROM GEAR TRAIN TO COASE

The gear train analogy creates transactions as each tooth turns and meshes with the teeth on the other gear. As the lean system is spread across more and more gears—related value streams—it eliminates and reduces transactions throughout. This results in the consumption of value streams all through the ever-growing lean enterprise, or as James Womack and Daniel Jones call it, the extended value stream. As Ronald Coase theorized, the enterprise grows until it is no longer cost effective for it to bring activities under the firm's roof, but instead leaves activity in the marketplace.

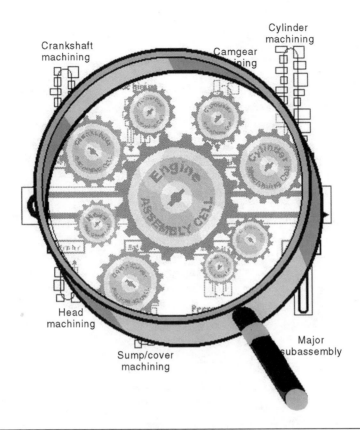

Figure 15.3 Model engine factory as a gear train

This movement of the lean enterprise into the market can expand to other plants within a particular company and into other companies.[12] Toyota has achieved this at a tremendous level. The Toyota Group companies are part of Toyota's huge gear train, which operates in near perfect synchronicity. Even though Toyota's group companies are separate firms, the group functions like a single entity entirely focused on each and every customer's needs. This function and its result amounts to Coase's theory in action. Many other companies that have successfully begun the transition into lean enterprises have been able to take advantage of what Coase discovered in the 1930s.

BACKFLUSHING

With flow (cellular style in one-piece flow manufacturing) and pull (inventory control and movement) in place, the lean factory can execute its operation like a gear train. And as Butt concludes, the system is designed to do just that. With this in mind, the lean system can now correctly and accurately function. If the engine factory model—the example used throughout this book—completes and ships an engine from its assembly line within takt time, a number of conclusions can be made.

The "If/Then" Loop

If the assembly line assembles an engine to be shipped, it has obviously consumed a crankshaft. And in turn, if the assembly/engine consumed a crankshaft, it was pulled from the inventory, which triggered the pull system to systematically move a crankshaft to replace it and, therefore, triggered the crankshaft machining line to machine another crankshaft to replace the one removed by the pull system. If the crankshaft machining line machines a new crankshaft to replace the one that was consumed, then it pulled a crankshaft casting from inventory, which triggered the crankshaft casting pull system to move inventory to replace it, which in turn triggered the foundry to cast a replacement casting. Figure 15.4 illustrates these activities.

Such a scenario may seem a bit cumbersome, but the important conclusion is that a right designed lean system does all activities automatically. Each "if/then" conclusion can be assumed to be correct and to have happened. Just like the gear train, if the assembly line gear (see Figure 15.3) rotates one tooth, by design, it can correctly be assumed that each of the other gears in the system rotated appropriately.

What the scenario above also indicates—and Figure 15.4 illustrates—is the ability of a lean system built upon flow and pull to self-execute needed activities at

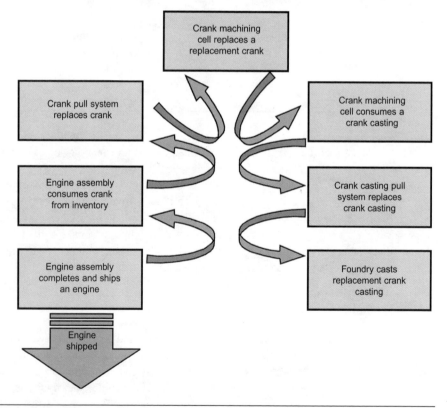

Figure 15.4 "If/Then" loops of a lean system

the right time in the right amount (ideally one by one) with the right part. The interconnection of the value stream flows and rigidity of the system to function and execute as needed allows for the great flexibility of the system to deliver exactly on time (just in time) the right part at the right location.[13] This system's capability is such that "the production process [is] so under control that WIP inventory is always much the same."[14] This is known as backflushing.

What Backflushing Does

The "if/then" of backflushing creates the ability for managers, or anyone, to intuitively know what has happened within the lean factory by simply knowing an output. For example, an engine was completed on the assembly line or a cylinder block was completed by the cylinder machining line. These physical events signify what has happened downstream or upstream in the system or in the value stream and any value streams that connect to it.

Backflushing can be applied to the supply base as well, assuming firms within the supply base are functioning as a lean enterprise. As noted earlier, this is exactly what Toyota and its supply base or group companies perform on a daily basis. Brian Maskell articulates what backflushing achieves through the supply base:

> The completion of the product can create a backflush that goes to the vendor. This is the logic:
>
> - If the product was made, the components must have been used.
> - If the components were used, they must have been received.
> - If the components were received, they must have been called off from the supplier.
> - If they were called off from the supplier, we must owe them money.
>
> A multitude of transactions and waste can be eliminated by this approach.... The supplier does not need to send an invoice because the backflushing can automatically create an invoice record in the accounts payable system.[15]

It must be remembered that whether or not the supply base is composed of separate companies, backflushing can function the same way. Maskell's example also shows the impact of transaction reduction in the backflushing scenario. Transactions within the plant—physical transactions that were discussed earlier—are eliminated, as are informational transactions involved with the traditional accounting and inventory tracking systems. Both the supplier and customer plants reap the benefit of no longer needing any of these transactions. With the lean system in place, one transaction—the shipment of an engine in the case of the model engine factory—can signify that a "factory load" of activities have successfully happened without the need to process transactions backstream, as with the traditional factory. Maskell acknowledges this very point: "This means we are getting very close to running the entire production plant on a single backflushing transaction ... we have eliminated virtually all of the traditional cost accounting transactions."[16] Maskell goes on to state how the speed of the lean system could even eliminate all production transactions as a result of back-flushing and would then need only the shipping transaction.[17]

Backflushing Benefits

The ability to backflush creates many benefits for any firm that can become a functioning lean enterprise. These benefits cover a wide range of areas in any manufacturing company, such as the factory floor, the shipping dock, production and inventory control, and accounting, to name a few more common areas. Backflushing eliminates and simplifies activities and transactions that would take place in a traditional operation. This ability is the result of right designing and executing the operational business system. The following are some benefits of backflushing:

- Elimination or reduction of material/inventory movement transactions
- Elimination or reduction of accounting transactions
- Elimination or reduction of shipping transactions
- Elimination of material searches
- Elimination of labor tracking
- Elimination (or great simplification) of daily, weekly, monthly, quarterly, and/or annual inventory counts
- Intuitive knowledge of operational activities ("if/then" scenarios) by anyone

Backflushing, Coase, and Church

Backflushing's "if/then" scenario contributes to a significant reduction of transactions in many areas. It could be stated that Coase's theory about transactions is a substantial factor in growing an operation's capability to deliver a product or satisfy the customer while shrinking the activities needed to accomplish this very action. Perhaps Coase would be very pleased with this situation, as it features physical proof of his theory.

Church would mostly likely also approve of the backflushing method, especially because of its easy and accurate costing. Since he put much effort and study into the ability to tie cost attributes directly back to the product and process, he would appreciate the tightness of the lean operational system that would allow for this very ability.

As the theme of this book is focused on cost management, it is important to note that backflushing significantly impacts cost information. As Harley-Davidson discovered, "backflush costing is typically associated with a highly simplified system in which relatively few transaction control points generate entries in the accounting system."[18] Yes, perhaps both Mr. Coase and Mr. Church would be pleased.

THE COMPUTER: THE THIRD
FACTOR FOR COST MANAGEMENT

The third factor that enables the cost-management system proposed here to be possible is the desktop computer. Perhaps Church would have been able to move his *Production Factors* method further into the mainstream during his era had the electronic technology been available. The gathering and tracing of information during his time had to be handled manually. The manual tracking of cost activities would have proved to be very cumbersome for most companies during the early twentieth century. Dr. H. Thomas Johnson states: "Until the advent of electronic information processing it was very difficult, and costly, to gather information about activities."[19]

The combination of manual tracking and lack of flow would have created an extremely burdensome environment to understand and tie cost activities to products or product families. This situation is as true today as it was in the pre-electronic industrial age of Church. Dr. Johnson also correctly believes that "user-friendly personal computer power enable companies to collect, manipulate, and analyze reams of real-time activity data at virtually no cost."[20] This is what Church was missing. Dr. Johnson and Kaplan point out that "of these systems, those designed to trace costs accurately to diverse lines of products disappeared after 1910, certainly by World War I. Perhaps the main reason for the disappearance was their high cost-to-benefit ratio. Existing information-processing technology made it costly to trace accurately the resources used to make each diverse product in a complex manufacturing plant.... The outcome ... might have been different had computers and electronic instruments been available."[21]

The difficulty of assigning cost activities to product value streams is the very reason the second factor, the implementation of flow production, for the proposed cost-management system is the most critical of the three. Implementing lean manufacturing and creating a lean enterprise not only allows for a host of benefits for any manufacturing company but also enables a company to directly assign cost activities to products and product families within a value stream.

Computers and software are relatively inexpensive. Today, virtually no company operates without a desktop computer involved with the business in some form. The software used for the method proposed here is inexpensive and usually resident on many computers purchased. The software used for the spreadsheet presented in this book is Microsoft Excel. Microsoft Excel is not exclusively needed for this method but is simple, inexpensive, and reasonably flexible. Any similar software spreadsheet would function just the same for this purpose. As will be discussed in detail in the next section. Hardware and software are the tools Church was missing and the tools lean firms can use today to achieve what Church could not. Spreadsheet programs and desktop computers make tracking and determining accurate product costs in the cost-management system easy and simple.

NOTES

1. Glenn Uminger used this analogy on May 6, 2003, during his presentation at the University of Michigan's Lean Manufacturing Conference.
2. The name Dennis Butt may be familiar to readers because he was the plant manager of the Kawasaki plant in Lincoln, Nebraska, introduced to many studying lean in the groundbreaking book Schonberger, *Japanese Manufacturing Techniques.*
3. Butt gave his presentation on November 8, 2001, at the Milwaukee School of Engineering's Lean Certificate Program in Milwaukee, Wisconsin.
4. Suzimori, Kusinoki, Cho, and Uchikawa, "Toyota Production System and Kanban System," 553–64.
5. Butt, "Toyota Production System," 4.
6. The original formula, called "Ohno's formula by Butt," is from a paper presented in 1977 by a group of engineers that work under Taiichi Ohno at Toyota. Suzimori, Kusinoki, Cho, and Uchikawa. "Toyota Production System and Kanban System," 553–64. The formula is discussed and presented on pages 561 to 564 of the article.
7. Butt, "Toyota Production System," 7.
8. Ibid., 5–6.
9. Butt's presentation and paper initiated my thought process about the tie between gear trains, flow, and Coase's theory and how these topics support Church's principles for cost management in a lean enterprise.
10. Rule 3 states that the pathway for every product or service must be simple and direct. This rule is taken from Spear and Bowen, "Decoding the DNA of the Toyota Production System."
11. Spear and Bowen, "Decoding the DNA of the Toyota Production System," 101.
12. Womack and Jones's *Seeing the Whole* addresses this concept and illustrates the value-stream mapping tool to help organizations achieve this. The analogy is adding gears to the gear train.
13. Recall the observation, rigidity and flexibility, made by Spears and Bowen in their article "Decoding the DNA of the Toyota Production System." By keeping strict adherence to the design and function of the system (flow and continuous improvement) the system has great flexibility to deliver whatever the customer needs quickly.
14. Maskell, *Making the Numbers Count*, 79.
15. Ibid., 87.
16. Ibid.
17. Ibid., 88.
18. Howell, Shank, Soucy, and Fisher, *Cost Management for Tomorrow*, 88.
19. Johnson, "Activity-Based Information," 24.
20. Ibid., 9.
21. Johnson and Kaplan, *Relevance Lost*, 127–28.

WHERE IS ABC?

In the pursuit of a cost-management system for the lean enterprise, it may be asked if activity-based costing (ABC)—or its more integrated form, activity-based management (ABM)—might be the answer.[1] It is a method and system that has gained attention in recent years, but it is *not* the solution that would benefit a lean manufacturer. A study of ABC methods, implementation process, and use proves it to be just another allocation accounting system, which is definitely not the direction for the lean manufacturer. As Orest Fiume and Jean Cunningham state, "The problem with ideas like ABC is one of narrow vision: they are based on old accounting concepts."[2] Fiume and Cunningham continue: "There are several problems with ABC. First, it is still an allocation method and wants estimates to be expressed in very precise terms. Second, it is expensive to establish and maintain.... In many cases, ABC may lead one to believe that the way to reduce costs is to produce in bigger batches."[3]

ABC is highly dependent on allocations, we do not see this as a desirable alternative.[4]

An ABC system does, in fact, greatly improve the allocation process and, in turn, clarifies cost information toward activities that create the cost. ABC is an improvement over traditional standard costing systems. But it is simply an improvement of a failed system. Dr. H. Thomas Johnson and Anders Bröms reveal the reality of ABC: "Unfortunately, management accountants quickly transform activity management into accounting-oriented costing exercise that today is known as 'activity-based management,' or ABM. ABM, as practiced today, is little more than an extension of ABC, which, of course, is nothing more than an extension of conventional cost accounting."[5]

THE DISADVANTAGES AND FAILURES OF ABC

In his book *Management Accounting Issues in Cellular Manufacturing and Focused-Factory Systems*, Dr. Dileep Dhavale lists the common problems with implementing and using an ABC system:

- ABC models are only a crude approximation of reality, not necessarily representing true causal relationships.

- Some practitioners feel that ABC models with a few dozen cost drivers and activity centers are overly complex for day-to-day operational use.
- Implementation of ABC systems creates significant additional demands on data collection, paperwork, computational time, and personnel.
- Some respondents feel that it is too cumbersome for lower-level operations staff (supervisors, foremen) to use ABC information because of its complexity.
- ABC possibly may encourage management of numbers instead of the business itself.[6]

As stated, ABC does greatly improve the accuracy of cost accounting during the allocation process, but it is still an allocation process, which is the very practice that should be eliminated. The key is to implement flow and move activities to align directly to products along their value stream.

Dr. Johnson strongly emphasizes why ABC is not the solution and how the lean enterprise is about different thinking:

> In the long run competitive businesses must change completely the way they organize people and work—to become responsive and flexible. Until a company changes the way it thinks about customers, people, and work, it undoubtedly will use ABC product cost information simply to improve how it does business as usual—that is, seeking economies of scale and speed in decoupled processes. The pathway to global competitive excellence is not reached by doing better what should not be done at all.
>
> But I firmly believe that the use of activity-based cost driver information to control operating activities—not just to reconfigure costs of products and other objects—leads companies to make decisions every bit as damaging to their long-term competitiveness as traditional standard cost information did in the last thirty years. Such uses of activity-based cost information commit "relevance lost" all over again![7]

Dr. Johnson made this statement in 1992; in 2002, he reveals who gave him this revelation and why ABC is nothing more than a collaborator of cost-cutting activities that, as discussed earlier, is the wrong approach for improving operational effectiveness. He states the following:

> I did not fully appreciate the depth of the question when it was first posed to me in the late 1980s by Richard Schonberger and Robert Hall, two renowned manufacturing authorities, and W. Edwards Deming, the world-famous authority on quality management. They suggested to me that overhead costs and the need for ABC systems would largely evaporate if companies organized work to meet customer requirements and spent less time striving to cut costs.[8]

Dr. Johnson continues: "ABM focuses attention on eliminating 'non-value activity,' a concept with which I grew increasingly disenchanted as I learned about Toyota's approach to organizing work."[9]

Johnson points out an interesting, but not commonly understood, view of lean manufacturing. When he references "Toyota's approach to organizing work," he is talking about the critical foundation of right designing the operational and, in turn, enterprise-wide system. ABC cannot support this approach, which underpins the successful transformation and execution of the lean enterprise.

ABC also fails—as does any cost-allocation–cost-accounting system—in having any ability to manage or control operations. This point was discussed in detail in Chapter 2, but Dr. Johnson summaries its failures in two basic points. He lists them in the following quote:

Accounting information—even activity-based cost information—is not an appropriate object to management for two reasons:

1. Accounting information does not identify what companies must do to be competitive; and
2. Cost information does not identify the root causes of costs.

Both deficiencies reflect the basic nature of accounting information, which is to measure results, not track what causes those results.[10]

JAPANESE MANUFACTURING AND ABC

Yasuhiro Monden clarifies why Japanese manufacturers using just-in-time (JIT) manufacturing systems do not feel it necessary to use the ABC approach. He writes: "Japanese automotive companies have not applied the ABC approach for these kinds of costs. Besides the fact that these costs are such a small portion of overall costs, they have also felt that companywide implementation of JIT techniques already works to minimize changeover and other drivers for these costs."[11]

Since effective lean manufacturers substantially reduce changeover times and other activities that exist much more extensively in traditional batch manufacturers, as Monden points out, they do not have the incentive to tie cost to activities. Their activities that create cost are either minimized or are already directly aligned to the product family. As previously discussed, Japanese lean manufacturers such as Toyota focus on target costing systems during product and process development, proper execution, and improvement (*kaizen* costing) of flow manufacturing instead of controlling costs via cost-accounting systems—ABC being one of these—during the product's life.

ABC VERSUS FLOW

Flow manufacturing is key in transformation into a lean enterprise and must be the central focus to achieve a useful cost-management system. Many companies, particularly traditional batch manufactures, use their cost systems to control and drive change in their operations and business. The managers of these companies focus on cost cutting and cost information, such as variances, to pound their agendas across their operations and personnel. They perceive ABC as a great tool to more strongly support an allocation strategy.

During my research and work as a consultant I have spoken with managers that have mistakenly viewed ABC as a key system to guide them to significant improvement and even to becoming a lean enterprise. They believed that ABC would give them the "control" to make the changes needed to transform to a lean firm. The very notion of control is a fundamental error in pursuing substantial change. Dr. Johnson fervently demeans this approach and its ability to support a transformation to a world-class manufacturer. He writes: "The belief that activity-based cost management tools will improve business competitiveness is a dangerous delusion! *No accounting information, not even activity-based cost management information, can help companies achieve competitive excellence*."[12]

Dr. Johnson also reveals that ABC, although an improvement over the costing method itself, is unquestionably not the solution a world-class enterprise would pursue or need. He writes: "As a tool to improve cost accounting information it is impeccable. But as a tool to improve the competitiveness of business it is pure snake oil. Any claims that activity-based cost management helps business become more competitive rest upon a poor understanding of what competitiveness means in the global economy."[13]

Perhaps the advice of two lean accounting practitioners that give the same message and warning about ABC systems should be followed. Glenn Uminger writes that he "does not like ABC accounting. Lean creates an environment where it is not needed! Creating excellent flow is much more important."[14] Fiume confesses that, "I just decided it was not the right way to go because it was just another method of allocating costs."[15]

Although it does, in fact, create much improved information than traditional standard costing methods, it misses the point developed throughout this book. Flow manufacturing is more effective in cost, delivery, and quality. Therefore, the point is to drop the traditional method of manufacturing, that is, batch manufacturing, and create flow manufacturing, which eliminates the majority of tracking issues that ABC works to resolve. Roy Harmon reveals that "companies continuing to pursue ways to apportion more 'accurately' costs that have no direct relationship between services performed and products benefited are engaging in an exercise in futility. The idea was a beautiful dream, but the reality is a nightmare."[16]

NOTES

1. The ABC methodology was originally developed at General Electric during the early 1960s as a result of efforts by finance and accounting people to develop better information for managing indirect costs. See Johnson, *Relevance Regained*, 132.

2. Fiume and Cunningham, *Real Numbers*, 3.

3. Ibid., 96.

4. Ibid., 99.

5. Johnson and Bröms, *Profit beyond Measure*, 166.

6. Dhavale, *Management Accounting Issues*, 106–7. These items are listed throughout pages 106 and 107.

7. Johnson, *Relevance Regained*, 149. This same point and much of the quote is also given in Johnson, "It's Time to Stop Overselling Activity-Based Concepts," 33. The same message is described in Johnson, Vance, and Player, "Pitfalls in Using ABC Cost-Driver Information to Manage Operating Costs," 26–32.

8. Johnson, "A Recovering Cost Accountant Reminisces," 2.

9. Ibid., 3.

10. Johnson, "Beyond Product Costing," 17.

11. Monden, *Cost Reduction Systems*, 339.

12. Johnson, *Relevance Regained*, 131–32.

13. Ibid., 132.

14. Uminger, "Lean: An Enterprise Wide Perspective."

15. Emiliani, Stec, Grasso, and Strodder, *Better Thinking, Better Results*, 220. This quote is from Orest Fiume.

16. Harmon, *Reinventing the Factory II*, 274.

PRODUCTION FACTORS: CHURCH'S METHOD APPLIED

Even though the early pioneers of the Industrial Revolution worked to achieve accurate product cost information through means other than allocation, use of these methods has risen only recently. Bruce Baggaley of BMA (Brian Maskell's consulting firm) states: "It now becomes important to know how much it costs to operate the value stream and the cost of products shipped from the value stream. In providing these needs we need to look for a better tool than is provided by the standard costing method in place in most traditional manufacturers."[1]

Perhaps when a manufacturing firm decides to become a lean enterprise its management should take the advice of James Womack and Daniel Jones when deciding both what to do about their business as a holistic system and, more specifically, what to do about the firm's accounting system. Womack and Jones advise: "Get rid of the system and start over, on a new basis."[2] Alexander Hamilton Church did just that when developing his ideas and principles for his cost-management system and production factors, as discussed in detail in previous chapters.

In this section, a method will be reviewed that could be considered a modern version of Church's method presented in 1910. Just as Church sought to redefine costs, this book contends that all costs should be shifted into direct costs, which in turn will assign costs to a product accurately. The method presented here can be achieved because the three factors that enable lean cost management are present. The three factors are the following:

1. Develop and implement flow production by utilizing and implementing:
   - One-by-one, one-piece flow
   - Flow, then pull
   - Right-design
   - A rigid and flexible system through standard operations and continuous improvement

2. Move all costs to be direct costs that are:
   - First presented by Church in the first decades of the twentieth century
   - Assignable
   - Actual
   - Accurate

3. Utilize desktop hardware and software that is:
   - Simple and inexpensive
   - Readily available

VALUE-STREAM ALIGNMENT

The first and second factors will be input into the third factor. Such a process of inputting will be shown and discussed using the engine factory model and a Production Factors spreadsheet. The configuration of the cost information in the spreadsheet is aligned along the value stream of each component; in the physical sense, it is aligned with each manufacturing cell (see Figure 17.1).

Maskell notes that value-stream information is the basis of cost information, as "activities and their related costs" are directly part of the value stream—or product family:

> Lean accounting uses the same value-stream cost-management information to determine product costs that was used to understand the value stream and its support processes. This information comes from the activities and activity costs associated with the value stream and support processes. These activities and their related costs are assigned to product families according to how much use each family makes of the activities.
>
> Value-stream cost management data provide excellent product family costs.[3]

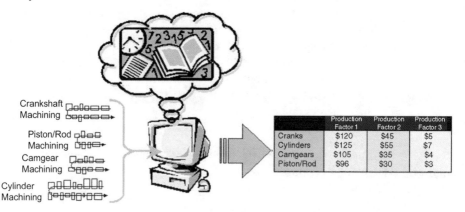

Figure 17.1 Information flow for the cost-management spreadsheet

Bruce Baggaley asserts the same conclusion and illustrates how all costs within the value stream are direct costs. He writes: "The value stream cost ... takes account of all the costs in the value stream. It makes no distinction between direct costs and indirect costs; all the costs within the value stream are considered direct."[4]

As discussed earlier, the need for cost information in the lean firm is much different from that of a traditional or batch manufacturer. The cost information in the lean enterprise is for planning and guidance, not for controlling operations as in a traditional manufacturer, which normally uses standard costing methods. Maskell states that "we need a clear understanding of costs if we care to achieve customer-focused price targeted through continuous improvement."[5] Maskell continues: "This cost information is used to understand the financial implications of the current processes and to assist with the prioritization of improvement initiatives."[6]

The main purposes of this cost information, as Maskell points out above, is planning and guidance to do the following:

1. Make decisions to manufacture or purchase
2. Accumulate component cost information for final product (the model engine factory used later in this chapter illustrates this point)
3. Maintain target cost
4. Allocate resources

Without solid and accurate cost information, these planning points are greatly compromised. This compromise is exactly what Church was concerned with in the early part of the twentieth century.

Cost information allows lean manufacturers to understand how well they have met their target costs and where resources must be applied to initiate improvements and countermeasures that will adjust activities to meet target costs. The same cost information provides guidance as to where future improvements and countermeasures may be needed. Also, it contributes to an understanding of where to shift and adjust resources for future activities and prioritization.

Cost information—which, unlike traditional costing methods, is accurate—allows for continued cost improvement and comparison to the target cost developed at the outset of a product's life. This ability to maintain accurate cost information is only accomplished via the value stream, as has been detailed throughout this book. Ansari, Bell, Klammer, and Lawrence state: "Target costing requires a shift away from traditional responsibility (department-focused) accounting systems to more process-oriented accounting information.... Process data focuses on interunit and interorganizational relationships. It collects cost data by how a product flows across the units/organizations."[7]

ACCURACY AND PRECISION

It has been continuously stressed that accurate cost information is critical for developing useable cost information, which will be useful for planning purposes. But the difference between accuracy and precision must be clearly understood. Traditional costing systems will produce cost information that is grossly distorted. Chapters 2 and 5 have discussed this problem in detail. But these same systems will calculate numbers up to five decimal places of a cent. This is ludicrous. Orest Fiume perhaps states it best: "And yet most companies believe they 'know' their product costs—out to four decimal places—a classic case of confusing precision with accuracy."[8] A distinction needs to be made between "precision" and "accuracy." Orest Fiume and Jean Cunningham define them: "Precision is knowing the answer down to the third decimal point. Accuracy is the answer that is correct for the decision you're trying to make."[9]

The same understanding must be part of lean cost management. Unless a product has absolutely no variety—that is, only one part number—and the processes within its value stream are totally stable, the cost will have some variability. Most products have various part numbers and various options and design specifics. For example, the crankshaft in the engine example has approximately thirty part numbers or variations. For the most part, these differences are minor dimensional differences; there are a few feature differences. Many of the engine components are subject to this same situation although they vary in the number of part numbers and feature differences.

The point of this discussion is that each crankshaft (or any of the other engine components or final engine assemblies) have various processing differences. Such differences will not be reflected in cost information developed in the cost-management spreadsheet. Cost information will give the correct cost of the product family in the value stream—for example crankshafts—but not the precise cost of each of the crankshaft part numbers, to continue using that example.[10] The breakdown and precision of cost information is completely unnecessary.[11] Figure 17.2 illustrates this point. Fiume would say: "I would rather be approximately right than precisely wrong."[12]

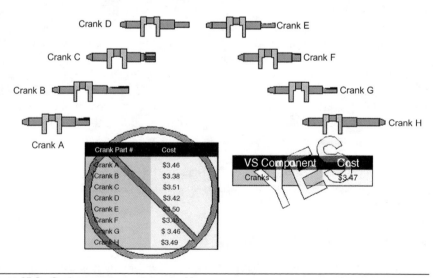

Figure 17.2 Cost accuracy versus precision

Figure 17.2 illustrates the unnecessary detailed breakdown of cost for of each part number for a component family. Only the cost for the product family, value-stream product, or component family should be tracked. Fiume's point about precision versus accuracy is more focused on the precision that is used in most traditional manufacturing companies that use standard costing. Many such companies' standard costing systems show costs down to four decimal places, or \$00.0000. This "precision" is absurd since, for one thing, the numerical figure is most likely wrong and not the actual cost. Second, why would any firm need a financial figure to the fourth decimal place anyway? The entire notion is inaccurate, completely unnecessary, and useless.

Even if an accurate figure is possible—as it is with the method proposed in this chapter—a precise and accurate figure is of no use. The accurate number developed by cost-management methods is used for planning and guidance. The accurate cost figure for the product family is ample information to serve this purpose.

THE COST-MANAGEMENT SPREADSHEET

The cost-management spreadsheet proposed and discussed here has a simple purpose. As presented in the "Accuracy and Precision" section of this chapter (and by Church), the spreadsheet simply provides a method to track and calculate an accurate cost figure for a lean firm's manufactured products for the purpose of planning and guidance. Its ability to achieve this information is based solely on the physical operation of the lean environment, which by its design physically aligns most of the activities to product families via their value streams. The spreadsheet simply takes the cost of the directly aligned activities along each product's value stream and compiles the total, in turn dividing the total cost by the total volume produced.

Maskell promotes the same simple method in an equation presented in his training material for product costs in cells:

$$\text{Total cell cost/Number produced}^{13}$$

In the same presentation, Maskell shows a slide that illustrates the same model and philosophy that the spreadsheet uses to achieve Church's objective—accurate product cost information (see Figure 17.3).

The Model Engine Focus Factory

The spreadsheet developed and used in this chapter focuses on the model engine focus factory. See Figure 17.4; it is virtually the same as Figure 11.3. Each department is actually a value stream for the major components manufactured within the model engine focus factory. The component value streams are one-piece flow lines or cells, which are self-contained and functional. They supply the final department or value stream, which is the final assembly of the complete engine per customer specifications and is shipped directly from the plant.

Summary Direct Costing

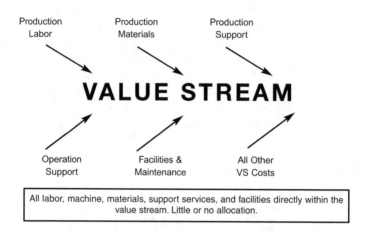

All labor, machine, materials, support services, and facilities directly within the value stream. Little or no allocation.

Figure 17.3 Direct costing via the value stream
Source: Maskell, "Lean Accounting Executive Briefing," slide 8.

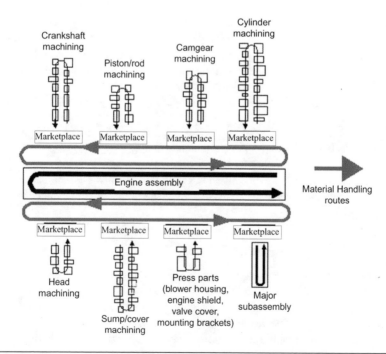

Figure 17.4 Engine focus factory and material handling routes

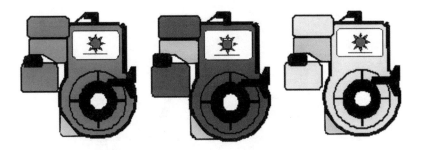

Figure 17.5   Engines manufactured in the model focus factory

Each component cell supplies a small marketplace from which the final assembly pulls what is needed as it assembles in a mixed-model fashion. Material handlers that move via standard routes and procedures accomplish the material movement between the marketplaces and the final assembly. The material handlers also supply the raw material—mostly castings and purchased parts—from marketplaces to the component cells as well as to the final assembly line.

The engine manufactured in this focus factory is a single cylinder, air-cooled engine for industrial and residential purposes, used, for example, in lawn tractors, generators, pumps, or mixers. See Figure 17.5 for an illustration of assembled engines.

A review of the Production Factors Spreadsheet (PFSS) will follow, but it will not be an all-inclusive review of every feature of the spreadsheet. It is meant to give an overview of what and how the spreadsheet tracks and calculates. It should be noted that the spreadsheet developed is not necessarily considered to be the absolute end for tracking and displaying cost information. It is one of many possible solutions based on the concepts, ideas, and proposals made in this book.

A variety of methods for allocation of less direct costs, such as those incurred by upper management, can be considered, and depending on a firm's individual needs, an organization may be required to give a more accurate cost picture. The development of the PFSS will also depend on the level of transformation in which a company is currently positioned in their lean journey, for example, whether they have yet implemented one-piece flow or right design.

Breakdown of the Spreadsheet

The PFSS tracks the costs of all incidences aligned with each value stream or cell. The crankshaft cell will be used as a specific example within the focus factory model. As Figure 17.6 shows, the complete machining of the crankshaft is accomplished within the one-piece flow cell from crankshaft casting to completed crankshaft, ready for assembly into the engine (also refer to Figure 14.1 for a breakdown of the operations to machine the crankshaft).

The spreadsheet captures the results of the physical changes made in the operation that allows the costs to be aligned with the product—crankshafts, in this example.

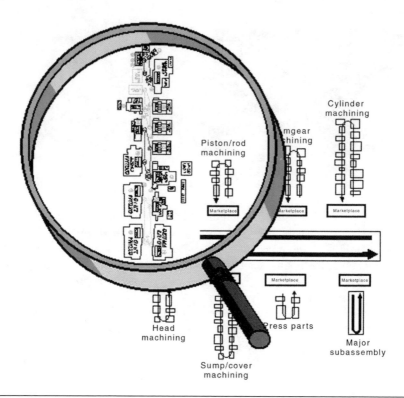

Figure 17.6 Zoom-in on crankshaft machining cell

As Figure 17.5 shows, equipment, machine tools, tooling, operators, utilities, and other support functions as directly part of the cell. All of these incidences are now directly associated with the cell and its machining of crankshafts; they are direct costs. These costs are captured in the spreadsheet.

Although the PFSS is a very helpful method to develop accurate (not precise) cost information for guidance and planning, it is simply a tool. As has been discussed in detail in previous chapters, the major foundation of lean cost management is the design and execution of the system. Accounting (particularly cost-management accounting) has very little to do with a company's lean cost-management system. The Production Factors Spreadsheet is the link between an accounting system and the lean enterprise from an operation management perspective. Figure 17.7 illustrates the connections between the lean enterprise, accounting, and the Production Factors Spreadsheet.

As stated in the section "Cost-Management Spreadsheet"—and as Figure 17.7 illustrates—the PFSS is an important, but small, tool for the lean enterprise. It is a supplement or, as stated at the beginning of this book, a reflection of manufacturing operations; it is simple and accurate cost information to guide managers in planning and decision making.

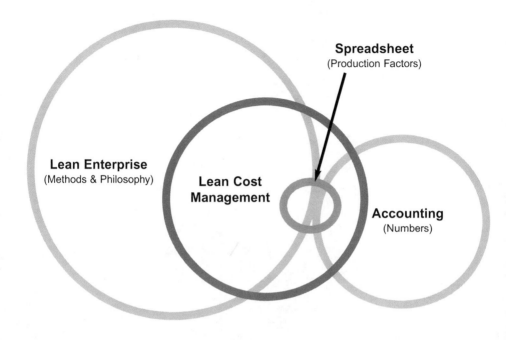

Figure 17.7 Connections between the lean enterprise, accounting, and the Production Factors Spreadsheet (PFSS).

THE PRODUCTION FACTORS SPREADSHEET

The PFSS was created in Microsoft Excel. Any applicable spreadsheet software would work, and the use of any desktop personal computer would be suitable. Simple desktop products fulfill the third factor of the factors for a lean cost-management system. Figure 17.8 illustrates the crankshaft-machining cell (or value stream) associated with the spreadsheet referenced in the following figures.

The Cost per Month Worksheet

The PFSS contains a worksheet for each month of the year (see Figure 17.9 for the Costs for January). Each monthly worksheet of the PFSS—titled the Costs per January, February, March, etc., on each worksheet tab—is identical in structure and each row in the worksheet represents an engine component value stream (listed in Figure 17.9 as "department" and "part/product," under label 1). The first group of costs attributed to each component value stream is labeled "overhead glob." Under this heading—label 2—are the costs associated with corporate costs, divisional costs, and focus factory support (managers, engineers, and so on).

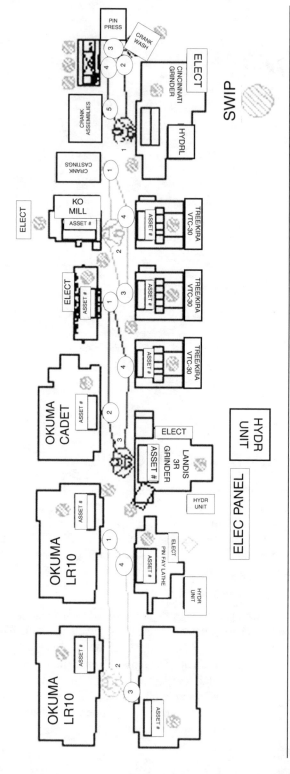

Figure 17.8 Component value stream, manufacturing cell with dedicated processes

The costs associated with these three overhead globs are the least direct of costs. The PFSS does break down their cost by a percentage that links to another worksheet, titled "overhead" in the spreadsheet. These costs are the most subjective included in the PFSS. It can also be legitimately argued that the corporate costs and divisional costs should not be included in the final product cost as developed by this type of cost information.[14] It has been included in this spreadsheet but should be done at the discretion of firms or manufacturing plants according to their needs.

Costs associated with the focus factory support, titled "focus factory overhead," are associated with the daily activities involved in the production within the value streams. This cost also is broken down by a percentage.

The rest of the costs listed on the Costs per January worksheet are directly associated with the production of the products. Label 3 or "direct costs (assigned costs)" includes the costs directly aligned with the value streams. These costs cover raw materials (castings and purchased parts), machine depreciation, operators, maintenance and repair, tooling, floor space, material handling, coolant, and utilities (air, electric, and heat or A/C). Such costs are all direct incidents of production. These costs are directly aligned with, associated with, and used by each product-family value stream as a result of the lean transformation, which was discussed in Chapters 8 and 11. Without the application of lean to the model engine focus factory, this claim would not be possible and, in turn, simple and accurate cost information would not be available.

The final information listed on the Costs per January worksheet in Figure 17.9 is simply the "cost per unit," label 4. This figure is calculated by simply dividing the costs accumulated in each value stream and dividing the sum by the quantity produced during the same period. The quantity produced, listed in the column "volume per period" is linked to a series of worksheets in the PFSS titled "Output for Month"— one worksheet for each of the twelve months—in Figure 17.10, which corresponds to each "Costs per Month" worksheet. In Figure 17.10, label 1 references the accumulated production output and is listed for each component value stream (manufacturing cell). Label 2 points out the column for the Engine Assembly daily output. These columns, one for each engine component value stream, track the daily and shift output for each value stream or manufacturing cell. The cumulative totals are tabulated at the bottom of the column. This total is also entered on the Costs per January worksheet – see label 4 of Figure 17.9. This allows an alignment of actual costs with actual production resulting in very accurate cost information during the period.

The Small Engine Focus Factory Worksheet

The next worksheet that will be reviewed in some detail is titled Small Engine Focus Factory (see Figure 17.11). This worksheet accounts for accumulated costs for each value stream during the year and calculates the total for each cost category and the cumulative total for the per-unit cost for each product family. It is laid out in the same manner with column titles as the Cost per Month Worksheets. The component value streams are listed as "department" and "part/product," or label 1. Label 2 shows

Cost Tracking (Cost Management System) — Generated on a PER PART Direct

1st day of the mo.	01/01/03
Day of the mo.	01/31/03
# working days	23

Boxes: **1**, **2**, **3**

Department	Part/Product	Corporate Overhead Percentage	Corporate Overhead Cost	Division Overhead %	Division Overhead Cost	Focus Factory Overhead M1X (General Factory) %	Focus Factory Overhead M1X (General Factory) Cost	Raw Materials Castings	Raw Materials Purchased Parts	Machines (Depreciation)	Operators per Period	Total Operator Cost per Period
L1A	Engine Assembly	36%	$2,800.00	36%	$8,925.00	30%	$30,000	$0.00	$23.45	$2,250.00	18	$69,000.00
M1A	Cylinders	20%	$1,600.00	20%	$5,100.00	15%	$15,000	$5.43	$0.00	$20,000.00	7	$26,833.33
M1B	Crankshafts	10%	$800.00	10%	$2,550.00	10%	$10,000	$1.20	$0.78	$16,666.67	4	$15,333.33
M1C	Camgears	8%	$840.00	8%	$2,040.00	5%	$5,000	$0.91	$0.00	$12,666.67	3	$11,500.00
M1D	Pistons/Rods	8%	$840.00	8%	$2,040.00	15%	$15,000	$0.88	$0.00	$9,333.33	3	$11,500.00
M1E	Heads	5%	$400.00	5%	$1,275.00	2%	$2,000	$0.45	$0.00	$3,900.00	2	$7,666.67
M1F	Sumps/Covers	2%	$160.00	2%	$510.00	3%	$3,000	$1.09	$0.00	$5,750.00	3	$11,500.00
M1G	Press Parts	5%	$400.00	5%	$1,275.00	5%	$5,000	$3.34	$0.04	$10,950.00	5	$19,166.67
M1H	Major Subassemblies	7%	$580.00	7%	$1,785.00	15%	$15,000	$0.00	$2.67	$1,300.00	5	$19,166.67

Total % = 100% (Cannot exceed 100%)

Total % = 100% (Cannot exceed 100%)

Total % = 100% (Cannot exceed 100%)

Cost per Operator	$40,000
Period	240
Cost per	$166.67

Period Key

Working Days	240
Working Weeks	50
Months	12

Maintenance Repair	Tooling (perishable & permanent)	Square Footage	Floorspace/ Building Cost (Sq. Footage Consumption)	Material Handling	Coolant	Air	Electric	Heat (Assigned by Sq. Footage)	Total Cost per Period ($)	Volume per Period	Cost per Unit this Period ($)
$567.00	$45.00	4,000.0	$3,000	$1,234.00	$0.00	$55.00	$500.00	$360.00	$625,654.65	21,617	$28.94
$56.00	$35.00	1,800.0	$1,350.00	$345.00	$56.00	$55.00	$500.00	$162.00	$188,157.70	21,559	$8.73
$78.00	$25.00	1,200.0	$900.00	$305.00	$58.00	$55.00	$500.00	$108.00	$89,535.16	21,292	$4.21
$34.00	$67.00	750.0	$582.50	$215.00	$450.00	$34.00	$500.00	$67.50	$53,041.32	21,615	$2.45
$58.00	$43.00	825.0	$618.75	$178.00	$42.00	$34.00	$500.00	$74.25	$58,620.71	21,583	$2.72
$234.00	$86.00	950.0	$712.50	$56.00	$25.00	$34.00	$500.00	$85.50	$26,648.32	21,497	$1.24
$5.00	$45.00	630.0	$472.50	$77.00	$32.00	$34.00	$500.00	$56.70	$45,595.73	21,517	$2.12
$123.00	$8.00	1,000.0	$750.00	$450.00	$15.00	$66.00	$500.00	$90.00	$111,744.21	21,583	$5.18
$154.00	$55.00	800.0	$600.00	$367.00	$0.00	$50.00	$500.00	$72.00	$96,870.49	21,446	$4.52
		Cost per Sq. Ft. per Mo.	$0.75				Heat Cost per Sq. Ft.	$0.09			

Figure 17.9 Production Factors Spreadsheet, Cost per Month Worksheet (January)

Volumes

Part/Product	Engine Assembly			Cylinders			Crankshafts			Camgears			Pistons/Rods			Heads			Sumps/Covers			Press Parts	
Department	L1A			M1A			M1B			M1C			M1D			M1E			M1F			M1G	
Day of the Month	1st Shift	2nd Shift	3rd Shift	1st Shift	2nd Shift	3rd Shift	1st Shift	2nd Shift	3rd Shift	1st Shift	2nd Shift	3rd Shift	1st Shift	2nd Shift	3rd Shift	1st Shift	2nd Shift	3rd Shift	1st Shift	2nd Shift	3rd Shift	1st Shift	2nd Shift
1	0	0		0	0		0	0		0	0		0	0		0	0		0	0		0	0
2	499	496		499	496		499	496		499	496		499	496		499	496		499	496		499	496
3	500	496		500	496		500	496		500	496		500	496		500	496		500	496		500	496
4	0	0		0	0		0	0		0	0		0	0		0	0		0	0		0	0
5	0	0		0	0		0	0		0	0		0	0		0	0		0	0		0	0
6	456	489		456	489		456	489		477	489		456	489		456	489		456	489		456	489
7	488	489		488	489		488	489		477	489		488	489		488	489		488	489		488	489
8	500	489		500	489		500	489		477	489		500	489		500	489		500	489		500	489
9	500	489		500	489		500	489		477	489		500	489		500	489		500	489		500	489
10	500	489		500	489		500	489		477	489		500	489		500	489		500	489		500	489
11	0	0		0	0		0	0		0	0		0	0		0	0		0	0		0	0
12	0	0		0	0		0	0		0	0		0	0		0	0		0	0		0	0
13	500	489		500	489		500	489		500	489		500	489		500	476		500	480		500	489
14	500	489		500	489		500	489		500	489		500	489		500	476		500	480		500	496
15	489	496		489	496		489	496		489	496		489	496		489	476		489	480		489	496
16	489	496		489	496		489	496		489	496		489	496		489	476		489	480		489	496
17	489	496		489	496		489	496		489	496		489	496		489	476		489	480		489	496
18	0	0		0	0		0	0		0	0		0	0		0	0		0	0		0	0
19	0	0		0	0		0	0		0	0		0	0		0	0		0	0		0	0
20	477	489		477	477		477	489		500	500		477	489		477	489		477	489		477	489
21	477	489		477	477		477	489		500	500		477	489		477	489		477	489		477	489
22	489	477		489	477		489	477		500	500		489	477		489	477		489	477		489	477
23	489	477		489	477		489	477		500	500		489	477		489	477		489	477		489	477
24	489	477		489	477		489	477		500	500		489	477		489	477		489	477		489	477
25	0	0		0	0		0	0		0	0		0	0		0	0		0	0		0	0
26	0	0		0	0		0	0		0	0		0	0		0	0		0	0		0	0
27	496	500		496	489		496	435		489	489		496	489		496	489		496	489		496	489
28	478	500		478	489		478	435		489	489		478	489		478	489		478	489		478	489
29	500	500		500	496		500	435		496	496		500	496		500	496		500	496		500	496
30	500	500		500	496		500	435		496	496		500	496		500	496		500	496		500	496
31	500	500		500	496		500	435		496	496		500	496		500	496		500	496		500	496
Total per shift =	10,805	10,812	0	10,805	10,754	0	10,805	10,487	0	10,746	10,869	0	10,805	10,778	0	10,805	10,692	0	10,805	10,712	0	10,805	10,778
Overall Total =	21,617			21,559			21,292			21,615			21,583			21,497			21,583			10,778	

1

Figure 17.10 Production Factors Spreadsheet, Output per Month worksheet (January)

Cost Tracking (Cost Management System) — Generated on a PER PART (M1A, M2A, ...) basis

| Department | Part/Product | Overhead Glob | | | Raw Materials | | Direct Costs (Assigned costs) | | |
		Cumulative Corporate Overhead	Cumulative Division Overhead	Cumulative Focus Factory Overhead M1X (General Factory)	Castings	Purchased Parts	Cumulative Depreciation (Machines)	Cumulative Operator Cost	Cumulative Maintenance & Repair
L1A	Engine Assembly	$47,800.00	$142,800.00	$360,000.00	$0.00	$23.45	$27,000.00	$829,333.33	$6,804.00
M1A	Cylinders	$27,600.00	$81,600.00	$180,000.00	$5.43	$0.00	$240,000.00	$329,500.00	$672.00
M1B	Crankshafts	$13,550.00	$40,800.00	$120,000.00	$1.20	$0.78	$200,000.00	$166,666.67	$912.00
M1C	Camgears	$10,840.00	$32,640.00	$60,000.00	$0.91	$0.00	$152,000.00	$125,000.00	$408.00
M1D	Pistons/Rods	$10,840.00	$32,640.00	$180,000.00	$0.88	$0.00	$112,000.00	$125,000.00	$672.00
M1E	Heads	$6,400.00	$20,400.00	$24,000.00	$0.45	$0.00	$46,800.00	$83,333.33	$2,808.00
M1F	Sumps/Covers	$2,160.00	$8,160.00	$36,000.00	$30,000	$1.09	$69,000.00	$65,750.00	$162,833.33
M1G	Press Parts	$6,400.00	$20,400.00	$60,000.00	$3.34	$0.04	$131,400.00	$208,333.33	$1,476.00
M1H	Major Subassemblies	$9,580.00	$28,560.00	$180,000.00	$0.00	$2.67	$15,600.00	$246,166.67	$1,848.00

1

2

Figure 17.11 Production Factors Spreadsheet, small engine focus factory costs

Cumulative Tooling (perishable & permanent)	Cumulative Floorspace/Building Cost (Sq. Footage Consumption)	Cumulative Material Handling	Cumulative Coolant	Cumulative Air	Cumulative Electric	Cumulative Heat	Total Cost	Cumulative Volume	Cost per Unit	Part/Product	Department
$540.00	$36,000.00	$14,808.00	$0.00	$660.00	$6000.00	$4,320.00	6,401,808.38	210,069	$30.47	Engine Assembly	L1A
$420.00	$16,200.00	$4,140.00	$672.00	$660.00	$6000.00	$1,944.00	2,238,415.04	248,528	$90.1	Cylinders	M1A
$300.00	$10,800.00	$3,660.00	$696.00	$660.00	$6000.00	$1,296.00	1,055,566.89	247,589	$4.26	Crankshafts	M1B
$804.00	$6,750.00	$2,580.00	$540.00	$408.00	$6000.00	$810.00	623,944.03	247,433	$2.52	Camgears	M1C
$516.00	$7,425.00	$2,136.00	$504.00	$408.00	$6000.00	$891.00	693,080.84	248,894	$2.78	Pistons/Rods	M1D
$1032.00	$8,550.00	$672.00	$300.00	$408.00	$6000.00	$1,026.00	313,822.68	248,263	$1.26	Heads	M1E
$540.00	$5,670.00	$924.00	$384.00	$408.00	$6000.00	$680.40	564,394.96	248,647	$2.27	Sumps/Covers	M1F
$96.00	$9,000.00	$5,400.00	$180.00	$792.00	$6000.00	$1,080.00	1,290.84543	248,495	$5.19	Press Parts	M1G
$660.00	$7,200.00	$4,404.00	$0.00	$600.00	$6000.00	$864.00	1,165,729.06	248,817	$4.69	Major Subassemblies	M1H

Total Engine Cost = $62.46

Figure 17.11 Production Factors Spreadsheet, small engine focus factory costs (*continued*)

the cumulative "overhead globs." The cumulative "direct costs (assigned costs)" are label 3. The cumulative "cost per unit" is label 4 and is based on the accumulated volumes linked from the Output for "each month" worksheets. And finally, the total cost for the final product—a small engine—is label 5.

Another worksheet, titled "Depreciation," which is included in the PFSS but not shown in any of the figures, provides a breakdown of equipment depreciation. In the case of the model factory, the depreciation is simplified and will not be discussed in detail, but it obviously plays a role in the cost of each product family's value stream. As was discussed earlier and is illustrated in a number of figures, the small engine focus factory has been right designed and each value stream has dedicated processes, machines, and equipment that are also right designed to accommodate one-piece flow in each process and are capable of meeting takt time.

The Cost Comparison Worksheet

The final worksheet that will be reviewed is one that shows a cost comparison of each component value stream (manufacturing cell) and is titled, "Cost Comparison" (see Figure 17.12). This worksheet simply takes each component value-stream cost from each month, calculated from the Cost per Month Worksheets—label 1—and lists them month by month. It also shows the total engine cost for each month, label 2, and an average cost for each value stream, label 3.

Today Is as Yesterday

An interesting point worth discussing is how the adoption of and transformation to a lean enterprise actually induces managers to function as their counterparts from early industry. As discussed in earlier chapters of this book, to truly understand an operation, as is required to design, execute, and improve a lean enterprise, managers and executives must become intimate with their own operation. Creating an environment where the cost-management spreadsheets examined above function simply and in a straightforward manner is simply not possible unless the managers and executives truly understand the operation and its support functions.

Cultivating this intimate understanding leads to a greatly diminished need for cost information. Cost information as put forth throughout this chapter is beneficial for planning and guidance but is only part of the knowledge base that supports the ability to make good business decisions.

What actually will happen in going through the lean transformation is that managers and executives revert back to the early industrial era when managers made solid decisions because they "knew" their business (products, processes, and customers). Cost information was a smaller part of their decision-making base and they relied more on their deep understanding of the operation.

Cost Comparison

Department	Part/Product	January	February	March	April	May	June	July	August	September	October	November	December	Total 2003
						Small Engine Focus Factory								
L1A	Engine Assembly	$28.94	$29.58	$29.47	$29.50	$28.34	$29.37	$29.52	$29.46	$29.26	$29.17	$29.55	$31.15	$30.47
M1A	Cylinders	$8.73	$9.17	$9.07	$9.07	$9.07	$8.99	$9.03	$8.91	$8.91	$8.83	$9.17	$9.99	$9.01
M1B	Crankshafts	$4.21	$4.35	$4.27	$4.23	$4.23	$4.24	$4.25	$4.18	$4.18	$4.11	$4.38	$4.88	$4.26
M1C	Camgears	$2.45	$2.59	$2.53	$2.47	$2.47	$2.50	$2.51	$2.47	$2.47	$2.41	$2.62	$2.99	$2.52
M1D	Pistons/Rods	$2.72	$2.87	$2.80	$2.73	$2.73	$2.77	$2.78	$2.73	$2.73	$2.66	$2.86	$3.32	$2.78
M1E	Heads	$1.24	$1.30	$1.28	$1.25	$1.25	$1.26	$1.27	$1.24	$1.24	$1.22	$1.29	$1.49	$1.26
M1F	Sumps/Covers	$2.12	$2.32	$2.29	$2.26	$2.26	$2.28	$2.32	$2.27	$2.27	$2.23	$2.33	$2.65	$2.27
M1G	Press Parts	$5.18	$5.25	$5.21	$5.17	$5.17	$5.19	$5.26	$5.16	$5.16	$5.10	$5.29	$5.74	$5.19
M1H	Major Subassemblies	$4.52	$4.76	$4.71	$4.70	$4.70	$4.65	$4.81	$4.66	$4.66	$4.60	$4.74	$5.35	$4.69
	Total Engine	$60.10	$62.19	$61.64	$61.36	$58.57	$61.24	$61.76	$61.89	$60.88	$60.33	$62.24	$67.56	$62.46

Figure 17.12 Production Factors Spreadsheet, Cost comparison for each month.

Glenn Uminger, Orest Fiume, Mark DeLuzio, Jean Cunningham, and Brian Maskell confirm this phenomenon.[15] They all focus on changes in the operation and how executive management must lead and understand the change process deeply.

The difference between today's manufacturing executives and yesterday's is that executives today have the principles, methods, philosophies, and tools of lean manufacturing. These concepts allow managers to more deeply understand their operation and significantly improve the design and execution of their facilities. Lean concepts (lean cost management, lean manufacturing, and the lean enterprise) are based on concepts from early industry. Flow was developed by Henry Ford's engineers[16] and later developed to a much deeper level by Toyota. But in the case of Ford and Toyota, the managers and engineers simply had a deep understanding and intimate contact with their operations, which enabled them to make outstanding decisions without the need for significant cost information—and definitely not a need for detailed accounting information.[17]

The change to a lean enterprise and the use of the PFSS actually guide today's manufacturers to function more like their predecessors in manufacturing.

NOTES

1. Baggaley, "Costing by Value Stream," 24.
2. Womack and Jones, *Lean Thinking*, 52.
3. Maskell, "Lean Accounting for Lean Manufacturers," 52.
4. Baggaley, "Costing by Value Stream," 25.
5. Maskell, "Lean Accounting Executive Briefing," slide 2.
6. Maskell, "Overview of Lean Accounting."
7. Ansari, Bell, Klammer, and Lawrence, *Target Costing*, 23.
8. Fiume and Cunningham, "Lean Accounting and Finance," 11.
9. Fiume and Cunningham, *Real Numbers*, 32.
10. Both Maskell and Fiume have stressed this same point—accuracy versus precision—in a number of conversations I have had with them since 1997. Fiume has also stressed the same point in presentations that I have attended.
11. In several conversations with Brain Maskell, Orest Fiume, and Glenn Uminger since June 1997, they all discussed that having continuous cost information and component product cost information may be the prevalent method for cost management. However, using the engine factory model, in order to figure the cost of the final engine assembly line, the cost of each component—that is, the component value stream—must be developed. This is exactly what the spreadsheet does.
12. Emiliani, Stec, Grasso, and Strodder, *Better Thinking, Better Results*, 228n8.
13. Maskell, "Lean Accounting Executive Briefing," slide 4.
14. Bruce Baggaley writes: "The costs and expenses associated with these non-value stream tasks are not allocated to the value streams. They are treated as sustaining costs of the business. They are budgeted and controlled, but they are not allocated.

There is no need for full absorption costing." Baggaley, "Costing by Value Stream," 28. As stated in this book, this position is a legitimate one. The simplicity of the Production Factor Spreadsheet allows for the easy removal of this cost information to fit a specific firm's needs.

15. The same point has been stressed by not only leaders in the accounting arena— as these individuals are—but also by mangers and executives in all types of manufacturing leadership positions. I have consistently heard this critical point from, and discussed it with, a variety of manufacturing managers and executives throughout the last ten-plus years.

16. Huntzinger, "Roots of Lean—Highland Park: The Cradle of Flow," 48–58.

17. Both Taiichi Ohno at Toyota and Charles Sorensen at Ford never discussed any reliance on accounting information and actually do describe issues they had with accountants at times. Church also emphasized the operations when discussing his production factors concept and methods.

A SUMMARY OF THOUGHT: LEAN COST MANAGEMENT

Alfred Sloan, the architect of General Motors, wrote: "The circumstances of the ever-changing market and ever-changing product are capable of breaking any business organization if that organization is unprepared for change—indeed, in my opinion, if it has not provided procedures for anticipating change."[1]

Lean accounting for the manufacturing enterprise, that is, cost management, is about design, function, and execution, not about accounting. The manufacturing enterprise must create a simple, straightforward, and accurate cost-information system. This cost-management system must be subservient to the manufacturing operations. It must support manufacturing needs, and not the other way around. Fred Garbinski[2] of the Parker Hannifin Company recapitulated lean accounting very well. He writes: "It's not finance, it's how you run the enterprise."[3]

HISTORY

This book explores and discusses the evolution of manufacturing between 1885 and 1925 and its effects on accounting activities, needs, and innovations. The strongest influence on cost management was the expansion of internal operations and processes, which drove cost information from the marketplace to become hidden inside the plant. Managers and engineers developed methods to understand and calculate internal costs for product manufacturing that had moved into larger operations as the proliferation of product families became more and more common. This specific need—product costs for internal decision making—was ever on the minds of these early managers and engineers. They needed product and process cost information to make competent decisions that impacted the future of their operations.

Unfortunately, in time, product-cost information became driven by external financial reporting, leading to gross distortion as simple methods of allocation became the standard. Since aggregate cost information was adequate for the needs of external reporting, the allocation process was acceptable. The developers of accounting methods had no intentions of using cost information for operational control, only for external financial reports and quoting. As it happened, these methods, particularly after World War II, were driven back into operations and became the standard and accepted control methods for managing the manufacturing operations. This mistake continues today.

ALEXANDER HAMILTON CHURCH

Alexander Hamilton Church, who recognized the potential issues of such aggregate information, strove to develop a method and philosophy that would provide accurate product-cost information for management and guidance purposes. Church's production-factors concept unfortunately did not take hold and establish a standard for cost-management practices, although it can be recognized today as truly innovative and as the best direction for cost information.

One of the major reasons for the failure of Church's production-factors concept to become a fixture in manufacturing was the lack of product processing alignment in manufacturers during Church's time, except for Ford's Highland Park plant. The second issue was the difficulty and cost of tracing and tracking the incidence of costs. During Church's time, information gathering had to be done manually. The combination of haphazard product movement and the inability to easily gather cost information steered manufacturers from his methods.

Today's lean enterprise and the modern desktop computer resolves the issues encountered by Church and directly allows his production-factors philosophy to become reality. A truly lean enterprise—best exemplified by Toyota and its group companies in its physical operations design—right designs the operation around products and product families, which creates an environment that aligns nearly all incidence of costs—both direct costs and support functions—directly to the products. Due to the very nature of a lean operation, the *production factors* are direct aspects of producing a product. This situation allows the simple, straightforward ability to directly associate costs with products. This ability satisfies Church's desire for accurate costing for products. The simple alignment of cost information with products is simplified even further with today's availability of desktop personal computers and software. Tracking and tracing nearly does not exist because of product value streams in the lean enterprise. The direct information that supports the product—known as resource consumption—is simply maintained in the computer at little to no effort and divided by the amount of product produced to meet the customer demand:

Value-Stream Costs/Output

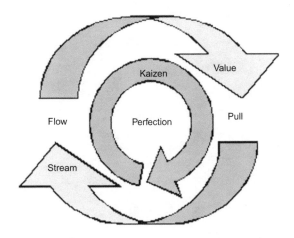

Figure 18.1   Continuous loop of improvement and change; flow, pull, *kaizen*, flow

THE THREE FACTORS

This simple equation satisfies the first of the three factors of a lean cost-management system and Church's philosophy: accurate cost information. The second two factors allow the first one to be possible: physical implementation of lean (that is, flow manufacturing) and desktop computers and software. These three factors are key to achieving the cost-management system proposed here.

Of the three factors, the implementation of lean manufacturing—applying one-piece flow—is the most basic foundation of the entire cost-management system. Flow manufacturing—including both product and information—is the focused objective for a lean enterprise. If flow cannot be achieved, pull must be the next order.[4] The constant pursuit of perfection, or the continual striving to create absolute one-piece flow, results in a continuous loop of improvement and change, that is, *kaizen* (see Figure 18.1).

In a truly lean enterprise the pursuit of perfection is understood and continually pursued under the premise of *kaizen*; again, refer to Figure 18.1. Even though the implementation of lean entails physical changes to the entire manufacturing enterprise, it is underscored by a *change in thinking*.

THINKING

The lean firm thinks in completely different way than does a traditional batch manufacturer. This different mentality is what underscores the ability of one firm over another to truly transform into a lean enterprise. Many companies try to transform into

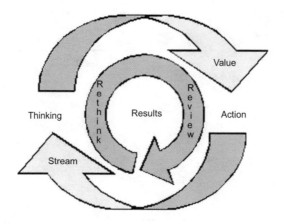

Figure 18.2 Continuous loop of improvement and change; think, action, results, think

lean, but until they achieve thoroughly different thinking, they will not succeed in changing into a lean enterprise.

Much of this book discussed the context of thinking that must be undertaken to transform into lean. The reason for this substantial discussion is that changed thinking must be present in order to achieve superior implementation of a lean system. Just like the loop depicted in Figure 18.1, thinking precedes action and creates a continuous flow of improvement and change. Figure 18.1 could easily be laid on top of Figure 18.2, because they are nearly one and the same; Figure 18.2 is the foundation for Figure 18.1.

Figure 18.2 can even be viewed as a simplified version of the Deming Circle (Figure 18.3).[5] This thought process drives change and knowledge on a continual basis, which is key to evolving the lean enterprise as well as a lean cost-management system.

Managers often discuss excellent thinking, yet they are not able to implement any action within their plants or companies. Likewise, managers have often taken good action, but did not have the thinking needed to understand or evolve the system any further than just some good lean tool implementation. Presently in industry, there are more and more companies and people "doing" lean, but there are very few lean enterprises or companies that have truly transformed both their thinking and action.

Thinkers

The ability to think is critical to understanding, implementing, and transforming a company into a lean manufacturer. Three key people who were discussed in these pages illustrate this type of critical thinking coupled with action. They were Church, Henry Ford,[6] and Taiichi Ohno.[7] They are listed in the table on the next page with comparisons of their thinking and actions.

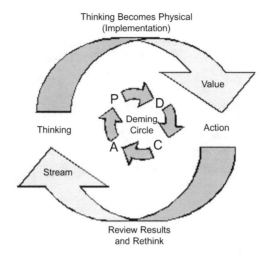

Figure 18.3 Continuous loop of improvement and change and the PDCA (Plan, Do Check, Act) Cycle

A number of philosophies (types of thinking, i.e. one-piece flow, MBM, direct cost, *kaizen*, etc.) that impact what companies do (action) have also been discussed in detail. These ideas are crucial in changing how companies and people operate and think. Although citing such thinking as "philosophy" tends to lead some to characterize it as nonaction, or as merely "fluffy" ideas, Toyota has smashed this misconception. Their Toyota Production System (TPS) is in fact soundly based on a philosophy that has led to dramatic methods, tools, and actions that have propelled them to be the most effective manufacturer in industry.[8]

	Thinking	**Action**
Alexander Hamilton Church	Accurate and useful cost information	Production-factors methods and philosophy
Henry Ford	Car for the masses	Led the design of the Model T and hired men that developed flow manufacturing at Highland Park plant
Taiichi Ohno	Must compete in a low volume and high variety market	Developed and implemented TPS and was famous for after-hours shop antics while trying out his ideas

The ideas, such as flow manufacturing and continuous improvement by solving problems that interrupt flow, that support Toyota's philosophies and guide the actions that make them—or any truly lean enterprise—truly successful, were discussed in detail in this book and will be reviewed below.

Economies of Scale

Economies of scale is the reigning business philosophy in the industrial world today. Its premise is that more output or volume leads to cheaper "per unit" costs. This premise is actually true, but its failure lies in the fact that it leads to overbuilding capacity. If overcapacity (or wrong sized/wrong designed) systems, processes, or machines are built or purchased, then increasing output will drop the cost of each unit. The lean enterprise uses a different approach—it designs and builds *only what is needed* to output *only what is required* by the customer and no more. As companies take this different approach—different thinking—they continually evolve their systems to have the ability to deliver this incremental cost to a higher level.

Toyota and other lean companies have been able to achieve this skill via their production system. They also deliver quicker and higher quality products at a lower or very competitive price.

MBR, MBM, and Execution

Another business philosophy that directly contributes to building a lean enterprise is MBM. Like economies of scale, MBR is the reigning method that companies use to manage their businesses. MBR is simply the belief that if the correct targets or objectives are given and monitored in the business, then the right actions will take place in order to reach the desired objectives and targets, or results.

The failure of MBR comes from the fact that most people do not know what to do to change their organization so that they may not only reach the desired results but also sustain and evolve the results over the long term. Organizations, that is the people within organizations, do not know how to execute properly to achieve, sustain, and advance the results of their business.

A fundamental failure of this understanding stems from viewing an organization as an accumulation of individual parts. It is assumed that the sum of these parts results in a linear addition of the whole or that improvement or savings in one part will translate to equal improvement or savings for the whole. This view is wrong because, as discussed in detail in Chapters 2, 4, and 11, an organization functions like a living entity. A change in one part directly affects the parts connected to the initial part and the parts connected to those parts and so on. All parts of a business are interconnected and changes impact many aspects of the business, which may or may not result in a benefit (improvement or savings) in the organization as a whole. Understanding this concept is key to using MBM. Flow manufacturing is a manifestation of applying MBM to a manufacturing business.

Spear's Rules-in-Use

Like Dr. H. Thomas Johnson and Anders Bröms's MBM, Dr. Steven Spear's Rules-in-Use are principles that underlie normally accepted lean principles. According to Dr. Spear, the Rules-in-Use represent the fundamental essence of the TPS.[9] Dr. Spear emphasizes that through the Rules-in-Use, the lean enterprise develops and actuates superior design, operation, and improvement.[10] These three aspects of the Rules-in-Use correspond directly to the application of the lean transformation presented in this book and its emphasis on system design (design), execution (operation), and feedback (improvement).

The Rules-in-Use guide the operation and development of TPS at Toyota, its group companies, and manufacturers that have worked directly with the Toyota Supplier Support Center (TSSC).[11] The Rules-in-Use guide the design of the complete business enterprise system from functions (see Figure 18.4). Dr. Spear's Rules-in-Use parallel the concepts proposed in this book of utilizing simplified flow through value streams.

Spear writes: "In the TPS managed organizations in which I gathered data, the expected functioning of [tending to] all activities, connections, and pathways be specified before they are used. Built-in-tests immediately diagnosed that the activity, connection, or pathway was actually working as expected in the specification. If not, then the activity, connection, or pathway was redesigned close in time, place, and person to the occurrence of a problem."[12]

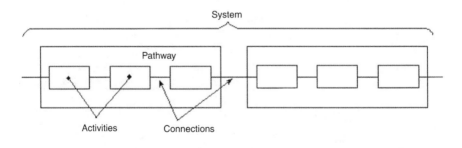

Figure 18.4 System design model based on Spear's Rules-in-Use and this book
Source: Based on Dr. Steven J. Spear's figures and discussion on nested modularity in "The Toyota Production System: An Example of Managing Complex Social/Technical Systems, 5 Rules for Designing, Operating, and Improving Activities, Activity-Connections, and Flow-Paths" (PhD diss., Harvard University, May 26, 1999), 21–29 and the design hierarchies in his "Just-in-Time in Practice at Toyota: Rules-in-Use for Building Self-Diagnostic, Adaptive Work-Systems" (Working paper 02-043, August 16, 2002), 2, 8.

Coase's Transactions

By understanding and applying the principles of flow and MBM and by moving away from economies of scale, transactions necessary in traditional batch manufacturers are greatly reduced. Lean manufacturers reap the benefit of most transactions being completely eliminated and the remaining ones being significantly simplified.

In his theorem, Ronald Coase proposed that organizations would grow in size when doing a transaction internally would cost less than doing the transaction in the marketplace. The lean enterprise accomplishes the same principles both internally and externally by reducing costs because transactions are eliminated or simplified. The key concept to achieve Coase's principle in the lean enterprise is flow manufacturing. The significant impact flow has on transactions was exemplified by Ford's Highland Park plant in the early nineteenth century and is exemplified by Toyota today.

Butt's Gear Train

A common analogy used for illustrating flow manufacturing is a linked chain, but perhaps a better analogy is a gear train. Chapter 16 presented Dennis Butt's concept of the gear train and explained that the equations developed by Toyota are actually a derivation of equations for gears.

The concept and analogy of a gear train for the lean enterprise can also be linked to the principles of MBM. MBM interlinks parts of an organization, and viewing a company as a gear train illustrates the organization as connected, meshed gears that directly react and respond to what happens to each respective gear (see Figures 15.2 and 15.3).

System Evolution

The concepts discussed throughout this book directly support the continued evolution of any lean system. Having an intimate understanding of how to apply these ideas, concepts, and principles is key to continually pushing the system to achieve new and improved levels of performance both in design and execution. The basic lean principle of *kaizen* can be applied in a number of avenues to move the system forward. Using the *kaizen* philosophy to promote and implement flow manufacturing—one-piece flow—is fundamental to further "leaning" in an already lean enterprise. Toyota is a master at continually developing and evolving their business system by pushing flow manufacturing via *kaizen* of existing and new system ideas and concepts.

A SMALL BUT IMPORTANT CONTRIBUTOR: THE SPREADSHEET[13]

Most of the chapters in this book discussed concepts, ideas, principles, and philosophies. These items create context or, as has been stated, a particular state of thinking. One conclusion then would be that context or thinking is fundamental to developing the lean enterprise as well as a lean cost-management system. This point is stressed throughout this book. The Production Factors Spreadsheet (PFSS) developed in Chapter 17 is simply a by-product of such thinking and the results of a need created by the physical lean systems designed and implemented.

The spreadsheet is thinking put into action. It is simply the result of Figure 18.3; it is the result of how thinking supports, drives, precedes, develops, and evolves action. In the spreadsheet, thinking manifests itself into a useful tool, which—as asserted at the beginning of the book—must be the purpose of the cost-management system; it must consist of methods and tools that are subservient to the operational system. The spreadsheet fulfills this purpose but must be part of the ongoing *kaizen* to continually support the overall progress of the business system and the enterprise.

IN THE END

As much of this chapter states, context is critical to enabling the ability to develop, implement, and evolve a lean enterprise. Different thinking is the cornerstone to developing this context on which the physical implementation is built. Therefore, most of this book focused on the context—or thinking—and physical design and implementation of the system itself; a smaller portion was devoted to an accounting method.

This book also purposely chooses the term cost-management accounting instead of managerial-cost accounting to illustrate the purpose and reason for the lean cost system. As this book asserts—and as was supported by leading lean practitioners with accounting backgrounds—the lean enterprise's accounting system has little to do with accounting in the traditional sense and is actually about the physical system itself—how the systems are developed, designed, and executed.

As the PFSS that was developed in Chapter 17 shows, it is only able to be supportive and successful if the physical system is designed properly for superior flow along value streams. Without this physical manifestation, Church's vision would remain only a vision, and it would continue to be lost in industrial obscurity. Instead, Church's concept of obtaining accurate cost information for guidance and decision purposes becomes a reality with the combination of flow and today's computer capabilities. The three factors of the lean cost-management system are fulfilled. This book and its conclusion by no way concludes the pursuit of a better cost-management system for the lean enterprise; instead it creates a good starting block for the continued development and implementation of cost-management systems that support the lean enterprise. As the fifth principle, perfection, from James Womack and Daniel Jones' book *Lean Thinking*, implies, the pursuit of perfection is ongoing and never ending.

The combination of thinking (context) and action (implementation) are necessary to build and evolve a superior system and, in turn, a superior manufacturing company. Church, Ford, and Ohno understood this need and vision, and worked to realize it for the benefit of industry and society. Perhaps Monden and Sakurai most simply and elegantly state the real purpose behind the work of this book and perhaps even the work of industry itself: "Knowledge and ideas without action result in the same outcome as ignorance."[14]

NOTES

1. Sloan, *My Years with General Motors*, 438.
2. Fred Garbinski is the recently retired director of cost accounting for the Parker Hannifin Company and has spent over twenty-four years with the firm starting as director of internal audit, then moving to the controller's staff. He has also held positions with responsibilities including reporting, government accounting, and cost accounting. Prior to his time at Parker Hannifin, Garbinski spent twelve years in public accounting with Deloitte & Touche.
3. Garbinski, director of Cost Accounting, phone conversation with the author, Mukwonago, WI, February 12, 2004.
4. This must always take place along a value stream with the actual value as it pertains to the customer. See Womack and Jones, *Lean Thinking*, chapters 1 though 5.
5. Walter Shewhart, the pioneering statistician who developed statistical process control in the Bell Laboratories in the United States during the 1930s, originally developed the concept of the PDCA (Plan, Do Check, Act) Cycle. It is often referred to as the Shewhart Cycle. It was taken up and promoted very effectively from the 1950s on by the famous quality management authority, W. Edwards Deming, and is consequently known by many as the Deming Circle.
6. Ford had the ability to hire men that understood his vision—creating a car for the masses—and continually worked in implementing and evolving a production system that would achieve the vision. The vision of both the car and the production system came into fruition at the Highland Park plant.
7. Some of Ohno's shop tales while trying to develop his production system are told in Shook, "Bringing the TPS to the US" in *Becoming Lean*, 47–55.
8. Recently the reality of Toyota's business philosophy has led them to change their term for their own system from the commonly known Toyota Production System (TPS) to what now is referred to as the Toyota Way. This change is the result of their business system being an enterprise-wide system and philosophy, not just a production system.
9. Spear, "Just-in-Time in Practice at Toyota," 9.
10. Throughout all of Dr. Steven Spear's work (see bibliography), specific examples are given describing actual operational events that illustrate the Rules-in-Use in action during daily operations. According to Dr. Spear's research, Toyota strives to properly design or prespecify work and responses to issues that arise during the use of their system.
11. The Toyota Supplier Support Center is a group of TPS experts that was established in the United States by Toyota to help manufacturers develop and implement TPS

principles within their own business. The TSSC works with both suppliers and nonsuppliers of Toyota.

12. Spear, "Just-in-Time in Practice at Toyota," 14.

13. Although it is out of the scope of this book, lean financial accounting information is also an important part of the lean transformation. Value-stream cost information, as proposed in this book and presented by the Production Factors Spreadsheet (PFSS), can contribute directly to the development and presentation of financial information for the lean enterprise. For details on this aspect of the lean enterprise, lean financial accounting, see Fiume and Cunningham, *Real Numbers*, 107–18; and Lean Enterprise Institute, "Creating the Course and Tools for a Lean Accounting System," 4–5. Fiume and Cunningham's book also includes an excellent discussion of the many aspects of accounting for the lean enterprise.

14. Monden and Sakurai, eds., *Japanese Management Accounting*, xvii.

19

HOW TO TRANSFORM TO
LEAN COST MANAGEMENT

Satoshi Hino, in his profound book *Inside the Mind of Toyota*, reveals that "unless we could grasp the structure of their minds, then even though we might be able to copy the Toyota Production System, we wouldn't be able to work out methods for going beyond it and we would never prevail. I concluded that I had to unravel *how* it was that their way of thinking came about" (emphasis added).[1]

How does a firm go about implementing changes that lead to a lean cost-management system? The path is not easy or for the faint of heart. In fact, to date there is probably no company that has been able to truly achieve this. Hino divulges that "methods advocated by Toyota are too far removed from the realities of most companies."[2] Toyota and its group companies do function in this manner and in fact exemplify a lean cost-management system. But they cannot definitively even explain themselves how they achieved this situation. Hino continues: "Very few companies have adopted the system with success. Parts are meaningful only in the context of a whole, and transplanting a part tends to results in less-than-perfect functioning. Companies need to adopt the system in its entirety."[3]

Many dynamics played a role in Toyota's development and their progress took place over six decades; there is not a defined path that they can explain. Firms scorching this road are truly burning a completely new path: one that has not yet been trodden. So how can one explain what will help a firm to succeed? The best "how-to's" are a combination of means and lessons learned by those who have spent time and energy out in the deep lean wilderness trying to figure it out. Lessons will be covered first.

LESSONS LEARNED

The first lesson *and* means is that time and energy must be spent trying to figure it out on your own! Making mistakes and experiencing misdirection are part of the path. Mistakes and misdirection must be accepted or there is no reason to venture forth, as frustration will kill the business and its leaders who either do not understand this or will not accept it. Those of us who have been deep in the wilderness know well that there are times that a decision will have to be made without completely knowing or understanding the eventual result of that decision. We recognized that it is part of the learning, and as long as the principles are adhered to, even if a mistake is made, a valuable lesson will be the actual result. This connects to lesson two: the journey is a series of lessons. It is as much (perhaps even more) about the learning experience as it is about applying lean methods.

A huge advantage today, which was not available to those who were thrown headfirst into the lean wilderness ten to twenty years ago, is that there are many stories and lessons about transforming to lean available.[4] Lesson three is to read and learn the stories and lessons from others. There are no guarantees that you will be able to directly apply what others have learned to your specific situation, but a broader and deeper understanding can and will supplement your own journey. Take advantage of it! Understanding other's thoughts, ideas, lessons, and failures will help to better articulate and highlight the learning and thoughts anyone will discover during their own transformation process.

Lesson four is realizing and accepting that many times you will not understand what you have discovered until weeks, months, or even years have passed. In other words, in order for you to really understand and fully articulate exactly what you have learned, time must pass. Lessons learned will become clearer and clearer with the passage of time, and additional lessons and experience will be piled onto these past lessons and experience. Time is perhaps the greatest teacher. Respect and accept this mentor!

Other organizations are in the same situation or a similar one as you and your firm. The fifth lesson is to find other pioneers and firms and collaboratively work together, or at least in tandem, to help each other through the lean and lean cost-management wilderness. The collective experience and knowledge from working with others in the same situation will accelerate progress and prevent, or at least lessen, the magnitude of mistakes and amount of misdirection. In many areas of the country, firms are forming both formal and informal networks and consortiums to help guide each other through the process of transformation. This is a valuable experience and provides advice and assistance during the active and fresh learning process. Ten to twenty years ago early pioneers longed for partners, but there simply were not enough companies working on these changes so that they could even be found.

Lesson six is to be bold. Your company will have to think differently and, in turn, try unique and different things. Many times the phrase "leap of faith" is common in this type of activity. This is part of the learning process and where the scientific method—which is the seventh lesson—more commonly referenced as PDCA (the Deming Cycle of "plan, do, check, act"),[5] is applied. Continually experiment with new ideas and improvements, but use a systematic approach (PDCA), which will result in better feedback, learning, understanding, and reapplication of ideas and changes.

The final lesson is patience. This lesson has been mentioned in the context of several of the lessons and must be accepted. Demands from the powers-that-be (CEOs, CFOs, COOs, presidents, and all other types of managers) for immediate results will *only* get you frustrated and lost. Taking the long-term view is simply a necessity. If it is not available with the firm for whom you are currently working or the boss to whom you report, *leave* and go somewhere else. If you truly desire to learn, you will not learn in such an environment. It takes years to learn and understand, even in a truly supportive and active learning atmosphere. Even within Toyota it is felt that at least ten to twenty years of solid well-mentored training is necessary for one to *begin* understanding what needs to be done and how to do it. It is a lifelong journey.

Robert Martichenko, who is a very knowledgeable and well-seasoned lean practitioner and thinker of fifteen-plus years stated that the more he learns in the area of lean and the Toyota Production System (TPS), the dumber he feels. What Martichenko is describing is an understanding that TPS is a lifelong learning process.

Mark DeLuzio, himself deeply involved in TPS for over twenty years and one of the lean pioneers in the United States, expressed that his Japanese mentor, a former member of Toyota's famed internal consulting group started by Taiichi Ohno and someone who worked directly for Ohno, told him that although he and his firm had made very good progress, they would still only be at the elementary-school level.

SUMMARY OF THE LESSONS

1. Accept mistakes and misdirection as a valuable learning tool.
2. View the journey as a series of lessons.
3. Learn and understand the lessons of those who have gone before you.
4. Time is the greatest teacher (practice patience and persistence).
5. Find and work together with others in the same or a similar situation.
6. Be bold and have the willingness to experiment.
7. Use the scientific method to learn.
8. Be prepared for and accept a long-term journey of at least ten to twenty years minimum.

WHAT ARE THE MEANS?

When broken down into detail, the means to accomplish a lean cost-management system are many. However, the two primary means are the implementation and philosophy of flow and the scientific method.

Flow, as presented throughout this book, is both a mechanical means to directly link customers with the fulfillment of their needs and wants and the philosophical means to provide the thinking for everyone involved in the value stream to build, support, and improve the link between the customer and their needs and wants.

Apply flow vigorously for all products and information that move under the scope of your organization. Spread this flow to your customers and supply base. Establish flow where it does not exist, and reestablish flow immediately when and where it breaks down (this is when scientific method is, as Satoshi Hino affirms, indispensable!). Remember that most of the lean tools and methods are simply manifestations of ways to establish flow. In situations where flow cannot be instituted yet, pull must be established.

Develop and implement pull systems to precisely move small batches (the smaller the better) according to customer demand. The scientific method is also used for the same purpose as flow: to establish pull where it is needed and to resolve breakdowns in the pull system when and where they happen.

Develop an infrastructure that thrives on building, supporting, and improving the link between the customer and their needs and wants using flow and pull while solving problems via scientific method.

The scientific method is a mechanical means to teach everyone involved with the value stream how to resolve problems associated with building, supporting, and improving the link between the customer and their needs and wants. The scientific method is accomplished through mentoring, Training Within Industry (TWI), PDCA, and other methods, and it is the best known process to quickly and effectively learn continuously—every day with every project and with every problem. Continuous learning, which is embedded within practicing scientific method, is a philosophical view on how individuals and organizations best serve the customer and provide long-term societal support—stable employment, stable income to all stakeholders, stable market satisfaction, and so on. Perhaps Hino states it best: "Good results can hardly be expected if efforts are haphazard. Independent hypothesis and an experimental approach to verification are indispensable.... It is important that managers, senior employees, and bosses urge their subordinates to experiment once a hypothesis has been established."[6]

The scientific method is a philosophical method, or belief, that views lifelong learning as the best method for developing and implementing customer satisfaction. It is built upon the belief that every learning event is simply a step to further learning—recall the "continuous loops of improvement and change" discussed and illustrated in Chapter 19. Learning enables learning. So every applied PDCA learning activity is simply another brick stacked upon previous bricks that continually build understanding and thought processes, which enables you to more quickly and effectively resolve the next issue that presents itself.

The scientific method provides the thinking and process means for everyone evolved in the value stream to build, support, and improve the link between customers and their needs and wants.

SUMMARY OF THE PRIMARY MEANS

1. Establish flow (one-piece flow is the goal and objective).
2. Immediately reestablish flow when and where it breaks down.
3. When you cannot flow, pull (for this, the smaller the batch size the better).
4. Immediately reestablish pull when and where it breaks down.
5. Use the scientific method (PDCA, TWI, or others) to establish flow or pull.
6. Use the scientific method (PDCA, TWI, or others) to reestablish flow or pull when and where it breaks down.
7. Use the scientific method as the learning philosophy and method to embed continual learning in everything people do daily.

SECONDARY MEANS

A number of secondary means are worth discussing but are essentially nothing more than manifestations of the primary means.

Right designing was a key element that was discussed in detail. It is important and has a variety of aspects to learn and consider when applying it to an organization. But it is, in effect, more than applying the concept of flow to machines, systems, and processes in manufacturing. It involves understanding how to apply design parameters so that a machine facilitates flow—ideally, one-piece flow—which enables a product to be moved as quickly as possible from its raw state into exactly what the customer wants and needs. Right designing also facilitates quicker learning of the scientific method by allowing the response feedback to a problem to surface immediately and inhibiting moving forward without the problem being addressed immediately and a countermeasure being applied. Intimate learning of what the issue is—discovery of the root cause—becomes necessary to enact a usable resolution or countermeasure to remedy the issue and move forward.

Takt time is another secondary means. It is the most basic design parameter for the entire system. Output, machines, systems, people, and resources all use takt time as the starting point to build the system upon. It is also the connection between the customer and the organization's ability to satisfy the customer. It must be adjusted continuously to maintain the management between the market (or customer) and the organization's system, which provides fulfillment of the want or need. It is the fundamental link that must be understood and sustained.

Standard operations are another secondary means. An analogy for standard operations could be that it is the glue that holds the system together. First, it gives cohesiveness to the systems as it functions—it tells the system what to do, when and where to do it, and the time frame in which to do it (takt time). Second, it gives the reference point from which to measure when issues or potential issues arise. Both Henry Ford and Taiichi Ohno stressed that without a standard there can be no improvement—no development, no evolution of the organization and its system. It is the measure for improvement both when activities are functioning well and when activities breakdown. Standard operations hold the key to measure and move everything forward. Interestingly, TWI was and is the scientifically based method that provides the skill to improve the system, prevent problems, and resolve problems. It is not a coincidence that TWI was the basis for the development of standard operations within Toyota and its group companies.

Another secondary means is target costing and the activities that surround it and the product development process. This activity includes *kaizen* activities made by engineers and staff in supervisory roles. It is mentioned here because of its valuable contribution to the development of lean cost management and the lean enterprise. It is estimated that the improvements made at Toyota in this aspect of its business organization contribute around 90 percent of Toyota's cost savings. In a study conducted by Koichi Shimizu of Okayama University, he states that "at Toyota: kaizen [target costing in the product development phase and kaizen costing in the production phase] made by the supervisory staff and engineers as their function [bring about the most] cost reduction and productivity increase [90 percent as stated above] within the cost management system at Toyota."[7] It cannot be overlooked and must be considered within the business enterprise. Shimizu goes on to state that "it is the group leaders, chief leaders and engineers whose responsibilities it is to execute these activities. These activities and the kaizen gains are supervised and controlled by management."[8] Shimizu's comments get to the heart of the conclusion of this text, that a lean cost-management system is actually the design, execution, and improvement of the managing system. Shimizu writes: "After all, it was organized kaizen under control of production efficiency management and cost management that constituted the source of Toyota's high performance for more than thirty years."[9]

Even though Toyota's effectiveness lies within the supervisory personnel and engineers, the company views the shop floor as "the necessity for nourishing [the] kaizen mind and ability of the workers."[10] In effect, the shop is the learning laboratory for Toyota people to grow in their intimate understanding (lessons learned) and ability (means) so that they can move upward in the organization with a deep knowledge of how to do things and why they do them. There is a story in circulation that Fujio Cho, then president of Toyota, was seen working directly on some issues on the assembly line during a group tour of one of Toyota's assembly plants in Japan. When asked later why he was working on the line—it seems an unusual activity for the head of a global organization to be working on line problems—he replied that he tries at least once a month to solve problems on the line because it keeps him intimate with what is important to his organization, and he simply stated that it was "part of his job."[11]

Mentoring is a critical means, which is completely overlooked. A mentoring structure is vital to develop and teach the thinking that is key to promoting and propagating the principles that underlie flow and scientific method. Without an embedded mentoring structure, the organization cannot deploy the deep understanding necessary for proliferating, or even sustaining, continued learning. Also, without a long-term commitment to mentoring employees, the learning developed in each employee would only reach a superficial level. A truly deep comprehension must exist at all levels but most importantly must exist at the leadership level. Cho of Toyota is a prime example of this deep understanding built upon a career-long mentoring process.[12]

The final secondary means to be discussed is binary linkage.[13] It is not a common aspect that is normally presented, but its understanding and application is very important.

In designing the functions of the system, the necessity to place within each link a binary signal is key to creating the most efficient functionality. This means that upon an action that takes place, the feedback signal ideally should be either a simple "yes" or "no." Did the container within the pull system move from the designated locations (point A to point B) at the correct time—yes or no? If the feedback is "yes," then the system is functioning as designed so no countermeasures need to be taken. If the feedback is "no" then immediate action must take place by a specific person (another binary response) using a specific procedure or method—which is another type of binary response. Designing binary response capability within each action and linkage creates an incredibly robust and highly responsive system and helps enforce the learning cycle.

Many may be curious about the lack of discussion on waste elimination in this "how-to" section. Waste elimination is important, and it is most often mentioned by many who speak and write about this subject. It is a foregone conclusion that it must be a part of developing and implementing an improved system. However, it is important to put waste elimination into the proper context. Waste elimination can exist within a traditional or batch manufacturer and in many cases does exist in batch-production organizations. But waste elimination must have a direction (or context) to properly apply it for a specific purpose. In the case of this text, waste elimination is embedded in the means.

Ohno stated many times that he was simply eliminating waste—and he was. But he was doing it in the context of implementing flow manufacturing or a pull system. His famous seven wastes have this context as an implied purpose: eliminate wasteful activities that impede flow or the continuous movement of product through the system. Waste elimination must have a framework to function effectively.

SUMMARY

In reading this chapter, many were probably hoping to find the definitive roadmap to how to implement a lean cost-management system. The desire would be to give an authoritative step-by-step procedure to successfully move from traditional accounting to a lean cost-management system, but unfortunately it simply does not exist. What does exist are valuable and successful lessons that will guide an organization to discover "their path" to accomplish the task. The way is long and can be treacherous, but if it is undertaken it will lead to much success and knowledge. Use the lessons to guide the way through the process that will develop through continued experiments and learning.

In this book, information was given through discussion and within a context of experience and history of what a lean cost-management system is, or the means. The lessons summarized in this chapter were embedded throughout the chapters and in some cases discussed directly. The means embrace the concepts of flow and designing the system to establish and accomplish flow—one-piece flow.

Next is learning to execute the system design for flow as effectively as possible, and then continually improving the system design by continually applying one-piece flow and reestablishing flow when and where it breaks down. Finally, one must execute in an exemplary manner while continually learning to execute better and better each day. Design, execute, and improve.

The how-to described in this chapter was purposely stated in a generalized and high-level way. The reason for this relates to statements that Shigeo Shingo made a number of years ago:

> Many people believe that when implementing a new system, only the know-*how* is required. However, if you want to succeed, you must understand know-*why* as well.
>
> With know-how, you can operate the system, but you won't know what to do should you encounter problems under changed conditions. With know-why, you understand why you have to do what you are doing and hence will be able to cope with changing situations.[14]

Shingo's comments are repeated in the statements made by Hino in the beginning of this chapter. The know-why is more important than the know-how. The only way to learn this is to apply it day-in and day-out, that is, learn by doing. You must go learn *why*! Shingo affirms just how important understanding the know-why is to the improvement of the overall system and its attachment to root cause discovery (Toyota's Five Whys[15]) and the means. Shingo divulges the following:

> Similarly, the Toyota Production System's focus on the "5 Whys" emphasizes the fact that we can discover the true causes of things by asking why, why, why, why, and why over and over again. Unless we are aware that goals and means trade places with one another, and unless we persist in tracking each issue to its source, our improvements will remain superficial and inconclusive and we will never be able to improve in essential, fundamental ways.[16]

You must get inside the mind of a lean thinker to forge and hone your own ability and thinking as a lean thinker. Sakichi Toyoda, who founded the original Toyota organization, Toyoda Shoten, in 1895,[17] believed "that invention only achieved its goal through practical application."[18] Toyoda's philosophy remains embedded in the DNA of Toyota to this day. Hino explains: "Sakichi's philosophy has become the traditional spirit of Toyota and the Toyota Group companies. It lives on as the ideology that binds the Toyota Group together."[19]

Other books, consultants, and conferences are excellent sources of knowledge, skills, and methods to help move along the path toward lean cost management.[20] Again, as mentioned in the third lesson, listed in the section "Lessons Learned," take advantage of these books. They provide a trail that leads you in the right direction. But, as Shingo warned, develop a deep understanding of your subject (recall from earlier in this book why James Womack and Daniel Jones titled their book *Lean Thinking*)—or the know-why—through applied learning. Applied learning will in time give you the deep philosophical comprehension to progress forward to a horizon beyond the one that your current understanding will allow you to see. When you reach such a point you will begin to understand just how to achieve a lean cost-management system.

NOTES

1. Hino, *Inside the Mind of Toyota*, xi.
2. Ibid., xvii.
3. Ibid., xxi.
4. This is in reference to the wealth of books, magazine articles, papers, Web sites, conferences, consultants, and individuals who are readily available. Take advantage of everything available.
5. Another form of the PDCA cycle is "plan, do, study, act" (PDSA), which may be a more appropriate way of stating this activity. Because of the learning associated with these changes during a transformation process, one must give a deeper "check" on the experiment being conducted. This deeper check is actually a study of how the experiment went that involves analyzing if it worked and whether it needs to be modified or completely rethought and applied again. Learn how to see what is happening by studying.
6. Hino, *Inside the Mind of Toyota*, 92.
7. Shimizu, "Transforming Kaizen at Toyota," 4.
8. Ibid., 5.
9. Ibid., 15.
10. Ibid., 27.
11. The author is indebted to Jim Warren, president and owner of Sunset Manufacturing Company in Tualatin, Oregon, for sharing this wonderful story that he experienced on a study tour with Toyota in Japan.
12. Taiichi Ohno was one of Cho's mentors.
13. In his research and writings, Dr. Steven Spear extensively stresses and discusses binary linkage and its function and importance. For more detailed information, see his work in the bibliography.
14. Shingo, *A Study of the Toyota Production System*, xxv–xxvi. Shingo also expresses the same ideas in his books, *The Sayings of Shigeo Shingo*, 102–3, and *Non-Stock Production*, xxiv, 59, and 106.

15. Toyota uses the Five Whys to discover the root cause of any problem. This means asking "why" at least five times until the answer to the question of why is the root reason for the problem in question.

16. Shingo, *The Sayings of Shigeo Shingo*, 68.

17. Sakichi Toyoda opened Toyoda Shoten in 1895 in Nagoya, Japan (Toyota Motor Corporation, *Toyota: A History*, 27), and in 1902 changed its name to Toyoda Shokai (Ibid., 28). In 1907, Sakichi dissolved his company, established Toyoda's Loom Works (Ibid., 30), and resigned in 1910 due to business differences with his other investors. In 1911, Sakichi secured personal financial backing to establish an independent, self-supporting plant so that he would not have to rely on outside capital again. With the growth his new organization gained, he established Toyoda Spinning & Weaving Co., Ltd. in 1918 (Ibid., 31–32). Interestingly, Sakichi Toyoda's first several attempts led to failure due to disagreements with his coinvestors, which taught him to become independent to pursue his vision freely and control his own destiny. This pattern is identical to what happened to Henry Ford with his own visions and pursuit and even occurred during nearly the same time period.

18. Hino, *Inside the Mind of Toyota*, 4.

19. Ibid., 3.

20. For current books on this topic, see Maskell and Baggaley, *Practical Lean Accounting*; Fiume and Cunningham, *Real Numbers*; Solomon, *Who's Counting*; and Johnson and Bröms, *Profit beyond Measure*. For reference to a conference on the topic of lean cost management, visit http://www.lean accountingsummit.com.

20

CONCLUSION

This book set out to establish that current managerial-cost accounting practices are not optimal or are even useless and misleading. A historical context was examined that revealed the intentions and needs of early nineteenth and twentieth century managers and industrial pioneers. These intentions and needs were driven by the internal expansion of products and processes in firms. The propagation of multi-product and multiprocess firms directed cost information away from the open marketplace and more internally toward the manufacturing operations. Managers needed methods to develop cost information to enable improved decision making but not to control their operations. These managers held an intimate understanding of their factories, and this knowledge allowed them to make well-informed decisions for the business.

In this book it has been established that the original intentions of cost information—guidance information for planning and decision making—changed when financial accounting took the leading role in most firms and forced financial-accounting-style information—today's managerial-cost accounting—to become the method for controlling manufacturing operations.

Most chapters of this book discuss and describe principles, philosophies, methods, and tools useful for transforming a traditional manufacturer into a lean enterprise. Undertaking and succeeding in a lean transformation is critical to a manufacturing firm maintaining or gaining success. But focusing on results (MBR), particularly financial results, as the driver behind this effort leads to failure, and this is the state of today's traditional batch, or economies of scale, manufacturers. As has been shown in detail, the focus for developing a superior manufacturing business is transforming into a lean manufacturer using the principles and methods of creating a superior system design, learning how to properly execute the system, and continually improving both the design and execution of the system. This ability is most profoundly manifested in understanding and utilizing MBM principles and the physical implementation of flow manufacturing (one-by-one, one-piece flow of product and information).

The use of MBM via flow is supported by several principles of business that span the entire twentieth century. The principles include Alexander Hamilton Church's accurate costs, Dr. Spear's Rules-in-Use, Dr. H. Thomas Johnson and Anders Bröms's MBM emulating living systems, Dennis Butt's analogy of gear trains, and Ronald Coase's theory of transactions. In the end, implementing lean principles by right designing the system, properly executing the system, and continually improving the system eliminates the need for traditional managerial-cost accounting methods and creates an enterprise in which lean cost management is possible (see Figure 20.1).

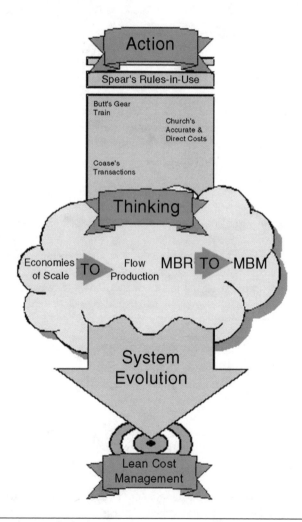

Figure 20.1 Development of a lean cost-management system

A lean cost-management system is created because products and all the incidents that create products (which also create costs) are directly aligned along value streams, and these value streams are greatly simplified and made straightforward. It has been shown that cost information can be simply and easily gathered from these value streams and used for accurate cost information for planning and guidance. This situation enables proper decisions to be made as they were by the early industrial managers. Thus, managerial-cost accounting in the traditional sense is no longer necessary.

Three factors transform a manufacturing firm into a lean enterprise: changing all costs into direct costs, developing and implementing flow production, and utilizing desktop hardware and software. The results of the first two factors allow for the third factor to easily become reality. The Production Factors Spreadsheet (PFSS) in Chapter 17 is a detailed example of the accomplishment of this process.

Toyota and its group companies exemplify the level of success that can be achieved by transforming into a lean enterprise. By understanding and implementing the ideas, principles, and methods proposed in this book, any manufacturing firm could successfully be transform into a substantial manufacturing force in the market-place. Having a lean cost-management system is a crucial support function to achieve this level of existence.

GLOSSARY

Batch production. Manufacturing large quantities of products without regard to demand or customer requirements in order to "seemingly" reduce costs of overhead, labor, and equipment by spreading the costs over a large amount of product.

Cell. The arrangement of people, equipment/machines, materials, and methods so that processing takes place in sequential order with continuous one-piece flow.

Continuous flow. A concept that, in its ideal state, means that items are processed and moved directly from one processing step to the next, one piece at a time. Continuous flow is also called "one-piece flow," "single-piece flow," "1 x 1," or simply "flow."

Cost management. The use of cost information to evaluate how efficaciously a business consumes resources to create products or services that have value to customers by developing and executing superior systems (instead of traditional cost-management accounting techniques) in which cost information is direct (see the glossary entry for "direct costs"), simple, and accurate. Cost management is a tool used to support and reflect operations, not drive operations and the behavior of those who manage it.

Cost-management accounting. The branch of accounting that uses both historical and estimated data in providing information that management uses in conducting daily operations, in planning future operations, and in developing overall business strategies, by accumulating manufacturing costs (Warren, Reeve, and Fess, *Accounting*, GL-3, GL-7).

Direct costs. Costs that can be directly associated with a product in the context of its incidence of manufacture. Be mindful that this is not its traditional definition, which is that direct costs are costing that treats only the variable manufacturing costs as a part of product cost and fixed manufacturing costs as period costs unrelated to product cost, which is also referred to as variable costing (Fess, "The Theory and Application of Direct Costing," 37; and Woelfel, "An Evaluation of the Advantages and Disadvantages of Direct Costing,").

Flow. The movement of a product through the value stream without stoppages or defects.

Flow manufacturing. Manufacturing operations that utilize continuous flow as the method of production.

Focus factory. Sometimes referred to as a factory within a factory. Usually a collection of manufacturing cells, which manufacture components that supply a value stream for a product or product family or a collection of component value streams that supply and are a part of a value stream for a product or product family. A focus factory will have its own autonomous support, resources, and management and will function as an independent entity and support resources. (Also called focused factory.)

Generally Accepted Accounting Practices (GAAP). Methods of accounting generally accepted as proper business practice for financial accounting.

Heijunka. In the production schedule, the overall leveling of the volume and variety of items produced in given time periods. Heijunka is a prerequisite for just-in-time (JIT) delivery.

Industrial Revolution. The change in social and economic organization resulting from the replacement of hand tools by machine and power tools and the development of large-scale industrial production during the period of 1885 through 1925 in the United States.

Jidoka. The ability to detect an abnormality and stop before moving to the next process. It supports the ability for manufacturing to build the part correctly the first time.

Just-in-time (JIT) production. A production system that manufactures and delivers exactly what is needed when it is needed and in the amount needed.

Kaikaku. The Japanese word approximately translated as rapid or radical improvement.

Kaizen. The Japanese word translated as continuous improvement. Continuous improvement is anything that eliminates waste or eliminates something that inhibits continuous flow. It is also a methodology of continuously improving operations to improve ergonomics, safety, operational downtime, scrap or rework, or productivity (based on takt time). The Training Within Industry (TWI) service developed the original methodology.

Kanban. The card system that controls inventory and movement in a pull system.

Lean production. The general term for the Toyota Production System (TPS), although Toyota would not accept this statement because they view TPS as a much deeper philosophy compared to how most companies apply lean production. A business system for organizing and managing product development, operations, suppliers, and customer relations that requires less human effort, less space, less capital, and less time to make products. Products have fewer defects and conform to more precise customer desires, as opposed to mass production. The term "lean production" was coined in the late 1980s by John Krafcik, a research assistant at

MIT's International Motor Vehicle Program. (Definition taken from "Capsule Summaries of Key Lean Concepts," Lean Enterprise Institute, http://www.lean.org/WhoWe Are/NewsArticleDocuments/key_lean_ definitions.html)

Management by means (MBM). Organizing work systematically. Business results that are an outcome that emerges spontaneously from mastering practices that harmonize with patterns inherent in the system itself (paraphrased definition taken from Johnson and Bröms, *Profit beyond Measure*, 50).

Management by results (MBR). Driving work with financial goals. The use of quantitative targets to run the operations of a business (paraphrased definition taken from Johnson and Bröms, *Profit beyond Measure*, 42).

Mass production. Manufacturing large amounts of product or producing large volumes. A traditional or lean manufacturer can be a mass producer. For example, Toyota and General Motors are mass producers because they both manufacture a large volume of products—automobiles.

Muda. Japanese term for waste or non–value added. See glossary entry for "waste."

One-piece flow. The same as flow but one piece at a time.

Pull system. A system in which product does not move to the next process unless signaled by the next process.

Right designing. Designing machines, processes, cells, and value streams for one-piece flow based on lean principles and techniques. (Sometimes referred to as right-sizing when referencing equipment or machine tools.)

Rules-in-Use. Rules that according to Dr. Steven Spear are the essence of the TPS. These rules specify how work is expected to occur before it is performed; imbed tests within the work itself signal immediately when work is not occurring as expected; and allow a quick response to signals with problem-solving processes (Spear, "The Essence of Just-in-Time: Imbedding Diagnostic Tests in Work-Systems to Achieve Operational Excellence," 6; Spear, "Just-in-Time in Practice at Toyota: Rules-in-Use for Building Self-Diagnostic, Adaptive Work-Systems," 9, 20; and (Johnston, *How Toyota Turns Workers into Problem Solvers*, 5).

Takt time. The rate of production that matches the rate of customer demand and is calculated by dividing available time by customer demand.

Toyota Production System (TPS). The methods, procedures, principles, philosophy, and enterprise-wide system that Toyota uses. TPS has its roots in Henry Ford's Highland Park plant, the TWI service, and its own needs and situation. Toyota has continuously evolved their system since before WWII. Its fundamental basis is eliminating or avoiding waste in order to implement continuous flow.

The production system, developed by Toyota to provide best quality, lowest cost, and shortest lead time through the elimination of waste, is comprised of two pillars, just-in-time (JIT) production and *jidoka*. TPS is maintained and improved through iterations of standardized work and *kaizen*, following the scientific method of the plan-do-check-act cycle (Definition taken from "Capsule Summaries of Key Lean Concepts," Lean Enterprise Institute, http://www.lean.org/WhoWeAre/NewsArticle Documents/key_lean_definitions.html).

Training Within Industry (TWI). The Training Within Industry (TWI) service was established in 1940 during World War II to increase production output to support the Allied Forces' war effort. It focused on the operator-supervisor interface and had four main training programs called the "J" programs (Job Instruction, Job Methods, and Job Relations). It was so successful that during the occupation of post-war Japan, it was extensively used to help rebuild and democratize Japanese industry.

The Five S's. Five words that represent the principles for cleanliness and organization. Originally based on five Japanese words: *seiri*, or sort; *seiton*, or straighten; seiso, or scrub; *seiketsu*, or systematize; and *shitsuke*, or standardize.

Value. Any activity that contributes to transforming a product or information into the customer requirements.

Value stream. The activities required to design, order, and manufacturing a product or information from raw material to the customer.

Waste. Any activity that takes time and resources and does not contribute to conforming a product or information into the customer requirements. Also known as *muda*.

Zero defect. The ability to manufacture products with no defects, scrap, or rework.

BIBLIOGRAPHY

Ahlstrom, Par, and Christer Karlsson. "Change Processes Towards Lean Production: The Role of the Management Accounting System." *International Journal of Operations & Production Management* 16, no. 11: 42–56.

———. "Change Processes Towards Lean Production: The Role of the Management Accounting System." Paper presented at the European Operations Management Association's International Conference, University of Twente, Enschede, The Netherlands.

Ansari, Shahid, Jan Bell, Thomas Klammer, and Carol Lawrence. *Management Accounting in the Age of Lean Production: A Modular Series, Management Accounting.* McGraw-Hill, 1997.

———. *Target Costing: A Modular Series, Management Accounting.* McGraw-Hill, 1997.

Baggaley, Bruce L. "Costing by Value Stream." *Journal of Cost Management* 17, no. 3 (May/June 2003), 24–30

———. "Solving the Standard Costing Problem." *Journal of Cost Management* 17, no. 2 (March/April 2003): 23–27.

———. "Solving the Standard Costing Problem." Northwest Lean Manufacturing Network, http://www.nwlean.net/article0803.htm (accessed August 2003).

Barclay, Hartley W. *Ford Production Methods.* New York: Harper & Brothers Publishers, 1936.

Butt, Dennis. "Toyota Production System: Little's Law, Ohno's Law, and Morgan's Formula." Conversation with the writer and presentation at Milwaukee School of Engineering's Lean Certificate Program, Milwaukee, Wisconsin. http://www.toyotaproductionsystem.net (accessed November 8, 2001).

Chandler, Alfred D. Jr. *The Visible Hand: The Managerial Revolution in American Business.* Cambridge, MA: Belknap Press, 1977.

Chatfield, Michael, and Richard Vangermeersch, eds. *The History of Accounting: An International Encyclopedia.* New York: Garland Publishing, 1996.

Church, Alexander Hamilton. "Comments." *Transactions of the American Society of Mechanical Engineers*. New York: American Society of Mechanical Engineers, 1913.

———. "Industrial Management," *Transactions of the International Engineering Congress*. Paper 238 (San Francisco, CA: 1915), 465.

———. "Machine Design and the Design of Systems." *American Machinist*, July 8, 1915, 61–62.

———. "The Meaning of Scientific Management." *The Engineering Magazine*, April 1911, 100.

———. "Organisation by Production Factors: VIII. Cost in Relation to the Financial Books." *Engineering Magazine* 35 (April 1910).

———. "Overhead: The Cost of Production Preparedness." *Factory and industrial Management*, January 1931, 38.

———. "Practical Principles of Rational Management." *Engineering Magazine* 44 (1913): 487–94, 673–80, 894–903; and vol. 45 (1913): 24–33, 166–73, 405–11.

———. *Production Factors in Cost Accounting and Works Management*. New York: Arno Press, 1976.

———. "The Proper Distribution of Establishment Charges." *The Engineering Magazine: A World Class Approach to Profit Management* 21 and 22 (1901): 508–17, 725–34, 904–12, 31–40, 231–40, 367–76.

———. "The Proper Distribution of Expense Burden." *American Machinist*, May 25, 1911, 22–23.

———. *The Science and Practice of Management*. New York: Engineering Magazine Company, 1914.

Ciulla, Joanne B. *The Working Life: The Promise and Betrayal of Modern Work*. New York: Times Books, 2000.

Clements, Ronald B., and Charlene W. Spoede. "Trane's SOUP Accounting: It's a System of Utter Practicality!" *Management Accounting*, June 1992, 46–52.

Coase, Ronald H. "The Nature of the Firm." *Economica* 4, no. 16: 386–405.

———. "The Problem of Social Cost." *The Journal of Law and Economics* 3 (October 1960): 1–44.

Cochran, David S. "The Design and Control of Manufacturing Systems." PhD diss., Auburn University, August 26, 1994.

Cooper, Robin. *When Lean Enterprises Collide: Competing Through Confrontation*. Boston: Harvard Business School Press, 1995.

Cooper, Robin, and Robert S. Kaplan. "Measure Costs Right: Make the Right Decisions." *Harvard Business Review*, September–October 1988, 96–103.

Darlington, John. "Lean Thinking and Mass Customisation: The Relationship Between Production and Costs." *Management Accounting*, November 1999, 18–21.

Davis, Ralph Currier. *The Fundamentals of Top Management*. New York: Harper & Row, Publishers, 1951.

DeLuzio, Mark. "Danaher is a Paragon of Lean Success." Interview by Richard McCormack. *Manufacturing News* 8, no. 12 (June, 29, 2001), http://www.manufacturingnews.com.

———. "Management Accounting in a Just-in-Time Environment." *Cost Management*, Winter 1993, 6–15.

———. "Management Accounting in a Just-In-Time Environment." Unpublished article, written circa 1992.

DeMarco, Tom. *Slack: Getting Past Burnout, Busywork, and the Myth of Total Efficiency*. New York: Broadway Books, 2001.

Dhavale, Dileep G. *Management Accounting Issues in Cellular Manufacturing and Focus-Factory Systems*. Montvale, NJ: IMA Foundation for Applied Research, Inc., 1996.

Downes, Larry, and Chunka Mui. *Unleashing the Killer App: Digital Strategies for Market Dominance*. Boston: Harvard Business School Press, 2000.

Emiliani, Bob. "The False Promise of 'What Gets Measured Gets Managed'." *Management Decision* 38, no. 9 (2000): 612–15.

Emiliani, Bob, David Stec, Lawrence Grasso, and James Strodder. *Better Thinking, Better Results: Using the Power of Lean as a Total Business Solution*. Kensington, CT: The Center for Lean Business Management, LLC, 2003.

Fess, Phillip Eugene. "The Theory and Application of Direct Costing." PhD, diss., University of Illinois, 1960.

Flinchbaugh, Jamie. "Beyond Lean: Building Sustainable Business and People Success through New Ways of Thinking." *Material Handling Management*, http://www.mhmonline.com/nID/2455/MHM/viewStory .asp.

———. "Connecting Lean and Organizational Learning." *Reflections: The Society of Organizational Learning Journal*, 1–13 (forthcoming), http://www.leanlearningcenter.com/downloads/Connecting_Lean_and_Organizational_Learning.pdf.

———. "Implementing Lean Manufacturing Through Factory Design." Master's thesis, Massachusetts Institute of Technology, May 1998.

———. "Is Lean a Fad?" *Manufacturer of Michigan Journal*, October 2001: 1–4, http://www.leanlearningcenter.com/downloads/Is_Lean_a_Fad.pdf.

Ford, Henry. *My Life and Work*. 1922. North Stratford, NH: Ayer Company Publishers, Inc, 1998.

Ford, Henry, and Samuel Crowther. *Today and Tomorrow*. Portland, OR: Productivity Press, 1988.

Fiume, Orest, and Jean E. Cunningham. "Lean Accounting and Finance." *Target* 18, no. 4 (2002): 6–14.

———. *Real Numbers: Management Accounting in a Lean Organization*. Durham, NC: Managing Times Press, 2003.

Fujimoto, Takahiro. *The Evolution of a Manufacturing System at Toyota.* New York: Oxford University Press, 1999.

Gantt, Henry. "The Relation Between Production and Costs." Lecture, American Society of Mechanical Engineers, Buffalo, NY, 1915.

Garner, S. Paul. *Evolution of Cost Accounting to 1925.* Alabama: The University of Alabama Press, 1974.

———. "Historical development of Cost Accounting." *Accounting Review* 22, no. 4 (October 1947): 385–89.

Geer, Howard C. "Cost Factors in Price-Making—Part I." *Harvard Business Review* 30 (July–August 1952): 45.

Gibbs, Lisa. "Are Earnings Meaningless?" *Money,* October 2002, 37–40.

Goodnight, James. "The Royal Treatment." *60 Minutes.* CBS. October 13, 2002.

Halberstam, David. *The Reckoning.* New York: William Morrow and Company, Inc., 1986.

Hall, Robert W. *Zero Inventories.* Homewood, IL: Dow Jones-Irwin, 1983.

Hammer, Michael. *Beyond Reengineering: How the Process-Centered Organization Is Changing Our Work and Our Lives.* New York: Harper-Collins Publishers, Inc., 1996.

Harbour, Ron. "Opinions & Analysis." *Automotive Industries,* December 2001, 10.

———. "Opinions & Analysis." *Automotive Industries,* February 2002, 16

———. "Opinions & Analysis." *Automotive Industries,* January 2002, 8.

———. "Opinions & Analysis." *Automotive Industries,* March 2002, 16.

———. "Opinions & Analysis." *Automotive Industries,* November 2001, 14.

———. "Opinions & Analysis: Good Plants, Like Art, Don't Just Happen." *Automotive Industries* (April 2003): 16.

Harmon, Roy L. *Reinventing the Factory II: Managing the World Class Factory.* New York: The Free Press, 1992.

Harris, Jonathon N. "What Did We Earn Last Month?" *N.A.C.A. Bulletin,* January 15, 1936, 501–26.

Hino, Satoshi. *Inside the Mind of Toyota: Management Principles for Enduring Growth* [*Toyota Keiei Shisutemu no Kenkyū*]. 2002. English edition, New York: Productivity Press, 2006.

Hiromoto, Toshiro. "Another Hidden Edge—Japanese Management Accounting." *Harvard Business Review,* July–August 1988, 22–26

Hounshell, David A. *From the American System to Mass Production, 1800–1932.* Baltimore and London: The Johns Hopkins University Press, 1984.

Howell, Robert A., John K. Shank, Stephen R. Soucy, and Joseph Fisher. *Cost Management for Tomorrow: Seeking the Competitive Edge.* Morristown, NJ: Financial Executives Research Foundation, 1992.

Huntzinger, Jim. "Roots of Lean—Highland Park: The Cradle of Flow." Independent study for master's degree, Milwaukee School of Engineering, November 17, 2002.

————. "Roots of Lean—Training Within Industry: The Origin of Japanese Management and Kaizen." Independent study for masters degree, Milwaukee School of Engineering, November 21, 2001.

————. "Roots of Lean—Training Within Industry: The Origin of Kaizen." *Target* 18, no. 2 (2002): 9–22.

Hyer, Nancy, and Urban Wemmerlöv. "Cost Accounting and Cellular Manufacturing." In *Reorganizing the Factory: Competing Through Cellular Manufacturing*. Portland, OR: Productivity Press Inc, 2002.

Imai, Masaaki. *Gemba Kaizen: A Commonsense, Low-Cost Approach to Management*. New York: McGraw-Hill, 1997.

————. *Kaizen: The Key to Japan's Competitive Success*. New York: McGraw-Hill, 1986.

Japan Management Association, ed. *Kanban: Just-in-Time at Toyota*. Cambridge, MA: Productivity Press, 1989.

Jelinek, Mariann. "Toward Systematic Management: Alexander Hamilton Church." *Business History Review* 45 (1980): 63–79.

Jenson, Richard L., James W. Brackner, and Clifford R. Skousen. *Management Accounting in Support of Manufacturing Excellence: Profiles of Shingo Prize-Winning Organizations*. Montvale, NJ: The IMA Foundation for Applied Research, Inc., 1996.

Johnson, Charles E. "Inventory Valuation—The Accountant's Achilles Heel." *The Accounting Review* 29, no. 1 (1954): 15–26.

Johnson, H. Thomas. "Activity-Based Information: Accounting for Competitive Excellence." *Target*, Spring 1989, 4–9.

————. "Activity-Based Information: A Blueprint for World-Class Management Accounting." *Management Accounting*, June 1988, 23–30.

————. "Beyond Product Costing: A Challenge to Cost Management's Conventional Wisdom." *Journal of Cost Management*, Fall 1990, 15–21.

————. "The Decline of Cost Management: A Reinterpretation of 20th-Century Cost Accounting History." *Journal of Cost Management*, Spring 1987, 5–12.

————. "Deming's Message for Management Accountants." *Management Accounting*, September 1992, 34.

————. "A Former Management Accountant Reflects on His Journey through the World of Cost Management." Based on a keynote presentation given to the Second International Symposium on Accounting History, Osaka City University, Osaka, Japan, August 8, 2001.

————. "How the Universe Story and MBM Can Save Business, Society, and the Earth from the Dictatorship of Strategic Financial Management." Paper presented to In2: InThinking Network Second Annual Forum, Los Angeles, CA, April 6, 2003.

————. "It's Time to Stop Overselling Activity-Based Concepts: Start Focusing on Total Customer Satisfaction Instead." *Management Accounting,* September 1992, 26–35.

————. "Managing by Remote Control: Recent Management Accounting Practice in Historical Perspective." In *Inside the Business Enterprise: Historical Perspectives on the Use of Information.* Peter Temin, ed. Chicago: The University of Chicago Press, 1991.

————. "A Recovering Cost Accountant Reminisces." Anticipated for publication for fall 2002 *Journal of Innovative Management.*

————. *Relevance Regained: From Top-Down Control to Bottom-Up Empowerment.* New York: The Free Press, 1992.

————. "The Role of Accounting History in the Study of Modern Business Enterprise." *The Accounting Review,* July 1975, 444–50.

————. "Toward a New Understanding of Nineteenth-Century Cost Accounting." *The Accounting Review* 56, no. 3 (1981) 510–18.

————. "Why Business Schools Focus on the Wrong Customer." In *Relevance Regained: From Top-Down Control to Bottom-Up Empowerment,* 178–83.

Johnson, H. Thomas, and Anders Bröms. *Profit beyond Measure: Extraordinary Results through Attention to Work and People.* New York: The Free Press, 2000.

Johnson, H. Thomas, and Robert S. Kaplan. "Management by Accounting is Not Management Accounting." *CFO Magazine,* July 1988, 6–8.

————. *Relevance Lost: The Rise and Fall of Management Accounting.* Boston: Harvard Business School Press, 1987.

Johnson, H. Thomas, Thomas P. Vance, and R. Steven Player. "Pitfalls in Using ABC Cost-Driver Information to Manage Operating Costs." *Corporate Controller,* January/February 1991, 26–32.

Johnston, Sarah Jane. "How Toyota Turns Workers into Problem Solvers." *HBS Working Knowledge,* November 26, 2001, http://hbswk.hbs.edu/ archive/ 2646.html.

Jones, Dan. "The Beginner's Guide to Lean." *Manufacturer,* December 2003.

Kaplan, Robert S. "The Evolution of Management Accounting." *The Accounting Review* 59, no. 3 (July 1984): 390–418.

————. "One Cost System Isn't Enough." *Harvard Business Review,* January–February 1988, 61–66.

————. "Yesterday's accounting undermines production." *Harvard Business Review,* July–August 1984, 95–101.

Kaplan, Robert S., ed. *Measures for Manufacturing Excellence.* Boston: Harvard Business School Press, 1990.

Kawahara, Akira. *The Origin of Competitive Strength: Fifty Years of the Auto Industry in Japan and the U.S.* New York: Akira Kawahara, 1997.

Kitano, Mikio "Mike." "Toyota Production System: One-By-One Confirmation." Keynote Address at Lean Manufacturing Conference, University of Kentucky, May 14–16, 1997.

Knoeppel, Charles E. *Installing Efficiency Methods*. Easton, NY: Hive Publishing Company, 1976.

Koenigsaecker, George. "The Cost Benefits of Going Lean." *CME*, October 2003.

———. "Lean Production—the Challenge of Multidimensional Change." In Liker, *Becoming Lean: Inside Stories of U.S. Manufacturers*, 466–67.

———. *Profit Engineering: Applied Economics in Making Business Profitable.* New York: McGraw-Hill, 1933.

Krafcik, John. "Triumph of the Lean Production System." *Sloan Management Review*, 41 (Fall 1988): 41–52.

Lean Enterprise Institute. "Creating the Course and Tools for a Lean Accounting System." Cambridge, MA: The Lean Enterprise Institute, 2003.

Liker, Jeffrey K., ed. *Becoming Lean: Inside Stories of U.S. Manufacturers*. Portland, OR: Productivity Press, 1997.

Liker, Jeffrey K. *The Toyota Way: 14 Management Principles from the World's Greatest Manufacturer*. New York: McGraw-Hill, 2004.

Litterer, J. A. "Alexander Hamilton Church and the Development of Modern Management." *Business History Review* 35, no. 2 (1961): 211–25.

Lutz, Robert A. *Guts: The Seven Laws of Business That Made Chrysler the World's Hottest Car Company*. New York: John Wiley & Sons, Inc., 1998.

Maskell, Brian. "Lean Accounting Executive Briefing: Introduction to Lean Accounting." Presentation at the AQC Conference, Rochester, NY, April 3, 2002.

———. "Lean Accounting Executive Briefing: Lean Accounting, Costing & Implementation." Presentation at the AQC Conference, Rochester, NY, April 3, 2002.

———. "Lean Accounting Executive Briefing: Lean Measurements, Transactions, & Financial Benefits." Presentation at the AQC Conference, Rochester, NY, April 3, 2002.

———. "Lean Accounting for Lean Manufacturers." *Manufacturing Engineering* (December 2000): 46–53.

———. *Making the Numbers Count: The Accountant as Change Agent on the World Class Team*. Portland, OR: Productivity Press, 1996.

———. "Overview of Lean Accounting." Cherry Hill, NJ: Brian Maskell Associates, Inc., 1999.

———. *Performance Measurement for World Class Manufacturing: A Model for American Companies*. Portland, OR: Productivity Press, 1991.

Maskell, Brian, and Bruce Baggaley. "Lean Management Accounting." Brian Maskell Associates, Inc, September 1999, http://www.maskell.com/Lean Article.htm.

———. *Practical Lean Accounting: A Proven System for Measuring and Managing the Lean Enterprise.* New York: Productivity Press, 2003.

McElroy, John. "Accounting as Weapon." *Ward's Auto World,* December 2003, 19.

Miller, Jeffrey G., and Thomas E. Vollmann. "The Hidden Factory." *Harvard Business Review* 63, no. 5 (September–October 1985): 142–50.

Monden, Yasuhiro. *Cost Management in the New Manufacturing Age: Innovations in the Japanese Automotive Industry.* Portland, OR: Productivity Press, 1992.

———. *Cost Reduction Systems: Target Costing and Kaizen Costing.* Portland, OR: Productivity Press, 1995.

———. *Toyota Management System: Linking the Seven Key Functional Areas.* Portland, OR: Productivity Press, 1993.

———. *Toyota Production System: An Integrated Approach to Just-In-Time.* 3rd edition. Norcross, GA: Industrial Engineering and Management Press, 1998.

Monden, Yasuhiro, and Michiharu Sakurai, eds. *Japanese Management Accounting: A World Class Approach to Profit Management.* Portland, OR: Productivity Press, 1989.

Nakajima, Seiichi. *Introduction to TPM: Total Productive Maintenance.* Portland, OR: Productivity Press, 1988.

Nevins, Allan, and Frank Ernest Hill. *Ford: The Times, The Man, The Company 1863–1915.* New York: Charles Scribner's Sons, 1954.

Noreen, Eric, Debra Smith, and James T. Mackey. *The Theory of Constraints and Its Implications for Management Accounting.* Great Barrington, MA: North River Press Publishing, 1995.

Ohno, Taiichi. "Arithmetic's Blind Spot." *Workplace Management,* 20–24.

———. "Overcoming the Obstacle of Accounting." *Lean Manufacturing Advisor,* July 2002, 1–4.

———. *Toyota Production System: Beyond Large-Scale Production.* Portland, OR: Productivity Press, 1988.

———. *Workplace Management.* Portland, OR: Productivity Press, 1988.

Parkinson, C. Northcote. *Parkinson's Law: And Other Studies in Administration.* Cutchogue, NY: Buccaneer Books, 1957.

Porter, Michael E. *Competitive Advantage: Creating and Sustaining Superior Performance.* New York: The Free Press, 1985.

Robbins, Harvey, and Michael Finley. *Learning To See: Value Stream Mapping to Create Value and Eliminate Muda.* Brookline, MA: The Lean Enterprise Institute, 1998.

———. *Why Teams Don't Work: What Went Wrong and How to Make It Right.* Princeton, NJ: Peterson's/Pacesetter Books, 1995.

Rother, Mike, John Shook, and Rick Harris. *Creating Continuous Flow: An Action Guide for Managers, Engineers & Production Associates.* Brookline, MA: The Lean Enterprise Institute, 2001.

———. "Do You Really Have Continuous Flow in Assembly?" Cambridge, MA: The Lean Enterprise Institute, 2002.

———. "Some Current Thoughts on the Management Side of Lean Manufacturing." January 2003. A copy of this unpublished article was sent to the author by Mike Rother.

Sakurai, Michiharu. *Integrated Cost Management: A Companywide Prescription for Higher Profits and Lower Costs.* Portland, OR: Productivity Press, 1996.

———. "Past and Future of Japanese Management Accounting." *Journal of Cost Management,* Fall 1995, 21–30.

———. "Target Costing and How to Use It." *Journal of Cost Management,* Summer 1989, 39–50.

Sakurai, Michiharu, and D. Paul Scarbrough. *Japanese Cost Management.* Menlo, CA: Crisp Publications, 1997.

Schonberger, Richard J. *Japanese Manufacturing Techniques: Nine Hidden Lessons in Simplicity.* New York: The Free Press, 1982.

———. *Let's Fix It!: Overcoming the Crisis in Manufacturing.* New York: The Free Press, 2001.

Schwarz, Emanuel F. *Internal Accounting: Advanced Presentation of the Chart of Accounts for Managerial Cost Accounting.* 1stBooks, 2000.

Shimizu, Koichi. "Transforming Kaizen at Toyota." Working paper, Okayama University, Japan, http://www.e.okayama-u.ac.jp/~kshimizu/ downloads/iir.pdf.

Shingo, Shigeo. *Non-Stock Production: The Shingo System for Continuous Improvement.* Portland, OR: Productivity Press, 1988.

———. *A Revolution in Manufacturing: The SMED System [Shinguru Dandori].* Portland, OR: Productivity Press, 1985.

———. *The Sayings of Shigeo Shingo: Key Strategies for Plant Improvement.* Portland, OR: Productivity Press, 1987.

———. *A Study of the Toyota Production System: From an Industrial Engineering Viewpoint.* Portland, OR: Productivity Press, 1989.

———. *Zero Quality Control: Source Inspection and the Poka-yoke System.* Portland, OR: Productivity Press, 1986.

Shook, John. "Bringing the Toyota Production System to the United States: A Personal Perspective." In Liker, *Becoming Lean: Inside Stories of U.S. Manufacturers,* 49.

———. "The Lean Enterprise." Ninth Annual Lean Manufacturing Conference, Japan Technology Management Program, University of Michigan, Ann Arbor, MI, May 6, 2003, Conference held in Ypsilanti, Michigan, 1–5.

Sloan, Alfred P. Jr. *My Years with General Motors.* New York: Doubleday, 1963.

Solomon, Jerrold M. *Who's Counting? A Lean Accounting Business Novel.* Fort Wayne, IN: WCM Associates, 2003.

Sorensen, Charles E. *My Forty Years With Ford.* New York: W. W. Norton & Company Inc., 1956.

South, John B. "A Modified Standard Cost-Accounting System Can Generate Valid Product Costs." *Production and Inventory Management Journal,* Second Quarter, 1993, 28–31.

Spear, Steven J. "Building Process Improvement Capacity: Structuring Problem Solving as Skill-Building Exercises." Working paper, 02–006, February 2003.

———. "The Essence of Just-in-Time: Imbedding Diagnostic Tests in Work-Systems to Achieve Operational Excellence." Working paper, 02–020, July 2002.

———. "Just-in-Time in Practice at Toyota: Rules-in-Use for Building Self-Diagnostic, Adaptive Work-Systems." Working paper, 02–043, August 16, 2002.

———. "Just-in-Time in Practice at Toyota: Rules-in-Use for Building Self-Diagnostic, Adaptive Work-Systems." Working paper, 02–043, January 7, 2002.

———. "The Toyota Production System: An Example of Managing Complex Social/Technical Systems, 5 Rules for Designing, Operating, and Improving Activities, Activity-Connections, and Flow-Paths." PhD diss., Harvard University, May 26, 1999.

Spear, Steven J., and H. Kent Bowen. "Decoding the DNA of the Toyota Production System." *Harvard Business Review.* Reprint 99509 (September–October 1999): 96–106.

Stec, David J. "Performance Measures for Lean Manufacturing." Master's thesis, Massachusetts Institute of Technology, May 1998.

Suzimori, Y., K. Kusinoki, F. Cho, and S. Uchikawa for the Toyota Motor Company. "Toyota Production System and Kanban System—Materialization of Just-In-Time and Respect-For-Human System." *International Journal of Production Research* 15, no. 6 (1977): 553–64.

Taninecz, George. "Cost Accounting Undercuts Lean: Switching to Simpler Accounting Methods Gives a More Realistic Reflection of Benefits." *Industry Week,* October 2002, 73–74.

Taylor, Audrey G. "Accounting for Lean Production." Quality Concepts Conference, The Engineering Society, Warren, MI, October 1993, 83–96.

Taylor, Frederick Winslow. "A Piece-Rate System." Paper presented at a meeting of the American Society of Mechanical Engineers, Detroit, MI, June 1885, 856–903. (Copy from the Linda Hall Library, Kansas City, MO).

———. *The Principles of Scientific Management.* Norcross, GA: Engineering & Management Press, 1998.

————. *Shop Management*. New York: Harper & Brothers Publishers, 1947.

————. *Taylor's Testimony Before the Special House Committee*. New York: Harper & Brothers Publishers, 1947.

Theeuwes, J. A. M. "Shortcomings of Traditional Accounting for Decision Support in Manufacturing Improvement." In *ISATA Proceedings*. Aachen, Germany: 27th International Symposium, 1994, 511–17.

Toyota Motor Corporation. *Toyota: A History of the First 50 Years*. Toyota City, Japan: Toyota Motor Corporation, 1988.

————. *The Toyota Production System*. Toyota City, Japan: Toyota Motor Corporation, Internal Public Affairs Division, Operations Management Consulting Division, 1995.

Turk, William T. "Management Accounting Revitalized: The Harley-Davidson Experience." *Journal of Cost Management*, Winter 1990, 28–39.

Uminger, Glenn. "Lean: An Enterprise Wide Perspective." Presentation at the Ninth Annual Lean Manufacturing Conference, Japan Technology Management Program at the University of Michigan, Ann Arbor, MI, May 6, 2003. Conference held in Ypsilanti, Michigan.

————. "Manufacturing Cost Management: A Practical Life-Cycle Cost Perspective." In *New Management Accounting: How Leading-Edge Companies Use Management Accounting to Improve Performance*, ed., William F. Christopher. Menlo, CA: Crisp Publications, 1998.

Urwick, Lyndall F., ed., part one, and William B. Wolf, ed., part two. *The Golden Book of Management: A Historical Record of the Life and Work of More Than One Hundred Pioneers*. 2nd ed. New York: American Management Association, 1984.

Vangermeersch, Richard., ed. *The Contributions of Alexander Hamilton Church to Accounting and Management*. New York: Garland Publishing, Inc., 1986.

Vangermeersch, Richard. *Alexander Hamilton Church: A Man of Ideas for All Seasons*. New York: Garland Publishing, Inc., 1988.

Vasilash, Gary S. "Lean Lessons." *Automotive Design & Production*, March 2001, 60–63.

War Production Board, Bureau of Training, Training Within Industry Service. *Job Instruction: Sessions Outline and Reference Material*. Washington DC: U.S. Government Printing Office, 1943.

————. *Job Methods: Sessions Outline and Reference Material*. Washington DC: U.S. Government Printing Office, 1943.

————. *Job Relations: Sessions Outline and Reference Material*. Washington DC: U.S. Government Printing Office, 1944.

————. *The Training Within Industry Report: 1940–1945*. Washington DC: U.S. Government Printing Office, 1945.

Warren, Carl S., James M. Reeve, and Philip E. Fess. *Accounting*. 20th ed. Cincinnati: South-Western Publishing Co., 2002.

————. *Financial and Managerial Accounting.* 5th ed. Cincinnati: South-Western Publishing Co., 1997.

Weber, Austin. "Lean Machines." *Assembly Magazine*, May 5, 2003.

Weber, Charles. *The Evolution of Direct Costing.* Urbana: Center for International Education and Research in Accounting, University of Illinois, 1966.

Weissman, Rich. "Bringing Lean to the Board." *Manufacturer*, December 2003, 42–43.

Wells, M. C. *Accounting for Common Costs.* Urbana: Center for International Education and Research in Accounting, University of Illinois, 1978.

Wells, M. C., ed. *American Engineers' Contribution to Cost Accounting.* New York: Arno Press, 1978.

————. *A Bibliography of Cost Accounting: Its Origin and Development to 1914.* Urbana: Center for International Education and Research in Accounting, University of Illinois, 1978.

Woelfel, Robert Charles. "An Evaluation of the Advantages and Disadvantages of Direct Costing." Master's thesis, University of Illinois, Urbana, 1962.

Womack, James P. *Here's to Toyota.* Cambridge, MA: The Lean Enterprise Institute, 2003.

————. Presentation at the AME Annual Conference, Chicago, IL, 2002.

Womack, James P., and Daniel T. Jones. *How the World Has Changed Since* The Machine That Changed the World. Cambridge MA: The Lean Enterprise Institute, Summer 2001.

————. *Lean Thinking: Banish Waste and Create Wealth in your Corporation.* New York: Simon & Schuster, 1996.

————. *Seeing the Whole: Mapping the Extended Value Stream.* Brookline, MA: The Lean Enterprise Institute, March 2002.

Womack, James P., Daniel T. Jones, and Daniel Roos. *The Machine That Changed the World: The Story of Lean Production.* New York: Macmillan Publishing Company, 1990.

INDEX